PHILOSOPHY, BLACK FILM, *FILM NOIR*

Philosophy, Black Film, *Film Noir*

DAN FLORY

THE PENNSYLVANIA STATE UNIVERSITY PRESS
UNIVERSITY PARK, PENNSYLVANIA

Library of Congress Cataloging-in-Publication Data

Flory, Dan.
  Philosophy, Black film, film noir / Dan Flory.
    p.   cm.
Includes bibliographical references and index.
Summary: "Examines how African-American as well as international films deploy
film noir techniques in ways that encourage philosophical reflection. Combines
philosophy, film studies, and cultural studies"—Provided by publisher.
ISBN: 978-0-271-03345-7 (pbk. : alk. paper)
  1. African Americans in motion pictures.
  2. African American motion picture producers and directors.
  3. Film noir—United States—History and criticism.
  I. Title.

PN1995.9.N4F59 2008
791.43'652996073—dc22
2007050089

Copyright © 2008 The Pennsylvania State University
All rights reserved
Printed in the United States of America
Published by The Pennsylvania State University Press,
University Park, PA 16802-1003

The Pennsylvania State University Press is a member of the Association of American
University Presses.

It is the policy of The Pennsylvania State University Press to use acid-free paper.
This book is printed on Natures Natural, containing 50% post-consumer waste, and
meets the minimum requirements of American National Standard for Information
Sciences—Permanence of Paper for Printed Library Material, ANSI z39.48–1992.

for Susan

CONTENTS

In order to understand white resistance to full equality for African Americans, black ex-slave, abolitionist, and civil rights leader Frederick Douglass argued more than once that we need to use philosophy.[1] I have sought to meet his requirement by writing a book that addresses how race functions in narrative fiction film. Although Douglass lived long enough to have overlapped with the invention of motion pictures, I do not know whether he ever actually saw any. However, had he seen those early films of Edison or Muybridge I think he would have understood at once that existing conceptions of race play a fundamental role in how human beings are represented. I believe he also would have understood that philosophical analysis would be necessary to disentangle the rat's nest of beliefs that make up most typical cinematic viewing habits. Douglass often argued that errant but enduring presumptions about black humanity distorted many whites' ability to perceive African Americans as fully human, so the transference of such beliefs to watching movies would have come as no surprise to him. On the other hand, more than a century after his death it still shocks many whites to discover that their cinematic perception may be raced.

Over the years makers of black films have frequently taken as one of their objectives the communication of this insight to audiences, and yet it has also frequently been misperceived, ignored, or deemed an exaggerated response to existing social conditions. Rather than seriously entertain such a possibility, many viewers—especially white viewers—resist this racialization of how they perceive film narrative because it would require too profound a change in their fundamental belief structure, too painful a shift in how they thought about their fellow human beings. Instead of considering the possibility of racial bias in their film viewing, many cling to the belief that they already see characters in films (as well as the world) from a humanly "universal" standpoint. A problem often confronting makers of black films, then, is how to convey this socially critical realization in a way that their audiences would readily comprehend.

1. See, for example, Frederick Douglass, "Introduction," in Ida B. Wells, Frederick Douglass, Irvine Garland Penn, and Ferdinand L. Barnett, *The Reason Why the Colored American Is Not in the World's Columbian Exposition*, ed. Robert W. Rydell (1893; repr., Urbana: University of Illinois Press, 1999), 14–15.

In contrast, filmmakers, critics, and audiences have long understood that *film noir* has a special capacity for providing readily accessible social criticism. Many have praised this group of films for how they make people think about existing structures of power and privilege. Although not typically directed at problems concerning race, *film noir's* capacity to raise questions about how things normally stand is a salient characteristic evident in many of its most representative works.

Film noir has fascinated me for a long time. I was first introduced to it as a child: an independent Minneapolis, Minnesota television station, no doubt inspired by the Brattle Theater in Cambridge, Massachusetts, showed Humphrey Bogart movies on Sunday afternoons, so I grew up watching *Dark Passage, Dead Reckoning, Knock on Any Door,* and similar films that made viewers think in order to figure out what was happening and cast a critical eye on the rich and powerful. At the same time, I was enculturated into a society wracked by the simultaneous promotion of social equality and racial inequality, and taught that it was nothing out of the ordinary. As I grew older "New Hollywood" filmmakers found inspiration in these movies I had enjoyed so much as a child and produced similar narratives that made viewers question how things were, something that I appreciated more and more as the late 1960s matured, ripened, and then rotted into the 1970s. Films that troubled me and made me reflect about existing social conditions seemed vitally important, particularly when focused, literally or metaphorically, on matters of justice and fairness. Like many of my era, *Chinatown* represented a personal landmark because it gave expression to my horror at a pervasive moral corruption revealed by the Watergate scandal that seemed to comprise the normal business operations of many governmental institutions.

At about the same time, racial progress seemed to stagnate, and in some cases recede. Resistance to integration and affirmative action, perhaps epitomized by former Alabama governor George Wallace's 1968 and 1972 presidential campaigns, indicated that many whites believed fairness to themselves called for unfairness toward everyone else. Often they felt that they had already "done enough" in favor of racial equality and saw continued complaints of racism as pleas for special treatment.

By this time, I had also become interested in philosophy. Aside from raising questions regarding what justice ultimately is, such principled inconsistency fascinated me because it generated Kantian-style questions regarding conditions of possibility for what we claim to know. For example, how is it possible for individuals to simultaneously hold clearly inconsistent beliefs? The issue seemed to me to be partly epistemological in that compatibility of our beliefs plays a fundamental role in any claim we might make that human beings (sometimes) act rationally. Such glaring inconsistencies required philosophical explanation if assertions of human rationality could ever be supported.

Thus when the new black film wave began to use *noir* techniques and themes in the middle and late 1980s, I came to perceive them as crystallizing many interests that I had had for a long time. Seeing *Do the Right Thing* for the first time I remember as particularly formative because I felt I was being challenged by ideas that I could not fully assimilate just then, but knew to be important socially, cinematically, and philosophically. When I saw the outright African-American *films noirs* released a few years later, such as *One False Move*, *Deep Cover, Juice,* and *Menace II Society,* the need to make those connections became imperative. It took me some time to figure out how to coherently absorb the ideas presented in these and other black *noir* films, and even more time to articulate that coherence, but one crucial feature in my efforts was realizing the insight expressed by Douglass: understanding white resistance to full social equality for African Americans often requires the integral use of philosophy.

This book is the product of my extended application of philosophy to the role race can play in our cinematic viewing as well as our social practices. In writing it, I hope to have foregrounded the reflective, analytical work either embodied or encouraged by many black *noir* films; that is, the techniques through which these films at times explore, at times urge *us* to explore, such matters as the theory and practice of "white privilege," the distorting effects of white supremacy, and the ways in which categories of race have defined and continue to direct much of our cinematic perception, our vision of the moral self, and what counts as appropriate moral sensibility. Part of my argument about these films is that they often function philosophically in the sense that they either provide or promote serious and systematic consideration of pre-conceived ideas in ways that make possible the fundamental alteration of our senses of self as well as the world in which we live. Their makers have directed *noir*'s capacities to trouble us and make us think toward matters of race and at times raised it to the highest level of reflective thought. By shaking white viewers in particular out of their ordinary modes of thinking, these films encourage the development of alternative systems of cognition that challenge dominant forms of moral knowledge as well as cinematic perception. Perspicuous representations of such matters are critical because they make clearer where we really are, morally speaking, and what we need to do in order to *fully* put ideals such as justice and equality into practice. I hope that the analyses and arguments I offer here will similarly inspire readers to reflect seriously and systematically on the interconnections between philosophy, race, film, and our social practices. At the very least, they should give readers a place to begin by offering them new ways to look at these films.

ACKNOWLEDGMENTS

Like many first-time authors, I have amassed numerous debts to those who have offered help, encouragement, or inspiration along the way. Three former teachers I wish to single out for praise are Gary Iseminger, Keith Gunderson, and Marcia Eaton. While I was an undergraduate, Gary taught me more about philosophy than I ever realized, the dividends of which are still paying off. As my dissertation adviser Keith gave me the latitude and sense of autonomy that I needed to finish—and to go on and become a colleague. Marcia sparked my desire to specialize in a field that I loved. She also suggested years ago that I combine my interests in philosophy and film, one product of which you have in your hands. I do not expect these or any other instructor I had to endorse everything I have written here, but from time to time I hope they can see their influence in turns of mind or phrase.

Old friends I wish to specially thank here are Garry Pech, Tom Atchison, Jonathan Munby, Karen Jüers-Munby, and Jim Glassman. While we were graduate students Garry and Tom listened to me for more than a decade while we spilled coffee and food on each other's books talking away hours about philosophy of psychology, Wittgenstein, ethics, and political theory. I probably learned more about philosophical thinking from these two than from anyone else. Traces of their different influences are evident throughout this book— Garry's sensibilities regarding philosophy of mind and psychology; Tom's regarding radical political philosophy and ethics. Jonathan and Karen became friends and introduced me to American studies and comparative literature during open-ended discussions that lasted over years and dissertations, and gave me confidence that I had worthwhile thoughts at a time when I was very unsure of myself. Their generosity, both intellectual and personal, is something I continue to appreciate. Jim has inspired me through decades spanning graduate student and professional lives with his political commitment, friendship, and intellectual insatiability. It was also Jim who first pointed out to me the problems regarding race in philosophy by telling me about those early articles by Harry Bracken and Richard Popkin criticizing Locke's and Hume's contributions to racialized thinking.

Colleagues I wish to thank include Charles Mills, who electrified me with a presentation on white supremacy as a concept of philosophical analysis in 1994. His arguments underscored my sense that philosophy needed to address matters of race. Charles has also provided friendship, advice, support, and criticism over the years since we first met. He even served as a reviewer for my book twice, so I feel doubly grateful to him for his willingness to plow through my work. Susan Kollin has read every word I have written, offered invaluable analysis and criticism of my ideas, arguments, and prose, and if I haven't followed all her advice properly, it is only because of my own stubbornness and lack of insight. Dan Shaw has managed *Film and Philosophy* since 2000 and I am proud to have had the opportunity to assist him in editing that journal. He also served as one of my manuscript reviewers and offered crucial recommendations that substantially improved it. Noël Carroll provided inspiration for years before we met through his work on the philosophy of film, and since has been a crucial colleague and peer. Murray Smith's work moved me to focus on morally ambivalent *noir* characters, but my interactions with him have been anything but *noirish*. His thoughtful advice and criticism have made this work far better than it would have been otherwise. Tom Wartenberg was actually the first to recommend that I write this book, and I deeply appreciate his encouragement. His comments and advice over the years have substantially improved my arguments. Simon Dixon has listened in his patient, open manner and provided thoughtful, generous comments from before the book was even an idea in my head. His collegiality was a crucial factor in my belief that the work I was doing was worthwhile.

Other colleagues I wish to thank include Sander Lee, Kevin Stoehr, Prasanta Bandyopadhyay, Richard Gilmore, Bill Lawson, Tommy Lott, Amy Coplan, Lester Hunt, Carl Plantinga, Richard Allen, Ray Pratt, Mitch Avila, Katherine Thomson-Jones, Leonard Harris, and Ron Sundstrom, whose comments, advice, or encouragements were crucial to the completion of this book. I also wish to thank my philosophy colleagues at Montana State University for providing me a welcome environment in which to do my work. My departmental chairs, Robert Rydell and Brett Walker, also came forward with support for my scholarship in the form of course releases, funding, and other assistance that facilitated the completion of this book.

For more than a decade, the Society for the Philosophic Study of the Contemporary Visual Arts has provided a welcome venue for my ideas. For nearly as long I have also enjoyed the acumen of American Society of Aesthetics members. Under the aegis of these professional organizations I have learned a great deal about the philosophical analysis of art, open-minded discussion, and intellectual generosity. I doubt my work would exist without the protective umbrellas they provide.

Many of my students offered inspiration as well. Calvin Selvey pushed me in ways that changed the direction of my thinking about how viewers perceived race in film. Other students whose names I should mention include John Glock, Ryan Moreno, Tim Oakberg, Matt Krug, Randy Krogstad, Brian Lande, Chris Ho, Andrew Edwards, Sheena Rice, Aaron Peterson, Bret Stalcup, and J. R. Logan. Their thoughtful responses to my ideas and arguments substantially improved this book.

I must also thank Montana State University's Office of the Vice President for Research, Creativity, and Technology Transfer, Office of the Provost, and

Office of the Dean of the College of Letters and Sciences for financial support. As heads or former heads of those offices, Thomas McCoy, David M. Dooley, Sara Jayne Steen, and George Tuthill deserve praise for their willingness to open the coffers of the university for a project that is probably one of the least likely to ever produce a financial return.

I also wish to thank Sandy Thatcher and the expert production assistants at the Pennsylvania State University Press. Sandy's enthusiasm, efficiency, and wisdom made the project much easier to finish, and the production staff offered all the help I could have wanted. In addition, I want to offer a special thanks to my friend and colleague Theo Lipfert for his patience in helping a technological inept to capture and prepare the images that accompany the text.

An earlier version of Chapter 1 appeared in the *Journal of Aesthetics and Art Criticism* 64 (2006). Ancestral versions of parts of the introduction, as well as parts of Chapters 3, 4, and 6, appeared in the *Journal of Social Philosophy* 31 (2000); and a shorter version of the section on *Deep Cover* in Chapter 6 appeared in *Film and Philosophy* 11 (2007). Earlier versions of parts of the introduction and the section on *Summer of Sam* in Chapter 8 first appeared in *Film and Knowledge: Essays on the Integration of Images and Ideas,* ed. Kevin L. Stoehr (© 2002 Kevin L. Stoehr, by permission of McFarland & Company, Inc., Box 611, Jefferson NC 28640); and part of the introduction saw light originally in a review essay in *American Quarterly* 56 (2004). I would like to thank the respective publishers for permission to reprint these essays or the parts of them that survived revision and integration into the manuscript: Blackwell Publishers; the Society for the Philosophic Study of the Contemporary Visual Arts; McFarland and Company, Publishers; and the Johns Hopkins University Press.

Last, I would like to thank my daughters, Michaela Kollin and Alexandra Flory, for their patience and equanimity in putting up with me working on a manuscript that they have never known me not to be working on in their young lives. My deepest appreciation, however, is to my friend, colleague, and partner Susan Kollin, who has read it all, seen every movie, and put up with more requests for critical comments than anyone ever should have. Without her, there would be no book, and I would be a greatly diminished human being.

FIG. I   Eunice Leonard (Theresa Harris) and her date (Caleb Peterson) warily answer the questions of private detective Jeff Markham (Robert Mitchum) (*Out of the Past,* 1947).

INTRODUCTION
philosophy and the blackness of *film noir*

The creation of film was as if meant for philosophy—meant to reorient everything philosophy has said about reality and its representation, about art and imitation, about greatness and conventionality, about judgment and pleasure, about skepticism and transcendence, about language and expression.

—Stanley Cavell, *Contesting Tears*

Men enjoy looking at images, because what happens is that, as they contemplate them, they apply their understanding and reasoning to each element.

—Aristotle, *Poetics*

It is knowledge itself that is dangerous in the noir world of American race relations.

—Paula Rabinowitz, *Black and White and Noir*

During the past two decades African-American and other filmmakers have refashioned the themes and techniques commonly associated with *film noir*[1] in order to redirect mainstream audience responses toward race and expose the injustices and inequities that typically frame black experience in the United States. By doing so, these filmmakers have created a new cinematic subcategory, "black *noir*."[2] Many of their films offer trenchant critiques of mainstream conceptions of race by encouraging audiences to reflect on such questions as what it means to be white, what it means to be African American, what it means to be treated equally, and what it means to be acknowledged as a full-fledged human being. By eliciting such responses, these black *noir* films aim to reorient and redirect, à la Cavell, the perceptions, imaginings, and dispositions of their viewers regarding race and its relations to morality and knowledge, thereby carrying their achievement beyond merely breaking new aesthetic ground and into the realm of philosophical reflection.

Black film's artistic development illustrates more generally how *film noir*, by virtue of its capacity to urge audiences to question the validity of assumptions

---

1. I have italicized *"film noir"* and *"noir"* throughout this book.

2. Ed Guerrero, "A Circus of Dreams and Lies: The Black Film Wave at Middle Age," in *The New American Cinema*, ed. Jon Lewis (Durham: Duke University Press, 1998), 328–52, names some of these films "funky noir" (346), but for reasons that will become obvious, I prefer the broader term "black *noir*." See also Guerrero's review of *Devil in a Blue Dress*, in *Cineaste* 22, no. 1 (1996): 40.

that guide their moral judgment, may function to criticize the unfairness of existing social orders. Although a dimension of *noir* films intermittently from their "discovery" by French criticism more than sixty years ago, recent African-American filmmakers in particular have sharpened these critical capacities in ways that highlight their potential for encouraging serious reconsideration of ordinary moral perception, thinking, and action—a potential for which I aim to promote greater appreciation.[3]

This book further examines African-American and related cinema for ways in which they orchestrate audience emotions of sympathy and empathy so as to encourage viewers to think philosophically about the racialized dimensions of film perception, the human condition, and current circumstances of human equality. By addressing these facets of narrative fiction film I draw particularly on recent work in philosophy, critical race theory, and cognitive film theory to make sense of how filmmakers have reconfigured *film noir* for the purposes of social critique and reflective inquiry into race. As a work of what might be called philosophically informed cultural studies, this book owes a significant debt to thinkers such as Cavell, Noël Carroll, Murray Smith, David Bordwell, Charles W. Mills, Lewis R. Gordon, Tommy L. Lott, Stephen Mulhall, and Richard Dyer, who opened up new possibilities for analyzing connections between film, culture, and philosophy. I extend their projects to the "black film wave" that began in the mid-1980s, its subsequent internationalization, and the employment of *film noir* techniques by these aesthetic movements to encourage what amounts to philosophical reflection in viewers.[4]

Ultimately, I argue that these thinkers' work helps to reveal how many African-American and other filmmakers have discovered innovative ways to spur a "Socratic impulse" regarding race by means of *film noir*. Numerous instances of black *noir*, for example, challenge us to use our reasoning capacities to think in sustained and focused ways about fundamental human questions, such as "What is it to be human?" and "How should I live?" By virtue of such challenges to reflect, we are encouraged to devise new *"ways to think"* that allow us to better understand ourselves and the world around us,[5] and that are here applied to race. From clearly recognizable black *noirs* such as Carl Franklin's *One False Move* (1992) to Spike Lee's *noir*-influenced *Bamboozled* (2000) and beyond, these films engage contemporary understandings of what it means to be a raced human being. Filmmakers as diverse as Franklin,

3. While Cavell analyzes the capacity of remarriage comedies and melodramas of the unknown woman to generate philosophical reflection on a kind of Emersonian perfectionism—and even notes the startling power of occasional *films noirs*—he does not attribute this capacity to *film noir per se*.

4. For more on the "black film wave," see Ed Guerrero, *Framing Blackness: The African American Image in Film* (Philadelphia: Temple University Press, 1993), and "A Circus of Dreams and Lies."

5. Stanley Cavell, "The Thought of Movies," in *Themes Out of School: Effects and Causes* (Chicago: University of Chicago Press, 1984), 9. See also Stephen Mulhall, *On Film* (London: Routledge, 2002), esp. 1–2.

Lee, Bill Duke, Charles Burnett, Kasi Lemmons, Ernest Dickerson, and the Hughes brothers have deployed and invigorated *film noir* conventions in order to portray matters such as African-American struggles with cinematic representation as well as racial injustice. In the process, they have created new possibilities for generating critical perspectives on contemporary American society and forms of racialized thinking that underlie standard conceptions of film perception, humanity, and how we should live.

With the exception of Africana Studies scholar Manthia Diawara's crucial pair of essays in the early 1990s, however, few scholars have addressed this development in detail.[6] Moreover, no work has examined the philosophical dimensions of black *noir* or its continuity into the twenty-first century. This book rectifies these oversights by analyzing how the use of *film noir* in the recent black film wave and elsewhere highlights representations of blackness in conjunction with moral and criminal transgression in order to provoke viewer analysis of racial inequities that encourage stereotypical representation as well as moral and criminal transgression in the first place. These works of art goad viewers to concentrate reflectively on typical conceptions of race, equality, and knowledge that often form the foundation of their moral action and thought. In this manner the films bring into focus presumptions that undergird the state of race in America and the world, and induce their viewers to do so as well, thereby mirroring comparable discussions now taking place at the intersection of critical race theory and philosophy. By promoting sustained and deliberate audience attention to fundamental questions of human existence such as the status of one's humanity and how its social ranking may contribute to the shape of one's overall moral treatment, these films urge viewers to contemplate race in ways that enhance, augment, and extend more formally philosophical discussions.

In order to better reveal these epistemological interconnections through cinema, I rely on recent advances in analytic philosophy of film, particularly those developed by Carroll and Smith. By theorizing how audience members may develop allegiances with different kinds of morally complex characters through modulation of the sympathy or empathy we typically feel toward them, these critics have made possible more precise understandings of how we evaluate figures such as those standardly found in *film noir,* in particular

---

6. Manthia Diawara, "*Noir* by *Noirs:* Toward a New Realism in Black Cinema," in *Shades of Noir,* ed. Joan Copjec (London: Verso, 1993), 261–78 (reprinted in slightly different form from *African-American Review* 27 [1993]: 525–37); Diawara, "Black American Cinema: The New Realism," in *Black American Cinema,* ed. Manthia Diawara (London: Routledge, 1993), 3–25, esp. 19–24. Other critics who have described black *noir* include Guerrero, "Circus of Dreams and Lies," 346–49; Foster Hirsch, *Detours and Lost Highways: A Map of Neo-Noir* (New York: Limelight Editions, 1999), 295–304; Alain Silver and James Ursini, "Appendix E1: Neo-Noir," in *Film Noir: An Encyclopedic Reference to the American Style,* 3rd ed., ed. Alain Silver and Elizabeth Ward (Woodstock, N.Y.: Overlook Press, 1992), 406–7, 412; James Naremore, *More Than Night: Film Noir in Its Contexts* (Berkeley and Los Angeles: University of California Press, 1998), 244–53; and Andrew Spicer, *Film Noir* (Harlow: Longman, 2002), 168–70.

those characters with whom we might not ordinarily sympathize or empathize in real life. Analytic philosophers of film, however, have addressed issues
of race rather less than their Continental counterparts, an omission that my
study helps remedy. By combining the theoretical structures analytic thinkers
provide with recent critical race theory and the reflective method for considering film worked out by Cavell, William Rothman, and Mulhall, I outline the
traditional themes and techniques of *film noir* that have sustained critical as
well as viewer interest over the years and that African-American directors,
writers, and other film artists have found advantageous to employ.

The narrative features in many black *noirs* tacitly recall elements found in
such classic *noir* films as *Double Indemnity* (Billy Wilder, 1944), *The Big Sleep*
(Howard Hawks, 1946), *The Naked City* (Jules Dassin, 1948), *Sunset Boulevard*
(Billy Wilder, 1950), and *The Asphalt Jungle* (John Huston, 1950). Classic *noir*
as well as African-American *noir* frequently address matters of power, confinement, determinism, and marginalization. Both regularly depict unknown or
inadequately understood forces that are far more powerful than their protagonists, who are marginalized from mainstream society or lured into unjust fates
from which there seems to be no escape. Both also encourage sympathetic
or empathetic responses from their audiences for morally ambivalent characters. In black American cinema, however, such *noir* elements often become
powerful tools for disclosing the inadequacies of racialized understandings of
humanity, justice, and morality. By urging viewers to think and reflect on their
presumptions about race, many of these films make knowledge dangerous,
as American Studies scholar Paula Rabinowitz would point out, in the sense
that questioning presuppositions has often incurred the wrath of those who
premise their lives on such beliefs. Of course, philosophy has been familiar
with such epistemological dangers since at least Socrates, but placing it in the
context of American race relations is something relatively new to the field, as
it is to mainstream U.S. cinema.

By deploying these and other features, many black *noir* films urge their
audiences to contemplate claims strikingly similar to those advanced by recent
philosophical theorists of race. Throughout this study, I reference the diverse
ways in which these theorists upset what Charles Mills calls an "epistemology
of ignorance" by providing insights into alternative systems of social cognition
that challenge dominant systems of moral knowledge.[7] In the process, I argue
that certain cinematic works, consistent with perspectives offered by critical
race theorists, demonstrate how racist oppression deforms African-American
life even as the majority of white Americans perceive it as nothing out of the
ordinary. Ultimately, the revelation of such perspectives calls for a reconsideration and redirection of aesthetic perception as well as moral thinking. Both
the philosophical and cinematic works provide critiques of moral or aesthetic
knowledge that place before us the obligation to question and rethink what

7. Charles W. Mills, *The Racial Contract* (Ithaca: Cornell University Press, 1997), esp. 17–
19, 91–109.

most people would otherwise observe as "normal" forms of life in America, and do so by mobilizing sympathetic and empathetic responses that promote a better understanding of the moral circumstances of many African Americans. Moreover, in the last few years international filmmakers have applied this critical focus of black *noir* to issues concerning human rights in a global context.

In this way, I argue that the recent intervention of critical race theory into the field of philosophy crystallizes much of the recent black film wave's innovative development of *film noir*. By bringing black *noirs* into dialogue with philosophical examinations of race, I explore such matters as the theory and practice of "white privilege," the distorting effects of white supremacy on justice and morality, and the ways in which categories of race have defined and continue to direct much of our vision of the moral self and what counts as appropriate moral behavior.

Crucial to note here is that I consider "race" to be a social construction that possesses very real consequences for human beings, even though it has no basis in any sort of objective reality. As such, race fails to be what philosophers of language call a "natural kind," like "gold," "water," or "tigers," which may lay claim to identifying essentialistic properties founded in something outside us.[8] Rather, racialized senses of the terms "black," "white," and so on designate sets of power relations that contingently depend on particular, historical circumstances existing between groups of human beings designated by these terms. Race and its attendant conceptions, then, turn out to be "*sociopolitical rather than biological, but . . . nonetheless real*"; that is, socially real rather than rooted in natural facts about the world.[9] Depicting the nonnatural and imposed character of race constitutes a fundamental dimension of many black *noirs,* which I bring out by means of placing them side by side with philosophical analyses of such concepts.

One reason I have chosen to focus on this particular group of films is that they exploit *film noir's* distinctive potential for encouraging viewers to question presuppositions that might otherwise go unnoticed. For example, as Mulhall has argued, among the most arresting aspects of *Blade Runner* (Ridley Scott, 1982) are its efforts to encourage viewers to think about what it means to be human.[10] It might also be argued that the iconic 1970s *noir Chinatown* (Roman Polanski, 1974) attracts many viewers because it elicits troubled reflections about the degree of corruption with which many municipalities are run. More classic *films noirs* such as *Force of Evil* (Abraham Polonsky, 1948), *Thieves' Highway* (Jules Dassin, 1949), *In a Lonely Place* (Nicholas Ray, 1950), and *The*

8. See, for example, Saul A. Kripke, *Naming and Necessity* (Cambridge: Harvard University Press, 1980), 116ff.

9. Mills, *Racial Contract,* 126.

10. Stephen Mulhall, "Picturing the Human (Body and Soul): A Reading of *Blade Runner,*" *Film and Philosophy* 1 (1994): 87–104. (Mulhall later revised this essay and incorporated it into *On Film,* 33–51.)

Damned Don't Cry (Vincent Sherman, 1950) operate analogously, bringing to the surface societal presumptions regarding class or gender in ways that invite critical examination on the part of the audience. Furthermore, film historian Sheri Chinen Biesen notes that generally, "Wartime *noir* films were provocative and challenging. They demanded thinking from filmgoers just to figure them out."[11] This subversive potential in *film noir* has served African-American and other filmmakers well, as it has paved the way for constructing new methods for eliciting sophisticated audience contemplation regarding justice, morality, knowledge, and their relations to race.

Recent Philosophical Theories of Race

An illustration from the autobiography of African-American writer Chester Himes might best serve to bring out a crucial, long-standing relation between race and philosophy. In *My Life of Absurdity,* Himes wrote that problems of race had created such complexities in his day-to-day existence that he often could not tell the difference between what was real and what was absurd in the existential sense of that term.[12] Himes's observation about his own life fittingly describes the general status of race in modern Western philosophy.[13] On the one hand, until well into the 1990s race had at best a marginal place in most philosophical discussions, particularly those taking place in the United States. Problems linked to the concept of race were predominantly considered to be of peripheral interest; empirical, nonphilosophical matters to be discussed after the "real" theoretical disputes had been settled.[14] On the other hand, since the seventeenth century, Western philosophy has profoundly influenced the treatment of nonwhites and their status as human beings, even while it outlined and established the bases for "universal" human rights and theories of liberalism. While providing the foundations for these cornerstones of modern Western society, philosophers such as Locke, Rousseau, Hume, Kant, and Hegel

11.   Sheri Chinen Biesen, *Blackout: World War II and the Origins of Film Noir* (Baltimore: Johns Hopkins University Press, 2005), 216. I argue for a similar conclusion about subversive *noirs* (in both classical and neo-*noir* forms) generally in "Black on White: *Film Noir* and the Epistemology of Race in Recent African American Cinema," *Journal of Social Philosophy* 31 (2000): 82–116, esp. 87–89.

12.   Chester Himes, *My Life of Absurdity: The Later Years* (New York: Paragon House, 1976), 1–2, 109.

13.   And, for that matter, the history of film. But that is a story that has already been well-documented. See, for example, Thomas Cripps, *Slow Fade to Black: The Negro in American Film, 1900–1942* (New York: Oxford University Press, 1977) and *Making Movies Black: The Hollywood Message Movie from World War II to the Civil Rights Era* (New York: Oxford University Press, 1993); Guerrero, *Framing Blackness;* and Daniel Bernardi, ed., *The Birth of Whiteness: Race and the Emergence of U.S. Cinema* (New Brunswick: Rutgers University Press, 1996).

14.   See, for example, John Rawls's *A Theory of Justice* (Cambridge: Harvard University Press, 1971).

also established the theoretical underpinnings for modern racism.[15] This contradiction continues to induce simultaneous dimensions of utter absurdity and brutal realism into discussions of race in Western philosophy. Because many scholars in the discipline have such difficulty admitting the fact that some of the "founding fathers" of human rights were also "founding fathers" of racism,[16] they have frequently had difficulty telling the real from the absurd with respect to race.

In contrast to this typical way of treating racial matters, some contemporary philosophers argue that while Western philosophy's influence on people of color has been profound, that influence has been consistently ignored, evaded, or obscured. They suggest that modern liberalism has historically and conceptually presupposed the systematic and racialized oppression of entire groups of human beings from whose domination whites, as the main beneficiaries of modern liberalism, have long benefited and from whose circumstances they continue to benefit. For these thinkers, the everyday, as configured through the category of race, emerges as a primary battleground. They argue, for example, that, like many standard conceptions of liberalism, the typical day-to-day lives of white Americans presuppose systematic and racialized oppression. In other words, the everyday life of persons counted as white in the United States takes for granted a system of dominance and advantage that, when examined in its actual, specific details, has as one of its dimensions the unconscious presumption of full human rights for whites while also presuming a lesser schedule of rights for nonwhites.

This social structure continues today as an implicit legacy of explicitly advanced white supremacy in the past. Being white in its typical configuration, then, continues to have its social, political, and moral advantages, a conclusion that should surprise no one. Perhaps the astonishing consequence broached here, however, is that typical whiteness also possesses and imposes implicit *cognitive* requirements, with moral consequences for both whites and nonwhites. When looked at as an entrenched social institution that continues to be supported and maintained by the practices of actual human beings, the standard form of whiteness amounts to an epistemological stance that fundamentally determines moral action and what is perceived as morally relevant.

These scholars thus contend that one overlooked aspect of race is how it permeates everyday cognitions as well as dominant sensibilities; that is, ordinary ways of perceiving, thinking, believing, and acting. Mills argues, for

15. See, for example, Robert Bernasconi, "Who Invented the Concept of Race? Kant's Role in the Enlightenment Construction of Race," in *Race*, ed. Robert Bernasconi (London: Blackwell, 2001), 11–36; Richard H. Popkin, "Eighteenth Century Racism," in *The Columbia History of Western Philosophy*, ed. Richard H. Popkin (New York: Columbia University Press, 1999), 508–15; Mills, *Racial Contract*, esp. 62–72; Emmanuel C. Eze, *Achieving Our Humanity: The Idea of a Postracial Future* (New York: Routledge, 2001); and the excerpts by these historical figures anthologized in *Race and the Enlightenment*, ed. Emmanuel C. Eze (London: Blackwell, 1997).

16. Mills, *Racial Contract*, 72.

instance, that whites normally operate by means of a structural blindness to their own power and privilege, as well as to the consequences of that lack of vision. "An idealized consensus of cognitive norms" informs their thoughts, beliefs, and actions, constituting a system of knowledge that imposes certain misperceptions, insensitivities, and presumed incapacities regarding persons counted as nonwhite.[17] Moreover, this epistemological blindness is a *condition* of whiteness in its idealized form, in the sense that to think and perceive from that subject position requires that one possess such cognitive incapacities. Whiteness, considered as a set of institutionalized power relations, rather than as an aspect of biology or heredity, has profoundly disturbing epistemological as well as moral consequences.[18]

Thomas E. Hill Jr. and Bernard Boxill concur with Mills's assessment of this cognitive deficiency on the part of many whites, even as these philosophers work from a strict Kantian moral perspective.[19] They argue that knowing the right thing to do can be tremendously difficult for such individuals because knowing the relevant moral facts is deeply problematic for those comfortably ensconced in power. Hill and Boxill elaborate: "Confident, complacent, well-positioned white people will not only find it difficult to do what they know to be right; they will find it still more difficult to know what is right, even when they sincerely claim that they are trying to do so" (470). This difficulty arises because whites may be easily deceived by their own social advantage into believing that it accrues to all, and unable to see with adequate vividness cases of racial injustice because these phenomena are so far removed from their experience (469–70). Such obstacles place whites at a cognitive disadvantage as a price of their social advantage. They are prone to self-deception regarding racial injustice because their social power seriously impairs their ability to grasp the morally relevant facts in such cases. Their "white privilege" thus typically blinds them to its absence in the lives of others. As a result, their capacity to know or "do the right thing" becomes substantially disabled.

From a phenomenological perspective Lewis Gordon argues similarly that most whites misperceive systematic misanthropy, abnormality, social pathology, and injustice involving African Americans as normal.[20] Rather than see what in the situation of fellow whites would be deemed unfair, iniquitous, or even morally perverse, one sees merely the ordinary lives of blacks, normalized by its presumed pervasiveness as well as by waves and waves of alleged explanation aimed at justification. In other words, it is "those people's" living

---

17. Ibid., 17–19.

18. See also ibid., 91–109, 126–27.

19. Thomas E. Hill Jr. and Bernard Boxill, "Kant and Race," in *Race and Racism*, ed. Bernard Boxill (Oxford: Oxford University Press, 2001), 448–71.

20. Lewis R. Gordon, *Fanon and the Crisis of European Man: An Essay on Philosophy and the Human Sciences* (New York: Routledge, 1995), 62–63.

conditions, their nature, social relations, economic circumstances, family structures, or overall potential for intelligence that are to blame.[21] Gordon notes that such misperceptions dehumanize whites and nonwhites both. Whites who presume—whether consciously or unconsciously—a racist outlook on humanity possess, as he puts it, a "misanthropic consciousness" that not only ignores, but is incapable of appreciating significant aspects of the social world.[22] Whole dimensions of human interaction, lifestyles, sensitivity, and even language become off-limits as a condition of presuming typical forms of whiteness. One aspect of having taken on these very ordinary forms of whiteness, then, is that they require cognitive, moral, and social constriction of one's full human potential, the results of which have disastrous consequences for one's self and others with whom one comes in contact.

A striking parallel to this point may be found in Mulhall's analysis of *Blade Runner*, in which he argues convincingly that one of the film's main focuses is the importance of recognizing and acknowledging the humanity of others in order to recognize and acknowledge the humanity in one's self. It is precisely this lesson that the main character, Deckard (Harrison Ford), learns from his encounters with the replicants.[23] Mulhall follows the lead of Cavell here, who analyzes in *The Claim of Reason* how taking a person seriously *as* a person must involve such acknowledgment and recognition.[24] Neither Cavell nor Mulhall applies his arguments to matters of race in film *per se*, even though both analyze the related issue of slavery and Cavell discusses issues of race in a more general context.[25] In a striking manner, however, their explorations of the importance of recognition and acknowledgment of humanity in others, and its consequences not only for others but one's self, correlates with Gordon's discussion of race. As we will see, the cinematic disclosure of this reciprocal relation between one's humanity and that of others plays a fundamental role in my discussion of black *noir*'s philosophical dimensions.

Critical race theorist David Theo Goldberg explores related points by examining how some racist exclusions may be justified by rational means. While

---

21. Examples of attempts to explain or justify such existing "normal" social relations include the Moynihan Report (1965); Charles Murray and Richard J. Herrnstein, *The Bell Curve* (New York: Free Press, 1993); J. Philippe Rushton, *Race, Evolution, and Behavior* (New Brunswick: Transaction Books, 1995); Seymour W. Itzkoff, *The Decline of Intelligence in America* (Westport, Conn.: Praeger, 1994); and Michael Levin, *Why Race Matters: Race Differences and What They Mean* (Westport, Conn.: Praeger, 1997).

22. Lewis Gordon, *Bad Faith and Antiblack Racism* (Atlantic Highlands, N.J.: Humanities Press, 1995), 182–84.

23. Mulhall, *On Film*, 33–51.

24. Stanley Cavell, *The Claim of Reason* (Oxford: Oxford University Press, 1979), esp. 372ff.

25. See, for example, ibid., 375ff. On the other hand, Cavell makes a few brief yet critically important observations about the representation of blacks in film in *The World Viewed: Reflection on the Ontology of Film*, enlarged edition (Cambridge: Harvard University Press, 1979), one of which I address later in the introduction.

many, perhaps most, forms of racism are indeed not rational—as we might expect—others, Goldberg argues, turn out to be consistent with accepted criteria of rationality such as providing sufficient evidence, accepting reasonable doubt, being open to criticism and revision, and the like. Those forms of racist belief that achieve the typical benchmarks for rationality thus become cognitively "normalized" by endorsement from the highest standard of human behavior. It becomes "perfectly reasonable," in other words, for whites to assume in everyday life that new, expensive clothing or valuable possessions operate as markers of criminal accomplishment if possessed by African Americans, but not whites; that skin color may be understood as a sign of criminal guilt or at minimum suspicion; or that neighborhood residencies may be taken as indicators of good or bad morals on the part of their inhabitants.[26]

More recently, legal scholar Jody David Armour has augmented Goldberg's arguments by considering how some versions of the philosophical position known as Bayesianism may actually support "rational discrimination" by whites. If one uses certain forms of probablistic reasoning to weigh statistics of violent felony convictions, overall criminality, and the like, then believing that, say, blacks possess a far higher potential to be violent assailants of one's person or property passes the test of rationality.[27] While Armour goes on to argue that such reasoning fails to meet a higher standard of reasonableness,[28] the point I wish to underscore here is that some forms of racism have an at least *prima facie* claim to being rational, which as Armour points out has been accepted by many U.S. courts as well as some philosophers (e.g., Michael Levin).[29] Elsewhere, I have noted how some forms of racism that were deemed rational in the past have served to explain racialized aesthetic response to melodrama.[30] These revelations about rationality's role in supporting some forms of racism would seem an unfortunate discovery for almost anyone working in

26. David Theo Goldberg, *Racist Culture: Philosophy and the Politics of Meaning* (London: Blackwell, 1993), esp. 139–47.

27. Jody David Armour, *Negrophobia and Reasonable Racism: The Hidden Costs of Being Black in America* (New York: New York University Press, 1997), 35–46. (As my colleague Prasanta Bandyopadhyay has pointed out to me, this is a rather crude form of Bayesianism.)

28. Armour argues that *acting* on rationally based factual assessments such as some Bayesian perspectives may offer would be unreasonable because it would fail to take into consideration other crucial factors, such as "the consequences of error if those factual judgments are mistaken" (ibid., 47). In other words, the cost of potential mistakes is too high for the threshold of *reasonably* acting on such beliefs to be breached. More generally, Armour explains that acting on these seemingly rationally justified racist beliefs ignores the value-laden dimension of reason (55–57). The fact that being reasonable requires a balancing of different values, some of which are the potential harms that may arise if one is inaccurate about one's assessments, militates against these discriminatory beliefs being endorsed by reason. Ultimately, he argues, such apparently rational assessments fall back on racial stereotypes for their foundation, rather than sound reasoning, so they may be rationally rejected (51–54).

29. Ibid., 1–46. See also Michael Levin, "Responses to Race Differences in Crime," in Boxill, *Race and Racism*, 145–79, and Levin, *Why Race Matters.*

30. See my "Race, Rationality, and Melodrama: Aesthetic Response and the Case of Oscar Micheaux," *Journal of Aesthetics and Art Criticism* 63 (2005): 327–38.

philosophy, to say nothing of those in the culture at large who would wish to support full and impartial equality for all.

One shared conclusion of these and other philosophical theorists who examine the epistemology of race is that instances of unfairness and injustice in black life frequently escape detection by whites. The task of the theorist thus becomes that of bringing attention to the epistemological misperception of everyday details, so we may reformulate and redirect typical white moral vision in ways that would recognize and acknowledge the unjust and unfair circumstances constituting many people's ordinary lives, rather than letting what Frantz Fanon calls the "white gaze" determine dominant moral perception.[31] Recent philosophical theorists of race have therefore worked to expose what Mills has called a racial fantasyland that undergirds white dominance and social advantage. The beliefs and presumptions that create this fantasyland constitute an epistemology of ignorance that typically prevents whites from perceiving the reality and effects of their own beliefs concerning racial difference.[32] As these theorists argue, such cognitive blindness requires fundamental revision, for it rests on what Mills calls a "consensual hallucination," an invented delusional world where standard white moral consciousness is filtered through norms of social cognition that derive from a typically unconscious sense of dominance and advantage in the world (18). The necessity of redirecting and reformulating this flawed white moral vision is forcefully brought home by many black American *noir*-influenced films.

Philosophy, Cognition, and Film Theory

In analyzing this recent wave of black filmmaking, I work from a theoretical position that synthesizes the broadly cognitivist outlook exemplified by the work of Smith, Carroll, and Bordwell with the more reflective, Wittgensteinian method employed by Cavell, Rothman, Mulhall, Richard Allen, and others. Such a theoretical approach might be called "analytic film theory," a term suggested by Allen and Smith in their collection *Film Theory and Philosophy*.[33] This approach focuses on investigating the actual linguistic practices and beliefs we employ regarding our efforts to understand films as an appropriate starting point for theoretical analysis. In doing so we might better understand and clarify such cognitive components for the sake of greater technical and theoretical facility (5). The point of such analysis, then, is to reveal "the conceptual structure [on] which such usage depends" rather than its literalization, replacement, or reformation (6). With theoretical hallmarks such

31. Frantz Fanon, "The Lived Experience of the Black" (1951), trans. Valentine Moulard, in Bernasconi, *Race*, 185. My use of Fanon's term, of course, also alludes to Laura Mulvey's "male gaze" in "Visual Pleasure and Narrative Cinema," *Screen* 16, no. 3 (1975): 6–18.

32. Mills, *Racial Contract*, 18.

33. Richard Allen and Murray Smith, "Introduction: Film Theory and Philosophy," in *Film Theory and Philosophy*, ed. Richard Allen and Murray Smith (Oxford: Clarendon Press, 1997), 3.

as philosophical clarification, precision, and "truth-tracking" to the greatest extent possible, this approach attends to argument, reasoning, accuracy, and recognition of complexity where it actually exists. It also seeks consistency with recent advances in other fields of study, such as those achieved by cognitive science, insofar as they inform our knowledge of human perception, psychology, and other matters crucial to a proper understanding of film (25–26). In this manner we might theorize about film in more interdisciplinary ways and diversify its foundations. Analytic film theory addresses artists' intentions as well, although these aesthetic aims in no way determine what might be important in a film. Rather, they are simply features relevant to an artwork that are as worth considering in our attempts to grasp what a film means as cultural considerations, political ideology, and other factors that contribute to the creation of art.

In bringing these aspirations to bear on film, Carroll argues that such theorizing should be provisional and piecemeal.[34] Rather than aim to achieve a unified, single theory that would explain all film for all time and all places, film theorizing—at least for now—would be better served by a variety of projects that accurately hypothesize, insofar as possible, about more limited objects of study, like the function of point of view editing or the operation of narrative suspense. Such theorizing, in other words, would "proceed at varying levels of generality and abstraction," depending on the needs of the project at hand (39). Such theorizing, "like most other forms of theoretical inquiry, . . . proceeds dialectically" (56), which accounts for its provisionality. In addition, attempts to formulate new theories take place in the context of past theoretical endeavors (57). Criticism and revision, then, will be fundamental to this philosophical style of inquiry into film (58). Insofar as such efforts will be "truth-tracking," the aim will be some sort of approximate truth rather than an absolute, Platonic conception (60).

Carroll, Smith, and other film theorists have further argued that film viewing in general should be understood as predominantly a matter of acentral imagining—that is, viewing a film from the outside, as if one were observing it, rather than experiencing it oneself. Whereas some forms of spectatorship from perspectives internal to a character remain possible, such a theoretical position directly opposes most stances that take "identification" as fundamental to film viewing, particularly those that require we perform some sort of "Vulcan mind-meld" with the characters, as Carroll puts it, so that we may grasp a film's chain of events and comprehend its meaning through imagining that we literally are the characters.[35] Unfortunately, most theories of film

---

34. See, for example, Noël Carroll, "Introduction," in *Theorizing the Moving Image* (New York: Cambridge University Press, 1996), xiii–xiv, and "Prospects for Film Theory: A Personal Assessment," in *Post-Theory: Reconstructing Film Studies*, ed. David Bordwell and Noël Carroll (Madison: University of Wisconsin Press, 1996), 40.

35. Noël Carroll, *The Philosophy of Horror, or, Paradoxes of the Heart* (London: Routledge, 1990), 89.

that invoke identification presume just that sort of undiscriminating, immediate imagining.[36]

Building on this insight, Smith constructs a theory to replace theoretical uses of identification in film and outlines a hypothesis to explain how we imaginatively engage with characters. He accomplishes this by introducing the interlocking concepts of recognition, alignment, and allegiance.[37] These concepts provide a more finely grained way to understand our grasp of characters than those offered by theories of identification. For example, recognition is a matter of how viewers assemble cinematically depicted traits into a specific character. By putting together narrative elements in analogy with ones we typically find and use in identifying human beings in the real world, such as the presumption that persons are embodied creatures, we construct characters that we understand as functioning in roughly the same way as actual individuals (82). Alignment, by contrast, "describes the process by which spectators are placed in relation to characters in terms of their access to their actions, and to what they know and feel" (83). Viewers' spatiotemporal attachment and subjective access to characters provide the means for audience members to acquire information about the characters, the plot, and other events taking place in the film. By specifying narrative range and restriction to their characters, filmmakers may determine what audience members know about the story they are telling. Alignment, then, accounts for the viewer's visual and aural congruence with characters and offers a theoretical structure through which audience limitation or freedom to gather information may be explained.

To have a relationship of allegiance to a character, on the other hand, is largely a matter of having a moral orientation to him or her; viewers evaluate characters from a moral point of view and respond accordingly. In its positive sense, allegiance will typically be a matter of feeling a broadly favorable moral connection to a character, such that the viewer approves of what the character thinks, believes, or does. Allegiance may be based on a variety of factors, but in general depends on reliable access to the character's state of mind, an understanding of the context of the character's actions, and a moral evaluation of the character based on this knowledge (84). Narrative understanding of such figures may be rooted in explicitly depicted features, such as the character's actions and statements, or in more subtle cues, such as iconography, music, or star persona (84). Smith also notes in passing a matter of primary significance to this book, that allegiance may be based partly on considerations stemming from presumptions regarding "ethnicity" (84).

---

36. See, for example, ibid., 88–96.

37. As Smith notes in his *Engaging Characters: Fiction, Emotion, and the Cinema* (Oxford: Clarendon Press, 1995), 108 n. 26, Carroll originally proposed the idea of allegiance and understanding characters by means of moral structure in "Toward a Theory of Film Suspense" (1984), reprinted in *Theorizing the Moving Image*, 94–117; see esp. 104–5. Of course, what Smith means by "recognition" here differs substantially from Cavell's sense of the term.

These interlocking concepts account for the structure of sympathy for characters in cinematic narrative and provide a theoretical explication of commonsense uses of the term "identification" (73). Of particular relevance to this study is how allegiance involves cognitive and emotional dimensions that result in a "moral orientation" to the character—a sense of moral approval, disapproval, or ambivalence toward what he or she does and believes. In this fashion we may explain in theoretically sophisticated ways how film viewers engage favorably, unfavorably, or ambivalently with characters. Of special note here is how Smith develops the idea that we might understand some morally complex characters as "alloys"—a "combination of culturally negative [and] culturally positive traits."[38] This alloying of good and bad characteristics can serve as a way to encourage audiences to sympathize with characters who hold aberrant social beliefs or commit immoral acts, such as theft or even murder. Smith explores this possibility mainly in regard to "perverse" beliefs about human sexuality,[39] but in applying this idea to *noir* characters I broaden it to incorporate beliefs about other forms of moral and social transgression.

In general, the good-bad structure of characters who are "alloys" in Smith's sense allows for audience sympathy with characters whom they might otherwise reject as unacceptable. Viewers are led to judge the characters in the story according to a system of preferences that they themselves construct from their experience through the film. These judgments, which may develop, evolve, or change over the course of the narrative, give the viewer a moral perspective toward the characters he or she has experienced cinematically. Viewers thus organize and rank characters according to a structure of character classification they create in response to what they see and hear.[40] In addition, certain characterological alloys can make us question our habits of moral judgment— interrogate typical applications of moral rules and principles and introduce greater subtlety into our moral assessments.[41]

As Cavell, Rothman, and Mulhall have still more generally argued, some films may provoke us to think deeply about fundamental human questions, such as what it is to be a human being or what acknowledgment of another as a full-fledged person might involve. Some films may even do some of this thinking for us and present it to us for our consideration, as Cavell argues some comedies of remarriage and melodramas of the unknown woman do, or as Mulhall argues *Blade Runner* does.[42] The idea that some films may encourage or even embody philosophical reflection harmonizes with the general cognitivist approach I have outlined, insofar as both theoretical positions seek

---

38. Smith, *Engaging Characters*, 209.

39. Murray Smith, "Gangsters, Cannibals, Aesthetes, or Apparently Perverse Allegiances," in *Passionate Views: Film, Cognition, and Emotion*, ed. Carl Plantinga and Greg M. Smith (Baltimore: Johns Hopkins University Press, 1999), 219.

40. Smith, *Engaging Characters*, 84.

41. Smith, "Gangsters, Cannibals, Aesthetes," 228.

42. Stanley Cavell, *The Pursuits of Happiness: The Hollywood Comedy of Remarriage* (Cambridge: Harvard University Press, 1981); Cavell, *Contesting Tears: The Hollywood Melodrama of the Unknown Woman* (Chicago: University of Chicago Press, 1996); Mulhall, *On Film*, 33–51.

to "make sense" of human experience while at the same time responding to the "claims of reason," as Cavell and Mulhall have stressed.[43] These positions also see theorizing—particularly philosophical theorizing—as matters of questioning, inquiry, outlining new ways of thinking, and dialectical criticism, without necessarily achieving definitive, final answers. The point over which these two theoretical positions differ most concerns where such reflective theorizing may legitimately occur. Cavell, Rothman, Mulhall, and their cohort believe that it may occur almost anywhere, as they do not see an essential break between ordinary human reflectiveness and more formally philosophical reflectiveness that professionals in the field might hope to achieve. As Cavell notes, they see the latter as an intensification or radicalization of the former, whereas many cognitivist philosophers of film argue for a more restricted sense of philosophy with closer links to formalized conceptions of argument and giving good reasons for or against a position in question.[44] While there exists considerable room for dispute regarding this difference, in my analyses of black *noir* I will exploit what I see as the productive affinities between these two theoretical camps.

What Is Black Film?

In "Aesthetics and Politics in Contemporary Black Film Theory," Tommy L. Lott argues that the "plethora of black film-making practices suggests that the political and aesthetic differences among black independent films cannot be captured by a single paradigm."[45] Noting not only the diversity of art objects designated by the term "black independent film," but also that the definitions offered to capture these works range from being too broad to too narrow, Lott advances instead the idea that the dialectic relations existing between black independent film and Hollywood are simply too strong to permit a clear and absolute division to be drawn between them. Rather than, say, focus on the supposed need for black film to be definitively and financially, aesthetically, or politically independent from mainstream cinematic products, Lott articulates a more complicated view that accommodates the reality of a symbiotic relation between these two kinds of cinema. He acknowledges black film's need to distinguish itself from the stereotypical themes and imagery of mainstream cultural representations, but adds that independent black films actually speak in both "mainstream" and "independent" voices. They are, in other words, "hybrid" or "polyvocal" cultural products (288). As an example, he analyzes director Melvin Van Peebles's *Sweet Sweetback's Baadasssss Song* (1971), which is often advanced as an exemplary instance of black independent cinema. Lott

43. Cavell, *Claim of Reason;* Stephen Mulhall, "Ways of Thinking: A Response to Anderson and Baggini," *Film-Philosophy* 7, no. 25 (August, 2003), paras. 4–6, http://www.film-philosophy.com.

44. Cavell, "Thought of Movies," 9; Mulhall, "Ways of Thinking," para. 10.

45. Tommy L. Lott, "Aesthetics and Politics in Contemporary Black Film Theory," in Allen and Smith, *Film Theory and Philosophy,* 288.

argues, however, that this film subverts the traditional Hollywood crime narrative and conventions of *film noir* in order to challenge the status quo and introduce the awakening of a black political consciousness (290–91, 300 n. 27). The film's hybridity makes it "politically ambiguous" (288), but viewers may nonetheless "read through," say, the film's sexism and conventionality, in order to grasp its political point (292–93). Such films often—perhaps even typically—create an ambivalence in their viewers and offer at best a complicated identification with their characters (294–95); however, by taking on some aspects of Hollywood's aesthetic codes, they can both reach an audience that understands and embraces such codes while at the same time subverting those codes to convey political messages that encourage their reformulation. Without ultimately offering a definition of black independent film himself, Lott effectively shows that historical factors such as the symbiosis between Hollywood and independent black film, as well as the possibilities of subverting standard Hollywood convention from within, cannot be ignored when seeking to formulate conceptions of what black cinema's independence is.[46]

As one might expect, the prospects for a straightforward, essentialist definition for the broader term "black film" are bleaker still. In an earlier essay Lott advances the suspicion that previous attempts to define black film founder because there are "no underlying criteria to which an ultimate appeal can be made to resolve [the] underlying issues," such as what counts as black identity itself.[47] Noting that here, too, definitions typically break down by being either too broad or too narrow (140), Lott argues that "biological criteria are neither necessary, nor sufficient, for the application of the concept of black cinema" (141). In place of "biologically essentialist view[s] of black cinema," he suggests a focus on the "plurality of standards by which black films are evaluated" (145). Black films require neither black filmmakers, nor actual black audiences (146), nor even some conception of a "monolithic black audience" to which one might appeal as an ideal (148). Instead Lott offers a *criterion* for such a definition that eschews the independent/mainstream distinction and emulates the currently existing political conditions of black people as a prerequisite for something to be a black film. Namely, "black film-making practices must continue to be fundamentally concerned with the issues that currently define the political struggle of black people," which will require any theory of black cinema to account for an "aim to foster social change," such that it "incorporates a plurality of political values that are consistent with the fate and destiny of black people as a group engaged in a protracted struggle for social equality" (151). Such struggle, of course, may occur either inside or outside mainstream cinematic practice, whether economically, aesthetically, culturally, or nationally.

---

46. See also Tommy L. Lott's "Hollywood and Independent Black Cinema," in *Contemporary Hollywood Cinema*, ed. Steve Neale and Murray Smith (London: Routledge, 1998), 211–28.

47. Tommy L. Lott, "A No-Theory Theory of Contemporary Black Cinema" (1991), in *The Invention of Race: Black Culture and the Politics of Representation* (London: Blackwell, 1999), 139.

By taking a step back from defining "black film" itself to focus on the difficulties surrounding the definition of what might count as being a black person, Lott suggests that offering definitions that provide necessary and sufficient conditions in this context may well be misguided. Instead he argues in favor of a criterion for such a definition: black films as currently and contingently configured must aim at values consistent with blacks' protracted struggle to achieve full social equality. Such a definitional condition will operate very loosely to include works from across the political spectrum and from a variety of sources. Certainly all the films discussed in this book meet Lott's criterion, but so do works not generally considered black films. For example, as Lott observes, some films about blacks made by white filmmakers, such as Michael Roemer's *Nothing But a Man* (1964) and John Sayles's *The Brother from Another Planet* (1984), would arguably require inclusion under any reasonable characterization of black film.[48] The same could be said of white-produced "race movies" like *The Scar of Shame* (Frank Perugini, 1927) and perhaps the Jack Johnson prizefight films (1908–16), as well as black director Bill Gunn's Blaxploitation-era, studio-produced *Ganja and Hess* (1973) and *Stop!* (1975), which Lott explicitly argues must be accommodated as well, even though most definitions of black film would exclude them.[49] While this criterion does not settle the issue of what definitively determines "black film" as a concept, it goes a long way toward indicating the shape that such a definition should take.

As Lott notes, a good part of the difficulty here is that "black film" must cover a very heterogeneous group of films, a collection of artworks arguably too diverse to be characterized as having any common properties. Since the term has been applied to "race movies" of the early twentieth century, the "Blaxploitation" films of the 1970s, and independent works of black filmmakers over the past two decades as well as isolated other movies, it should hardly be surprising that "black film" holds out little hope of being described by means of a single shared characteristic. Lott's outlining of a condition for such a definition, then, may well be the best we can hope for in aiming to delineate what these films have in common. On the other hand, Lott's analyses provide a useful delineation of the general context for black *noirs* and their examination in this book.

What Is *Film Noir?*

Even though critics have frequently addressed this question, for good reasons no one seems to have answered it satisfactorily. Perhaps most important, in Anglophone film and literary studies applications of *film noir* and its related

48. Ibid., 139–40.

49. See Thomas Cripps, "'Race Movies' as Voices of the Black Bourgeoisie: *The Scar of Shame* (1927)," in *American History/American Film: Interpreting the Hollywood Image*, ed. John E. O'Connor and Martin A. Jackson (New York: Ungar, 1979), 39–55; Dan Streible, "Race and the Reception of Jack Johnson Fight Films," in Bernardi, *Birth of Whiteness*, 170–200; and Lott, "Aesthetics and Politics," 286–88, and "Hollywood and Independent Black Cinema," 215–16.

critical terms have been ones of ever broadening scope. From its initial reference to a small group of Hollywood movies made during the 1940s to its designation of ongoing aesthetic forms in both film and fiction, English-language *noir* studies have grown in ways that few might have imagined. Yet even prior to this development, French critics used the term *noir* in similar ways. For example, the term was initially employed during the nineteenth century to describe British gothic novels—*littérature noire.*[50] Slightly better known was its use to describe French cinematic works of poetic realism such as *Pépé le Moko* (Julien Duvivier, 1937) and *Le Quai des brumes* (Marcel Carne, 1938) just before World War II—*films noirs,* but of an indigenous variety.[51] Just after the war Gallimard publishers adopted the term to title their new line of American hard-boiled detective fiction translated into French—*Série Noire.*[52] Then most famously French film critics Nino Frank and Jean-Pierre Chartier, seeing American films again for the first time since before the war, proclaimed a handful of them *films noirs.* Over the next several years *noir* became a critical term of art in France for discussing American cinema.[53]

The term *film noir* then took another dozen years or so to cross the Atlantic, arising both in French and in English translation in Charles Higham and Joel Greenberg's *Hollywood in the Forties* (1968) and exclusively in French in essays by Raymond Durgnat, Paul Schrader, and others a few years later.[54] The latter school won the battle terminologically, so to speak, largely because another kind of "black film" or "black cinema" arose in America at the time—a rather ironic result from the point of view of this study. The focus of scholarship subsequent to the term's introduction into English was mainly the "classic" period of American *noir* films, 1941–58, a bracketing apparently first suggested by Schrader, but very quickly adopted as the benchmark for discussing American

50. *The Film Encyclopedia,* ed. Ephraim Katz (New York: Perigee Books, 1979), s.v. *"film noir,"* 418.

51. Charles O'Brien, "Film Noir in France: Before the Liberation," *Iris* 21 (1996): 7–20; Janice Morgan, "Scarlet Streets: Noir Realism from Berlin to Paris to Hollywood," *Iris* 21 (1996): 31–53; Ginette Vincendeau, "Noir Is Also a French Word: The French Antecedents of Film Noir," in *The Book of Film Noir,* ed. Ian Cameron (New York: Continuum, 1992), 49–58; Robin Buss, *French Film Noir* (London: Marion Boyars, 1994).

52. Etienne Borgers, *"Série Noire,"* in *The Big Book of Noir,* ed. Ed Gorman, Lee Server, and Martin H. Greenberg (New York: Carroll and Graf, 1998), 237–44.

53. For a useful chronology of the history of the French term *noir,* see James Naremore, "American Film Noir: The History of an Idea," *Film Quarterly* 49, no. 2 (Winter 1995–96): esp. 12–18. For a sampling of early French critical works, see *Film Noir Reader* and *Film Noir Reader 2,* ed. Alain Silver and James Ursini (New York: Limelight Editions, 1996, 1999), and Raymond Borde and Etienne Chaumeton, *Panorama du film noir américain, 1941–1953* (Paris: Editions de Minuit, 1955), or its recent English-language translation, *A Panorama of American Film Noir, 1941–1953,* trans. Paul Hammond (San Francisco: City Lights Books, 2002).

54. Charles Higham and Joel Greenberg, *Hollywood in the Forties* (New York: A. S. Barnes, 1968), 19–36. The Durgnat, Schrader, and other early English-language essays are reprinted in Silver and Ursini, *Film Noir Reader* and *Film Noir Reader 2.*

film noir in general.[55] There followed a fairly stable period of roughly two decades in film studies where most *noir* scholarship focused on whether this collection of films was a genre, cycle, style, mood, historical period, and so on, as well as cataloging what might be called the *noir* canon. Although there were raging controversies over the definition of the term, exactly which films should or should not be counted as actual or exemplary *noirs*, and whether the concept was a legitimate one at all, few scholars contested whether the term applied (in English) to anything but films to be found predominantly within Schrader's bracketing.

Overlapping with this *de facto* research program but becoming particularly prominent in the last decade and a half, more and more *noir* scholars—both inside and outside the academy—broadened the term's application to incorporate films far outside the classic period. This generalizing tendency had always been an internal problem anyway, as even most classic *film noir* critics could not help offering examples beyond Schrader's time span.[56] In addition, the term's use in English evolved to include *film noir*'s origins in literature, thus mimicking earlier French practice. Further areas of scholarship included *noir*'s relation to the urban landscape and television shows and British *film noir*. French *film noir* was discovered by English-language researchers and extended far past the prewar years; and hard-boiled detective fiction was redubbed *noir* literature, both in classic forms such as works by Hammett, Cain, and Chandler, and contemporary, such as works by James Crumley, Elmore Leonard, and Andrew Vachss.[57] *Noir*'s racial dimensions came under scrutiny as well, in film, fiction, and the critical literature.[58]

Even as some critics over the years have suggested putting aside the term in favor of more conventional film genre concepts (for example, crime melodrama, gangster film), others have embraced a more general "*noir* sensibility" and sought out its central meanings by analyzing objects at or near

55. See Paul Schrader, "Notes on *Film Noir*" (1972), in Silver and Ursini, *Film Noir Reader*, esp. 58–61, and Naremore, "American Film Noir," 26 n. 2.

56. See, for example, the many entries for pre-1941 as well as post-1958 films in Silver and Ward, *Film Noir: An Encyclopedic Reference*.

57. Mike Davis, "Sunshine or *Noir*?" in *City of Quartz: Excavating the Future in Los Angeles* (1990; repr., New York: Vintage, 1992), 17–97; James Ursini, "Angst at Sixty Fields per Second," in Silver and Ursini, *Film Noir Reader*, 275–87; Tony Williams, "British *Film Noir*," in Silver and Ursini, *Film Noir Reader 2*, 243–69; Buss, *French Film Noir*; William Marling, *The American Roman Noir: Hammett, Cain, and Chandler* (Athens: University of Georgia Press, 1995); Woody Haut, *Neon Noir: Contemporary American Crime Fiction* (London: Serpent's Tail, 1999).

58. See, for example, Diawara, "*Noir* by Noirs," 261–78; Eric Lott, "The Whiteness of Film Noir," *American Literary History* 9 (1997): 542–66; Flory, "Black on White"; James Sallis, "Chester Himes: America's Black Heartland," in *The Big Book of Noir*, 273–80; Woody Haut, "Chester Himes," in *Pulp Culture: Hardboiled Fiction and the Cold War* (London: Serpent's Tail, 1995), 34–46; and the series of Easy Rawlins mysteries by Walter Mosley. For an interesting non-American example, see Jakob Arjouni, *Happy Birthday, Turk!* (1987), trans. Anselm Arno (Harpenden: No Exit Press, 1993).

its conceptual borders. By "*noir* sensibility," these critics mean a feeling or attitude that invokes the features and effects of *noir,* especially its ability to critically examine existing social institutions.[59] For example, in 1996 James Naremore published "American *Film Noir:* The History of an Idea," at the conclusion of which he observed that in the closing years of the twentieth century the term *noir* was no longer confined to describing films or literature, but could be used to sell fashion in the *New York Times.* Other scholars discerned similar uses of the term in pointing to perfumes named "*Noir!*" or its employment to sell hamburgers in McDonald's commercials.[60] Naremore took this broadening application and general ubiquity to signify that *noir* really operated more like "a discourse—a loose, evolving system of arguments and readings, helping to shape commercial strategies and aesthetic ideologies" (14). Rather than being merely about the objects themselves (a bunch of moldering old Hollywood movies in cans), *noir* was also a highly malleable but nonetheless useful way of talking about them that could be readily applied elsewhere. Paralleling Naremore's analysis, Rabinowitz employs the term *noir* as a tool of historical analysis to understand wartime photographs of single working women, African-American literature, the Popular Front and melodrama's influences on documentary, novels about female "juvenile delinquency" and social work, women's shoes (especially stiletto-heeled pumps), and avant-garde film. Through a strategy of juxtaposing such borderline items with classic *noir* films, she extends as well as delineates more clearly what *noir* might mean.[61]

This method of considering *noir* from a historical perspective yields a loose collection of traits, various groupings of which might constitute different objects as *noir.* Naremore and Rabinowitz's analyses thus approach *noir* as a sort of aesthetic "cluster concept," which as Berys Gaut argues provides many advantages in discussing and analyzing aesthetic concepts.[62] Film scholar Ben Singer has deployed this strategy in discussing the related idea of "melodrama" because such a theoretical approach provides more coherent and accurate possibilities for understanding what the term means.[63]

59. Naremore, *More Than Night,* 11; Paula Rabinowitz, *Black and White and Noir: America's Pulp Modernism* (New York: Columbia University Press, 2002), xi, 14–15ff. Of course, the idea that *noir* embodies a kind of sensibility reaches back at least to Robert G. Porfirio, "No Way Out: Existential Motifs in the *Film Noir*" (1976), in Silver and Ursini, *Film Noir Reader,* 77–93 (see, e.g., 77, 80). Philosopher Mark T. Conard, "Nietzsche and the Meaning and Definition of Noir," in *The Philosophy of Film Noir,* ed. Mark T. Conard (Lexington: University Press of Kentucky, 2006), 7–22, also argues for the idea that *noir* is best understood as a sensibility, although from a different philosophical perspective (see esp. 17–19).

60. Naremore, "American Film Noir," 24–25; Rabinowitz, *Black and White and Noir,* 15–16; Jans B. Wager, *Dangerous Dames: Women and Representation in the Weimar Street Film and Film Noir* (Athens: Ohio University Press, 1999), 123.

61. Rabinowitz, *Black and White and Noir.*

62. Berys Gaut, "'Art' as a Cluster Concept," in *Theories of Art Today,* ed. Noël Carroll (Madison: University of Wisconsin Press, 2000), 25–44.

63. Ben Singer, *Melodrama and Modernity: Early Sensational Cinema and Its Contexts* (New York: Columbia University Press, 2001), 44.

The point of my brief history of *noir* is that as a critical term it has never been strictly circumscribed in its use. Even Frank's and Chartier's famous essays use it to characterize what otherwise apparently quite different films had in common. The group of movies to which these critics referred specifically as *films noirs* were *The Maltese Falcon* (John Huston, 1941), *Murder, My Sweet* (Edward Dmytryk, 1944), *Double Indemnity* (Billy Wilder, 1944), *Laura* (Otto Preminger, 1944), *The Postman Always Rings Twice* (Tay Garnett, 1946), and *The Lost Weekend* (Billy Wilder, 1945).[64] Perhaps as surprising is the fact that another American *noir* classic, director Fritz Lang's *The Woman in the Window* (1944), was released at the same time in France but did not strike critics there as a *noir*—only a "bourgeois tragedy."[65] Subsequent attempts to delineate the boundaries of *noir* have fared little better, as shown by the 1970s and 1980s controversy in Anglophone scholarship concerning its definition.[66] In spite of decades of arguments seeking to outline the *noir* canon as well as its proper conceptual limits, knowledge of those limits seem little improved from the sketchy contours provided by midcentury French critics. For all its vagueness and ambiguity, Borde and Chaumeton's *Panorama du film noir Américain, 1941–1953* remains in many respects the benchmark for those who wish to define *noir*.[67]

On the other hand, this brief history also indicates that there is a clear sense in which *noir* operates as a useful category, even if it does not precisely fit into standard definitions of "genre." As Steve Neale argues in *Hollywood and Genre*, "it is in essence a critical category" whose "corpus can only be established by means of critical observation and analysis."[68] Although I disagree with Neale that the concept of *noir* is "incoherent" (154), I concur that it may hardly be confined by means of necessary and sufficient conditions. Rather, *noir*'s definition is "fuzzy" at its edges, as is its canon, aspects that can deeply frustrate those who like clean and easily delineated boundaries to their ideas. In a sense it is a paradigmatically "open" concept, to use terminology made famous by Morris Weitz, one about which we must constantly make decisions

64. For translations (by Alain Silver) of Frank and Chartier's works, see Silver and Ursini, *Film Noir Reader 2*, 15–23.

65. Noted in Naremore, "American Film Noir," 15.

66. Several of the central essays concerning the definition of *film noir* are anthologized in Silver and Ursini's *Film Noir Reader*, esp. 27–127. I should add in passing that this difficulty continues to dog many more recent essays that seek to delineate *film noir*, such as those contained in *The Philosophy of Film Noir* (see especially the essays by Conard, Holt, and Schuchardt), which seek to reify *noir* by advancing quasi-definitional conditions regarding its "meaning" or "essence" for which there exist numerous counterexamples that illustrate these claims' unsuitability for serving as any sort of essentialistic criterion for this film form.

67. Borde and Chaumeton, *Panorama of American Film Noir*, esp. 5–13. Recently, Biesen has argued that early instances of *noir* films have more in common than I seem to allow, namely, as part of the "red meat" cycle of films following the success of *Double Indemnity* (*Blackout*, esp. 96–123). Her argument has much to say in its favor. However, I stand by the claim that these early *noir* films as well as their successors are at least *prima facie* dissimilar, partly because their *noir* characteristics have proven so elusive, historically speaking, in the critical literature.

68. Steve Neale, *Genre and Hollywood* (London: Routledge, 2000), 153.

regarding what to include or exclude, rather than being a closed concept, one for which necessary and sufficient conditions may be more straightforwardly provided.[69]

For all that, however, *noir* is not much different from many other genre concepts, which also frequently possess unclear borders, changing characteristics, and expanding canons. To take *noir*'s generic cousin, melodrama, as an example, the latter's core features have changed considerably. As Smith explains, melodrama's notorious flexibility derives fundamentally from significant shifts in its use over the course of a more than two-hundred-year history, a conclusion with which Neale concurs, especially with respect to melodrama's more recent development in the history of film.[70] *Noir* has developed with even greater flexibility, as reflected in Naremore's and Rabinowitz's studies, which foreground, in part, an interplay between noun and adjective, the distinction between *noir* and *noirish*, and the ways in which adjectival uses may influence the employment of a term as a noun. In this way their studies concur with film scholar Rick Altman's work on the noun/adjective distinction in the creation of film genres, which he explains is often a matter of adjectival uses being offered to characterize various films becoming nominal ones over time, which is precisely how he characterizes *noir*'s development in English.[71]

The danger here, of course, is to avoid slipping into theorizing about *noir* by "inventing your own" genre, a common strategy employed by philosophers (!), according to Deborah Knight and George McKnight.[72] As they admit, however, internal coherence among films or their "family resemblances" to one another may offer ways out of such a dilemma (332, 338). Cavell, with his studies of comedies of remarriage and melodramas of the unknown woman, has employed just such strategies in order to argue for the unity of his "philosopher's genres."[73]

On the other hand, I think that *film noir* has a stronger claim to coherence than a philosopher's genre, even of the sort Cavell proposes. Namely, its application as a term is rooted in generally consistent viewer as well as critical practices that, while perhaps not definable as a genre in the strict sense that scholars like Neale would require, nonetheless stem from ways of thinking and talking that make sense and possess their own internal logic. The use of the term *noir* has, for example, yielded a relatively stable set of films that are recognized as canonical. Recent extensions of its uses are moreover understandable and explicable, even if they are at times arguable.

---

69. Morris Weitz, "The Role of Theory in Aesthetics" (1956), reprinted in *The Philosophy of Art*, 183–92.

70. Smith, *Engaging Characters*, 166. See also 197–223, and Neale, *Genre and Hollywood*, esp. 179–202.

71. Rick Altman, *Film/Genre* (London: BFI Publishing, 1999), 30–62. Altman analyzes *noir*'s evolution in English from adjective to noun, 60–61.

72. Deborah Knight and George McKnight, "Whose Genre Is It Anyway? Thomas Wartenberg on the Unlikely Couple Film," *Journal of Social Philosophy* 33 (2002): 331–32.

73. Ibid., 338. See also Cavell, *Pursuits of Happiness*, esp. 19–32, and *Contesting Tears*, 3–8.

References to *noir* mean something significant and nontrivial to people when they use it or extend its employment to other areas. Such characteristics indicate that its application to art objects may be considered illuminating, interesting, or aesthetically pleasing, as Gregory Currie describes Cavell's genre of comedies of remarriage.[74] Grouping films as *noir* is, in other words, critically useful because it facilitates the study of "their commonalities, responses, and progressions in relation to one another."[75] As a recognizable even if not always clear category of film, *noir* may also serve to "criterially pre-focus" audience expectations regarding what sorts of characters to look for, situations to think likely, themes to anticipate, and so on.[76] It is thus a worthwhile, historically based concept that helps us to better describe, explain, and analyze viewer's actual psychological engagement with art objects they perceive as similar.[77] In other words, *noir* operates like other genres in the sense that Currie theorizes for the term, even if it does not function as a genre in the more strictly classic sense presumed by, say, Neale.[78] Although discussing films as *noir* may not always be rooted in artists' first-order intentions, advertising, or other clearly specifiable features, it remains a worthwhile critical practice to discuss certain films *as noir*, particularly when attempting to describe, explain, or analyze viewer's expectations and presumptions about artworks, because it makes particular aspects salient that would otherwise not be.[79] This perspective on *noir*, in Currie's sense of "genre," becomes especially effective when reflecting on its use as a form of "critical cinema"—that is, *noir's* use as a form of social criticism.

Film Noir's Subversive Possibilities

From its inception in the 1940s, classic American *film noir's* convergence of diverse techniques and themes has offered ways of persuading audiences to

74. Gregory Currie, "The Film Theory That Never Was: A Nervous Manifesto," in Allen and Smith, *Film Theory and Philosophy*, 53. See also Currie's *Arts and Minds* (New York: Oxford University Press, 2004), 57–58. (As will be evident from the rest of this paragraph, I am deeply indebted here to Currie's discussion of genre in *Arts and Minds*.)

75. Currie, "The Film Theory That Never Was," 53; see also *Arts and Minds*, 57–58.

76. Noël Carroll, "Film, Emotion, and Genre," in Plantinga and Smith, *Passionate Views*, 31, 34–35. See also Currie's *Arts and Minds*, esp. 49–53.

77. Currie, *Arts and Minds*, esp. 57–58.

78. Some may object that *noir* may not work in genre-like ways if the film itself is not presented generically *as a noir*, either intentionally by the artists, through advertising, or in other ways. But I would argue that if David Bordwell is accurate that films have their own "primacy effect" of raising viewer anticipations and expectations by means of their opening sequences, then such presentations need not be necessary. Rather, the *noir*-like qualities of a film need only arise at some point early in the film to prepare viewers to see the film as *noir*. See David Bordwell, *Narration in the Fiction Film* (Madison: University of Wisconsin Press, 1985), 38. Moreover, as Currie argues, the conferral of genre may also be "retrospective," particularly when such conferrals "allow us to see unexpected and worthwhile commonalities" (*Arts and Minds*, 58).

79. Currie, *Arts and Minds*, 45–50.

willingly see protagonists cross lines of bourgeois acceptability, transgress established laws, and infringe on underlying moral codes. Outlaw and marginalized groups have regularly counted *noir* characters among their members, and have just as often drawn others into their orbit. The doomed or damaged fates of many *noir* protagonists often reflected an implicit pessimism and dissatisfaction felt by audience members against prevailing established orders. While *noir* films typically urge audiences to sympathize with moral transgression as well as underworld economies,[80] I want to suggest a different but related point, namely, that these standard themes and conventions of classic American *film noir* may also be directed toward critical examinations of knowledge. For instance, a convention such as confinement to circumstances from which there seems no escape may function in *film noir* to compel characters or audience members to seek knowledge that might profoundly alter their systems of belief, perceptions, or actions. Such techniques open up possibilities for some *noir* narratives to serve as cognitive searches aimed at the transformation of one's existing belief structures.

Such possibilities arise not all that rarely in classic *noir* as well as its post-1960s descendants, generally described in the critical literature as neo-*noir*. *Out of the Past* (Jacques Tourneur, 1947) depicts its main character trying desperately to uncover the details that will allow him to escape his sordid past. *Try and Get Me* (Cy Enfield, 1950) explicitly condemns (nonracialized) lynching.[81] *In a Lonely Place* examines the latent violence that typically informs American masculinity. *Chinatown* reveals a pervasive corruption by power that thrives in the way most municipalities are run. *Noir* narratives frequently operate as cognitive investigations aimed at some sort of epistemological transformation, particularly of their audiences. Some do so explicitly (e.g., *Try and Get Me*), while others may be more subtle (e.g., *In a Lonely Place, Chinatown*), but many offer up to their viewers knowledge and perspectives meant to change how they believe, think, perceive, and act morally.

In spite of this well-established subversive capacity, *noir* can function in both radical and conservative manners. I would contend, however, that it is

80. Numerous critics have noted *film noir*'s critical function since the beginning of the American cycle's "discovery." See, for example, Nino Frank, "A New Kind of Police Drama: The Crime Adventure," in Silver and Ursini, *Film Noir Reader 2*, 15–19; Borde and Chaumeton, *Panorama of American Film Noir*, 7–13; Carlos Clarens, *Crime Movies* (New York: W. W. Norton, 1980), 191–233; Brian Neve, *Film and Politics in America: A Social Tradition* (New York: Routledge, 1992), 147–70; Davis, *City of Quartz*, esp. 18–46; and Bert Oliver, "The Logic of *Noir* and the Question of Radical Evil," *Film and Philosophy* 8 (2004): 122–37, esp. 122–24.

81. As I will discuss more fully in Chapter 8, this deracializing is odd because the post-1860s history of lynching in America would lead one to believe that the lead characters who suffer this fate should have been black; see, for example, Philip Dray, *At the Hands of Persons Unknown: The Lynching of Black America* (New York: Modern Library, 2003) and *Without Sanctuary: Lynching Photography in America*, ed. James Allen et al. (Santa Fe: Twin Palms Publishers, 2000). Yet the victims are played by white actors, and no references to race are made in the narrative. On the other hand, *Try and Get Me* remains an emotionally powerful condemnation of an unjust practice that has a long history in America.

noticeably duller as right-wing critique; who, after all, admires *film noir* for such works as *I Was a Communist for the FBI* (Gordon Douglas, 1951) or those abysmal features cranked out under the aegis of Howard Hughes at RKO? Like cultural critic Mike Davis and others, I find *noir's* radical affinities more attractive,[82] and many African-American filmmakers have likewise been drawn to these elements. In one of the best articles written describing this appropriation, Diawara explains how various examples of the recent black film wave employ *film noir* tropes to depict social injustice and the need for its rectification.[83] Rather than merely highlight moral or legal transgression, black and darkness tropes foreground the oppression forced on African Americans by white society. For example, crucial to the aims of many *noir* narratives is their strategic use of an "underlying determinism."[84] Long recognized as a staple of *noir* narratives, recent filmmakers interested in race have deployed this thematic element to convey how African Americans are "held captive" by "a way of life that has been imposed on black people through social injustice."[85] The fatalistic strain evident in films such as *Double Indemnity, Scarlet Street* (Fritz Lang, 1945), and *Detour* (Edgar Ulmer, 1945) thus becomes an instrument for making racialized oppression visible as well as comprehensible by showing how institutions of white authority often impose criminality and lawbreaking on African Americans through giving them such meager alternatives.

Depicting black life through *noir* conventions, Diawara argues, allows many films to deconstruct white racism and its intricacies by exposing how the forces of white privilege fracture and distort African-American existence (263), thereby making possible improved reflections by audience members regarding the immorality and injustice of dominant institutions. Unlike typical Marxist or feminist forms of *noir* criticism, however, Diawara focuses mainly on thematic elements in *film noir* to support his analyses, rather than offering a form of criticism based more squarely on *noir's* stylistic features (262). Diawara's strategy is one I draw upon frequently in my own analyses of black *noir* films.

In addition, I want to briefly note that the use of *noir* themes such as crime and transgression as "metaphors of resistance" to the values of the dominant white culture is something that Tommy Lott has pinpointed as a key element in the early success of rap and hip-hop music.[86] By noting that among the

---

82. See, for example, Davis, *City of Quartz*, 18–46; Oliver, "Logic of Noir"; Clarens, *Crime Movies*, 191–233; Neve, *Film and Politics in America*, 147–70; and Lary May, *The Big Tomorrow: Hollywood and the Politics of the American Way* (Chicago: University of Chicago Press, 2000), 220–30.

83. Diawara, "*Noirs by Noirs*," 263.

84. Silver and Ward, "Introduction," in *Film Noir: An Encyclopedic Reference*, 4.

85. Higham and Greenberg note *noir's* use of "narrow corridors," "cramped apartments," and faces "barred deeply with those shadows that usually symbolized some imprisonment of body or soul" (*Hollywood in the Forties*, 19, 20). For the quotations from Diawara, see "*Noirs by Noirs*," 263.

86. Tommy L. Lott, "Marooned in America: Black Urban Youth Culture and Social Pathology," in *The Invention of Race*, 121. See also Bill E. Lawson, "Microphone Commandos: Rap Music and Political Ideology," in *A Companion to African-American Philosophy*, ed. Tommy L. Lott and John P. Pittman (London: Blackwell, 2003), 429–35.

dominant media images of black men are those of criminals and describing how hip-hop and rap work to invalidate those images by recoding them for other purposes, Lott explains that these musical forms convey different meanings to their intended audiences from those grasped by individuals in power (120–21).[87] For example, one result of this recoding is a transformation of the meaning of knowledge: "to be *politically* astute" (122), rather than the unreflective possessor of some dominant outlook. Another is the value of defiance in the face of oppressive circumstances for the purpose of reinforcing a sense of self-respect (122), without necessarily endorsing the form that defiance takes in the real world. In these and other ways, rap and hip-hop use crime and transgression as metaphors of resistance in order to critique the values of the dominant white culture.

Much like rappers who have exploited stereotypical gangster and thug life images to critique white power, makers of black *film noir* have used and recoded the components of this film form to expose and criticize white ways of knowing and acting. By bringing these structural elements of race to the surface and relying to some extent on the tropes of rap and hip-hop,[88] black filmmakers offer audiences the opportunity to see how life operates from the racial underbelly of institutional forces, particularly those connected to epistemologically embedded dimensions of whiteness. On the other hand, such artistic practices from rap and hip-hop merely serve to reinforce potentials already latent in *film noir*. As critics from Nino Frank to Jonathan Munby have pointed out, classic American *film noir* frequently represented dissatisfaction with existing power structures by means of narratives focused around committing crime, which makes the combined use of this musical form and film format surprisingly symbiotic.[89]

Finally, as I will explain more fully later, a good deal of *film noir* is about cultivating sympathy for or empathy with socially marginalized characters and others somehow distanced from mainstream culture. Its narrative strategies for presenting characters who are complex moral alloys of good and bad traits provide ways to elicit these responses for what are frequently openly criminal characters who occupy a *noir* underworld. More than half a century ago Borde

---

87. Lott contends that only black audiences have this capacity, but this recoding of black men's stereotypical images is something that I believe has been understood to some degree by at least some (but by no means all) of the young white suburban audiences that allowed rap and hip-hop to grow exponentially in the decade and a half since Lott originally wrote his essay in 1991.

88. For a fuller analysis of how recent black films have borrowed from rap and hip-hop (although without connecting them to *film noir*), see S. Craig Watkins, *Representing: Hip-hop Culture and the Production of Black Cinema* (Chicago: University of Chicago Press, 1998).

89. Diawara, "*Noir by Noirs,*" 272–73, explicitly notes this symbiosis. For more on crime as a metaphor of resistance in *film noir*, see Frank Krutnik, *In A Lonely Street: Film Noir, Genre, Masculinity* (London: Routledge, 1991), 136–63, and Jonathan Munby, *Public Enemies, Public Heroes: Screening the Gangster from "Little Caesar" to "Touch of Evil"* (Chicago: University of Chicago Press, 1999), esp. 186–220. As Krutnik and Munby observe, like *noir*'s critical function, its use of criminality to express dissatisfaction with the status quo was recognized from the very beginning. See Frank's and Chartier's essays in Silver and Ursini, *Film Noir Reader 2,* 15–23.

and Chaumeton pointed out that *films noirs* encourage viewers to sympathize and even identify with gangsters, criminals, and other morally dubious characters, and a surprising number of entries in Silver and Ward's *Film Noir: An Encyclopedic Reference to the American Style* refer to sympathetic portrayals of morally complex or even criminal characters.[90] This fact about *film noir* provides an entry point for many black filmmakers to tell stories to mainstream audiences about complicated, underclass African-American characters and the difficulties they face in dealing with problems of race. These possibilities for cultivating sympathy and empathy thus allows black artists to offer pathways of understanding for their audiences regarding how problems of race often work, as these types of audience responses also make possible better understandings of the situations, perspectives, and decisions that nonfictional blacks often face in America.

What Is Black *Noir?*

It may surprise many readers to discover that *noir* is not new to African-American aesthetic production. By the late 1940s, for example, a noticeable portion of black literary resistance to racism had taken on the trappings of *noir* and directed them against presumptions of white supremacy and racial hierarchy. Although they remain an undervalued dimension of black literature, *noir* techniques frequently conveyed resistance to white oppression and depicted everyday black life as that of full-fledged human beings rather than something less, as was often the case in literature written by whites—the latter point having been made clear by novelist and critic Toni Morrison.[91] For example, Mike Davis points out that Chester Himes employed *noir* conventions in his Los Angeles novels *If He Hollers Let Him Go* (1945) and *Lonely Crusade* (1947).[92] Diawara argues similarly by describing how recent African-American filmmakers have appropriated features of classic *noir* films and comparing these appropriations with Himes's 1957 novel *A Rage in Harlem.*[93] The Coffin Ed Johnson/Grave Digger Jones series that this novel inaugurated were originally commissioned for Gallimard's *Série Noire* and are now commonly recognized as *noir* literary classics.[94] More generally, elements of *noir* run throughout Himes's literary output, a point underscored by Diawara's comparison of it with early black *noir* films.[95]

90. Borde and Chaumeton, *Panorama of American Film Noir,* 8, 12; Silver and Ward, *Film Noir: An Encyclopedic Reference,* 15, 35, 159, 171, 215, 270.

91. Toni Morrison, *Playing in the Dark: Whiteness and the Literary Imagination* (Cambridge: Harvard University Press, 1992).

92. Davis, *City of Quartz,* 43.

93. Diawara, "Noir by Noirs," 261–78.

94. Sallis, "Chester Himes"; Haut, *Neon Noir,* 21–23, 106–7, and elsewhere. In contrast, Davis, *City of Quartz,* notes that as of 1990 Himes was "ignored in most critical treatments of the *noir* canon" (43).

95. Diawara, "Noir by Noirs."

Yet Himes is hardly unique among black writers for exploiting the trappings of *noir* to portray racialized oppression. As Rabinowitz points out, Ann Petry and Gwendolyn Brooks used them to convey the limits of black female possibilities by portraying African-American women as caught in a racist, *noir* world. Even though classic *film noir* visualized "many of the issues lurking within [white] proletarian literature," particularly those connected to class, its racial and gender-biased myopia typically curbed *film noir*'s vision.[96] For example, Rabinowitz argues that a "black femme fatale [could] not be visualized within [mainstream] film" (73) during the classic *noir* era, although her life could be recorded on the pages of novels, like Petry's or Brooks's, aimed mainly at black readers. Pathways to escape and freedom in America were much more severely circumscribed for black than for white women during the 1930s and 1940s, Rabinowitz observes, and their marginal status in, for example, classic *noir* films stems directly from insights lacking in the source materials of these movies, as well as black women's material conditions in the era. Petry's *The Street* (1946) and Brooks's *Maud Martha* (1953), as sister texts to white proletarian literature, offer compelling insights into why black *femmes fatales* were "'invisible (wo)men'" in classic *film noir* (80), as well as why these novels themselves fit solidly into a tradition of black *noir* literature alongside the work of Himes. The worlds portrayed in Petry's and Brooks's novels are ones of *noirish* confinement, restriction, and marginalization. The characters find themselves hemmed in by circumstance and social institutions that severely limit their freedom. Yet those restrictions are clearly due to racism and all its consequences—poverty, disadvantage, limitation of opportunity, and so on.

Rabinowitz also argues for the consideration of Richard Wright's 1953 novel *The Outsider* as an instance of black *noir* literature. She analyzes this novel "as a literary version of film noir" rather than tracing the more characteristic development from novel to film (84). But Wright's novel requires this reversal, she reasons, because he imbibed classic *noir* films and their historical sources in order to use their ingredients in his work (90). According to Rabinowitz this appropriation made imminent sense, for "African Americans already lived the noir world, guilt and betrayal the central theme of their American experience" (91). As is so often true in classic *film noir*, "it is knowledge itself that is dangerous in the noir world of American race relations" (92), a point to which I have already alluded. Wright uses a Du Boisian sense of double consciousness to focus on the status of blacks in America (90), thereby exposing depths of knowledge and desire that drive his protagonist mad with rage and send him on a murderous rampage that extends from Chicago to New York City. As Rabinowitz observes, "racial differences appear only skin deep; however, their imbrication in virtually every aspect of American life, from sexuality to economics, makes them profoundly significant. The fact of depth—that the surface masks hidden, profound, secret truths—is central

96. Rabinowitz, *Black and White and Noir*, 64.

to noir sensibility. That not everything can be immediately discerned at first sight" (97), particularly in regard to race, becomes Wright's root insight for the novel and propels his main character through its pulpy narrative. "Like the noir detective, [Wright] was obsessed with the sleaze spreading across the nation, hiding yet quite obviously there" (102)—only, as Rabinowitz argues, this sleaze was the corruption of racism and its damaging effects on the national psyche, particularly in the case of African Americans, which Wright illustrates through the tortured mind of his main character, Cross Damon.

One may see, in addition, that *The Outsider* and these other literary texts become aesthetic archetypes for "flipping" *noir*'s standard meanings in favor of exposing racial inequities, making the everyday "ordinariness" of racism seem strange, and calling for justice in rectification obvious. These works reverse perspectives on race by incorporating into their stories *noir* ingredients found in many classic films of the era as well as *noir* literature's pulpy sensibility— that is, its feeling of working-class "street" modernism, its attitude of casting a critical vernacular eye on existing social institutions, by way of suggesting such background presumptions are flawed and should be changed for the better.[97]

It is further worth noting that just as black literature borrowed from classic *film noir*, classic *film noir* borrowed from black literature. The 1949 film *Knock on Any Door*, directed by Nicholas Ray and starring Humphrey Bogart, was based on the critically acclaimed novel of the same name by African-American writer Willard Motley, published in 1947. Both the film and the novel, a best-seller in the naturalist vein of Theodore Dreiser and Frank Norris, portray a white protagonist who runs afoul of the law.[98] Despite the apparent raceless-ness of both the novel and the film, traces of racial hierarchy may still be found in the central character, Nick Romano (John Derek), whose upbring-ing and life in the slums inexorably propel him into crime. Poverty, lack of opportunity, brutality, and stereotypical presumptions about what we might call "probationary whites" like the Italian-American Romano doom him to a thug's life, in spite of his best efforts to go straight.[99] Many of the film's flash-backs, which are consistent with descriptions in the novel, depict the warp-ing of Nick's humanity by the harsh circumstances of destitution, prejudice, judicial unfairness, and plain bad luck, all features that would resurface forty years later in black *noirs*. The salient point to notice here, though, is the film's faithful use of a narrative from black literature to construct a film that was recognized from very early on as *noir*.

Other critics have noted the later deployment of *noir* and *noir*-like features in "black experience" novels of the 1960s and 1970s written by Donald Goines

---

97. Ibid., esp. 6–10.

98. Silver and Ward, *Film Noir: An Encyclopedic Reference*, 161–62; Willard Motley, *Knock on Any Door* (New York: Appleton-Century-Crofts, 1947); Robert E. Fleming, *Willard Motley* (Boston: Twayne Publishers, 1978), esp. 59–63.

99. For more on "probationary," "borderline whites" and internal hierarchies of whiteness, see Mills, *Racial Contract*, 78–80.

and Robert Beck (better known as "Iceberg Slim").[100] Goines's novels have
been incorporated into Gallimard's *Série Noire,* and some of them have been
made into films, one of which will be analyzed later in this book.[101] The novels
of Goines and Beck depict an underside to 1940s, 1950s, and 1960s ghetto
life seldom (if ever) found in mainstream literature. As *noir* critic Woody Haut
notes, they conform to the aesthetic of black *noir* fiction outlined by Chester
Himes more than half a century ago.[102]

More recently—as well as more famously—Walter Mosley has utilized *noir*
conventions extensively in his books. The first of his Easy Rawlins mysteries,
Devil in a Blue Dress, was made into a movie in 1995.[103] Another of his books,
Always Outnumbered, Always Outgunned (1998),[104] became an HBO movie the
year it was published. Both these films will also be analyzed at length later in
this book.

The use of *noir* in black literature thus has a solid if underappreciated
tradition that might be seen to serve as an ambient aesthetic circumstance for
the germination of later appropriations of *film noir* by the black film wave. It
also provides a set of models for transforming the *noir* genre in favor of foregrounding racial injustice and providing critiques of American conceptions of
race. In some cases, such as those of Himes, Mosley, and Goines, it also has
provided the bases for actual black *noir* films.

One might even argue that earlier black film and some more mainstream
Hollywood productions used the techniques of *film noir* to depict problems of
race. One of the earliest examples might well be *Dark Manhattan* (Ralph Cooper, 1937). As black film historian Thomas Cripps notes, "It could be said that
with the release of *Dark Manhattan* in 1937, race movies had anticipated postwar *film noir,* perhaps because the actuality of black life echoed the dark street
scenes of the genre."[105] Cripps also observes that black director Spencer Williams made two *films noirs* in the 1940s,[106] and arguments similar to Cripps's

100. Munby, *Public Enemies, Public Heroes,* 226; Munby, personal communication; Haut, *Neon
Noir,* 212–13. See also Donald Goines, *Dopefiend* (Los Angeles: Holloway House, 1971), *Black Girl
Lost* (Los Angeles: Holloway House, 1973), *Daddy Cool* (Los Angeles: Holloway House, 1974), and
White Man's Justice, Black Man's Grief (Los Angeles: Holloway House, 1973), and Robert Beck,
Pimp: The Story of My Life (Los Angeles: Holloway House, 1969) and *Trick Baby* (Los Angeles:
Holloway House, 1970).

101. Borgers, "*Serie Noire,*" 240; Lola Ogunnaike, "Credentials for Pulp Fiction: Pimp and
Drug Addict," *New York Times,* March 25, 2004, http://www.nytimes.com.

102. Haut, *Neon Noir,* 214.

103. Walter Mosley, *Devil in a Blue Dress* (1990; repr., New York: Pocket Books, 1991).

104. Walter Mosley, *Always Outnumbered, Always Outgunned* (New York: Washington Square
Books, 1998).

105. Thomas Cripps, "Introduction to 1929–1940: Hollywood Beckons," in *Instructor's Guide
to African Americans in Cinema: The First Half Century,* ed. Phyllis R. Klotman (CD-ROM, Urbana
and Chicago: University of Illinois Press, 2003), 19.

106. Cripps, *Making Movies Black,* 148. The films in question are *The Girl in Room 20* (Spencer
Williams, 1946) and *Dirty Gertie from Harlem USA* (Spencer Williams, 1946). Cripps writes that
these films are "flawed."

FIG. 2   Dr. Luther Brooks (Sidney Poitier) asks Edie (Linda Darnell) to recognize the humanity of the man who just shot him, Ray (Richard Widmark), and assist in saving his life (*No Way Out*, 1950).

regarding *Dark Manhattan* could possibly be made about some aspects of the work of black film pioneer Oscar Micheaux.[107]

Another noteworthy antecedent is the Hollywood production *No Way Out* (Joseph Mankiewicz, 1950). Although clearly made as a social problem film intended to be consistent with other relatively mainstream works about blacks in this era, such as *Home of the Brave* (Mark Robson, 1949) and *Pinky* (Elia Kazan, 1949), and no doubt inspired by the critical and financial successes of the *noir* classic *Crossfire* (Edward Dmytryk, 1947), which strongly criticized American anti-Semitism, as well as its more mainstream doppelganger, *Gentleman's Agreement* (Elia Kazan, 1947), the Mankiewicz film dares to depict a race riot (where blacks triumph) and the unadulterated bigotry of some whites, chiefly that of the petty crook Ray (Richard Widmark). Advertised as "entertainment that challenges your own ability to experience the emotions of others," the film foregrounds the institutional presumption that blacks are incompetent, here directed primarily against a medical resident, Dr. Luther

107. For example, Charles Musser, "To Redream the Dream of White Playwrights: Reappropriation and Resistance in Oscar Micheaux's *Body and Soul*," in *Oscar Micheaux and His Circle*, ed. Pearl Bowser, Jane Gaines, and Charles Musser (Indianapolis: Indiana University Press, 2001), 114, argues that a technique used by Micheaux in *Body and Soul* (1925) is "*noirish*."

Brooks (Sidney Poitier), who in the final scene teaches a white female character, Edie (Linda Darnell), to acknowledge even the racist Ray's humanity, in
spite of the fact that this criminal has just shot him.[108] Borde and Chaumeton
explicitly mention this film as a work that was at least influenced by *film noir*,
and nearly three decades later critics Foster Hirsch and Jon Tuska discuss
it as a *noir* outright.[109] Although frequently ignored by works on classic *film
noir* and race, it constitutes a crucial precursor to the later cycle discussed in
this book, even if I agree with Ralph Ellison that films like this one generally failed aesthetically because they focused more on "what whites think and
feel about" blacks than depicting compelling representations of actual black
human beings.[110]

Another classic *film noir* brush with race is *The Set-Up* (Robert Wise, 1949).
Cripps notes that this boxing film starring Robert Ryan was based on writer
Joseph Moncure March's eponymous poem and further claims that March's
poem is "a black literary source."[111] Yet Cripps is inaccurate here. March was
not black, but a white jazz-age vernacular poet (an Amherst graduate and
protégé of Robert Frost) who hoped to write a tragedy about racial prejudice.
While "The Set-Up" (1928) is indeed about a black boxer who never gets a title
shot because of his race and as the years slip by becomes a palooka, that feature of the poem does not make it a black literary source—at least not in the
sense that Cripps means.[112] Still, Cripps is on firm ground when he points out
that the filmmakers had originally planned to make "a *film noir* that revealed
the bigotry visited upon blacks because they were black" starring African-
American actor James Edwards (213). Unfortunately, the greater potential of
profiting financially from a story about a white boxer enticed the filmmakers
into changing the racial character of the film and its star. Edwards received a
minor role as another boxer who briefly shares the fight arena's dressing room
with Ryan's character.[113] In March's own words, "the whole point of the narrative had been thrown out the window. Ah, Hollywood . . . !"[114]

108. See the theatrical trailer and other materials on *No Way Out*, DVD, directed by
Joseph L. Mankiewicz (1950; Twentieth Century Fox Home Entertainment, 2005).

109. Borde and Chaumeton, *Panorama of American Film Noir*, 119; Foster Hirsch, *Film Noir:
The Dark Side of the Screen* (1981; repr., New York: Da Capo Press, 1983), 10, 160, 180–81; Jon
Tuska, *Dark Cinema: American Film Noir in Cultural Perspective* (Westport, Conn.: Greenwood
Press, 1984), 229. It is also worth noting that the film's DVD version was released as part of the
"Fox Film Noir" series.

110. For examples of *No Way Out* being ignored by critics, see Lott, "Whiteness of Film Noir,"
and Kelly Oliver and Benigno Trigo, *Noir Anxiety* (Minneapolis: University of Minnesota Press,
2003), esp. 1–26. For the Ellison quotation, see Ralph Ellison, "The Shadow and the Act" (1949),
reprinted in *Shadow and Act* (New York: Vintage, 1972), 277.

111. Cripps, *Making Movies Black*, 214.

112. Joseph Moncure March, *The Wild Party / The Set-Up / A Certain Wildness* (Freeport,
Maine: Bond and Wheelwright, 1968), esp. 53–54, 149–297; "Joseph Moncure March," *Contemporary Authors Online*, 2000, http://galenet.galegroup.com (accessed March 24, 2006).

113. *Making Movies Black*, 212–14, 348–49 nn. 94, 95. See also Robert Wise, commentary,
The Set-Up, DVD, directed by Robert Wise (1949; Warner Brothers Entertainment, 2004).

114. March, *The Wild Party / The Set-Up / A Certain Wildness*, 58–59.

More generally, while I agree with American Studies scholar Eric Lott's claim that racist exclusions seriously mar a good deal of classic American *film noir*, the problem is more complex than his "totalizing" argument allows—as he himself implies in the last few pages of his essay, "The Whiteness of Film Noir." Nevertheless, films like *Knock on Any Door, No Way Out,* Robert Montgomery's *Ride the Pink Horse* (1947), Anthony Mann's *Border Incident* (1949), Joseph Losey's *The Lawless* (1950), Michael Curtiz's *The Breaking Point* (1950), Elia Kazan's *Panic in the Streets* (1951), Orson Welles's *Touch of Evil* (1958), Robert Wise's *Odds Against Tomorrow* (1959), and Sam Fuller's *The Crimson Kimono* (1959) make the possibility of "occasional" exceptions to which he refers much more difficult to dismiss than his argument suggests.

In the Mann film, its address of race is "honorable," even if it is also considerably weakened by the depiction of clownish Mexican thugs, as Lott notes (561). *The Lawless* (which Lott does not mention), on the other hand, follows the gradual realization of a white small-town newspaper editor regarding the racialized presumptions under which Mexican fruit pickers must live and work. In many ways it improves on the racial politics of *Border Incident,* and Borde and Chaumeton single it out for special praise in their discussion of classic *noir*-influenced films on race.[115] In *The Crimson Kimono* (which Lott does not mention either), its focus on the rather selfish personal feelings of its white male protagonist obscures to some extent a fairly probing exploration of anti-Asian sentiments. Still, the film's antiracist point is not lost. *Odds Against Tomorrow,* which Lott describes as a "civil-rights noir" and "politically interesting" but "cinematically dull" (561), deserves more serious consideration than he gives it, in part because it illustrates what classic American *film noir* was capable of when directed squarely at race. Its *noirish* ending, for example, offers a devastating comment on the misguidedness of race prejudice. In the Welles film, Charlton Heston's star personality, performance, and total lack of an accent admittedly tend to obscure the fact that he plays a Mexican national. We as viewers cannot completely forget who is up on the screen under all that greasepaint (see Lott, 562–63). At the same time, the film clearly sides with this racial "other" and against Hank Quinlan (Orson Welles), such as when the corrupt white police detective tries to frame the Mexican-American shoe clerk Manelo Sanchez (Victor Millan) for the bombing that famously opens the film—even if it also turns out, ironically, that Sanchez ultimately confesses to having planted the bomb. The point being made by the film here is that framing even a guilty man is morally wrong, particularly if it is motivated by racism.

Curtiz's *The Breaking Point* (also unmentioned by Lott) is especially noteworthy for the changes it makes in the Ernest Hemingway novel on which it is based, *To Have and Have Not,*[116] and the shocking twist in its final shot that challenges viewers to think about race in a way rarely found in Hollywood

115. Borde and Chaumeton, *Panorama of American Film Noir,* 119.

116. Ernest Hemingway, *To Have and Have Not* (New York: Charles Scribner's Sons, 1937).

FIG. 3   A crowd disperses, leaving Joseph (Juan Hernandez) alone on the dock (*The Breaking Point*, 1950).

productions of the era. As Morrison points out, the novel provides a black character who is crucial to the story, but through the first five chapters is referred to only as "the nigger."[117] Later in the novel he does acquire a name (Wesley) and a voice, but as Morrison notes he uses it only to grumble, apologize, and whine (74–76). Curtiz's film changes all that by providing Wesley (Juano Hernandez) with a far more independent and humanized character. Moreover, the protagonist, Harry Morgan (John Garfield), treats him fairly and equitably, a marked contrast from the novel. The plight of Wesley's family even becomes the final focus of the film. As Cavell has argued, *The Breaking Point*'s last shot invokes "a massive evil about which this film has nothing to say," namely the sort of racist presumption regarding the greater value placed on Morgan's loss of an arm than on Wesley's death and its impact on his family, here represented by his son, who waits silently on the dock for the return of a father who will never come home.[118] Unfortunately, no one tells him, so consumed are the other characters (including Morgan himself) by the prospect of bodily

117. Morrison, *Playing in the Dark*, 70–76. It is perhaps worth noting that even though Lott cites Morrison's work as an inspiration (e.g., 542, 566), he does not make the connection between *To Have and Have Not*, which serves as one of Morrison's central examples, and the Curtiz film, which is based on it.

118. Cavell, *World Viewed*, 34.

disability. While it remains the case that neither Wesley nor his family become the film's primary focus, their roles in the story are substantially augmented and dignified, to the point that its final image directs many viewers to reflect, even if only for a moment, on their own unthinking racial prejudices.

Even in a politically "mainstream" *film noir* like *Panic in the Streets,* one occasionally finds explicitly egalitarian presentations of racial diversity, as in the scene where the Navy doctor Clinton Reed (Richard Widmark) questions both black and white longshoremen looking for work. Although a good deal of that effect is undone by an earlier scene where two Chinese sailors are stereotyped and played for laughs, as well, perhaps, by naming the primary antagonist "Blackie" (which Lott notes, 558), its depiction of race is more nuanced than Lott's passing reference would suggest.[119]

Finally, let us consider the complicated case of *Ride the Pink Horse,* which seems to be, like John Ford's *The Searchers* (1956), a racist film that nonetheless manages to offer insightful criticisms about racism. While superficially embracing the prejudices of its time, *Ride the Pink Horse* also clearly subverts them by valorizing the lives, actions, and values of its racial "others" in contrast to those of its largely uncomprehending *noir* protagonist Gagin (Robert Montgomery), whose alienation and moral myopia are thereby even more prominently displayed. The Mexican-American Pancho (Thomas Gomez) and the Native American Pila (Wanda Hendrix) assist and even take brutal beatings for Gagin, because they think of him as a friend as well as someone who needs help. In contrast, Gagin declares, "I'm nobody's friend," and acts almost exclusively to promote his own self-interest. The film also clearly depicts these racial "others" as members of a social network, a community, whereas Gagin's isolation and alienation are evident from the moment he steps off the bus in the first scene. The film suggests as well that these diverging relations to one's community have serious implications for prospects of personal happiness and contentment with one's life.

These examples show that while Lott may be correct in general, the whiteness of *film noir* is neither as monolithic nor as pervasive as he suggests. Rather than being "a nightmarish world of otherness and racial aliens" into which whites were imaginatively cast—and one that captivated "*all* of noir's creators" (Lott, 562; italics mine)—*film noir* provides a catalog of many different stances that whites took in regard to race, ranging from white racial paranoia, which Lott perceptively identifies, to far more liberal, at times perhaps radical, outlooks on race. Again, this more complex view of *noir* agrees with Mike Davis's insight, as well as with the fact that black fiction writers found literary *noir* amenable to portraying racial unfairness. Many of white racism's subtleties are lost by means of Lott's totalizing interpretation of *film noir*—subtleties that we must grasp if we are to fully comprehend the diverse

---

119. The first two points regarding this film are made by James Ursini and Alain Silver in their commentary on the DVD release of the film; see *Panic in the Streets,* DVD, directed by Elia Kazan (1951; Twentieth Century Fox Home Entertainment, 2005).

F I G . 4   Pancho (Thomas Gomez) moves to protect the injured Gagin (Robert Montgomery), as Pila (Wanda Hendrix) cradles him in her arms (*Ride the Pink Horse*, 1947).

phenomena comprising whiteness and their consequences, let alone begin
working to eradicate them.

Also worth noting as a precursor to the more recent films analyzed in this
book is Van Peebles's *Sweet Sweetback's Baadasssss Song*, which black critic Nelson George describes only slightly hyperbolically as "essentially a European art
film set in Watts."[120] As Cripps more accurately observes, "Sweetback's transformation experience [from hustling picaro to political outlaw] would have
been implausible but for borrowings from the genre of *film noir*. Van Peebles,
a lifelong moviegoer, saw how to use that genre's darkened streets, glistening
half-lights, bumbling and villainous cops. Even the raspy sound, some of it,
one guesses, unintentional, contributes to the urban streetscape."[121] Van Peebles also uses other *noir* techniques such as low-key and single-source lighting
as well as swinging lamps, and his main characters are clearly from a black
noir underworld, far from the middle-class domesticity of most mainstream

120. Nelson George, *Blackface: Reflections on African-Americans and the Movies* (New York:
HarperCollins, 1994), 52.

121. Thomas Cripps, *Black Film as Genre* (Bloomington: Indiana University Press, 1978),
135–36. Tommy Lott also observes that "Van Peebles employed the social realism of *film noir* to
engage in hyperbole" ("Aesthetics and Politics," 300 n. 27). I should note as well that the point of
Cripps's analysis of *Sweetback* via *film noir* is negative, although Lott's is not.

films. *Sweetback* proved that representations of disreputable figures from the black community (often referred to as "bad niggas" in black folklore) had an audience,[122] and Van Peebles's use of *film noir* techniques allowed him to portray them sympathetically.

Arguably, other "Blaxploitation" features—for example, *Shaft* (Gordon Parks, 1971), *Super Fly* (Gordon Parks Jr., 1972), *Coffy* (Jack Hill, 1973), *Black Caesar* (Larry Cohen, 1973), and *Foxy Brown* (Jack Hill, 1974)—use the techniques and themes of *noir* to tap into audience sympathies for violent, "bad" black male and female characters. For example, the moral ambiguity and pervasiveness of evil in *Coffy* makes it at least plausible to think of this film as much more *noir* than most critics have realized, particularly in regard to its final sequence. Although slowly drained from later Pam Grier vehicles, themes such as the female protagonist's defeat by overwhelming corruption and personal betrayal, as well as her morally complex character, indicate that *noir* influences here deserve greater attention.[123]

What most Blaxploitation pictures did not do was find ways to develop and aesthetically enhance *noir* themes and conventions beyond the conditions in which they previously existed. That is, most of these movies (with the exception of *Sweetback* and perhaps a few others) did not transform the cinematic elements they utilized into critical tools that could promote more than occasional, fleeting audience reflection on racial injustice. That would take another decade and a half, as well as greater black artistic control over the content and style of films. Ultimately, it would take Spike Lee and other black filmmakers kicking in the door to Hollywood before the sorts of *noir* innovations I describe in this book could be made. Of course, as has frequently been pointed out, one of the main stumbling blocks to this possibility being actualized earlier was financial.[124] Political economist and film scholar Jesse A. Rhines notes that it was not until the early 1990s offered new and unprecedented opportunities to African-American directors and filmmakers who could produce gritty "urban dramas"—a genre that lends itself especially well to *film noir* conventions as well as fitting white producers' preconceptions about black

122. Lott, "Aesthetics and Politics," 290–91. For an account of the bad black man figure in African-American folklore, see John W. Roberts, *From Trickster to Badman: The Black Folk Hero in Slavery and Freedom* (Philadelphia: University of Pennsylvania Press, 1989), 171–215, and Lawrence W. Levine, *Black Culture and Black Consciousness: Afro-American Folk Thought from Slavery to Freedom* (Oxford: Oxford University Press, 1977), 407–20.

123. Aside from occasional *noir* shots using "mystery lighting" or "criminal lighting" such as described by famous *noir* cinematographer John Alton in *Painting with Light* (1949; repr., Berkeley and Los Angeles: University of California Press, 1995), 44–56, the film's writer/director Jack Hill states on his commentary for *Coffy* that he thinks the last great American film was *White Heat* (Raoul Walsh, 1949), one of the best-known late-1940s gangster *noir* pictures; see Jack Hill, commentary, *Coffy*, DVD, directed by Jack Hill (1973; MGM Home Entertainment, 2001).

124. See, for example, Jacquie Jones, "The New Ghetto Aesthetic," *Wide Angle* 13, no. 3–4 (1991): 33; Watkins, *Representing*, esp. 187–95; Guerrero, *Framing Blackness*, 164–65, 182ff.; and Jesse Algernon Rhines, *Black Film/White Money* (New Brunswick: Rutgers University Press, 1996), 4, 12–13, 57–78.

film—that the new black film wave really got off the ground.[125] I would further conjecture that it took some subtle shifts in general audience presumptions as well, helped along by, for example, the advent of hip-hop, a point that should become evident from later discussions. At the same time, the antecedents I have outlined remain important because they establish a tradition of *noir* use in African-American literary and visual art that until recently has largely escaped detection by nonblack critics, but that provided a solid foundation for more recent appropriations of *film noir*, in much the same way that hard-boiled detective fiction and gangster films have provided a basis for other forms of *film noir* since the 1940s.

In the following chapters, I analyze and explain how the foregoing elements come together in many black *noirs* and their cinematic descendants. The works I examine here use *noir*'s subversive potential to offer their viewers occasions to reflect in sophisticated and fundamental ways on presuppositions regarding race, a possibility that black filmmaker and critic Jacquie Jones noted very early in the cycle.[126] Like Socrates, who goaded his peers to reflect on virtue,[127] black *noirs* and their aesthetic progeny challenge audiences to think carefully and intensely about the relations between race, morality, and justice. Many of these films prompt their viewers to seriously reconsider their usual patterns of thought and action, especially their presumptions about themselves and other human beings, and the role those presumptions play in acts of recognition and acknowledgment of humanity that have all too often been integrated into, or at times even blocked by, presumptions of racialized inferiority and superiority—that is, by unconscious senses of racial hierarchy and "white privilege."

125. Rhines, *Black Film/White Money*, 89–90.

126. Jones, "New Ghetto Aesthetic," 37.

127. Plato, *Apology* 29d–30e, trans. Hugh Tredennick, in *Plato: The Collected Dialogues*, ed. Edith Hamilton and Huntington Cairns (Princeton: Princeton University Press, 1963), 15–17.

SPIKE LEE AND THE SYMPATHETIC RACIST

Know thyself.

—Inscription on the Temple of Apollo at Delphi

In his recent book *White*, film scholar Richard Dyer argues that racial whiteness has operated in Western film and photography as an idealized standard against which other races have been judged.[1] Making his case inductively using instruction manuals, historical theories of race, traditional lighting and makeup practices, as well as the dominant ideals for human beauty utilized in developing film stocks and camera equipment over the last 150 years and more, Dyer maintains that Western visual culture has presented whites as the norm for what it is to be "just human" or "just people," whereas other human beings have been presented as raced, as different from the norm (1–2). This manner of depicting whiteness has invested the category itself with the power to represent the commonality of humanity. Furthermore, Dyer argues that this historical function of whiteness's normativity continues to profoundly influence current practices and instruction.[2]

Dyer's argument is in accord with what Charles Mills and Lewis Gordon have advanced in broader theoretical terms regarding the operation of whiteness as a norm against which nonwhites—and particularly blacks—have been negatively judged.[3] Like Dyer, these philosophers argue that presumptions of whiteness institutionalize racial beliefs at a level of background assumptions that most people would not even think to examine. Based on this claim, they reason that whiteness functions not only as a social norm but also at an epistemological level as a form of learned ignorance that may only with considerable effort be brought forward for explicit critical inspection.[4]

1. Richard Dyer, *White* (London: Routledge, 1997).
2. Ibid., esp. 70–142.
3. Mills, *Racial Contract*, esp. 53–62; Lewis R. Gordon, "Critical Reflections on Three Popular Tropes in the Study of Whiteness," in *What White Looks Like: African-American Philosophers on the Whiteness Question*, ed. George Yancy (New York: Routledge, 2004), 173–93, esp. 175–76, 181–82.
4. Mills, *Racial Contract*, especially 17–19, 91–109; Gordon, *Fanon and the Crisis of European Man*, 22–26, 38ff. See also Peg O'Connor, *Oppression and Responsibility: A Wittgensteinian Approach to Social Practices and Moral Theory* (University Park: Pennsylvania State University Press, 2002), especially 1–59, 128–131.

Similarly, many of Spike Lee's films place into question presumptions about whiteness's normativity. One crucial aim of his ongoing cinematic *oeuvre* has been to make the experience of racism understandable to white audience members who "cross over" and view his films. Because seeing matters of race from a nonwhite perspective is typically a standpoint unfamiliar to white viewers, Lee has sought to make more accessible such an outlook through the construction and use of specific character types. One way he achieves this goal is by offering depictions of characters who function as what I will call "sympathetic racists": characters with whom mainstream audiences readily ally themselves but who embrace racist beliefs and commit racist acts. By self-consciously presenting white viewers with the fact that they may form positive allegiances with characters whose racist bigotry is revealed as the story unfolds, Lee provokes his viewers to consider a more complex view of what it means to think of one's self as "white" and how that affects one's overall sense of humanity.

Lee thus probes white audiences' investment in what might be called their "racial allegiances," a dimension of film narrative pertaining to the manner in which audiences become morally allied to characters through categories and presumptions about race.[5] Foregrounding racial allegiances allows him to depict how ideas of race may affect characters' and audience members' behavior at much deeper levels cognitively, emotionally, and morally than many of them realize. Through offering a critical perspective on their investment in race, Lee issues his viewers a philosophical challenge, both within the context of their narrative understanding and their lives generally. By focusing audience attention on a character toward whom they feel favorably while also revealing that character's racism, Lee constructs a film that philosophizes by developing a conception of what it means to be racist that fundamentally challenges typical white viewers to inspect their own presumptions about how they see themselves and others.

Lee depicts sympathetic racist characters so that white viewers may forge positive allegiances with them in spite of those characters' antiblack beliefs and actions, which in earlier stages of the narrative may seem trivial, benign, or unimportant, or may even go unnoticed. He often then alienates viewers from such characters by revealing the harmfulness of these typically white beliefs and actions. Through this technique, Lee contests the presumed human commonality attached to being white by providing viewers with an opportunity to see their conceptions of whiteness analytically. By introducing a critical distance between them and what it means to be white, Lee makes a Brechtian move with respect to race. As Douglas Kellner points out, he "dramatizes the necessity of making moral and political choices" by forcing his viewer "to come to grips" with certain crucial issues and "adopt a critical approach" to the emotions and cognitions involved.[6] The opportunity offered to white viewers

---

5. The idea of a racial allegiance was suggested to me by Calvin Selvey.

6. Douglas Kellner, "Aesthetics, Ethics, and Politics in the Films of Spike Lee," in *Spike Lee's "Do the Right Thing,"* ed. Mark A. Reid (New York: Cambridge University Press, 1997), 75;

who cross over to see these films is that of experiencing what they have been culturally trained to take as typical or normative—being white—and see it depicted from a different perspective, namely, that of being black in America, which in turn removes white viewers from their own experience and provides a detailed access to that of others. Exploiting this kind of anti-egoist strategy regarding fiction's capacities to give audiences access to the perspectives of others is something that theorists such as Kendall Walton, Iris Murdoch, Martha Nussbaum, Alex Neill, and others have long recognized.[7] It is just this strategy that Lee takes advantage of in his films.

Given this characterization of Lee's goals, I would argue that we should recognize the opportunity he offers typical white viewers as a chance to imagine whiteness "from the outside"—see it acentrally and sympathetically, as opposed to imagining it centrally and empathetically. Both kinds of responses are modes of imaginative engagement; sympathy, however, is generally a more distanced attitude in which we imagine *that* such-and-such were the case, whereas empathy calls for something closer to imagining from one's *own* situation.[8] By encouraging viewer response to be more sympathetic than empathetic, Lee promotes a mode of detached critical reflection that is not merely Brechtian, but philosophical, for it involves reflectively considering presuppositions of the self and humanity that are among the most fundamental in contemporary conceptions of personal identity, namely, those regarding race.[9] In this sense Lee challenges his white viewers to know themselves along the lines of the Delphic inscription made famous by Socrates.

Similarly, a narrative technique also frequently employed by Lee and other filmmakers allows for the presentation of what would be otherwise unsympathetic black characters with whom many audience members might feel little or nothing in common. Through encouraging empathy for characters that audiences might in different circumstances dismiss as apprentice criminals

Bertholt Brecht, *Brecht on Theatre: The Development of an Aesthetic,* ed. and trans. John Willett (New York: Hill and Wang, 1962), 23, 101.

7. Kendall Walton, *Mimesis as Make-Believe: On the Foundations of the Representational Arts* (Cambridge: Harvard University Press, 1990), 34; Iris Murdoch, *The Sovereignty of Good* (1970; repr., London: Ark Paperbacks, 1985), esp. 64–67; Martha Nussbaum, *Love's Knowledge: Essays on Philosophy and Literature* (New York: Oxford University Press, 1990), esp. 77–79; Alex Neill, "Empathy and (Film) Fiction," in *Post-Theory: Reconstructing Film Studies,* ed. David Bordwell and Noël Carroll (Madison: University of Wisconsin Press, 1996), 179–80; Smith, *Engaging Characters,* 235–36.

8. For more on the distinction between central and acentral imagining, see Bernard Williams, *Problems of the Self* (Cambridge: Cambridge University Press, 1973), esp. 36–38; Richard Wollheim, *On Art and the Mind* (Cambridge: Harvard University Press, 1974), 58ff., and *The Thread of Life* (Cambridge: Harvard University Press, 1984), 73ff.; Carroll, *Philosophy of Horror,* 88–96; and Smith, *Engaging Characters,* 76ff.

9. The claim that modern personal identity is intimately linked to race has been argued for by philosophers at least since Fanon. See Fanon, "Lived Experience of the Black," 184–201; Gordon, *Fanon and the Crisis of European Man;* O'Connor, *Oppression and Responsibility;* and Mills, *Racial Contract.*

or incorrigible gang members, filmmakers can delineate and contextualize ways in which the presumed guilt of young black men and women frequently impose on them the expectation, both internally and externally, that they live degraded human lives that are somehow worth less than those of whites. By inducing viewers to imagine these characters "from the inside" through providing detailed access to the context, reasons, and motivations for their actions and beliefs, filmmakers like Lee enrich the grounds for empathy for individuals that viewers might in other settings dismiss out of hand as already hopeless delinquents, a technique I will examine closely in subsequent chapters.

A crucial insight here regarding both sympathetic racist and empathetic black characters is that, analogous to most white viewers' generally favorable "internal" predisposition to white characters, such viewers also frequently have trouble imagining what it is like to be African American "from the inside"—engaging black points of view empathetically—because they do not understand black experience from a detailed or intimate perspective. It is frequently too far from their own experience of the world, too foreign to what they are able to envision as ways in which human life might proceed. Hill and Boxill argue that this limitation in imagining other life possibilities makes it difficult for whites to make correct moral choices because they may be easily deceived by their own social advantages into thinking that such accrue to all, and thus will be unable to perceive many cases of racial injustice. This cognitive insensitivity may thus affect even well-meaning, sincere individuals who wish for nothing more than to act morally in situations where questions of racial injustice might arise, a phenomenon that Janine Jones refers to as "the impairment of empathy in goodwill whites."[10]

To counteract such an imaginative limitation in film viewing, Lee offers depictions that invite a deeper imagining with respect to blackness. Not only does he provide numerous detailed representations of African-American characters in his films, but he also offers sympathetic racist character types who provide a conception of how it might be possible for a white person to act favorably toward blacks but still be racist. In this sense, Lee constructs the sympathetic racist character type as an "alloy" of morally good and bad characteristics in the terminology developed by Murray Smith in *Engaging Characters* and elsewhere.[11] As Smith notes, the moral complexity of such characters can force us "to question certain habits of moral judgment," which is precisely what Lee achieves in many of his films.[12]

What Lee offers, then, is a more acentral access (that is, detached access "from the outside") to white characters so that white viewers in particular may look at these characters more critically. This type of access might be thought

---

10.   Hill and Boxill, "Kant and Race," 469–70; Janine Jones, "The Impairment of Empathy in Goodwill Whites for African Americans," in Yancy, *What White Looks Like*, 65–86. Mills, *Racial Contract*, 95, also notes this problem of empathetic impairment in many whites.

11.   Smith, *Engaging Characters*, 209ff., and "Gangsters, Cannibals, Aesthetes," 217–38, esp. 223ff.

12.   Smith, "Gangsters, Cannibals, Aesthetes," 228.

of as the first step in giving whites a sort of "double consciousness" regarding their own race. If W. E. B. Du Bois was correct in observing that African Americans possess a sort of "twoness" regarding themselves racially in American society, then the "single consciousness" of whites would make them particularly susceptible to narrative allegiances based on whiteness and resistant to seeing white characters from other perspectives.[13] The presupposition of white racial experience in much film narrative, then, contingently predisposes viewers, especially white viewers, to understanding characters from a racialized point of view. Thus, counteracting this phenomenon and creating an incipient white double consciousness might be conceived as another way to think of Spike Lee's overall goal with regard to his white viewers. As Linda Martín Alcoff has explained, such a perspective would involve a critical sense that white identity possessed a clear stake in racialized social structures and inequalities as well as some sense of responsibility in helping to rectify these inequities.[14] In this sense, the technique of self-consciously depicting sympathetic racists throws into question white racial allegiances, for the explicit use of this character type aims to provoke in white viewers a self-reflective examination of why one might feel favorably toward such characters, in spite of their racist beliefs and actions.

Lee also encourages his viewers to reflect how whiteness possesses specific characteristics that make white experience different from nonwhite experience, and vice versa. African-American experience, for example, is constituted by specificities that involve a history and legacy of racialized slavery, as well as the ongoing "scientific" research project that has time and again ranked blacks at the bottom of what was claimed to be an empirically verified racial hierarchy, and that frequently served as grounds for arguing that blacks possess lesser capacities to be moral, intelligent, and law-abiding. African Americans have been subject to the burden of representation established across decades (one could also now say centuries) by stereotypes that arose out of blackface minstrelsy, as well as a history of having been subject to lynching on the basis of one's skin color.[15] These features need to be kept in focus when thinking about and assessing the actions, beliefs, and emotions of black American characters in many films, as it is not unusual for blacks in real life to have the capacity to imagine that whites who are sympathetic toward them might also harbor racist beliefs or act in racist ways. History bristles with examples of African Americans having to deal with such individuals, among them Abraham Lincoln.[16] Thus it would not be difficult to transfer this cognitive capacity

13. W. E. B. Du Bois, *The Souls of Black Folk* (1903; repr., New York: Signet, 1969), 45.

14. Linda Martin Alcoff, "What Should White People Do?" *Hypatia* 13 (1998): 6–26, esp. 24–25.

15. For more on the history and legacy of racialized existence of blacks, see Mills, *Racial Contract*, esp. 81–89, 109–20.

16. Eze, *Achieving Our Humanity*, 27, as well as some of the title cards in D. W. Griffith's *The Birth of a Nation* (1915). For examples from the abolition movement, see *Against Slavery: An Abolitionist Reader*, ed. Mason Lowance (New York: Penguin, 2000).

over to understanding film narratives. On the other hand, neither this history nor its related imaginative capacities are generally shared by whites. Lee's self-conscious use of sympathetic racist character types, then, aims to assist whites in acquiring the rudiments of these imaginative capacities.

Spike Lee is not the only filmmaker to employ the narrative technique of constructing sympathetic racist characters, but his work seems to be the locus classicus for such figures in the new black film wave. From 1989's *Do the Right Thing* through *Jungle Fever* (1991), *Clockers* (1995), *Summer of Sam* (1999), and even *The 25th Hour* (2002), Lee's films have self-consciously foregrounded allegiances with sympathetic racists or similar morally complex "good-bad characters" for the inspection and contemplation of his audiences.[17] In this fashion he has sought to make white viewers more critically aware of anti-black racism and fear of difference. I should add here that I do not believe that Lee and other filmmakers necessarily devised these narrative techniques with exactly the theoretical goals I describe or by using the philosophical considerations I outline in this chapter. Rather, while I assume that there is some overlap between their goals and the ones I describe, filmmakers use these techniques because they work well in depicting certain character types and narrative situations. In contrast, what I provide here is a theoretical explanation and clarification of what these techniques are, how they work cognitively, and why they achieve the effects that they do. I would further argue that these techniques also represent singular achievements of black American *film noir* as it has developed during the last two decades. Character types like the sympathetic racist develop in new and innovative ways the morally complex "good-bad character" types so common to *films noirs* and whose multifaceted allegiances with audiences Murray Smith has explored in other contexts.

Even as Lee offers his white viewers an opportunity to contemplate their racial allegiances, it is important to note that one problem associated with the depiction of sympathetic racist characters is that its critical use may not always be evident. Some audience members may not detect such characters as racist; others will. What I offer next is a detailed analysis that makes clear what Lee seeks to accomplish by presenting this character type, as well as an explanation addressing why some viewers are unable to apprehend it as racist.

Who—and What—Is Sal?

In an otherwise astute examination of *auteur* theory, Berys Gaut argues that the Italian-American pizzeria owner, Sal (Danny Aiello), in *Do the Right Thing* is not a racist figure.[18] Aiello's performance, Gaut asserts, overcomes Lee's

17. As Smith notes ("Gangsters, Cannibals, Aesthetes," 223), the original source for the concept of the "good-bad" character is Martha Wolfenstein and Nathan Lietes, *The Movies: A Psychological Study* (Glencoe, Ill.: The Free Press, 1950), 20ff.

18. Berys Gaut, "Film Authorship and Collaboration," in *Film Theory and Philosophy*, ed. Richard Allen and Murray Smith (Oxford: Clarendon Press, 1997), 166.

FIG. 5   Sal (Danny Aiello) angrily racializes the confrontation about which pictures should hang on the wall of his pizzeria (*Do the Right Thing*, 1989).

explicit directorial intention of revealing racist beliefs in a character who is for many viewers the film's richest, most complex, and sympathetic figure.[19] Despite Lee's clearly stated aim to portray this character as a racist, Aiello allegedly trumps that aim through his rendition of Sal.[20] Gaut sees this conflict between Lee and Aiello as an "artistically fruitful disagreement" that contributes to "the film's richness and complexity" (166), in spite of Sal's "complicity in a racial tragedy culminating in a horrifying murder" (165). Gaut quotes film scholar Thomas Doherty to support his point, noting that "on the screen if not in the screenplay [Aiello's] portrayal wins the argument" by depicting Sal's character as someone who is not racist.[21]

Other viewers, however, have regarded Sal's character differently. Ed Guerrero argues that despite Sal's humanity and reasonableness throughout most of the film, when confronted with Radio Raheem (Bill Nunn), Smiley (Roger Guenveur Smith), and Buggin' Out's (Giancarlo Esposito) demands at the end of a long, hot day, "Sal's good-natured paternal persona quickly cracks and out

19. See, for example, Vincent Canby, "Spike Lee Tackles Racism in *Do the Right Thing*," *New York Times*, June 30, 1989, C16, and "Spike Lee Raises the Movies' Black Voice," *New York Times*, May 28, 1989, sec. 2, p. 14; Joe Klein, "Spiked? Dinkins and *Do the Right Thing*," *New York Magazine*, June, 26, 1989, 14–15; and Salim Mawakkil, "Spike Lee and the Image Police," *Cineaste* 17, no. 4 (1990): 36.

20. See, for example, Spike Lee, with Lisa Jones, *Do the Right Thing: A Spike Lee Joint* (New York: Fireside, 1989), 45, and Marlaine Glicksman, "Spike Lee's Bed-Stuy BBQ," in *Spike Lee: Interviews*, ed. Cynthia Fuchs (Jackson: University of Mississippi, 2002), 18–19. Gaut notes ("Film Authorship and Collaboration," 166) that Lee also makes this point during a read-through of the script with Aiello in St. Clair Bourne's documentary *Making "Do the Right Thing"* (1989).

21. Thomas Doherty, review of *Do the Right Thing*, *Film Quarterly* 43, no. 2 (1989): 39; Gaut, "Film Authorship and Collaboration," 166.

comes a screed of racist invective about 'jungle music,' accompanied by egregious racial profanities, the likes of 'black cocksucker,' 'nigger motherfucker,' and so on."[22] Guerrero's point is that by using these terms nonironically and ascriptively with respect to black characters in the narrative, Sal reveals himself as a racist. Similarly, African-American studies scholar Clyde Taylor notes that it is Sal who explicitly racializes this confrontation by insulting his adversaries' choice of melodic accompaniment with the angry exclamation, "Turn that jungle music off! We ain't in Africa!"[23] Following this declaration, racial epithets spew from Sal's mouth.

Taylor and Guerrero's observations concur with those of Media Studies scholar S. Craig Watkins, who notes that "Sal is very much a patriarchal figure," by turns attached, paternal, mistrustful, and hostile toward the African-American community his business serves.[24] This critic, too, would agree that Sal, even as portrayed on the screen, is a racist character, although Watkins eschews the point and prefers to discuss the film in terms of its varied characterizations of whiteness. Specifically, he argues that the film represents some of the subtle differences between different forms of whiteness—for example, between Sal, Pino (John Turturro), and their third family member, Vito (Richard Edson)—all of whom represent different white responses to African Americans. As Watkins argues, when in control Sal's attitude toward blacks is benevolent and patriarchal, but when confronted or challenged, he reveals a form of racialized thinking that clearly mark blacks as inferior. The film reveals this attitude by the way he uses racial categories to verbally put blacks "in their place"; when placed on his guard, denigrating insults pour from his mouth with a full conviction of the derogatory force behind them (156–58). Sal's son Pino, on the other hand, is more openly racist. He clearly shows contempt for the people to whom he serves his father's pizza and consistently distances himself from them through language similar to that ultimately employed by Sal, using terms such as "niggers," "animals," "apes," and "*moolingan*" (Italian for eggplant) to describe as well as demonize all blacks in general (see Watkins 158); while at the other end of the spectrum Pino's brother Vito tends to accept people for who they are as individuals and forgoes racialized categorizations and markers.[25] As the film makes clear, Vito even prefers the pizzeria's delivery person Mookie's (Spike Lee) company to that of his older brother.

22. Ed Guerrero, *Do the Right Thing* (London: BFI Publishing, 2001), 75.

23. Clyde Taylor, *The Mask of Art: Breaking the Aesthetic Contract—Film and Literature* (Bloomington: Indiana University Press, 1998), 269.

24. Watkins, *Representing*, 156.

25. In Bourne's *Making "Do the Right Thing,"* actor Richard Edson explains his character Vito with the following remarks: "[He is] the sympathetic one, the one who likes the neighborhood, who likes black people . . . as opposed to Pino, who's racist . . . [Vito] doesn't think too much . . . [he] thinks that people are people." In the audio commentary on *Do the Right Thing*, Lee remarks that the conflicts between Pino and Vito are due to the fact that "Pino thinks that Vito is too friendly with the *moolingans*." Spike Lee, commentary, *Do the Right Thing*, DVD, directed by Spike Lee (1989; The Criterion Collection, 2001).

"He listens to me. You don't," he tells Pino as his sibling lectures him about racial loyalty and how whites should allegedly relate to blacks. Vito is the white character who clearly has the best rapport with other members of the community and often tries to smooth relations out between them and his other family members. For these efforts Pino tells his brother, "Just remember who you are, right? Your name is Vito Frangione—not Vito Muhammad," an explicit reference to Vito's potential as a "race traitor" in Pino's eyes. From this range of depictions of whiteness, we can see that Lee offers his viewers a broad context from which to understand the character Sal and his relations to whiteness, blackness, and ideas of race in general. Furthermore, it is worth noting that reviewers in the popular press have also sometimes seen Sal as a racist.[26]

Unlike these critics, many white viewers tend not to notice or acknowledge the racist dimension of Sal's character. Instead, like Gaut and Doherty, they often see him as a good person who does a bad thing, or a rational person defeated by an irrational world, but not as someone who is a racist.[27] This form of explanation also seems to have been actor Danny Aiello's own understanding of Sal. In St. Clair Bourne's documentary *Making "Do the Right Thing,"* Aiello remarks during an early read through of the script that "I thought [Sal is] not a racist—he's a nice guy; he sees people as equal." In a later discussion of his character, Aiello further explains: "The word ['nigger'] is distasteful to him." Finally, after acting out Sal's explosion of rage that sparks Raheem's attack and brings down the New York City Police Department's fatal intervention, Aiello summarizes: "Is he [Sal] a racist? I don't think so. But he's heard those words so fucking often, he reached down. . . . If it was me and I said it— I'm capable of saying those words; I'm *capable.*—And I have said them, but I'm not a racist." Aiello thus consistently believed, in developing and acting out his character during the production of the film, that Sal was not a racist, but rather a fair and equal-minded character who *in this one case* made a mistake and did something that was racist. In his anger and fatigue, he "reached down" into himself and found the most insulting words he could to throw at those who made him angry and thus ended up acting *like* a racist, even though he himself was not one. This understanding of Sal would thus seem to be a common strategy for white viewers to use in explaining the character.

Such a conflict in viewers' understanding presents an interpretational dilemma, which I argue the concepts of racial allegiance and the sympathetic racist help to resolve. Accordingly, the explanation for why many white viewers—and Aiello himself—resist seeing Sal as a racist might be formulated in the following way. A white audience member's understanding of a white character's actions often accrues from a firm but implicit grasp of white racial

26. See, for example, Jacquie Jones, "In Sal's Country," and Zeinabu Irene Davis, "Black Independent or Hollywood Iconoclast?" both in *Cineaste* 17, no. 4 (1990): 34, 37.

27. See, for example, Richard Corliss, "Hot Time in Bed-Stuy Tonight," *Time,* July 3, 1989, 62; Murray Kempton, "The Pizza Is Burning!" *New York Review of Books,* September 28, 1989, 37; and Stanley Kauffmann, *"Do the Right Thing,"* *New Republic,* July 3, 1989, 25.

experience, which presupposes the many ways in which the long histories of world white supremacy, economic, social, and cultural advantage, and being at the top of what was supposedly a scientifically proven racial hierarchy, underlie and remain influential in white people's lives. After all, the circumstances that resulted from hundreds of years of pursuing the goals of presumed European superiority—namely, global domination by whites in economic, cultural, social, religious, intellectual, national, political, and various other ways—remain structurally in place.[28] Such dimensions of white experience are part of the "co-text," what Smith refers to as the internal system of "values, beliefs, and so forth that form the backdrop to the events of the narrative" for individuals raised in white-dominated cultures, regardless of their race.[29] As dimensions of white experience in particular, they operate as implicit, nonconscious presumptions and expectations that form the background for viewing narrative fiction films. For white viewers, this co-text is part of what Smith calls their "automatized" or "referentially transparent" belief-schemata,[30] which here I take to form a crucially important and racially inflected ground for understanding and empathizing with white characters. This system of beliefs, values, emotional responses, and so on amounts to a set of readily available, albeit largely unconscious, cultural assumptions concerning what it is to be white that have been implicitly built into much Western visual media like film.

Because white viewers are rarely called upon to imagine their whiteness from the outside, they tend to have difficulty looking at it critically. This circumstance of rarely having their background beliefs put to the test means that many white viewers find it hard to question or give up their racial allegiances to characters like Sal. In fact, they resist *not* empathizing with him and seeing him from a nonwhite perspective. Unlike nonwhite viewers, who, often out of necessity, develop a critical sense of race or double consciousness merely to function and survive in cultures like America's, most white viewers lack the cognitive tools that would allow them to recognize and question the typically presumed cinematic viewpoint of whiteness. Their life experiences as well as their viewing experiences are such that they typically have neither opportunity nor need to develop such forms of cognition. Thus, when confronted with narratives that call for them to utilize such cognitive forms or to incorporate new information concerning them, they react in confused or myopic ways. They resist the possibility of race being an issue and thus overlook crucial pieces of information that would require them to revise their typical ways of thinking about race because their previous experience has prepared them cognitively neither for the possibility of changing their standard ways of thinking nor for properly incorporating such information.

Clearly, it is not that such audiences are logically incapable of doing so, but rather that given their strongly ingrained and reinforced "initial schema"

28. Mills, *Racial Contract*, especially 1–40, 91–109; Eze, *Achieving Our Humanity.*
29. Smith, *Engaging Characters*, 194.
30. Ibid.

for conceptualizing race, there is little or no cognitive space for perceiving certain critical details offered by Lee's narrative. Were this flaw pointed out and explained to them, no doubt many audience members would modify their viewing stance toward race and seek to properly absorb the critical points advanced. From a cognitive perspective, this epistemological limitation should not be particularly surprising; as art theorist E. H. Gombrich noted decades ago, sometimes when our initial belief schemata for artworks "have no provisions for certain kinds of information . . . it is just too bad for the information."[31] We simply lack the requisite tools for absorbing it, although with some conceptual assistance we could make the necessary changes.

Because many whites may easily live lives oblivious to how matters of race have had and continue to have an impact on their lives, it is quite possible for them to wholeheartedly embrace the belief that race is no longer a major factor in *anyone's* existence. This deracialized outlook is one version of the cognitive insensitivity stressed in the work of Hill, Boxill, Jones, Mills, Gordon, and others.[32] As they point out, absent from such an outlook is a sense that race could be of any major importance in human life experience. Those who believe otherwise, by contrast, appear to be paranoid, morbidly focused on the past, or otherwise psychologically impaired.

When watching films, then, many white viewers may strongly resist the invitation to reconsider their racial allegiances because, from their perspective, such a reconsideration does not make sense. It flouts a system of beliefs, values, and emotional responses presupposed by their everyday lives as well as their typical film viewing and would require a fundamental upheaval in their overall belief-schemata if those elements were to be substantially revised or abandoned. Such an invitation asks them to consider as a problem something that they believe to have been resolved long ago. To accommodate a character like Sal and make the least disruptive changes in their system of belief—which unconsciously presupposes aspects of white advantage and power—rather than seeing Sal as a sympathetic racist character, they view him as an empathetic and morally good character. The hateful, bigoted dimensions of his racist beliefs and actions thus drop out; these aspects of his character are seen as not really racist. Perhaps for some viewers, these beliefs are explained away as an accurate reflection on "how things are" with respect to nonwhites, and are therefore not thought to be racist because they are believed to be true, alluding back to explicit racial hierarchies of times gone by. More frequently, however, white viewers explain away Sal's racist actions at the end of the film as not truly representative of his character. Instead, his actions are

31. E. H. Gombrich, *Art and Illusion: A Study in the Psychology of Pictorial Representation*, 2nd ed. (Princeton: Princeton University Press, 1972), 73. This general point regarding cognition is also noted in Smith, *Engaging Characters*, 121.

32. Hill and Boxill, "Kant and Race," 469–71; Jones, "Impairment of Empathy"; Mills, *Racial Contract*; Gordon, *Fanon and the Crisis of European Man*; Arnold Farr, "Whiteness Visible: Enlightenment Racism and the Structure of Racialized Consciousness," in Yancy, *What White Looks Like*, 143–57.

seen as an aberration, an exception to his overall good character. Many white viewers thus empathize with Sal and do not understand him as a "good-bad" moral alloy, but simply a morally good character who is trying to do the right thing—an "amalgam," in Smith's terminology.[33] He becomes a good person who does a bad thing, or a rational person defeated by an irrational world, as some reviewers described him, a character who is not racist but through a bad moral choice toward the end of the narrative is unfortunately complicit in a racial tragedy that culminates in a horrifying murder.[34] Such explanations of the character fit better into their existing schemata for viewing racial matters on film as well as in life than do alternative explanations, such as that Sal is a sympathetic racist.

A major task facing viewers of *Do the Right Thing* is that of constructing Sal such that his actions, beliefs, and characteristics fit together coherently.[35] However, white racial allegiances can distort this process in such a way that Sal's racism may seem peripheral or temporary rather than central and ongoing. An ignorance of the fundamental role race plays in currently existing versions of human identity—especially white identity, as explained by the philosophers noted above—may prevent viewers from seeing racism's centrality to Sal's character. Again, the monocular nature of white racial consciousness may well prevent viewers from constructing Sal's character in a way that coherently assembles his actions, beliefs, and primary characteristics.

A careful examination of the film, however, indicates that such an approach would be to misunderstand Sal as the narrative presents him. A variety of cues provide ample support for the idea that the film directly addresses the problem of antiblack racism at the core of Sal's character and militates against the interpretation that he is merely the victim of a bad moral choice. In closely watching the scene depicting the confrontation between Sal, Radio Raheem, Smiley, and Buggin' Out, for example, audiences may detect Lee signaling to them that the issue of racism will be explicitly raised. As Buggin' Out and his associates stand in the doorway of Sal's, one hears on the soundtrack Raheem's boom box playing once again Public Enemy's song "Fight the Power." Specifically, the lines sung by Chuck D. blast forth, observing that "Elvis was a hero to most but he never meant shit to me . . . a straight-out racist sucker; it's simple and plain." The function of the music in referring to Elvis Presley, who appropriated from black culture the music, clothes, and movements that originally made him famous, is to foreshadow what will be presented as the scene unfolds—namely, that issues of race that normally remain hidden will be brought to the surface and scrutinized.[36] In other words, the music

33. Smith, *Engaging Characters*, 203.

34. Corliss, "Hot Time in Bed-Stuy Tonight"; Kempton, "The Pizza Is Burning!"; Gaut, "Film Authorship and Collaboration," 165–66.

35. For more on the viewer's need to construct characters in ways that make sense of them as fictional agents, see Smith, *Engaging Characters*, especially 120ff.

36. See Theodore Gracyk, *Rhythm and Noise: An Aesthetics of Rock* (Durham: Duke University Press, 1996), 191–92; Ray Pratt, *Rhythm and Resistance: Explorations in the Political Uses of Popular*

FIG. 6   Radio Raheem (Bill Nunn), Smiley (Roger Guenveur Smith), and Buggin'
Out (Giancarlo Esposito) enter Sal's Famous Pizzeria (*Do the Right Thing*, 1989).

operates as a cinematic narrative prompt employed by Lee to encourage viewers to imagine that the sequence to follow will address antiblack racism.[37]
Moreover, during the sequence itself Sal's insults to blacks are underscored by
other characters repeating them indignantly and resentfully. Sal's initial racial-
izing of the incident through use of the terms "jungle music" and "Africa"
to denigrate Raheem's choice of acoustic accompaniment is explicitly noted
by Buggin' Out, who argues that such terms are irrelevant regarding what
pictures should hang on the wall of Sal's Famous Pizzeria. "Why it got to be
about *jungle music?* Why it got to be about *Africa?* It's about them fucking pictures!" Buggin' Out doggedly protests, refusing to let Sal get off the subject.
Similarly, Sal's initial use of the term 'nigger' in threatening to tear Buggin'
Out's "fucking nigger ass open" is repeated indignantly and resentfully by the
group of teenagers waiting for one last slice before the pizzeria closes. Lastly,
after Sal has smashed Raheem's boom box, he looks its erstwhile owner in the
eye and unapologetically declares, "I just killed your fucking radio." By explicitly stating that he has destroyed the source of the "jungle music," the source
of the unwanted "African" melodic presence, as well as Raheem's pride, joy,
and sense of identity, Sal underscores his own violently imposed and racially
inflected dominance.

Perhaps most damning of all, however, is Sal's immediate reaction to
Raheem's death. With the eyes of the entire community looking to him for

Music (New York: Praeger, 1990), 135–39; Peter Guralnick, *Last Train to Memphis: The Rise of Elvis
Presley* (Boston: Little, Brown, 1994), esp. 3–54.

37. I borrow here the idea of a textual "prompt" from Murray Smith's "Imagining from the
Inside," in Allen and Smith, *Film Theory and Philosophy*, 417.

some sort of appropriate response, Sal can think of nothing better to say than the tired old saw, "You do what you gotta do," as if he had just stepped out of some John Wayne movie, rather than offering any hint of an apology or regret for his complicity in the events that led to Raheem's death. Sal's response self-servingly portrays his violent destruction of Raheem's boom box as justified, as the best and most appropriate reaction to the situation, given the circumstances. Of course, his listeners in front of the pizzeria shout him down in anger and resentment at the outrageousness of such a stance. Getting Raheem to turn down his boom box did not require Sal to destroy it, then rub his triumph in with a humiliating remark. Plus, in no way does Sal's alleged justification of his actions speak to the events that ensued, specifically, Raheem's murder at the hands of the police.

As much as any other factor, Sal's breathtaking callousness at this point of the narrative, in seeking to exonerate himself and unfairly justify his actions as appropriate, brings on the riot that follows. His moral insensitivity is at least threefold. First, he lacks an understanding of the racial issues involved in his own response to the confrontation between himself, Radio Raheem, Smiley, and Buggin' Out. Second, he does not grasp the racial dimension of Raheem's death by means of the famous "choke hold" that urban police forces long argued affected African Americans more lethally than whites.[38] Third, his overall lack of compassion over Raheem's death sparks the neighborhood's revulsion, which surprises him to such an extent that he has no further response except to exclaim, "What'd I do?" and yell for the crowd not to destroy his business. In this way the narrative shows that Sal values his property over Raheem's life. All these factors mix and combust to the point that community members lose control and riot, burning and gutting Sal's business in an angry riposte to his racial and moral callousness. Specifically, Sal's insensitive remark is, as I will argue more fully in the next chapter, primarily what spurs Mookie to throw a trash can through the front window of the pizzeria, the act that sparks the riot.

It is also worth noting in this context that the morning after the riot, when Mookie returns to receive his week's pay, Sal is still unapologetic and defensive about his role in Raheem's death. While he acknowledges that Raheem is dead ("I was there, remember?"), he also blames it entirely on Buggin' Out ("He's dead because of his buddy"), rather than seeing himself as being in any way responsible. Sal's inability to admit having made any sort of mistake in his actions here as well as immediately after Raheem's murder further harks back to an earlier scene in which Mookie asks Sal whether or not the address on a pizza to be delivered is correct. Mookie remarks that he is making sure because sometimes Sal "makes mistakes." To this accusation Sal immediately and categorically declares, "I don't make mistakes. I don't make 'em." Mookie responds to Sal's claim of absolute infallibility by questioning skeptically, "You don't make mistakes?" to which Sal emphatically replies, "No." These incidents collectively establish that Sal is someone who is not capable of seeing

38. Davis, *City of Quartz*, 272.

himself as having made errors in judgment, which most of us would agree is a flaw in one's moral character. What is important to notice here, however, is that this flaw, combined with other aspects of Sal's character, contributes significantly to the eventual destruction of the pizzeria.

Spike Lee foreshadows Sal's subtly racist character earlier in the film as well. When describing to his son Pino why they cannot move their business from the African-American neighborhood of Bedford-Stuyvesant to their own Italian-American neighborhood of Bensonhurst, Sal refers to the community's residents as "these people," thereby using language that distances himself from them, that "others" them by using the phrase made infamous by onetime U.S. presidential candidate Ross Perot. For Sal, there may well be the added tension of being part of an ethnic population that in America had only recently been admitted into the category of full-fledged whiteness. As someone who has within his lifetime escaped being "othered" himself, Sal may feel only insecurely white and in need of establishing a category beneath his own.[39] Earlier still in the narrative, when Buggin' Out first questions the absence of African Americans on the "Wall of Fame" in Sal's restaurant and suggests that Sal put up pictures of Nelson Mandela, Malcolm X, or even Michael Jordan because African Americans are the mainstay of the business, Sal ridicules the black vernacular use of the term "brother," scorning it so maliciously that even mild-mannered, passive Vito tells him, "Take it easy, Pop." A moment later Sal threatens Buggin' Out with the same baseball bat that he eventually uses to destroy Raheem's radio. We should note that, particularly during the late 1980s in New York City, baseball bats were symbolic of white on black violence due of their use in a number of racist incidents involving whites beating blacks for being in the wrong neighborhood, being there at the wrong time, dating the wrong (i.e., white) girl, and so on.[40]

After Sal commands the expulsion of Buggin' Out from the pizzeria for suggesting that the Wall of Fame might display famous people of color, Mookie defends Buggin' Out's freedom of expression by declaring, "People are free to do the hell whatever they want to do." To this very typical American declaration of freedom, Sal replies, "What 'free'? What the hell are you talking about, 'free'? 'Free'? There is no 'free' here. What—I'm the boss. No freedom. I'm

39. See the essays in *Are Italians White? How Race Is Made in America,* ed. Jennifer Guglielmo and Salvatore Salerno (New York: Routledge, 2003), and Mills, *Racial Contract,* 78–81, where he discusses "borderline" whiteness and hierarchies developed within the category itself. In particular, Mills notes black awareness of the gradations of whiteness: in the film *Zebrahead* (Anthony Drazan, 1992), two black teenagers discuss whether Italians are white (79). It is also worth noting that Lee directly references Italian Americans' insecurity as whites in *Do the Right Thing.* In order to discourage Pino from using the word "nigger," Mookie notes the kinkiness of Sal's older son's hair and muses, "You know what they say about dark Italians."

40. During incidents in the New York City neighborhoods of Bensonhurst and Howard Beach in the late 1980s, young black men were either beaten to death or threatened with bats in ways that led to their deaths. Noted in Lee and Jones, *Do the Right Thing: A Spike Lee Joint,* 32–33, 46, and Watkins, *Representing,* 157, 270 n. 43.

the boss." For Sal, the application of this prized American value has limited scope. Although he couches his response in terms of a businessman setting the rules for frequenting his establishment, because of other factors—primarily, the racial one that Sal and his sons are virtually the only whites consistently in the neighborhood and his customers are almost exclusively nonwhites—it amounts to saying that in his establishment only white Americans like himself may exercise freedom of expression, not his African-American or Puerto Rican-American patrons. They, in contrast, must abide by his (the white man's) rules. For African Americans then, there is no freedom inside the confines of Sal's Famous Pizzeria. Sal is the boss. No freedom. As Guerrero notes, "Sal is the congenial and sometimes contentious, but always paternal, head of what amounts to a pizza plantation, a colonial outpost in native territory."[41]

Given these redundant narrative cues, I would argue that utilizing the concepts of racial allegiance and the sympathetic racist helps to make better sense of Sal than other possible interpretational strategies. Such an analysis coheres more completely with what the film actually presents, even if it does not cohere with typical white presumptions regarding race. Seeing Sal as a good-bad character, an alloy who possesses both positive moral traits as well as negative ones, synthesizes him much more consistently and comprehensively than competing possibilities. This narrative figure coheres better if one attributes to him a racist character, even if he is also sympathetic in other ways, than if one seeks to explain away his actions late in the narrative as that of a morally good character who makes a bad decision that leads him to do racist and immoral things, even though he himself is not racist.

Sal's explosion of anger, then, serves as what George M. Wilson has described as an "epistemological twist" that prompts audience members (especially many white audience members) to suddenly see Sal's earlier actions from a different perspective. Wilson uses the term to generally describe films that introduce narrative revelations that force viewers to entirely rethink their perspectives regarding what they believe has happened in a narrative as presented to that point in a film, as is done in director David Fincher's *Fight Club* (1999), when the main character (Edward Norton) and Tyler Durden (Brad Pitt) are revealed to be the same character.[42] Similarly, I would argue that the idea may be usefully applied to characters themselves, and in particular to Sal's explosion of racist anger, which aims to prompt changes in many viewers' perception of who he is and what he is really like. For white viewers in particular, the explosion aims to jolt them from seeing Sal as a generally sympathetic character who shows compassion and understanding toward blacks to one who at the same time holds racist beliefs—that is, it aims to shock them into thinking of him as a sympathetic racist character.

---

41. Guerrero, *Do the Right Thing*, 35.

42. George M. Wilson, "Film and Epistemology" (paper presented at the sixty-second annual meeting of the American Society of Aesthetics, Houston, Tex., October 29, 2004). See also his "Transparency and Twist in Narrative Fiction Film," *Journal of Aesthetics and Art Criticism* 64 (2006): 81–95, esp. 91–93.

Many white viewers tend to miss or overlook the details of Sal's antiblack racism because these particulars do not easily fit into their preconceptions of where their moral allegiances should lie. These viewers tend to more readily empathize with white characters like Sal than black characters like, say, Raheem, who, in spite of his intimidating character and bullying ways, was nevertheless murdered by the police and therefore deserves something more than to be forgotten or valued as less important than the destruction of Sal's business, which is what many white viewers, mimicking Sal's own presumptions, did.[43]

Some empathy for Sal, of course, must be attributed to nonracial factors. To present a nuanced sympathetic racist character for whom viewers might initially establish a solid favorable outlook, Lee makes him central to the narrative and treats him compassionately much of the time. This strategy carries with it a certain risk—namely, that viewers will find it difficult to judge him negatively as a racist because they know him well and have become firmly attached to his character. White viewers in particular might be inclined to overlook or excuse the depth of Sal's wrongdoing because their attachment to the character—based on both racial and nonracial elements of the narrative—is too powerful. On the other hand, it should be noted that Lee counterbalances this possibility by making the film an ensemble piece. The story focuses not just on Sal, but on the whole neighborhood, including numerous African-American characters who receive significant screen time, such as Mookie, Raheem, Da Mayor (Ossie Davis), and Mother Sister (Ruby Dee). I would argue that this narrative counterbalancing aims to keep viewers from investing themselves too heavily in Sal by presenting other, nonwhite characters with whom viewers might also ally themselves. Of course, these other character allegiances may be partly or even wholly blocked by racial factors as well, but one can see that from the viewpoint of narrative construction, these figures operate to spread out audience allegiance rather than investing it in just one central character such as Sal.

On the other hand, from the point of view of epistemology, white viewers may resist developing a critical distance from Sal and instead find ways to explain his actions that downplay or eliminate the matter of racism as constituent of his character. Rather than question their own deep-seated habits of judgment and imagine whiteness from the outside, as the narrative encourages them to do, they find fault in the narrative's inconsistency with their current, racially influenced beliefs and expectations. In this sense, the pull of empathy for Sal, and specifically the pull of white racial allegiance, is too strong for many white viewers to overcome and begin reexamining their habits of moral judgment. For these viewers, it seems less disruptive cognitively and emotionally to ignore or leave aside certain uncomfortable details in the narrative than to substantially change their belief-schemata—the narrative's

43. For example, David Denby, "He's Gotta Have It," *New York Magazine*, June 26, 1989, 53–54; Klein, "Spiked? Dinkins and *Do the Right Thing*."

co-text—to accommodate those details. Rather than work to develop a rudi-
mentary white racial double consciousness, many viewers choose to embrace
their already existing white single consciousness and use it as best they can
to understand the film's narrative, even if that white-privilege-influenced perspective requires them to ignore certain clearly presented details and can only
poorly explain others. If Gombrich has accurately identified our typical use of
"initial schemata" in understanding visual artworks, these narrative details
would be precisely the ones that white viewers would tend to overlook in any
case, given the cognitive background from which they work. Whites typically
lack sensitivity to the importance of these features because they tend not to see
race as cognitively important in the sorts of situations presented by the film.
Thus *Do the Right Thing* tends to come up short when measured by means of
such an interpretive stance.

This problem of cognitive insensitivity may be further explained by means
of Janine Jones's analysis of "empathetic impairment." She argues that if
whites—even whites of moral good will who desire not to be racist—are
unable to detect the cognitive importance of race in situations where antiblack
racism impinges on African Americans in day-to-day interactions with whites
(such as those depicted in *Do the Right Thing*), then they will also be impaired
and perhaps even unable to analogize from their own circumstances to those
of African Americans. The construction of analogy between white and black
experience, which would be critical to any sort of successful empathizing
here, breaks down because certain crucial elements of the former experience
are seen as strongly disanalogous to the latter. White viewers may empathize
incorrectly or even not at all with black characters, and therefore misunderstand the situations and outlooks of African-American characters. Empathy,
Jones points out, requires being able to produce an accurate system of mapping between another person's life and some aspect of our own. Empathic
understanding thus begins with an appreciation of the other person's situation.[44] If that situation is not well appreciated or understood, then empathy
will go awry or perhaps fail to occur.

This failure of "mental simulation" also makes clear why many whites fail
to see Sal from what is for them the acentral, African-American perspective
offered by Lee's film.[45] They empathize with Sal because they fail to grasp the

---

44. Jones, "Impairment of Empathy," 71. See also Mills, *Racial Contract*, 95.

45. I use the term "mental simulation" here with some reservations because, although I think
that work by Robert Gordon, Gregory Currie, and others on this concept has greatly increased our
knowledge of the workings of the mind in general and empathy in particular—especially with
respect to literary fiction and film—I am not yet ready to embrace the claim that when we imagine, empathize, and so on, we are running our belief systems "off-line" and operating as if our
brains were just like computers, as in Currie's *Image and Mind: Film, Philosophy, and Cognitive Science* (New York: Cambridge University Press, 1995), esp. 141–97. I find these descriptions of how
human brains work too literally digital to feel comfortable endorsing them. For a fuller argument
detailing reservations about mental simulation, see Noël Carroll, *A Philosophy of Mass Art* (Oxford:
Clarendon Press, 1998), esp. 342–56.

importance of certain details that the narrative presents to them—namely, the way in which his actions and statements build up to a kind of subtle, mostly unconscious presumption of racial advantage that is a part of his character, as opposed to being attributable to a single bad decision or two. They empathize with him, even though Lee indicates again and again through narrative cues that they should ultimately want to qualify their attitude toward Sal. The details of Sal's character are meant to operate cumulatively as signals to mitigate ultimate viewer empathy for him, even if the narrative to some extent courts that imaginative stance toward him earlier. Lee urges viewers to distance themselves from Sal by the film's end and look at his character critically, instead of embracing him as someone close to their hearts. Again, nonwhite viewers, who typically possess a more finely tuned racial awareness, tend to see this suggestion much more clearly, but it is by no means beyond the cognitive capacities of whites to develop this sharper racial awareness. It is just that socially and culturally, such an awareness is not encouraged in white viewers. Rather, as Dyer argues, Western visual media tends to presume and reinforce presumptions of whiteness as the norm, even to the extent that racial whiteness functions as the assumed standpoint from which to perceive popular film narrative. The typical viewer is presumed to be white or to at least have a full working grasp of what it is to engage films from a white perspective.

A further way to characterize this problem of audience asymmetry with respect to responses involving race is by comparing it to an example analyzed at length by Jones. She builds much of her case around the divergent ways in which many whites viewed the videotapes of the Rodney King beating on the one hand, and the attack on Reginald Denny on the other. Infamously, King, an African American, was stopped in 1991 for a traffic violation by the LAPD and was severely beaten as he lay on the ground by several police officers using riot batons. Denny, a white truck driver, was pulled from his rig by several black youths who used bricks and other objects to beat him during the riots that followed more than a year later in the wake of those same police officers being found not guilty of assaulting King. Both men were hospitalized for extended periods and suffer from permanent disabilities as a result of their injuries. Both incidents were also secretly videotaped. What Jones noted was that in viewing the videotapes of these incidents whites did not react emotionally in the same way toward both individuals, in spite of the similarity of their situations. As one white professor of law who viewed the tapes put it, "For King I felt sympathy; for Denny, empathy."[46]

46. Cited in Jones, "Impairment of Empathy," 75. As she notes, Jones bases her analysis on the work of Joe R. Feagin, Hernan Vera, and Pinar Batur, *White Racism*, 2nd ed. (New York: Routledge, 2001), 117–51, esp. 141–42. It should also be noted that the white professor of law quoted here, David B. Oppenheimer, was sharply critical of this racial asymmetry with regard to empathy. His position is actually consistent with the one I have outlined. See Oppenheimer's "The Movement from Sympathy to Empathy, Through Fear; The beatings of Rodney King and Reginald Denny provoke differing emotions but similar racial concerns," *Recorder*, June 9, 1992, 14.

I would argue that the difference in response to the two cases here may be readily explained as one of racial allegiance. White viewers of the videotapes felt closer to the situation, possibility, and overall experience of Denny than to those of King, even though both tapes depicted brutal beatings of helpless individuals by multiple attackers using clubs, bricks, and other blunt instruments. Constructing an appropriate experiential analog in the case of Denny came much more easily for most white viewers because of a shared experience of whiteness, an analog not extended in the case of King. White viewers' racial commonality permitted a much more immediate response—empathy for Denny, as opposed to the more distanced attitude of sympathy for King.[47]

Like the allegiance that many white viewers felt while watching the videotape of Denny's beating, responses to Sal often seem to be based more on racial allegiance than on close attention to narrative details. Thus these audience members are more inclined to empathize with Sal than to distance themselves from his character. They ignore, miss, reject, or downplay the African-American perspective offered by Lee's film in favor of another racially inflected one already embedded in their typical responses to popular film narratives, in spite of ample evidence that this latter perspective fails to fully explain many details presented. At the same time, this aspect of the film allows us to see how it aims to trouble viewers into making a closer examination of their background assumptions concerning film viewing, race, and personal identity.

Critical Reflection and Sympathetic Racists

By self-consciously depicting a character who is both sympathetic and racist—and goading his viewers to think about how such a character may be both at the same time—Spike Lee casts a critical eye at the assumptions that underlie white racial allegiance. In this manner he hopes to move white audience members toward a more complex perspective on race. I would further argue that through this provocation Lee summons his audience members to think philosophically about race. By means of *Do the Right Thing*'s narrative and the character type of the sympathetic racist in particular, Lee encourages his white viewers to reflect on and devise a new belief schema for understanding race. In addition to the film's explicit calls for viewers to reflect in its final scenes, such as Mr. Señor Love Daddy's (Samuel L. Jackson) exclamations that we "Wake Up!" and think about the question "How are we going to live together?" as well as the famous contradictory quotations from Martin Luther King Jr. and Malcolm X that end the movie, Sal's depiction as a seemingly paradoxical figure aim to trouble the viewer, especially the typical white viewer,

---

47. Empirical studies of empathy in psychology also support the idea that race is a form of "in-group bias" that impedes one's ability to empathize; see, for example, Martin L. Hoffman, *Empathy and Moral Development: Implications for Caring and Justice* (2000; repr., Cambridge: Cambridge University Press, 2003), 207.

into considering the question, "What is it to be a racist?" and come up with a considerably more complicated response than most had previously embraced. In ways perhaps not unlike many students in introductory philosophy courses, however, many white viewers resist this invitation because the prospect of replacing their old way of cognizing would call for them to perform too radical an epistemological revision, require too much of a change in their existing belief structures for them to feel comfortable exploring such a possibility. At some level, perhaps they realize that such a reexamination and replacement of background assumptions would not only concern their film viewing, but also their understanding of their own identities and humanity itself, thereby touching them at their core.

As philosophers and other theorists have frequently pointed out, our senses of personal identity in Western culture are strongly raced.[48] For whites, however, this dimension of self-understanding is largely invisible and unacknowledged. To compel them to recognize this invisibility, then, is a daunting and difficult task. Still, it is possible, and in fact many whites have done so, in film viewing as well as in their own senses of identity. But many others have not. Facilitating this possibility, which concerns cinematic as well as existential presuppositions, has guided Lee's efforts, I would argue, to present and depict a sympathetic racist character like Sal. Through narrative characters like him, Lee encourages white viewers to look critically at their racialized sensibilities and assess what they see.

In this sense, Lee presents his viewers with a philosophical challenge: to evaluate the contents of their souls, so to speak, and gauge how those contents influence them to perceive matters of race. This critical self-questioning was one of Socrates' highest aspirations, as evidenced in the *Apology* as well as dialogues with Euthyphro, Meno, Laches, and others. It has also inspired philosophers through the ages to the present day, such as Alexander Nehamas.[49] Socrates aspired to meet, both in his own case and that of others, the old Delphic injunction used as an epigraph for this chapter. More recently, Noël Carroll has argued that Orson Welles's *Citizen Kane* (1941) stages a debate meant to "afford the opportunity for the general audience to interrogate prevailing cultural views of the nature of human life by setting them forth in competition." The Welles film is "similar in purpose to many philosophical dialogues" because it seeks "to animate a debate" about human life and personal identity.[50] In the same spirit we may recognize Spike Lee as encouraging viewers to take up that sort of philosophical task regarding race through his construction of character and narrative in *Do the Right Thing*. One could say, then, that

48. Fanon, "Lived Experience of the Black"; Mills, *Racial Contract*, 53–62, 91–120; Dyer, *White*, 41–81.

49. Alexander Nehamas, *The Art of Living: Socratic Reflections from Plato to Foucault* (Berkeley and Los Angeles: University of California Press, 1998), esp. 40, 106, 185–88.

50. Noël Carroll, "Interpreting *Citizen Kane*," in *Interpreting the Moving Image* (New York: Cambridge University Press, 1998), 163.

Lee not only induces his white viewers in particular to perform a Brechtian maneuver—that is, critically distance themselves from certain characters and narrative situations in order to consider moral and political choices—but charges them with a properly philosophical task as well. By drawing them into a favorable stance with Sal only to alienate them from his character by means of the realization that he is also fundamentally a racist, Lee has produced a film that philosophizes, a film that calls on viewers to think philosophically about questions regarding race, identity, and cinematic viewership. Lee urges viewers to critically reflect on their *own* senses of self, humanity, and personal identity, which is a hallmark of most if not virtually all persuasive conceptions of philosophy.

In addition, Lee's film offers indications regarding the proper shape that answers to such self-questioning might take. For example, having a fuller sense of the role race has played in the formation of one's identity as well as one's overall cognitive perspective is strongly implied as a better epistemological stance to take than one that does not possess these features. For all of Sal's compassion and patience toward neighborhood members like Da Mayor or Smiley, his lack of racial self-awareness condemns him to incomprehension regarding much of what goes on around or even inside his pizzeria, and this incomprehension contributes significantly to his downfall. The film's narrative thus suggests that having a greater racial awareness—a "double consciousness" about race, particularly for whites—would serve one better than lacking such a capacity. This attempt to not only pose but to shape fundamentally the answers to questions, to provide some sort of positive, in-depth contribution to the topic being discussed, is a further hallmark of many stronger senses of what counts as philosophy.[51] Meeting this requirement thus implies that the film's call for critical reflection is indeed philosophical rather than merely social, psychological, or political. Some viewers may resist this invitation by means of alternative interpretive strategies, but, as I have argued, the cost of that choice is failure to achieve full coherence in grasping narratives like those presented in *Do the Right Thing*, to say nothing of the costs such choices exact in one's life or from the lives of one's fellow human beings.

Spike Lee and Institutional Racism

From what has been argued so far, it should be clear that Lee focuses his artistic energies in *Do the Right Thing* on depicting racial beliefs mainly at the level of institutions, as opposed to that of individually chosen beliefs. According to this way of thinking, many racial beliefs are embedded in cultural ways

---

51. For more discussion on what sorts of capacities philosophy has and whether film can mimic them, see Mulhall, *On Film*, esp. 1–10; Julian Baggini, "Alien Ways of Thinking: Mulhall's *On Film*," *Film-Philosophy* 7, no. 24 (August 2003), http://www.film-philosophy.com; Mulhall, "Ways of Thinking"; and many of the essays in *Journal of Aesthetics and Art Criticism* 64, no.1 (Spring 2006).

of believing and acting typically conveyed through the unconscious learning of social practices rather than chosen by means of an individual's consciously employed decision processes.[52] Sympathetic racist characters like Sal, then, provide Lee with the capacity to aim his criticisms at ways in which whites typically albeit unconsciously live, rather than at aberrant individuals who knowingly embrace morally evil belief structures. While criticism of the latter is depicted through characters such as Sal's older son, Pino, whose ignorance and inarticulateness Lee holds up for special scorn, Lee devotes most of his narrative attention to outlining the unconscious racism possessed by the paterfamilias at Sal's Famous Pizzeria.

Similarly, recent philosophers of race have invested much of their time arguing for the existence of racist beliefs at the institutional level.[53] Crucial to their criticisms is that presumptions of racial advantage, privilege, and superiority have seeped into how people see, think, and act without their even knowing that these dimensions of their lives have been suffused by such presumptions. As I noted in the introduction, Mills has dubbed the inability to see this level of racism the "epistemology of ignorance," a *pattern of localized and global cognitive dysfunctions (which are psychologically and socially functional)*" that morally impair whites, preventing them from seeing and doing the right thing when race is a factor.[54] As he argues, "they will experience genuine cognitive difficulties in recognizing certain behavior patterns *as* racist" (93) because their moral psychology—their very way of thinking and perceiving morally—has been racialized by centuries of detailed, carefully explained reconciliation with ideas of white supremacy, black inferiority, and a racial hierarchy based on skin color. This reconciliation, it should be further noted, was actively sought and performed by mainstream science, philosophy, history, anthropology, legal theory, and other fields of knowledge. Moreover, only within the last five decades or so have such efforts been unambiguously discredited and pushed out of the mainstream of these disciplines.[55] Yet this long-term, sustained reconciliation of whites' "ordinary" thinking with Western conceptions of racial hierarchy remains inadequately confronted and disentangled, as it continues to have disastrous effects for not only the psychology of whites, but for nonwhites in general and African Americans in particular.

The ongoing racialization of moral psychology by social institutions is something of which most whites remain overwhelmingly ignorant. Few have

52. For more regarding this point, see O'Connor, *Oppression and Responsibility*, esp. 1–18.

53. See, for example, Gordon, *Fanon and the Crisis of European Man*, 21–23, and passim.

54. Mills, *Racial Contact*, 18, 93.

55. Stephen Jay Gould, *The Mismeasure of Man*, rev. ed. (New York: W. W. Norton, 1996); Elazar Barkan, *The Retreat of Scientific Racism* (Cambridge: Cambridge University Press, 1992); Thomas Gossett, *Race: The History of an Idea in America*, new ed. (New York: Oxford University Press, 1997); Mills, *Racial Contact*; Eze, *Achieving Our Humanity*, 3–111; Popkin, "Eighteenth Century Racism"; Robert Bernasconi, "Kant as an Unfamiliar Source of Racism," in *Philosophers on Race: Critical Essays*, ed. Julie K. Ward and Tommy L. Lott (London: Blackwell, 2002), 145–65; Bernasconi, "Who Invented the Concept of Race?"; Farr, "Whiteness Visible."

seen through their veil of privilege and advantage to grasp that embedded in
the background of much of their thinking and upbringing are assumptions
that, were they to consider these presumptions consciously and explicitly,
they would deem as out-and-out racist.[56] Many whites are unprepared to think
about race and white supremacy at the level of being embedded in institutions
and expressed in our perceptions and actions, rather than as being personal,
individually chosen beliefs knowingly embraced and under the control of particular human beings, because such a perspective takes the problem of racism
out of the sphere of individual influence and places it at a level over which no
one person has any decisive say. To contemplate such profoundly embedded
beliefs goes, for example, against one of the basic tenets of modern liberalism,
namely that we are autonomous individuals who may self-consciously determine our own behavior as well as our personal beliefs.[57] Thus many whites
no doubt feel that they have ample grounds for rejecting the idea that racism
might exist at a level other than that at which it is under the conscious determination of specific individuals.

As I suggested earlier, many whites consider this sort of racism incomprehensible and overwhelming. To avoid confronting it, they cling to the perspective to which they are accustomed. When they attempt to interpret a film
like *Do the Right Thing* from within this imperfect belief structure, they tend
to blame Lee for any lack of fit between their interpretation and the details of
the film. This is how white viewers may build what appears to them to be a
plausible if still troubled case for why it is legitimate to empathize with Sal in
a way that does not see him as racist.

This difficulty, of course, can be easily linked to why it is important to be
able to analogize from white experience to that of African Americans in viewing narrative fiction films. However, consistent with the points just summa-
rized, it is also worth emphasizing how racial allegiances may impair whites'
ability to navigate well in the real world itself, which would seem to be one of
the primary reasons that knowledge is of value at all. As Janine Jones puts it,

> insofar as humans are seeking something as grand as truth, our inves-
> tigations are often carried out for truth's instrumental value. People
> seek truth in order to *navigate* their world, not for truth's own sake.
>
> Possessing good evidence that our beliefs are true (i.e., that they
> allow us to map our beliefs onto the world) may aid our navigation, not
> to mention manipulation, of the world.[58]

Moreover, while white racial allegiance and insensitivity to the commonalities
of all human beings may have positive survival value in what Du Bois called

---

56. Hill and Boxill, "Kant and Race," 469–71; Jones, "Impairment of Empathy"; O'Connor,
Oppression and Responsibility, esp. 41–59, 127–31.

57. See, for example, Steven Lukes, *Individualism* (Oxford: Basil Blackwell, 1973), 56.

58. Jones, "Impairment of Empathy," 70.

"the white world,"[59] it can seriously impede one's ability to navigate in a world where significant numbers of nonwhites exist, which is of course the one in which human beings actually live, if not always cognitively, emotionally, or locally. Such impairments will thus inevitably cause their possessors problems, even if one is not fully able to appreciate what these problems might be. This troubling matter of the construction of one's "inner eye," then, will be as much a disadvantage as any other impairment that one may at times but never in all cases avoid.[60]

As already noted, whites need not be insensitive to these factors, for racially inflected cognitive insensitivity may indeed be overcome. For example, in the case of *Do the Right Thing*, *Newsweek* film reviewer David Ansen wrote during its initial release that he saw Sal as "a sympathetic figure . . . who's arguably an unconscious racist."[61] In addition, *New York Times* film reviewer Vincent Canby saw Sal as a sympathetic character who was nonetheless racist.[62] Clearly it is possible for whites to successfully analogize from their own experience to that of African Americans, even when numerous cultural and cognitive factors militate against it. Moreover, if one is prepared to think of race as institutional rather than merely a matter of personally and knowingly embraced beliefs, then a character like Sal offers more than sufficient justification for careful and detailed reflections on whiteness as well as antiblack racism in the actual world, in addition to fictional ones, because this character opens up whole new grounds for understanding the origin and sustainability of such beliefs in real as well as in fictional contexts. If one wishes to navigate the real world competently and have some measure of control over it, then confronting the sorts of difficulties represented by white racial allegiances and empathetic impairment would seem a necessity. Thus the creation of Sal provides fertile bases for improving not only one's ability to grasp fictional narratives, but advantages for the world in which human beings actually live their ordinary, day-to-day lives.

The invention of this sympathetic racist figure may well have been a happy accident, the result of Lee and Aiello's adversarial collaboration in developing this fictional character. Given what Lee has said about working with Aiello in *Making "Do the Right Thing"* as well as on the audio commentary of the Criterion Collection version of the film, such a possibility seems likely. Lee's remarks thus support Gaut's broader point that collaborative artistic disagreements may sometimes be aesthetically beneficial for an artwork by adding to

59. See, for example, Du Bois, "The Forethought," in *The Souls of Black Folk*, xi.

60. For the metaphor of whites' inner eye as impaired, see Ralph Ellison, "Prologue," *Invisible Man* (New York: Random House, [1952]), 3.

61. David Ansen, "How Hot Is Too Hot; Searing, Nervy, and Honest," *Newsweek*, July 3, 1989, 65. Contrast this view with that of Jack Kroll on the facing page, who argued that *Do the Right Thing* would incite race riots; see "How Hot Is Too Hot; The Fuse Has Been Lit," *Newsweek*, July 3, 1989, 64.

62. See Canby, "Spike Lee Tackles Racism in *Do the Right Thing*" and "Spike Lee Raises the Movies' Black Voice."

its richness and complexity.[63] On the other hand, it clearly makes better sense to understand Sal as a sympathetic character who is also a racist than not being a racist character at all, as Gaut and others have claimed, because the former interpretation more coherently and comprehensively organizes the narrative as well as the presumed psychological belief structures necessary for understanding who Sal really is—as well as for knowing who we are ourselves.

63. Gaut, "Film Authorship and Collaboration," 166.

What is interesting is that [Spike Lee] cuts through these barriers and you suddenly *see*
people, and you understand you have the same feelings, you have the same dreams, you
have the same anger, and I think this is an extraordinary contribution of his pictures.

—Martin Scorsese, interview

At the same time that *Do the Right Thing* encourages viewers to reflect on how
a white character can be both sympathetic and racist, the film also urges its
audience to imagine from the inside the situations, thoughts, and perspectives of its black characters. In this way the film extends the manner in which
many classic *films noirs* gave audiences a foundation for identifying with and
understanding socially marginalized, morally good-bad characters. In a fashion similar to but distinct from the strategies used to present a narrative figure
like Sal, Spike Lee depicts his black characters as complicated, flawed individuals who respond to the social pressures around them in sometimes morally
praiseworthy, sometimes morally blameworthy ways. In contrast to his presentation of characters like Sal, however, he generally provides more grounds for
evaluating these black narrative figures positively, as well for understanding
them from an internal perspective, by making clear not only that they are just
like everyone else, but also that many social pressures in their lives are fundamentally raced.

Furthermore, in the same way that Lee provides a range of representations
of whiteness through Sal's family and other characters, so does he provide an
accessible range of representations of American blackness and their various
responses to racism. At one end of the spectrum is Radio Raheem, who trucu-
lently demands respect and recognition from everyone around him by means
of his boom box. At the other end is Da Mayor, who resolutely practices civility
and respect toward others, and seeks more than anyone else to "always do the
right thing," a principle that distinctly echoes Martin Luther King Jr.[1] Somewhere in between are Mookie and the other black characters, who negotiate
the racialized pressures exerted on them as best they can, given the restricted
alternatives at their disposal.

In this chapter I analyze how Lee depicts this broad cross-section of what
it means to be African American using narrative techniques that were honed
and popularized in classic American *film noir*, thereby exemplifying Diawara's

1. See Martin Luther King Jr., *Why We Can't Wait* (New York: Signet, 1964), 74, 126.

observation that Lee's work could be described as *"film noir* with a vengeance," as well as *noir* scholars Alain Silver and James Ursini's claim that *film noir* constitutes a "major influence" on Lee's work.[2] Through a complex set of *noir*-influenced narrative strategies, this filmmaker offers his viewers access to striking insights into his black characters as well as their social marginalization. In doing so he also provides a sort of object lesson regarding the employment of empathy to better understand race that will be taken up again and again in later black *noir* films.

Moral Ambiguity, Suspense, and *Noir* Characterization

Private investigator Sam Spade (Humphrey Bogart) in *The Maltese Falcon* is a protagonist whose appearance of moral complexity and ambiguity is critical to the film's narrative. While on the one hand he ultimately upholds the moral law—for example, by doing his duty and turning in Brigid O'Shaughnessy (Mary Astor) for his partner's murder—on the other he is willing without a moment's hesitation to use bribes or withhold information from officials in order to achieve his goals. Moreover, earlier in the film he appears strangely insensitive when first told of his partner's murder and seems complacent about throwing in his lot with thieves and murderers when potential profits look great enough. While his reasoning in these circumstances is later clarified and his character ultimately vindicated as morally positive, for much of the narrative the film emphasizes his appearance of moral ambiguity as well as the complexity of his moral character, even to the point of explicitly indicating their role in understanding him. "Don't be too sure I'm as crooked as I'm supposed to be," he tells Brigid just before he turns her over to the police. "That sort of reputation might be good business, bringing high-priced jobs and making it easier to deal with the enemy." Critical to the trade he plies is his appearance of being "shady," an insight that retrospectively helps viewers to make better sense of his motivations and actions. Spade's apparent attributes of criminality and amorality thus substantively influence viewers because while watching the film (initially, at least) they cannot always predict how he will act, given the complex set of conflicting moral traits he apparently possesses.[3] The questions of how and why Spade will respond occurs repeatedly through the narrative for viewers because his character is morally ambiguous, his motivations complex and mysterious. Thus viewers experience anxiousness and suspense regarding what he will do next.

2. Manthia Diawara, cited in Houston A. Baker Jr., "Spike Lee and the Commerce of Culture," in *Black American Cinema*, ed. Manthia Diawara (New York: Routledge, 1993), 154; Alain Silver and James Ursini, *Film Noir*, ed. Paul Duncan (Köln: Taschen, 2004), 9. According to Baker, Diawara made his remark about the *noir* aspects of Lee's master's thesis film, *Joe's Bed-Stuy Barbershop—We Cut Heads* (1982).

3. In a similar vein, part of the pleasure of re-viewing the film is trying to see Spade's moral complexity as a coherent whole.

FIG. 7   Philip Marlowe (Humphrey Bogart) threatens an off-camera Eddie Mars (John Ridgeley) (*The Big Sleep*, 1946).

Similarly, in *The Big Sleep* private detective Philip Marlowe (Bogart again) operates in a sort of moral netherworld that necessitates compromise, but nevertheless is, in his creator Raymond Chandler's words, "a man of honor."[4] Yet in this film, too, as in Chandler's novels, Marlowe has morally negative as well as positive traits. Other characters describe him as insolent and rude (which he is, typically to hilarious effect), and when we first meet him, Marlowe admits to having been fired from the district attorney's office for insubordination. He is also not above taunting an opponent into attempting something stupid, so that he may then beat him all that much more brutally, as he does when he throws down his gun so that he may then viciously kick and knock out the young killer Carol Lundgren (Thomas Rafferty) when the thug foolishly lunges for it. Marlowe is also not above exacting a certain degree of petty revenge, as he does when he shoots Eddie Mars (John Ridgeley) in the arm for trying to double-cross and kill him.

As with Spade, this combination of positive and negative moral characteristics makes the audience slightly anxious and uncertain about what Marlowe will do in the course of the narrative, which adds to their interest in him as a character. Viewer anxiousness and uncertainty add to the suspensefulness of

4. Raymond Chandler, "The Simple Art of Murder," in *The Simple Art of Murder* (New York: Ballantine Books, 1980), 20.

this *noir* narrative because often audiences do not feel secure in being able to predict accurately whether he will respond morally or immorally in specific narrative contexts. Marlowe's moral ambiguity operates in favor of sustaining audience interest for what is happening in the film because viewers must repeatedly ask themselves, "What will Marlowe do?"

This type of curiosity and anticipation aroused by the character is, of course, consistent with what cognitive film theorists like Noël Carroll and David Bordwell have been arguing for decades about the erotetic, question and answer, nature of much film narrative.[5] As these theorists maintain, classic Hollywood narratives typically prompt questions in viewers' minds that they expect will be satisfied as the story proceeds. In this sense, suspense becomes a subcategory of erotetic narrative. It raises questions that engage the viewer in anxiously anticipating what will happen next.[6] We can see this sort of suspense at work through the *noir* characters just described. In *The Big Sleep*, Marlowe's moral complexity gives rise to questions regarding his future actions, as viewers must seek answers later in the narrative in order to resolve some of the complexity and ambiguity about his character. More generally, Humphrey Bogart made a career out of playing this type of morally complex, ambiguous character during the 1940s, both in and out of *noir* films such as *Casablanca* (Michael Curtiz, 1943), *To Have and Have Not* (Howard Hawks, 1944), *Key Largo* (John Huston, 1948), *The Treasure of the Sierra Madre* (John Huston, 1948), and *In A Lonely Place*. Although the characters he played typically made overall positive moral choices by the end, they did not always do so, and their moral complexity and ambiguity were such that viewers often could not be sure what his characters would do, morally speaking. This uncertainty made the narratives themselves more suspenseful and interesting by actively engaging viewers in anticipating what would happen next. French *noir* critics Raymond Borde and Etienne Chaumeton directly address *noir*'s moral "ambivalence" and "ambiguity" by referencing Bogart's role in determining these characteristics of American *film noir* in their book. "Humphrey Bogart is the model here," they tell us.[7] Taking advantage of Bogart's star persona, the films in which he acted often exploited the moral ambiguity of his past performances by integrating audience expectations about that quality into the story itself, making the narratives that much more engaging for the viewer.[8]

5. Noël Carroll, "Toward a Theory of Film Suspense" (1984) and "The Power of Movies" (1985), both reprinted in *Theorizing the Moving Image*; Bordwell, *Narration in the Fiction Film*, esp. 55–57, 64–70; David Bordwell and Kristin Thompson, *Film Art: An Introduction*, 6th ed. (New York: McGraw-Hill, 2001), esp. 60–64. Of course, as noted by both theorists, this critical position reaches back to Russian formalism. See, for example, V. I. Pudovkin, *Film Technique and Film Acting*, trans. and ed. Ivor Montagu (1958; repr., New York: Grove Press, 1970), 69–78.

6. Carroll, "Toward a Theory of Film Suspense," 95–100.

7. Borde and Chaumeton, *Panorama of American Film Noir*, 9.

8. A work that interestingly explores further dimensions of complexity and ambiguity with regard to Bogart's star persona is Robert Sklar, *City Boys: Cagney, Bogart, Garfield* (Princeton: Princeton University Press, 1992).

FIG. 8   Jeff (Robert Mitchum) confesses to Ann (Virginia Huston) his mysterious past (*Out of the Past*, 1947).

Similarly, the viewer's anxious uncertainty regarding Jeff Bailey (Robert Mitchum) in *Out of the Past* contributes to the interest this *film noir* produces. Jeff's girlfriend Ann (Virginia Huston) relates in the scene that introduces him that other people in their town talk about him as "the mysterious Jeff Bailey"; moreover, his actions, as well as the narrative in general, confirm that description. Ann herself admits to knowing very little about him and frustratedly describes him as "a secret man," someone who avoids telling others about himself, where he came from, and what he did before he showed up one day out of the blue to open a gasoline station in their small town of Bridgeport, California. Although we find out a great deal more about Jeff as the narrative proceeds, perhaps one of the most intriguing aspects of *Out of the Past* is that for much of the film audiences have difficulty telling exactly who he is, how he will act, and what motivates his behavior. In particular, it is unclear whether he will choose the film's dark-haired, sexy *femme fatale* Kathie Moffat (Jane Greer) or his wholesome, blonde "good girl," Ann. Again, as with Bogart's characters, for significant stretches of the film the narrative is constructed so that viewers are anxiously uncertain about Jeff's moral character and how he will act. Audience interest is partly driven by questions the narrative generates regarding this character's lack of "moral resolution," which engages them more closely than they would be otherwise because Jeff's moral opacity encourages them to anticipate more intensely what will happen next.[9]

A related type of *noir* character is Dave Bannion (Glenn Ford) in *The Big Heat* (Fritz Lang, 1953), who quits his job as a police detective when legalities prove to be too confining for his pursuit of personal vengeance. Finding that most of his law enforcement colleagues are either corrupt or apathetic, Bannion veers from being an honest, hard-working cop into self-righteous vigilantism (albeit, for understandable reasons), showing at times a breathtaking insensitivity for others in his single-minded pursuit of revenge, before ultimately realizing that he is going too far. The narrative largely constructs this *noir* protagonist in a positive manner, so that audiences will generally be morally allied with him throughout his quest. But that allegiance is at times stretched thin by the cold brutality of his actions, and his character is such that for at least certain segments of the narrative viewers will typically feel unable to predict what he will do—for example, whether he will continue his blinkered, extralegal pursuit of revenge or return to his earlier, more principled stance of operating within the law.[10] Bannion's internal moral struggle and his resultant character ambiguity thus help drive the narrative forward for viewers, engaging their interest and sympathy for a "good-bad" character and increasing the film's overall suspense.

These *noir* protagonists may be readily understood and explained by means of Noël Carroll's and Murray Smith's related hypotheses concerning audience allegiance to characters based on their positive moral traits. However, there are other kinds of *noir* characters to whom audiences typically develop positive allegiances whose appeal may not be so easily explained. In order to clarify the workings of this other set of narrative figures, let me first recount an associated investigation into the role of morality in determining audience pro-attitudes toward characters.

Hitchcockian "Subjective Suspense" and the Spectrum of *Noir* Characters

In analyzing the moral structure of suspense in some of Alfred Hitchcock's works, film theorist Richard Allen argues that the old master does these *noir* protagonists one better, for some narrative figures for whom we cheer in Hitchcock's films are not merely morally complex but positively immoral. Amazingly, Hitchcock manages to induce his audiences to ally themselves positively with morally bad characters in some suspenseful situations. Thus the director not only complicates, but positively subverts conventional moral coordinates by inducing audiences to hope for the unlikely triumph of villainous

9. The term "moral resolution" is Murray Smith's; see *Engaging Characters*, 213.

10. See also Daniel C. Shaw, "Lang *contra* Vengeance: *The Big Heat*," *Journal of Value Inquiry* 29 (1995): esp. 540–44, where Shaw more fully analyzes Bannion's struggles between his lust for revenge and his commitment to moral decency.

characters. As Allen puts it, viewers are "encouraged to root for the successful completion of an action whose success would contribute to an immoral outcome to the story by being placed in sympathy with the predicament of a morally undesirable character whose likelihood of success is presented as being improbable."[11]

As Smith and Carroll have argued, one way to create this inversion is to foreground in these figures positive moral traits such as generosity, kindness, or solicitousness toward secondary characters, so that they will seem less evil overall.[12] This strategy is indeed one way in which Hitchcock lures his audience into having "sympathy for the devil"—here, the desire that immoral characters be successful, based on a positive allegiance to them because of minor, morally praiseworthy actions. This kind of character is a moral alloy in Smith's terminology, as is Sal in *Do the Right Thing*, but here a mixture of morally bad traits rather than good ones clearly dominates, even if that is not our subjective experience of these characters within certain film sequences. Audiences hold just enough positive moral allegiance to these characters within the narrative to wish them some limited or occasional triumphs. As Allen notes, one such moment occurs in *Psycho* (1960), when we wish for Norman Bates's (Anthony Perkins) success at covering up his "Mother's" murder of Marion Crane (Janet Leigh) by sinking her car into a swamp (166). In a similar fashion we can see this narrative strategy often at work with regard to *noir* protagonists such as those I just described, even as we remain unsure of our overall moral evaluation of the character.

Allen also brings to our attention a second way in which Hitchcock endows morally undesirable characters with a positive allegiance, namely through nonmoral but nonetheless socially admirable traits of the "dandy," such as flamboyance, grace, charm, intelligence, wit, and so on (165).[13] In this way Allen's argument extends an observation made by Berys Gaut, namely that "our sympathies can be based on other than moral characteristics."[14] Allen notes that Hitchcock self-consciously marks both this and the form of moral inversion explicable by means of Smith's and Carroll's theories so that audiences will understand and enjoy their transgression of moral convention. Ordinary morals are characterized as "a set of prohibitions that it is desirable to breach"

---

11. Richard Allen, "Hitchcock and Narrative Suspense: Theory and Practice," in *Camera Obscura, Camera Lucida: Essays in Honor of Annette Michelson*, ed. Richard Allen and Malcolm Turvey (Amsterdam: Amsterdam University Press, 2003), 166.

12. Carroll, "Toward a Theory of Film Suspense"; Noël Carroll, "The Paradox of Suspense," in *Beyond Aesthetics: Philosophical Essays* (Cambridge: Cambridge University Press, 2001), 254–70; Smith, *Engaging Characters*, 209ff.; Smith, "Gangsters, Cannibals, Aesthetes," 223ff.; Allen, "Hitchcock and Narrative Suspense," 166.

13. Allen is, of course, taking his cue regarding Hitchcock's dandyism in his aesthetics from Thomas Elsaesser's "The Dandy in Hitchcock" (1981), reprinted in *Alfred Hitchcock: Centenary Essays*, ed. Richard Allen and S. Ishi Gonzales (London: BFI Publishing, 1999), 3–13.

14. Berys Gaut, review of *Engaging Characters: Fiction, Emotion, and the Cinema*, by Murray Smith, *British Journal of Aesthetics* 37 (1997): 97.

(180), so that audiences will enjoy these immoral characters' success at doing so. Furthermore, in many of Hitchcock's films grotesque humor serves to supplement this desirability. For example, the immoral character's mordant wit may attract us to him or her, or the narrative situation may be presented in such a way that an immoral character's predicament is humorously revealed, making us more sympathetic toward him or her. By using humor, Hitchcock further encourages viewers to wish for the success of an immoral character's actions while knowing full well that what they wish for is immoral.

One example of allegiance through grotesque humor arises in *Strangers on a Train* (1951) when the fey killer Bruno Antony (Robert Walker) attempts to retrieve a cigarette lighter from a sewer drain, where he has accidentally dropped it while on his way to plant this incriminating object as evidence against the nominal hero, Guy Haines (Farley Granger). Audience members wish for Bruno's success at retrieving the lighter, in spite of the fact that it will create a much worse situation for Guy, for at least two salient reasons. First, Bruno possesses socially attractive, dandyish characteristics such as wit and charm, qualities that by contrast his opponent Guy lacks. Audiences thus ally themselves with Bruno to some extent based on his social attractiveness. In addition, the sequence uses grotesque humor to make this morally perverse allegiance stronger and more self-conscious, for Bruno's horror at dropping the lighter, as well as his exertions in retrieving it, are exaggerated and played for laughs by Hitchcock.

A third way of encouraging audience allegiance for immoral characters that Hitchcock employs is to reveal a character's vulnerability, as the director does by showing us Alex Sebastian's (Claude Rains) susceptibility to manipulation by strong, intelligent women in *Notorious* (1946). As a Nazi leader guiding some of Hitler's former scientists to develop an atomic bomb, he is certainly villainous, yet he also attracts audience sympathy by means of his kindness, solicitude, and clear romantic love for Alicia (Ingrid Bergman), the American spy whom he marries. His weakness at being so utterly duped by Alicia again contrasts with the nominal hero Devlin (Cary Grant), who coldly and knowingly manipulates Alicia into marrying Alex, despite a strong mutual attraction between himself and this young woman.[15]

Alex's vulnerability generates sympathy for him above and beyond the allegiances prompted by his occasional positive moral acts. His romanticism and delight in the much younger Alicia's attentions endear him to audience members because they make him charming as well as pitiable, given the personal frailties they reveal.[16] Based on these and other discernable narrative strategies, Allen argues that some "Hitchcockian suspense is bound up with the subversion of conventional moral co-ordinates" because this filmmaker "encourages the audience to enjoy morally iniquitous deeds" (167, 168).

---

15. Allen, "Hitchcock and Narrative Suspense," 165–66.
16. Hitchcock's ability to generate sympathy for Sebastian by means of his unreserved love for Alicia is also noted in Silver and Ward, *Film Noir: An Encyclopedic Reference*, 215.

FIG. 9   Nazi ringleader Alex Sebastian (Claude Rains) succumbs to the charms of American spy Alicia Huberman (Ingrid Bergman) as his mother (Madame Konstantin) suspiciously looks on (*Notorious,* 1946).

These alternative forms of allegiance particularly contrast with the theory of character engagement developed by Smith in *Engaging Characters,* for Allen essentially argues, as does Gaut, that some truly immoral characters may nonetheless acquire positive audience allegiance by means of nonmoral but nonetheless socially admirable traits. Audiences may wish for villainous characters' success because of their dandyish qualities—charm, wit, grace, urbanity, and so on. At least some such allegiances would seem to be truly perverse from a moral point of view. Smith has subsequently acknowledged that his theory as originally stated cannot account for these kinds of cases, although he also suggests that such allegiances are rare.[17] Similarly, Carroll argues that viewer allegiance is secured predominantly through the narrative's depiction of positive moral character virtues. While he introduces some flexibility regarding what might count as a virtue by noting that those he has in mind are broadly Greek rather than Christian, Carroll has been adamant that such allegiances stem overwhelmingly (even if not quite exclusively) from them and not other characteristics.[18]

17.   Smith, "Gangster, Cannibals, Aesthetes," 222.

18.   Carroll, "Toward a Theory of Film Suspense," 104–5; Carroll, "The Paradox of Suspense," 259; Carroll, "Film, Emotion, and Genre," 45. In a personal communication, Carroll characterized these moral factors as "VERY dominant," rather than exclusive.

In contrast, Allen demonstrates that Hitchcock repeatedly creates suspenseful situations in his films where the opposite is true. Rather than work in concert with viewers' positive moral inclinations, Hitchcock frequently works against them by establishing audience allegiances based on socially admirable but amoral characteristics. Allen chronicles several narrative strategies utilized by Hitchcock in order to create suspense using this sort of amoral allegiance, of which I have highlighted three. In some cases, Hitchcock provides truly immoral characters who nevertheless gain audience favor with regard to their hoped-for success through nonmoral but socially admirable traits; in other cases he exploits the use of humor to extend audience sympathy to villainous characters. "Humor allows us to sympathize with the anti-hero," Allen explains, because it detaches "us from the moral consequences of what we see, enabling us to find amusement in the absurdity of the situation." In short, it aestheticizes the moral dimension of the circumstances and allows us to laugh at Hitchcock's macabre jokes embedded in the narrative (169). A third set of cases exploits a villain's weaknesses to encourage audience sympathy. We become solicitous or even pity villains because of their vulnerability. These and other strategies allow Hitchcock to establish what Allen calls, following the filmmaker himself, "subjective suspense." Moreover, Allen stresses that "moral ambiguity is a factor that informs, and is indeed sustained by" this type of suspense (177).

What I hope to extract here from Allen's argument in terms of theories regarding audience allegiance to characters and suspense narrative is that moral ambiguity—and even some forms of immorality—may be exploited to further engage film audiences, as Hitchcock's example shows. These factors of ambiguity and immorality, I would argue, are among those traits that often crucially ally us to *noir* protagonists. We are attracted to them not only for their positive moral qualities, but also for socially admirable but amoral, or at times immoral traits.

Thus wicked humor becomes a way of bonding us favorably with characters such as Spade, Marlowe, and Bailey. Their wisecracks, talent for stichomythia (the witty exchange of one-liners), and sardonic irony engage us positively with them, just as Hitchcock's use of grotesque humor often secures audience allegiance to morally undesirable characters. It is true that some moral philosophers such as Aristotle and Hume offer "wit" and other socially admirable traits as moral virtues,[19] and Smith and Carroll are inclined to follow their example.[20] But I would hesitate to call these traits "moral" because such a categorization raises the possibility of equivocating on the term. It is not clear what "moral" means if such traits are included under its meaning; nor does it seem to have a basis in how we ordinarily speak. On the other hand, I would agree that a quality like wit remains socially admirable and agreeable, even if it is not moral, and because of that admirability and agreeability offers

19. Aristotle, *Nicomachean Ethics*, 2nd ed., trans. Terence Irwin (Indianapolis: Hackett, 1999), 65–66; David Hume, *An Inquiry Concerning the Principles of Morals*, ed. Charles W. Hendel (Indianapolis: Bobbs-Merrill, 1957), 84–85.

20. Smith, "Gangster, Cannibals, Aesthetes," 226–27; Carroll, "Toward a Theory of Film Suspense," 104–5; Carroll, "Film, Emotion, and Genre," 45.

a means of allegiance that circumvents positive moral value. Other socially admirable, but nonmoral characteristics that might encourage audience allegiance include intelligence, resourcefulness, and beauty, such as those often possessed by the stars who portray *noir* characters. Thus, I would argue that protagonists such as Spade, Marlowe, and Bailey exemplify alternative forms of (nonmoral) allegiance through their use of wit and other socially agreeable traits, in addition to cultivating more standard forms of allegiance by virtue of being moral alloys, as described by Carroll and Smith.

In an essay that concedes many of these points, Smith amends his original theory regarding audience allegiance by agreeing that attractive, nonmoral traits may sometimes ally us positively with immoral characters.[21] For example, Smith argues that Hannibal Lecter (Anthony Hopkins) is an "attractive-bad" character in *The Silence of the Lambs* (Jonathan Demme, 1991) to whom audiences have some positive allegiance because he is "charming, witty, urbane, genteel, and learned" (226). Although he is morally repellant overall—he is, after all, a cannibalistic murderer—as viewers we see just enough of his attractive traits to find him subjectively sympathetic and generally wish him well, particularly at the film's conclusion when he famously tells Clarice Starling (Jodie Foster) that he would love to chat longer, but he is "having an old friend for dinner."[22] As Smith notes, the various humiliations to which the narrative subjects Lecter, such as the restraints in which he initially appears, also win him some limited favor, as does Hopkins's star persona (227). In addition, as we now know, this allegiance to Lecter has proven strong enough to sustain multiple sequels.

Some *noir* protagonists make use of similar socially admirable but not positively moral traits as well. *The Big Heat*'s Dave Bannion is a relatively humorless character, much more memorable for his earnestness than his sardonic wit. But I would argue that a certain sympathy for an otherwise unattainable personal revenge is a factor in securing audience allegiance for him. The narrative presents his quest for vengeance as just. He seeks redress against a group of thugs who brutally murdered his wife Katie (Jocelyn Brando), a possibility that may not be pursued by means of ordinary channels of legal justice because they are clogged with payoff money from the local crime boss, Mike Lagana (Alexander Scourby). Thus Bannion's actions are narratively sanctioned as the best available recourse through which he might achieve success in pursuing a kind of rectificatory justice. Moreover, there are some who would argue that, at least sometimes, vengeance is a virtue; and seeking revenge is in any case seen by a good deal of Western culture as socially admirable, particularly when it seems to be the only viable avenue of rectification.[23]

21. Smith is responding specifically to Gaut's distinction between morally desirable and non-morally desirable traits. However, his remarks also pertain to Allen's argument regarding Hitchcockian suspense. See "Gangster, Cannibals, Aesthetes," 225.

22. Ibid., 225–28.

23. See, for example, Peter French, *Cowboy Metaphysics: Ethics and Death in Westerns* (Lanham, Md.: Rowman and Littlefield, 1997), 114–15, 125–26, 151, and *The Virtues of Vengeance* (Lawrence: University Press of Kansas, 2001).

On the other hand, I would hesitate to sanction personal vengeance itself as a moral virtue because it would seem to be not only an excess by definition, but also to collapse into justice when redress is proportionately appropriate—that is, fair.[24] Leaving these considerations aside, however, my point is that *The Big Heat*'s narrative uses Bannion's perhaps morally questionable desire for personal revenge to curry audience favor and sympathy for his character, partly because that desire is seen by many audience members as morally admirable, and partly because in some circumstances it may be arguably portrayed as morally just and appropriate.

To extend Allen's analysis of Hitchcockian suspense even further, we should note that even otherwise egocentric and morally repellant *noir* protagonists, such as the openly dishonest private detective Mike Hammer (Ralph Meeker) in *Kiss Me Deadly* (Robert Aldrich, 1955) and the politically apathetic, caustically sarcastic pickpocket Skip McCoy (Richard Widmark) in *Pickup on South Street* (Samuel Fuller, 1953), are not beyond explicability in terms of how audiences ally with them. In fact, Allen's examination of Hitchcockian villains, coupled with Smith's amendment of his own theory, make explanation of viewer allegiance to them much easier. For example, while both of these *noir* characters prominently embody morally repugnant traits, such as selfishness and insensitivity, they also display socially admirable, dandyish traits such as wit and intelligence, and both further show a kind of resourcefulness that encourages positive audience allegiance to them, thus making them "attractive-bad" characters.

Of course, *noir* films also use other features to encourage audience sympathy that are consistent with more conventional moral structures, as Carroll and Smith emphasize, such as these characters' occasional solicitude or kindness toward secondary characters and the existence of even worse villains within the narrative to make these characters look less repellant by comparison.[25] Still, over and above these narrative strategies the filmmakers use nonmoral, socially admirable traits to boost our sympathies for these characters. We laugh at their nasty comments and respect their intelligence because we see its usefulness in the narrative dilemmas presented by the films. We also frequently appreciate their beauty, as in the case of McCoy. Director Sam Fuller uses Richard Widmark's physical attractiveness to at least partly curry our favor toward the character he plays in *Pickup on South Street*.[26] A similar argument could be mounted in the case of Meeker's character, at least in terms of his well-cut clothes, carefully coiffed hair, properly lit face, and manly physique. The film treats Hammer as an object of beauty, in spite of his reprehensibility,

---

24. Aristotle, *Nicomachean Ethics*, 71–72.

25. Smith, *Engaging Characters*, 190–91; Carroll, "Toward a Theory of Film Suspense," 105; Carroll, "The Paradox of Suspense," 261.

26. Samuel Fuller acknowledges that he uses Widmark's beauty in just this way in "Sam Fuller on *Pickup on South Street*" (an interview with Richard Schickel), on *Pickup on South Street*, DVD, directed by Samuel Fuller (1953; The Criterion Collection, 2004). Gaut also makes the observation that beauty could be used in this way *en passant* in his review of Smith's book (98; see note 14).

FIG. 10   Caustic pickpocket Skip McCoy (Richard Widmark) baits his police depart-ment rival, Captain Dan Tiger (Murvyn Vye) (*Pickup on South Street*, 1953).

thus securing some limited nonmoral allegiance for him on those grounds. More broadly, then, I would argue that we significantly ally ourselves with *noir* characters like Hammer and McCoy through their socially admirable traits, rather than *merely* because of their meager positive moral actions or their moral ranking relative to other characters in the film. Collectively, however, *all* these narrative strategies help to engage us sympathetically with them.

I would also argue that such narrative strategies are common to *noir* films in general. We acquire positive allegiances with immoral characters not only in ways that utilize conventional morality or relative moral ranking in a story but also in ways that utilize what David Hume referred to as "agreeable" quali-ties. How else could we become allied so closely with clearly immoral figures such as McCoy and Hammer—or for that matter, Bruno Antony and Alex Sebastian, who *film noir* encyclopedists Silver and Ward argue are sympa-thetic *noir* villains?[27] Dandyish traits such as Allen has identified at work in Hitchcock would seem to be critical for fully explaining such *noir* allegiances, even if graduated moral rankings and occasional acts of kindness or solicitude play a crucial role as well.

Let me summarize what this analysis of *noir* characters and audience engagement has yielded to this point. First, these characters' moral complexity,

27. Silver and Ward, *Film Noir: An Encyclopedic Reference*, 270, 215.

ambiguity, and at times their immorality help to foster greater suspense and interest in many *noir* narratives because such traits help to create still greater uncertainty in the viewer. In some cases, such as with Spade and Marlowe, we become positively allied with these characters mainly through their morally good actions, which are a noticeable and significant subset of all the actions they perform in the narrative. Yet viewers are nevertheless frequently anxious about what these figures will do next because such characters are not "pure," morally speaking. As in the case of the sympathetic racist character type analyzed in Chapter 1, they are alloys of morally good and bad characteristics. But here, I wish to stress that from very early in the narrative their mixture of traits creates anxiousness and uncertainty in viewers because such characters remain morally ambiguous—they lack full transparency in terms of their moral motivations. This lack of resolution yields audience uncertainty and adds to suspense, as it does in many of Hitchcock's films. In classic *noirs* it adds to audience interest in these protagonists because they are to some extent unpredictable. Moral complexity and ambiguity operate to increase our engagement with the characters as well as the narrative because our predictive capacities are limited by ignorance of these individuals' full characters and how they work. In some ways, then, many *films noirs* operate as character studies, focusing audience attention on who characters are and what they will do because moral unclarity precludes reliable foretelling of their actions by the audience.

Of course, the trick in terms of narrative construction is to portray these characters' complexity and ambiguity in ways that are simultaneously mysterious and convincing—that is, in ways that engage our anxious curiosity as believably as possible and at the same time remain cognitively elusive. In other words, these characters must embody what Cavell calls "individualities"— types of human beings, or the kinds of characters that certain people are, such that we could imagine ourselves as having met them or as meeting them in other circumstances[28]—and be simultaneously partially opaque to our efforts to understand them. I would argue that many *noir* protagonists embody precisely these sorts of individualities. Moreover, such character types are not unfamiliar to us in our everyday lives, or indeed to philosophy, as may be seen in the voluminous literature on the problem of other minds—that is, the problem of how it is possible for human beings to recognize and understand one another.[29] *Noir* protagonists like these might be seen as a subset of those perplexing individualities that engage our curiosity partly because we do not fully understand them.

28. Cavell, *World Viewed*, 33–34, 35.

29. A recent sampler of work on the philosophical problem of other minds as influenced by cognitive science may be found in *Mental Simulation*, ed. Martin Davies and Tony Stone (London: Blackwell, 1995). More traditional presentations of this problem include John Wisdom, *Other Minds* (Berkeley and Los Angeles: University of California Press, 1968); Gilbert Ryle, *The Concept of Mind* (1949; repr., New York: Barnes and Noble Books, n.d.); Ludwig Wittgenstein, *Philosophical Investigations*, 3rd ed., trans. G.E.M. Anscombe (New York: Macmillan, 1968); and Thomas Nagel, "What Is It Like to Be a Bat?" *Philosophical Review* 83 (1974): 435–50.

In regard to more predominantly amoral, immoral, or "attractive-bad" characters, a set of similar points can be made. For example, dandyish characters may acquire our favor, but do so more on the basis of socially agreeable traits rather than positively moral ones. We ally with morally repugnant *noir* characters like Antony, McCoy, or Hammer significantly because they exhibit attractive, socially admirable traits such as wit, intelligence, and beauty. In other cases, we ally with villainous characters in part because of their weakness or vulnerability, as in the case of Sebastian. Of course, moral graduation as well as these characters' occasional good deeds help to cement our positive allegiance, but such factors are simply not enough by themselves to explain fully our sympathetic allegiance to such characters. Instead, we are often seduced into having sympathy toward them on the basis of characteristics that facilitate human interaction and are generally desirable traits for humans to have, even while not being moral ones. Similarly, we may become allied to figures because we pity or feel solicitous toward them because of their human weaknesses. Finally, the narrative may use humor to diffuse our enmity toward a character and turn our attitude to a more favorable orientation. Thus, in addition to Carroll and Smith's forms of positive moral allegiance, our pro-attitude toward characters may be acquired amorally or even immorally by means of socially attractive or agreeable characteristics, by means of humor, or by soliciting audience members' compassion for human frailty.

In this sense, the foregoing analysis yields a spectrum of *noir* characters, ranging from somewhat ambiguous but ultimately positive moral alloys like Spade and Marlowe, to clearly immoral but socially attractive "dandies" like McCoy, Hammer, and Antony, and ultimately to pitiably flawed villains like Sebastian. Probably, some of these latter characters serve as logical limits to what might count as allegiance, as opposed to mere alignment, with a character. That is, they serve as limits to our sympathies, as opposed to our mere knowledge and understanding of the actions characters perform. These characters are moreover figures with whom we may not be particularly strongly allied. As Smith and Carroll would point out, were there more positively moral characters significantly featured in the narrative, all other things being equal, we would probably ally with them instead.[30]

Do the Right Thing and *Noir* Characterization

One of Spike Lee's innovations in constructing *Do the Right Thing* is that he uses this range of characterological possibilities to his advantage in portraying African-American figures. He turns *noir* "sympathy for the devil" in favor of his black characters by depicting them in ways that foreground their complexity and ambiguity, prominently displaying their flaws and weaknesses, as well as their mitigating attributes, but in a way that demystifies his characters

---

30. Smith, *Engaging Characters*, 215–16; Carroll, "Toward a Theory of Film Suspense," 104–5.

enough to make them envisionable as "individualities," and such that overall audiences may develop positive allegiances with them. Most of Lee's African-American characters fall on the morally "good-bad" side of the scale, becoming figures with whom audiences will typically have a morally based sympathy; however, he does not shy away from presenting black characters whom audiences may find morally ambiguous or even alienating—"attractive-bad" narrative figures, as Smith has named them—or worse.

Typically, Lee provides moderating dimensions even for black characters at this far end of the spectrum, such as when he humorously shows us Radio Raheem's vulnerability. After time and again hearing this character's boom box pound out the confrontational song "Fight the Power" and seeing how Raheem uses it to threaten and annoy those around him, we suddenly hear the lyrics warble and distort as the box's batteries die, which amusingly shows us one of this character's weaknesses, namely, his dependence on the boom box's ability to project his implied threat. Raheem's subsequent attempt to buy new batteries from the Korean vegetable stand further stress his weakness, for without these very ordinary technological devices he is considerably diminished, more socially naked, and exposed to the racialized social pressures that impinge on his fragile sense of self. These scenes give Raheem a certain vulnerability that mitigates his threatening presence by portraying him in ways analogous to Alex Sebastian in *Notorious*. As Hitchcock did with his character, Lee diffuses audience antipathy for Raheem by depicting his weakness and his quiet desperation at covering it up, as well as by using humor to present these dimensions of his character.

A similar case can be made for the way in which Lee humorously exposes Buggin' Out's (Giancarlo Esposito) cowardice. As this volatile, rather obnoxious young man argues with the gentrifying yuppie colonizer Clifton (Jon Savage) over the damage done to his $100 sneakers, Lee amusingly reveals Buggin' Out does not quite have the fortitude to back up the vehement threats he is making. This aspect of his character gives the viewer insight into the gap between Buggin' Out's rhetoric and his follow-through, while at the same time it mitigates our condemnation of his character.

A more general argument could be made regarding how Lee and his fellow filmmakers deploy the socially agreeable trait of beauty. It is fairly well known that during the shooting of Lee's previous film *School Daze* (1988), his regular cinematographer at the time, Ernest Dickerson, developed a combination of innovative techniques using different lamps, film stocks, makeup, and other technologies of light to display African-American characters in more complimentary ways. Dickerson's cinematic technology is crucial in the present context because it allowed different subtleties of African-American hue and skin tone to come through on film in a way that was not previously done (or at least, not commonly). One reason Dickerson's innovations become crucial for *Do the Right Thing*'s characters is that these cinematographic developments enhanced possibilities for presenting African Americans more beautifully. Under Lee's aegis as writer, director, and producer, Dickerson devised procedures that enabled the film's black characters to solicit further audience allegiance by means of enhancing this socially agreeable, nonmoral trait.[31]

Utilizing this range of possible *noir* characteristics further complicates the depiction of Lee's black narrative figures and draws in viewers because of the additional ways in which these traits encourage as well as deepen audience allegiance. For example, his characters' frequent lack of moral resolution, far from being a drawback, helps drive the narrative forward by that much more actively engaging the interest of his audience members. In addition, their socially agreeable, amoral traits such as beauty, wit, intelligence, and so on operate to further secure audience approbation. By using these traits in the ways that he does, Lee is thus able to make more explicit the racialized pressures exerted on such characters as being part of their everyday lives and why they act as they do. Our more intimate and positive attachment to the narrative figures in his films transforms *noir*'s social marginalization as a form of alienation from conventional morals into a sort of racialized alienation from "white" justice, which might be understood congruently with the traditional African-American aphorism: "When white people say 'Justice,' they mean 'Just us.'"[32] In this fashion Lee converts the moral underworld of *noir* protagonists into the racialized social underworld of blacks, thereby revealing an entire realm of humanity previously hidden by the blinkers of white advantage from the view of many audience members.[33]

In arguing for a *noir* influence on *Do the Right Thing*, I am not claiming this work is a *film noir*. I am asserting more modestly that, like many of Lee's other films, this one has been substantially influenced by *noir*, a claim that concurs with Silver and Ursini's assessment noted earlier. Still, a related set of questions arise concerning this issue of *noir*'s influence on Lee. For example, are his uses of *noir* techniques intentional? Has he consciously brought the techniques of *film noir* to bear on problems of race in this and other films? I do not propose to answer these questions at the moment, but I will point out that given Lee's apparent knowledge of *film noir* as well as its obvious influence on many of his films, exploring such possibilities are not without merit. While I will allude to these matters later in this chapter, I will take up a more focused examination of them later by analyzing *Clockers* (1995), *Summer of Sam* (1999), and *Bamboozled* (2000) in Chapters 4 and 8.

What I do wish to indicate at the moment is that by the late 1980s *noir* characterizations had become part of the repertory of urban narrative filmmaking, in the sense that such narrative constructions had seeped into the standard array of techniques at the disposal of filmmakers to depict characters.

31. Ernest Dickerson, interview, in Linda Lynton, "*School Daze:* Black College Is Background," *American Cinematographer* 69, no. 2 (February 1988): esp. 70.

32. Cited in Mills, *Racial Contract*, xiv, 109–10, 133.

33. As noted in the introduction, Manthia Diawara suggests in "*Noir* by *Noirs*" the general idea of a transformation of *film noir* with regard to race through the utilization of the determinist forces impinging on criminal characters. For the observation regarding ideas of race hiding an entire realm of humanity, see Cavell, *World Viewed*, 34.

This possibility held true across the spectrum of American cinema, but particularly for those telling stories that take place in cities. Just as Carroll has observed that suspense "is a genre classification that cuts across other genre classifications,"[34] so I would argue that *noir* influences by that time cut across various generic categories, commonly arising in melodramas, gangster films, comedies, and so on. Seeking to confine them solely to a certain type of film would seem to be not only foolhardy, but false. One may see this mixing of *noir* influence with other genres in much of the work of Martin Scorsese and Jim Jarmusch, to name just two major influences on the early Spike Lee.[35] Genre mixing is moreover typical of classic Hollywood narrative and its legacy, so why would we expect anything less from this filmmaker?[36]

Last, I will note that, like the strategy of creating a sympathetic racist character such as Sal, the *noirish* moral ambiguity with which Lee invests his black characters is greatly complicated for many audience members by embedded preconceptions of race. Positive character traits or actions will be much more difficult to grasp for these viewers because they are to some extent anesthetized to the possibility of black moral goodness or admirability by the background assumptions that are a part of their existing belief schemata.[37] In other words, certain racialized assumptions regarding the morality and humanity of blacks that form a part of their presumed belief structure make it much more difficult for them to recognize African Americans as acting morally or admirably, thereby making such viewers relatively insensitive to narrative representations of positive black traits. As in the case of sympathetic racist characters, however, Lee offers narrative strategies that aim to counteract this anesthetization regarding black fictional characters—strategies that also evince a *noir* influence. In the remainder of this chapter I demonstrate these claims by analyzing three of Lee's black characters from *Do the Right Thing*.

Empathy for Radio Raheem?

For most of *Do the Right Thing*, Radio Raheem does not encourage either sympathy or empathy. With his huge boom box constantly blaring Public Enemy's

34. Carroll, "Film, Emotion, and Genre," 43.

35. For an analysis of *noir* influences on Scorsese, see Richard Martin, *Mean Streets and Raging Bulls: The Legacy of Film Noir in Contemporary American Cinema* (Lanham, Md.: Scarecrow Press, 1999), esp. 63–143. For *noir* influences on Jarmusch, see especially his earlier films, such as *Stranger Than Paradise* (1986). For the influences of Scorsese and Jarmusch on Lee, see Fuchs, *Spike Lee: Interviews*, 11, 18, 131.

36. For a philosophical analysis of genre mixing, see Deborah Knight, "Aristotelians on *Speed*: Paradoxes of Genre in the Context of Cinema," in Allen and Smith, *Film Theory and Philosophy*, 343–65, esp. 346–47. For other arguments regarding how genres mix in classical Hollywood narrative, see Neale, *Genre and Hollywood* (see Introduction, n. 68); Altman, *Film/Genre*; and various essays in *Film Genre Reader III*, ed. Barry Keith Grant (Austin: University of Texas Press, 2003).

37. See Smith, *Engaging Characters*, 194; O'Connor, *Oppression and Responsibility*, esp. 2–7.

"Fight the Power," and the way he uses it to create a sonic force field around him, Raheem tends to repel and alienate viewers as well as other characters in the film. It may be getting difficult to remember the impact of rap in the late 1980s, when it was new to those outside the black underclass neighborhoods where it initially developed. As music critic Tricia Rose has argued, works such as those by Public Enemy were perceived as "noise" that violated traditional Western conceptions of music involving harmony, melody, and tonality.[38] As a form of acoustic expression based in "rhythmic and percussive density and organization" and crucially dependent on its overwhelming volume, rap struck many early, first-time listeners as "unintelligible yet aggressive sound" that hardly qualified—and to some less thoughtful listeners failed to qualify—as music.[39] Thus rap songs such as "Fight the Power" would have served at that time as especially effective ways to aurally offend and alienate those people unacquainted with the complexity, history, and meaning of the music.

At the same time, as I noted in the introduction, rap could also thereby operate as a powerful "metaphor of resistance" because of these alienating qualities, in the sense that it permitted the recoding of crime and images of black male criminality into symbols that represented a rejection of the status quo. As Tommy Lott and Bill E. Lawson explain, rap artists often take on such stereotypes in order to invalidate and recode them, which allows these artists to express their rejection of currently existing social institutions as racist.[40] This characteristic further gives rap powerful affinities to classic American *film noir*, as Diawara has noted, because both artistic forms frequently represent dissatisfaction with existing power structures by means of narratives focused around committing crime.[41]

Lee deftly employs these *noir*-like qualities of rap to characterize Radio Raheem. In his initial appearance, Raheem uses his boom box to distance himself from his peers Punchy, Ella, Cee, and Ahmad (Leonard Thomas, Christa Rivers, Martin Lawrence, and Steve White), who warily recognize his acoustic power and demand for respect. The implied threat of Raheem's call for recognition and respect by means of rap is underlined later when he menaces Punchy and Cee until they stop the fire hydrant they have opened from spraying into the street so that Raheem may cross, something that they do for no one else. The older corner men, Sweet Dick Willie, ML, and Coconut Sid (Robin Harris, Paul Benjamin, and Frankie Faison), are put off and complain bitterly about Raheem's jarring presence as well, as do Stevie (Luis Ramos) and his Puerto Rican cohorts who live down the block. In fact, Raheem challenges

38. Tricia Rose, *Black Noise: Rap Music and Black Culture in Contemporary America* (Middletown: Wesleyan University Press, 1994), 65–66. For an arthritic philosophical defense of Western music's characteristics as well as what amounts to an attack on what Rose calls the "blackening" of popular music as a "decline of musical culture," see Roger Scruton, *The Aesthetics of Music* (Oxford: Clarendon Press, 1997).

39. Rose, *Black Noise*, 65, 63.

40. Lott, "Marooned in America," 121; Lawson, "Microphone Commandos," 429–35.

41. Diawara, "*Noir* by *Noirs*," 272–73.

Stevie and his friends to a contest of "dueling boom boxes" for no better reason than to prove his acoustic superiority. Raheem leaves them alone only when the contest ends with Stevie acknowledging Raheem's greater sonic power by means of rap, which overwhelms the more delicate sounds of Ruben Bladés that these Latino neighborhood residents had been playing. Even Buggin' Out complains that Raheem's musical choices offer too little variation.

On the other hand, Raheem would not have it any other way. For him, the boom box that plays his favorite rap song is a weapon that forces others to recognize and acknowledge his presence, that cancels out his social invisibility. Like a child who can only secure her parents' notice when she does something bad, Raheem revels in the belief that negative attention is better than no attention at all. Of course, as I noted earlier, his utter dependence on a boom box reveals a certain vulnerability, a fragility, to Raheem's ego that will become crucial in his final confrontation with Sal, but most of the film explicitly foregrounds the external consequences of Raheem's acoustic aura rather than its internal implications, even if it also compels us ultimately to acknowledge the latter.

Lee presents Raheem's character as a threatening presence in other ways, too. For example, when he shows off the origins of his massive gold-plated knuckle rings to Mookie, the camera momentarily takes the diminutive pizza deliverer's place to depict Raheem's story of LOVE and HATE as it would be seen from the smaller man's point of view. Shot in close-up through a wide-angle lens and from a tilted-up angle, Raheem looms over the camera as he uses boxing moves and metaphors to mimic and at the same time reinterpret Robert Mitchum's terrifying performance as the murdering misogynist preacher Harry Powell in *The Night of the Hunter* (Charles Laughton, 1955), a scene that offers a clear homage to this *film noir* icon.[42] Early in the Laughton film, Powell offers a lunatic sermon about the story of good and evil by using the words "LOVE" and "HATE" which are tattooed just below the knuckles on the fingers of his right and left hands respectively. Similarly, Raheem enthusiastically provides what cinematographer Dickerson calls this character's "philosophy about love and hate, [and] how people should treat each other,"[43] by using figures of speech and movements derived from boxing as well as his outsized knuckle rings to represent the arduous but ultimate triumph of good over evil. Raheem ends his explanation with the implied threat to Mookie, "If I love you, I love you. But if I hate you . . . ," which the smaller man cautiously and deftly sidesteps by noting noncommittally, "There it is, love and hate."

The point of the scene is clear. Raheem seeks to intimidate even his friends, for menace is his primary mode of relating to others. He is a character around whom peers and enemies alike are continually wary and on their guard because he threatens to break into violence at any moment, if he suspects any lack of respect or slight to his humanity, a narrative element that Lee underscores by

---

42. Lee explicitly notes this homage in Lee, with Jones, *Do the Right Thing: A Spike Lee Joint,* 78. Lee also describes this scene as an homage in his commentary, *Do the Right Thing,* DVD.

43. Ernest Dickerson, commentary, *Do the Right Thing,* DVD.

FIG. 11   A shot from Spike Lee's *homage* to Robert Mitchum (*Do the Right Thing,* 1989).

shooting most of this character's scenes in the same way that the exchange with Mookie is shot: namely, in close-up using a wide-angle lens from a tilted-up camera, all of which serve to exaggerate Raheem's size and menacing presence. Again and again the film presents him as neither likable nor sympathetic, which makes the audience's response to his murder all that much more crucial. As a large, intimidating African-American male who imposes himself on others through his boom box and his implied physical threat, he easily fits the stereotype of being a black thug—a gangsta—someone around whom white audience members in particular would probably be suspicious, were they to meet him in real life, as well as being a figure who fits readily into *noir* categories.

At the same time, Lee wants us to understand that Raheem is still a character who represents a human being. As Cavell, Mulhall, and others would point out,[44] the value of this character's life should be taken as morally equivalent to that of any other human being represented by the narrative, not something to be placed below the value of property, such as Sal's Famous Pizzeria, which as I noted is what many viewers did at the time of the film's release and unfortunately continue to do.[45] In this way Raheem is not unlike the fictionalized version of boxer Jake LaMotta (Robert De Niro) in Martin Scorsese's neo-*noir* *Raging Bull* (1980), another morally reprehensible character who has little besides his fragility and humanity to recommend him.[46]

44.   Cavell, *World Viewed*, 33–34, 35; William Rothman, *The "I" of the Camera: Essays in Film Criticism, History, and Aesthetics*, 2nd ed. (New York: Cambridge University Press, 2004), 96–109; Mulhall, *On Film*, esp. 33–51.

45.   See, for example, Klein, "Spiked? Dinkins and *Do the Right Thing*," 14–15, and Kroll, "How Hot Is Too Hot."

46.   For a characterization of *Raging Bull* as a neo-*noir*, see Martin, *Mean Streets and Raging Bulls*, esp. 7, 96–97.

FIG. 12   The first of four shots depicting Radio Raheem's (Bill Nunn) lifeless stare
(*Do the Right Thing*, 1989).

It is all the more astonishing, then, when Lee prompts viewer empathy for
Raheem late in the film—namely, when he is murdered by the police. Once
he is killed, Lee offers three extended close-ups of Raheem's lifeless stare as
he lies prostrate on the sidewalk, while in the background the police franti-
cally try to figure out what to do in the wake of their overreaction to Raheem's
threat. Lee also offers an additional medium shot of Raheem lying dead-eyed
and motionless in the back of a police car, as his body is spirited away from
the shocked and stunned witnesses to his murder. Narratively speaking, these
shots provide viewers with the chance to absorb fully what has taken place.
Thus they may be profitably compared to what film studies scholar Carl Plantinga has described as a "scene of empathy," in which audiences are presented
with "a character's face, typically in close-up, either for a single shot of long
duration or as an element of a point-of-view structure alternating between
shots of the character's face and shots of what she or he sees," which noticeably slows the narrative and offers viewers the opportunity to contemplate and
absorb the character's interior emotional experience.[47] Similarly here, through
these four shots the narrative momentarily slows and invites the audience to
reflect on the fact that Raheem will have no more interior emotional experience, that he will have no more thoughts in his life, that he will see nothing
else. In this way the film redirects our feelings of antipathy or fear of Raheem
to empathy by compelling us to retrospectively apply to him a sense of human
solidarity. Lee shocks his viewers into contemplating an enforced equality for
all human beings through these images; namely, the fact that none of us will
escape this mortal coil alive. Just as Raheem has died, so too will we.

47. Carl Plantinga, "The Scene of Empathy and the Human Face in Film," in Plantinga and
Smith, *Passionate Views*, 239.

In this manner the scene recalls the bleak ending of Robert Wise's *Odds Against Tomorrow*. As the two antagonists, the white racist ex-con Earl Slater (Robert Ryan) and black jazz musician Johnny Ingram (Harry Belafonte), lie dead and burnt to a crisp among the wreckage they have jointly created, a morgue worker asks one of the policemen standing nearby, "Which is which?" The policeman shrugs and responds, "Take your pick." Death here becomes a great equalizer, erasing racial distinctions that mean so much to so many in life. Likewise, Lee uses the phenomenon of death to *noirishly* indicate the ultimate fate that all human beings share, and by implication everything else they have in common.

Moreover, Raheem's manner of death reveals a distinct unfairness in failing to recognize these facts. For anyone's life to be ended unjustly, as Raheem's is, constitutes what is perhaps the worst of iniquities, and by presenting the repeated shots of Raheem's lifeless stare, Lee seeks to summon these thoughts into his viewers' consciousness. By redundantly stressing that Raheem's eyes, his windows to the soul, no longer reflect animate activity, Lee urges his audience to consider not only a fundamental commonality with Raheem—namely, that our mortality is something that makes us all human, even large, intimidating young black men such as this character represents—but also that his life has been taken from him without adequate justification. In spite of Raheem's intimidating manner and overall audience lack of sympathy for him, he did not deserve to die. His life should have been considered of equal value to anyone else's in the narrative, and being an obnoxious and imposing young black male with a jarringly loud boom box does not cancel that fact out.[48]

These shots, which are intercut with the shocked and outraged reactions of onlookers we have come to know and feel close to over the course of the narrative, also compel us to empathetically understand the weight of his unjust death on them, and their feeling that such an end could befall any African-American member of the neighborhood precisely because of their skin color. Alluding to decades of racial violence committed against blacks by urban police forces such as those in New York City or Los Angeles,[49] Lee and his collaborators design the sequence as a whole to evoke audience empathy for his other black characters as well, and for the feelings of horror and outrage that they experience at having witnessed Raheem's murder. As New York City police officer Gary Long (Rick Aiello) chokes Raheem to death, Lee cuts to a shot of Raheem's feet kicking, an allusion to lynching. Such allusions have a special resonance for African Americans because in the past, and arguably still, they were frequently the targets of such actions, which were similarly extralegal killings that involved explicit cruelty, immoral excess, and racially

---

48. Of course, I am not arguing that this sequence is a scene of empathy as Plantinga describes the concept. More modestly, I am offering here what I hope is an instructive comparison, even while recognizing that there are distinct differences between the scenes that make up this sequence and the type described by Plantinga.

49. Feagin, Vera, and Batur, *White Racism*, 117–51; Davis, *City of Quartz*, 267–317.

motivated violence.[50] The other black characters' responses in reaction shots as Raheem is being killed—anguish, crying, and screaming for the police to stop, facial expressions that convey recognition that Raheem is being killed rather than merely subdued, and other actions that transmit their grief, shock, and outraged anger at seeing the police overreact and murder Raheem before their eyes—redundantly emphasize that they grasp the horror of what is happening. The sequence's structure forcefully conveys this understanding to viewers, so that the thoughts and feelings of both narrative figures and viewers are congruent. As further reminders, after Raheem's death characters call out the names of actual African Americans who were murdered by "New York's Finest," Michael Stewart and Eleanor Bumpers; and it is worth remembering that Lee dedicates the film itself to the families of these and other victims of officially "exonerated" police violence.

In these ways viewers are called upon to imagine the narrative from a non-white perspective, and specifically to feel empathy for these characters' sense of outrage at the fact that they are "not safe in [their] own fuckin' neighborhood," as the character Cee exclaims in frustration over seeing his friend executed by the police. By using these strategies to depict Raheem's death, the film seeks to make clear to its viewers the fact that African Americans remain subject to institutional injustice on the basis of race by eliciting in viewers thoughts and feelings distinctly similar to those possessed by the narrative's African-American characters. Such features thus give viewers, especially white viewers, a basis for cognitive analogues from which they might build a bridge from their own experience to that of these African-American characters by breaking down the horrific features of such a racially motivated murder into cognizable bits. As Jones, Mills, Hill, Boxill, and others have indicated, such analogues are the necessary basis for constructing any sort of empathetic understanding that could successfully link differently racialized experiences.[51]

Of course, efforts to construct cognitive bridges for empathetic understanding across racial lines may be readily blocked or misunderstood by many white viewers, who possess a wealth of resources to prevent the building of such connections. However, my point here is that Lee has worked hard to structure his narrative to militate against the employment of those resources. The redundancy of shots depicting Raheem's lifeless stare, as well as the many reaction shots of outraged witnesses, prompt again and again audience empathy for African-American characters and aim to destabilize the standard use of thoughts and feelings stemming from presumptions of racial hierarchy and white supremacy. As I explain more fully in the next section, the film has

50. See also Jonathan Markowitz, *Legacies of Lynching: Racial Violence and Memory* (Minneapolis: University of Minnesota Press, 2004), esp. 45–50, and Dray, *At the Hands of Persons Unknown.* Obviously, I disagree with Markowitz's claim that this lynching is not connected with "broader racist social structures" (49).

51. Jones, "Impairment of Empathy," 65–86; Mills, *Racial Contract*, 95–96; Hill and Boxill, "Kant and Race," 469–71; Farr, "Whiteness Visible."

frequently overcome these epistemological impediments and provoked Lee's intended emotional response.

Mookie *Agonistes*

At the end of the previous chapter, I noted that, in contrast to typical reactions based in racial allegiance, some white viewers readily grasp how *Do the Right Thing* calls upon them to see its events from an African-American perspective. Film critic Roger Ebert, for example, explicitly describes the film as "a call to empathy": "It seemed to me that any open-minded member of the audience would walk out of the movie able to understand the motivations of every character in the film—not forgive them, perhaps, but understand them." Ebert goes on to call this feature of the film a result of Lee's "evenhandedness" and "detached objectivity" that is "yet invisible to many of his viewers and critics."[52] Another striking feature of Ebert's remarks is that he argues *Do the Right Thing* is constructed so that viewers may insightfully "identify" with its characters, which concurs with the observation made by Martin Scorsese about Lee's films that serves as the epigraph for this chapter. Of course, Ebert also acknowledges that many viewers cannot make this cognitive leap, but it is noteworthy that he does so by describing their inability as a failure to answer a call to empathy. In other words, he, too, feels that many have an empathetic impairment with regard to imagining the events and characters depicted in *Do the Right Thing* from an African-American perspective.

Ebert's assessment agrees with the conception of empathy described in Chapter 1. He presumes that this emotional response is one in which a person takes on another's psychological perspective (or something near to it) and imagines experiences at least congruent to those that the other person experiences. It is perhaps unsurprising that he should agree with such a characterization, given that it agrees with our commonsense intuitions about empathy, but it is worth pointing out here that there remains a possibility under this conception for permitting racial asymmetry. Perhaps this divergence is made possible by the fact that, as Amy Coplan points out, when empathizing we do not lose our sense of self, but retain it even when imagining what the other experiences.[53] Given such an understanding of empathy, it is easy to see how this emotional response could be racially asymmetrical. One of the ways in which white viewers might not lose their sense of self while empathizing could be by not losing a sense of their racialized identities. Given the many philosophical arguments noted in Chapter 1, both recent and historical, regarding the raced nature of

52. Roger Ebert, pamphlet essay for *Do the Right Thing*, DVD. Salim Mawakkil, "Spike Lee and the Image Police," 35–36, also argues that Lee's depiction of his black characters is "empathetic" (35) and that Sal "is easily the film's most sympathetic character" (36).

53. Amy Coplan, "Empathetic Engagement with Narrative Fictions," *Journal of Aesthetics and Art Criticism* 62 (2004): 143.

personal identity in Western cultures, it is understandable, if not justifiable, that many whites would find difficult leaving aside the racial aspect of their identities when empathizing.

I should note that Ebert does not himself attribute the failure to answer this call for empathy to racism, but to being "thoughtless or inattentive or imbued with the unexamined values of our society."[54] In contrast, I would argue that here Ebert is being too narrow in his application of what it means to be racist, which for him seems to be due to personally chosen beliefs rather than broader institutional underpinnings that might cause individuals to have beliefs that they themselves do not consciously embrace. I agree with Ebert that many unaffected viewers of *Do the Right Thing* are being thoughtless, inattentive, or too closely adherent to the unexamined values of our society, but would add that some of those "unexamined values" amount to aspects of institutionalized racism—and of course, as I noted in the previous chapter, I think that Spike Lee would agree.

Ebert's sense that *Do the Right Thing* is a movie about empathy is further supported by the fact that Lee depicts major black characters in ways that cultivate this imaginative response from viewers across racial lines. Mookie, for example, is shown as having extraordinary talents as a "middleman . . . negotiating all the neighborhood's varied racial factions and ambushes," as Guerrero notes.[55] Mookie handles the threats, predicaments, and implied violence posed by Raheem, Buggin' Out, Sal, and Pino with equal aplomb. He also shows patience and tolerance toward the mentally disabled secondary character Smiley, a narrative technique that as noted earlier both Carroll and Smith point out is often employed to elicit positive moral evaluation toward primary characters.

Mookie even tries calmly and long-sufferingly to encourage Pino to reflect on why he uses the word "nigger" to exemplify his hatred of blacks. Quietly taking Pino aside after hearing him mutter, "How come niggers are so stupid?" Mookie points out that even as Pino universally denigrates blacks by using this most insulting of terms, most if not all of Pino's favorite people are black. After Pino shows himself completely unable to explain this inconsistency, Mookie provocatively suggests that perhaps the reason Pino hates blacks so much is that, deep down, he wishes he were black. Pino responds by breaking into nervous laughter, possibly in fear that this suggestion might at some level be true.

By foregrounding Mookie's positive moral traits and negotiating abilities in very trying circumstances, Lee offers ample grounds for audiences to attach themselves sympathetically as well as empathetically to this character. Mookie

---

54. Ebert, pamphlet essay for *Do the Right Thing*, DVD.

55. Guerrero, *Do the Right Thing*, 33. Guerrero undervalues Mookie's talents in this regard, describing Mookie as "feckless," and implying that he is self-centered and lazy, but as I argue more fully later in the chapter, in spite of his shortcomings Mookie's talents for patience and negotiating should be valued more highly, especially given their importance to the overall narrative of the film.

shows characteristics that we not only generally admire, but in many cases believe we have—or wish we did—such as patience, tolerance, generosity, and the ability to confront difficulties with practiced skill. Viewers find themselves not only sympathizing but empathizing with Mookie because situations that call for these traits are common ones in our day-to-day lives. In general we share his aspiration to treat everyone by means of these virtues, even if we also share his frustrations over not always feeling like doing so.

Mookie shows these positive moral traits throughout the film. Early on we see him treating Mother Sister and Da Mayor with respect. Much later, just before the riot begins, Mookie tries repeatedly to stop the confrontation building between Sal, Buggin' Out, and Raheem because he foresees that it might erupt into a conflict beyond the control of any of its participants. He even appears to have grown by the end of the film by adding to these traits some quality of maturity and reliability, for he seems to be consciously attempting to shoulder a greater share of his responsibilities regarding his girlfriend Tina (Rosie Perez) and their son Hector (Travell Lee Toulson).

By virtue of being broken down into readily recognizable components with which many of us identify (or think we can), these and other actions prompt viewers not only to sympathize with Mookie, but to empathize with him across racial lines—imagine his experience from inside his raced perspective. Again and again, the narrative studiously shows us not just *how* Mookie acts but *why*—the situations he must face, the racialized pressures he must constantly negotiate as a part of his everyday life, and how his actions in the context of those pressures are mostly admirable. In spite of his less praiseworthy traits, such as being preoccupied with money, controlling about his sister Jade's (Joie Lee) sexuality, or having a certain lackadaisical attitude toward his parental responsibilities and his job, by means of seeing his actions depicted in recognizable detail viewers can grasp that Mookie typically makes a conscious and determined effort to do the right thing, thus giving us grounds for establishing an overall positive moral allegiance with him as well as a congruent, if perhaps not exactly identical, sense of his thoughts and feelings.

At the same time, a mixture of good and bad moral traits provides Mookie with a complexity and ambiguity that bespeaks a *noir* influence. Like Spade, Marlowe, and Bailey, his moral assets and flaws make him seem like someone we could imagine as an actual person—an individuality, in Cavell's terms— even if he remains unpredictable in many circumstances. His moral flaws, while on the one hand making him seem more "real," also make him harder to figure out as a moral agent. But these traits, too, bring him closer to us as audience members. Seemingly amoral when we see first him, counting his money and teasing his sister, Mookie nonetheless develops into a character whose traits are readily identifiable and identifiable with.

We have, then, all the more reason to have a certain critical empathetic understanding—but not a justification—for his action of throwing the garbage can through the front window of Sal's Famous Pizzeria and starting the

FIG. 13　Da Mayor (Ozzie Davis) pleads with neighborhood residents to calm down, think rationally, and act accordingly (*Do the Right Thing*, 1989).

riot. Because he is a figure whose character we know about as well as anyone's in the narrative, audience members have the materials necessary to grasp why he might finally break down, morally speaking, and express his anger and frustration in the form of initiating the destruction of Sal's property. Outraged by Raheem's death and his boss's moral insensitivity, Mookie reaches his limit regarding his capacity to remain patient and negotiate the racial and other pressures ceaselessly imposed on him. On the other hand, the narrative is explicit in not endorsing Mookie's action. For example, Da Mayor repeatedly urges everyone (including Mookie) to remain calm and not act out of anger or frustration in response to Raheem's death and Sal's morally obtuse response to it. If anything, Da Mayor acts as the voice of reason at this point in the film.[56] "If we don't stop this and stop it now," he tells those gathering around the pizzeria, "we gonna do something that we gonna regret for the rest of our lives." Furthermore, Da Mayor cries "Noooo!" in response to Mookie's shout of "HATE!" as he hurls the garbage can through Sal's windowfront. Mookie's exclamation clearly alludes back to Raheem's story about good and evil and explicitly indicates that evil has won out, in direct contradiction to both Da Mayor and Raheem's moral philosophies.

The narrative makes redundantly clear that Mookie is doing the *wrong* thing, even while striving to make redundantly clear *why* he is doing it: he has just seen his friend murdered by the police and heard Sal falsely deny any sort of complicity in the matter. In fact, Sal has characterized his own actions as

56. This claim is made by Lee himself in his commentary on the scene: he defends Da Mayor as not being an "Uncle Tom," but as voicing reason (*Do the Right Thing*, DVD).

FIG. 14   Mookie (Spike Lee) agonizing over what to do (*Do the Right Thing*, 1989).

just and appropriate, when clearly they were not. As I argued in the previous chapter, Sal's response shows no real understanding of the fact that what has just taken place has a deeply racialized meaning. Raheem's murder evokes a moral outrage in neighborhood residents because they know that they too could suffer racial injustice at any time. Lee flags these features in his narrative by making explicit reference to them in what his African-American characters say and do, as well as in how iconographically Sal and his sons are often isolated in opposition to the other community members. Thus when viewers see Mookie visibly agonizing over the conflicting pressures bearing down on him, as they do in a medium shot inserted into the crowd scenes just prior to the riot, it should be readily discernible why Mookie acts as he does—why he strides resolutely over to the trash can, empties it, carries it over to Sal's, and hurls it through the glass front of the pizzeria.

This is not to say, however, that such a realization need be immediate. Like many *noir* characters, Mookie's decision here may well trouble us long after the film is over. We may only come to grasp his decision after reflecting on it at length. Yet this aspect of encouraging us to reflect on dilemmas faced by morally ambiguous characters and the decisions they make regarding them are aspects common to many *noirs,* from *The Maltese Falcon* to *Memento* (Christopher Nolan, 2001).

Mookie initiates the riot, even though it is precisely the wrong thing to do, because he is expressing his outrage at Raheem's racially unjust death and Sal's inability to admit any complicity. Even though Mookie's act is morally wrong and the film marks it as so, the depiction of the film's events, situations, and the characters involved provide abundant evidence to explain why Mookie acts as he does. Of course, in the absence of empathy for Lee's African-American characters, that difference between explanation and justification will be difficult, if not impossible, to grasp.

Lee is able to present this complicated stance regarding Mookie because he is a *noir*-influenced, morally complex good-bad character with whom the narrative has led viewers to be allied, in spite of his shortcomings. This complexity means that even as audience members have sympathy as well as empathy for him and understand his perspective intimately—that is, if they have been thoughtfully following the narrative—they may still judge his actions negatively. In the same way that viewers can judge classic *noir* characters such as Walter Neff (Fred MacMurray) in *Double Indemnity* or Frank Chambers (John Garfield) in *The Postman Always Rings Twice* for far more iniquitous deeds (namely, murder) even while empathizing with them,[57] so Lee employs narrative strategies to allow his viewers to judge Mookie's far less dastardly act critically even as they empathize with him regarding why he did it.

Lee also uses Mookie's lack of transparency due to his moral complexity to his advantage by employing it to add to the suspense immediately preceding the riot. Mookie is more actively engaging as a character and his agonizing more suspenseful because viewers do not know what Mookie will do in response to Raheem's death and Sal's callous reaction to it. Moreover, given the injustice of Raheem's death many viewers are probably not sure themselves what they want him to do.[58] This character's unpredictability, like that of many *noir* characters, adds to the audience's uncertainty regarding how black community members ought to respond to Raheem's murder and Sal's role in it. Mookie, who has negotiated relations among neighborhood residents and Sal's family throughout the narrative, thus personifies the black community's need to decide what to do in the face of these events. As both someone whom Sal considers a part of his family and a member of the community, Mookie has his feet firmly planted in both camps. To represent this "dual citizenship," in the pre-riot sequence he wears a "Sal's Famous Pizzeria" bowling shirt, even as his physical features mark him as a neighborhood resident. Mookie's *noirish* moral ambiguity thus crystallizes the relentless conflicting pressures that bear down on African Americans—their Du Boisian twoness, from which they must still make choices and live their lives. Small wonder, then, that occasionally they make mistakes and decide to do the wrong thing. These difficulties of position and choice are precisely what the narrative seeks to convey through the character of Mookie to audience members. As such, the film offers here another *noir*-influenced possibility for grasping what it might feel like "from the inside" to possess a "double consciousness" regarding race.

---

57. Regarding our empathy for these classical American *noir* protagonists, see Pauline Kael, Film Note on *Double Indemnity, New Yorker,* November 29, 2004, 46; R. Barton Palmer, *Hollywood's Dark Cinema: The American Film Noir* (New York: Twayne, 1994), 47–48; and Bruce Crowther, *Film Noir: Reflections in a Dark Mirror* (New York: Continuum, 1988), 100.

58. Allen, "Hitchcock and Narrative Suspense," 172–74, also makes the point that suspense is heightened when the viewer herself is not clear which outcome she wishes for.

Da Mayor and Moral Orientation

Do the Right Thing also prompts empathy for Da Mayor, which is crucial for a proper understanding of the film because he is in many ways its moral center. He announces, for example, the narrative's theme: "Always do the right thing." His character also tellingly illustrates how much more unnecessarily difficult racism makes following that adage for African Americans. Although it is a seemingly simple moral directive, through Da Mayor (as well as characters like Mookie) the film makes clear that racial oppression often forces African Americans to work much harder to uphold that moral principle than they should have to.

The narrative squarely focuses on this adage's deceptive simplicity as well as the difficulty of its implementation in racialized contexts. For example, when Da Mayor announces the film's moral imperative to Mookie, the younger man tellingly undervalues it. "That's it?" he responds in astonishment. "That's it," Da Mayor tells him. "I got it; I'm gone" is Mookie's parting remark. The impression is that this sage advice has gone in one ear and out the other, an underestimation that comes back to haunt Mookie as well as everyone else in the narrative. In contrast, Da Mayor is, perhaps a bit oddly given his alcoholism, the character most consistent in upholding this principle. Despite his inebriation, he is polite and courteous to everyone. After he saves the youngster Eddie (Richard Habersham) from being run over by a car, he apologizes to the child's mother when she takes umbrage at Da Mayor's suggestion that she not hit or spank her son in punishment for not looking as he crosses the street. He addresses cordially and even gives flowers to Mother Sister, in spite of the fact that she calls him "an old drunk" and a "fool," and for most of the film apparently has little besides enmity for him. He also tries hard to stop the fight between Sal and Raheem, once it spills out onto the sidewalk in front of the pizzeria. Failing that, he then puts himself at risk by attempting to stop the riot before it starts, persisting even after members of the crowd threaten to harm him for his defense of Sal and his sons. Once the riot begins, he further risks his life to put Sal, Vito, and Pino in a safe place so that they will be out of harm's way. He even tells Sal to stop yelling and not to draw attention to himself so that he will remain unnoticed. In analyzing Da Mayor's moral character, it is also worth noting that earlier he had wisely rejected Buggin' Out's suggestion to boycott Sal's as "damn foolishness," an assessment the accuracy of which is forcefully driven home by the riot.

Other actions ring true to Da Mayor's efforts to "always do the right thing" as well. He refuses to identify the neighborhood youths who direct the open fire hydrant to soak the belligerent white antique Cadillac driver played by Frank Vincent. This sort of integrity becomes especially important later when the neighborhood group of which these youths are members attack Da Mayor for sending Eddie to the store to buy him some beer, which is perhaps Da Mayor's most glaring moral error within the narrative. Punchy, Cee, and Ahmad sharply criticize Da Mayor for this misstep and go on to impugn his personal character as that of a lazy old drunk who does not deserve the respect he commands in the neighborhood. In explaining himself, Lee gives Da Mayor what might be thought of as his central scene for generating empathy. The older man defends himself by explaining to the neighborhood teens:

> What you know about me? . . . What you know about anything? . . .
> Unless you done stood in the door and listened to your five hungry
> children crying for bread and you can't do a damn thing about it. Your
> woman standing there, you can't even look her in the eye. Unless you
> done done that, you don't know me, my pain, my hurt, my feelings, you
> don't know shit! . . . Don't call me "bum." Don't call me a "drunk." . . .
> Don't call me nothing! It's disrespectful. I know that your mamas and
> your papas raised you better.

For Da Mayor's trouble in explaining himself, Ahmad reacts so viciously that even Cee and Punchy, who had earlier agreed with their friend's criticisms, move to calm him and tone down his rhetoric. Eventually, they physically carry Ahmad away because he refuses to stop verbally savaging Da Mayor. Afterward, the one female member of this neighborhood group, Ella, looks at Da Mayor with shame and embarrassment, as if in apology for her friends, who we are to understand through her look have gone too far, stepped over the line in dissing Da Mayor and been truly insensitive to his pain, his hurt, his feelings. Clearly, Lee provides this medium shot of Ella's embarrassed look so that audiences will take their cue for proper response from her, not her calumnious friends. Like Ella, we are to feel empathy for Da Mayor and understand that past racial oppression more than adequately explains his broken-down, alcoholic state.

Given the idleness or underemployment of many younger African-American men in the narrative, audiences should furthermore be able to extrapolate that these forces of discrimination remain in place, albeit in perhaps attenuated forms, even when black men would seek betterment and willingly shoulder their responsibilities. Ahmad, for example, speaks the vocabulary of continued personal effort and striving for accomplishment in response to Da Mayor's plea for empathetic understanding, arguing that he would "do anything" to put food on the table for his children, thus implying that Da Mayor just did not try hard enough, that he gave up too easily. In advocating such an outlook, however, Ahmad overlooks the fact that such extraordinary efforts might still mean nothing in the face of overwhelming racial discrimination, both in its institutionalized and personally embraced forms. As Guerrero notes, fear that this possibility might be real in his own future readily explains Ahmad's vociferous anger at Da Mayor.[59] More generally, this incident reflects how even for Da Mayor, the character who seeks more persistently than any other in the

---

59. Guerrero, *Do the Right Thing*, 49.

narrative to always do the right thing, there are times when such principled-ness may seem futile or even pernicious, because of antiblack racism.

These scenes and others provide Da Mayor with a certain moral authority, in spite of his alcoholism and lapse in judgment in sending Eddie to the cor-ner store to buy a bottle of beer. As in many *noirs*, this moral center is flawed. *Do the Right Thing*'s narrative offers no easy answers, but compels us to think about what doing the right thing entails in ways similar to *The Maltese Fal-con, The Big Sleep,* or *Out of the Past.* Da Mayor, then, like the protagonists of these classic *noirs*, offers a sort of flawed integrity from which we might judge the events taking place around him (even if we have to think about it before realizing this insight). By announcing the film's standard for moral action and showing how unnecessarily difficult it can be for African Americans to remain consistent with that standard, Da Mayor provides the audience with a "moral orientation" within the narrative, a center of positive moral value, even if that moral orientation is substantially complicated by moral flaws and the exposure of pressures that are exerted on African Americans because of racial oppression. Despite these complications, through providing a moral center Lee offers an axis around which viewers may organize their moral judgments regarding other actions depicted in the film. Most important, it provides a critical standpoint from which to judge Mookie's action of throwing the trash can through Sal's windowfront, even as it also provides additional grounds for an empathetic understanding of why this action was done.[60]

Critical Reflection and the Role of Empathy in *Do the Right Thing*

Tracing the role of empathy provides a crucial key to understanding Lee's film. Of course, empathy is not evenly distributed to every character. Lee does not call for viewers to *so* closely empathize with his white characters, for example, even though empathy is clearly involved there as well. We feel empathy for Sal—and we are meant to feel empathy for Sal—when he watches the busi-ness he has built over twenty-five years with his own two hands burnt to the ground.[61] But more important, Lee uses Sal's largely unconscious racism to introduce a distance between viewers and Sal, while simultaneously working to improve white viewers' abilities to empathetically analogize from their own experiences to those of African Americans. Lee further casts a critical eye at the assumptions that underlie white racial allegiance by depicting characters who are both empathetic and black—and goading his viewers to think about how these characters may be both at the same time, and how presumptions involving white identity and advantage might often preclude this insight.

60. Regarding moral orientation and moral centering, see Smith, *Engaging Characters,* esp. 213–16.

61. Production designer Wynn Thomas points out the importance of this kind of empathy for Sal in his commentary on the burning of the pizzeria on the DVD of *Do the Right Thing.*

Again, through such techniques he hopes to move white audience members away from having a single consciousness, racially speaking, and toward a more complex perspective on race, a "white double consciousness" through which they might critically understand the legacies of white supremacy as well as the possibilities for its transformation.[62]

I would additionally argue that Lee's construction of narrative makes us reflect on fundamental human questions. Raheem forces us to reflect on the commonalities of life and death for all humanity, Mookie on the grounds for explanation as well as justification of moral acts, and both Mookie and Da Mayor on the difficulty of facing up to the task of doing the right thing, day in and day out, in the face of obstacles such as overwhelming racial oppression and disadvantage. In these ways as well, *Do the Right Thing* is a film that compels viewers to reflect deeply on matters concerning what it means to be human, what it means to be moral, and what it means to be identified as raced.

Lee's provocations to his viewers to reflect on these dimensions of basic human perplexities moreover concur with arguments regarding film as philosophizing put forth by Cavell and Mulhall, who contend that films that prompt viewers to reflect on such questions regarding humanity should be considered themselves philosophy because they contain philosophical promptings of the first order.[63] In particular, the question of acknowledging another's full humanity is a central philosophical concern, as is the claim that acknowledgment frequently depends on empathy, as Mulhall's analysis of *Blade Runner* makes explicit.[64] By means of its African-American characters in particular, *Do the Right Thing* similarly urges its viewers to reflect in focused and sophisticated ways on these matters—namely, on what it is to be a human being, what is allowable conduct, and what implications follow from differently racialized responses to these questions.

Analogously, these sorts of reflections and reconsiderations are precisely what recent philosophical theorists of race have urged. Mills, Gordon, and others have argued that we must thoughtfully reconsider how race continues to influence our thinking about these questions, as well as their relations to one another. The ideas of personhood, morality, justice, and how they have been misapplied because of unexamined presumptions of white supremacy and advantage all require a thorough conceptual inspection, if the racialized flaws in typical moral thinking—both in its philosophical and its everyday forms—are to be overcome.[65] By eliciting our sympathies and empathies for characters in *noir*-influenced ways, Spike Lee has contributed significantly to this conversation. In filmmaker and critic Jacquie Jones's words, *Do the Right*

    62. Alcoff, "What Should White People Do?" 25.
    63. Cavell, *World Viewed*, 33–34, 35; Mulhall, *On Film*, esp. 33–52.
    64. Mulhall, *On Film*, esp. 34–37.
    65. Mills, *Racial Contract*, 53–62, 91–133; Gordon, *Bad Faith and Antiblack Racism*, 182–84; Gordon, *Fanon and the Crisis of European Man*, esp. 38–42; the essays by Mills and Gordon in Yancy, *What White Looks Like*.

Thing depicts the terrible "humanity of racism," a feature we must examine and understand thoroughly if we wish to have any hope of dismantling it.[66] Moreover, because white viewers are commonly blind to this feature by virtue of their misperception of moral phenomena because of an epistemology of ignorance, Lee has sought to employ and refashion narrative strategies such as *noir*-influenced characterizations, so that he might bring such matters explicitly to his viewers' attention.

In the next several chapters, I examine African-American films that are more straightforwardly *films noirs*. These works carry forward many of the *noir*-influenced strategies employed by Lee and his fellow filmmakers in creating *Do the Right Thing*. In particular, these films continue to develop the narrative depiction and presentation of sympathetic racists and empathetic black characters, especially the figure of the gangsta. While we may see the germination of new uses for *noir* techniques in *Do the Right Thing*, they ultimately blossom into black *noir* in the works that follow.

66. Jones, "In Sal's Country," 34.

African Americans have been well-acquainted with the noir world since their arrival in America.
—Ed Guerrero, "A Circus of Dreams and Lies"

Like Spike Lee, other African-American filmmakers have used sympathetic racist characters in order to focus on how racialized presumptions truncate the social world of whites by impairing their moral perception in ways that make them incapable of appreciating or living fully human lives. The work of director Carl Franklin provides at least two such depictions. In perhaps the best known and certainly the most easily recognizable of black *noirs*, *Devil in a Blue Dress* (1995), Franklin offers the secondary figure of Todd Carter (Terry Kinney). When the protagonist Easy Rawlins (Denzel Washington) first meets this rich and powerful white man, Franklin means for his viewers to see that Carter is the most sympathetic white character in the film because he is the first such figure given significant development to treat Easy civilly and fairly. His actions are particularly noticeable given that they occur more than halfway through the film, after we have seen Easy treated with condescension, fear, or presumed superiority by nearly all the other white characters.

Although Walter Mosley's novel, on which the film is based, conceives of this character differently by describing him as treating Easy with "the worst kind of racism" because Carter is "so rich that he didn't even consider [Easy] in human terms" and therefore engages him as if he were a pet dog,[1] in the film Franklin depicts Carter as one human being recognizing another. Because of changes made in the plot, while this rich white man later bristles when Easy inquires into what is really happening between him and the woman Easy is trying to find, Daphne Monet (Jennifer Beals), and becomes increasingly annoyed when Easy gouges him for his fee to find her and insists on a cash retainer, Carter's overall treatment of the budding detective remains noticeably different from that of other white characters—as well as from his characterization in the novel—because he speaks to Easy without condescension right from the beginning. Thus viewers are encouraged to respond favorably to Carter and regard him as a narrative figure toward whom they should be sympathetically disposed. Of course, because he is a minor character that disposition is not strong.

---

1. Mosley, *Devil in a Blue Dress*, 119.

On the other hand, by the end of the film when it is revealed that Daphne is actually a light-skinned black woman who has been passing for white, Carter cannot bring himself to cross the color line and marry her, even though the two of them had planned to do so earlier and Easy's actions have made certain that the facts of her origin will remain hidden. Although Carter explicitly states that he loves Daphne and viewers have no reason to doubt his word, this rich and powerful white man still fears transgressing the color line, even secretly. As a cue for the viewer, the film offers Easy's bluntly critical voiceover in assessing the rich man's dread at the thought of interracial matrimony. The narrative thus urges viewers to disapprove of Carter's moral cowardice, in spite of his being the most sympathetic white character in the film. His fear of racial intermarriage, even when no one would know, is presented in ways that mean to alienate viewers' positive disposition toward him. While Carter remains civil toward Easy and fair in dealing with him, the film makes it clear that Carter will do no more than what prevailing restrictions concerning race in the late 1940s would permit, in spite of loving Daphne and having a veil of secrecy drawn to protect his possible actions. In this way the film aims to make us see how he ultimately chooses to act as a racist, in spite of being a sympathetic character who otherwise acts honorably toward the film's black protagonist.

A Hurricane of Sympathy and Racism

Franklin's 1992 *One False Move* presents viewers with a much more explicit and nuanced example of a sympathetic racist, a character who powerfully draws audience allegiances in conflicting directions. Its lead character, Dale "Hurricane" Dixon (Bill Paxton), is the eager, energetic, but naïve "good ol' boy" of a police chief who presides over the sleepy little Southern town of Star City, Arkansas, where most of the film's action takes place. His job, as he admits, consists mostly of "busting peeping toms and stop-sign runners" until the big-time robbery/murder investigation around which the film revolves descends upon his tiny hamlet. He's "never even had to draw [his] gun," as he tells the Los Angeles Police Department homicide detectives, Dud Cole (Jim Metzler) and John McFeely (Earl Billings), who come to Star City in pursuit of this case to which they have been assigned. As seasoned and slightly jaded police officers, they look on in nearly dumbfounded amazement at Hurricane's ignorance over how to proceed in such a dangerous case—and most other law enforcement situations, for that matter. Where they would advance with extreme caution, Hurricane barges right in, as he does when he blithely approaches and questions one of the suspects' reclusive, near-deaf uncle about when he last saw his wayward nephew. As the detectives later argue with Hurricane, his actions left all of them completely "exposed"—vulnerable to all sorts of potential mayhem or death for which they should have been looking out, given the gravity of the case. But as the film makes clear, impulsively jumping into something without thinking is Hurricane's standard operating procedure. Through an alignment with these big-city characters' perceptions of his actions, viewers realize that Hurricane's brash, unreflective police methods are woefully inappropriate for the apprehension of the dangerous criminals being pursued here.

In spite of his professional ineptitude, Hurricane cannot wait to become part of the case. When first talking over the telephone with his LAPD counterparts, Hurricane is so thrilled to join the investigative team that he cannot wait for them to respond to what he has just said before he begins to speak again or offer more suggestions about how to proceed. Once Cole and McFeely arrive in Arkansas, he meets them at the border of his jurisdiction flashing the lights and siren of his police cruiser and pulling up alongside their rental car as they speed across a narrow two-lane bridge. He manically introduces himself through his open car-door window while the two vehicles streak side-by-side toward Star City in the face of oncoming traffic. Hurricane then rushes them through their first meal together so that they may all proceed to what he believes is their best lead. His wife Cheryl Ann (Natalie Canerday) later confides to Cole that she's never seen her husband more excited. "I guess that this [case] is about the biggest thing that's ever happened to him," she tells the more seasoned detective. As McFeely observes, "Hurricane is waiting on the bad guys the way a kid waits for Christmas."

At the same time, his recklessness and enthusiasm have a certain charming effect on the viewer. Just as Hurricane looks forward to helping solve the case and works vigorously to bring it about, so he draws the audience into the narrative and generates a desire that his involvement play some substantive role. His appeal is partly that of someone who makes things happen, who relentlessly presses forward in his excitement and can hardly wait to see what will turn up next. In this way his character operates as a catalyst, an agent whose introduction causes other actions to occur. For the viewer, this characteristic means that whenever he is onscreen, additional events are bound to take place, so his presence is welcome because he inevitably moves the story forward. I take this point to be related to the fact that, like many other *noirs*, *One False Move* is partly a detective thriller. It thus frequently conforms to a question-and-answer, erotetic narrative structure that draws viewers in by virtue of inducing them to pose questions and seek answers regarding what is going on in the film.[2] Hurricane, then, not only generates additional narrative questions (such as "What in the world will this country bumpkin of a police officer do next?") but by virtue of his heedless, plunge-ahead attitude also facilitates the creation of answers to them.

In addition, his insouciance toward the danger he and the other law enforcement officers face gives him a kind of *de facto* bravery, although as Aristotle would point out his actions more approximate rashness.[3] Hurricane

2. Pudovkin, *Film Technique and Film Acting*, 69–78; Carroll, "Power of Movies," 88–91; Bordwell, *Narration in the Fiction Film*, 64–70.
   3. Aristotle, *Nicomachean Ethics*, 41–42.

will dare to do things that his more cautious Los Angeles colleagues will not, and so great is his enthusiasm for the case that he delights in doing them. As something close to the generally admirable trait of bravery, this feature of his character works to further attract the viewer. The humor that his lack of police skills generates, on the other hand, influences viewers to appreciate his presence for that aspect of his character as well.

Overall, his dynamism, rashness, enthusiasm, and laughably inept, down-home approach to police work help endear him to audience members, creating a positive attachment to the character in spite of his shortcomings. This attachment is especially pronounced in the early part of the film, since the narrative initially foregrounds the more positive and humorous dimensions of his traits rather than their drawbacks. In addition, actor Bill Paxton plays the role of Hurricane with a great deal of charisma. He even gives Hurricane a certain misguided nobility, in the sense that he makes clear that the character usually aims to do the right thing even when he blunders into a situation and makes it worse. Thus, as audience members actively establish who characters are and with whom they might feel comfortably allied in the early part of the film, the narrative provides them with details about Hurricane such that they will feel positively disposed toward him, even if they are also encouraged to be critical of his impulsiveness and lack of professionalism. In constructing a sense of Hurricane's character, his vitality, eagerness, rashness, and astonishing fool's luck make him a narrative figure with whom viewers establish a favorable, sympathetic connection.

We also see that within his rural environment Hurricane sometimes possesses a limited competence at what he does. When he is forced to take a detour from the case and stop an irate husband from potentially murdering his wife, viewers witness Hurricane's ability to calm an out-of-control, axe-wielding drunk through simply restraining him and talking to him as a friend, rather than resorting to overt violence or coercive physical intimidation. He even manages a kind of reconciliation between husband and wife, who both ask him to convey greetings to Cheryl Ann and his daughter as he leaves. After this harrowing episode, over which the L.A. detectives have drawn their guns in anticipation of a far messier outcome, he dismisses their concerns and tells them, "It's OK, boys. Hell, I'm out here twice a week." Although hardly a comprehensive solution to the abusive situation presented here, Hurricane's ability to deal with the husband's violent threat illustrates that he possesses a certain capacity to successfully confront some local law enforcement dilemmas. Furthermore, it is largely through Hurricane's hard work that the murder case bringing Cole and McFeely to Star City is solved. This constabulary rustic maintains the necessary stakeouts for longer hours than anyone else, and his local knowledge allows him to grasp more immediately why these criminals seem intent on coming to Star City.

Hurricane's complex combination of positive and negative traits makes him attractive overall as a character, especially in the first two-thirds of the film. In many respects he is out of his depth, but in other ways he possesses admirable or attractive traits that favorably ally the viewer with him. Even the black detective McFeely, whom he manages to insult repeatedly by casually using terms like "colored boys" and "niggers" around him, never getting his name straight, and consistently slighting him in favor of his white partner Cole, admits, "I like old Hurricane." Similar to McFeely and to some extent taking their cue from him, viewers also find the character alluring in spite of his shortcomings.

In addition, there is the matter of white viewers' racial allegiance to Hurricane.[4] He appeals to many of them because he is like them racially. As I explained in Chapter 1, his character generally meshes with their automatized or referentially transparent belief-schemata that form a racially inflected ground for allying positively with white characters in fictional film. Perhaps more important here, however, his casual racism is probably not unfamiliar to many audience members. Many white viewers can likely identify with the character's racial *faux pas* because they have occasionally committed such lapses themselves, or perhaps at least worried about doing so. Many of them probably feel a forgiving sense of embarrassment for Hurricane as he obliviously insults McFeely because his racial indiscretions seem relatively minor—a bad choice of words, say, or the remnants of an old-fashioned way of speaking—especially given the black detective's tolerant and amused reactions to them.

However, as the narrative approaches its conclusion viewers come to see Hurricane differently. He devolves from being a likable, impulsive hick cop to being the ultimate cause of the evil that invades his town—not so much because he is evil or diabolical himself, but because his ignorance and impulsiveness extend in directions neither he nor viewers had anticipated. For white viewers in particular, his seemingly casual racism acquires an astonishing depth that becomes clear once the role of Fantasia (Cynda Williams), the fugitive whom Hurricane knows as Lila Walker, becomes apparent. She and her criminal companions are headed to Star City because of her ardent wish to go there, not because her lover, the trigger-happy "white trash" thug Ray (Billy Bob Thornton), has a doddering old hermit of an uncle living outside of town. Before she became "Fantasia," Lila grew up in the black part of Star City and had a son when she was seventeen, whom she left behind in her mother's care when she decided to take off for Hollywood—"to become a movie star," as Hurricane puts it. Fantasia reminds Ray at one point that the only reason she got involved in the drug money heist that begins the film and culminates in more than a half-dozen grisly murders was so that she could return home and "see [her] people," in particular her young son, whose last four birthdays she has missed.

From this point in the film viewers become progressively more aware of Hurricane's past relationship with Lila. To the Los Angeles police detectives he admits to having arrested her for shoplifting and "trying to help her out—you

---

4. I owe this insight to Calvin Selvey, who originally made his observation about different audience members' racial allegiances regarding *One False Move*.

know, talk to her" rather than prosecute her for petty theft. But his behavior subtly betrays a deeper involvement that becomes clearer once she arrives in town to see her family. Hurricane and Lila have had an affair, orchestrated by Hurricane under the guise of "helping" Lila and facilitated by the hierarchical race relations existing in the town—and for that matter, America in general. As sociologist F. James Davis and others have noted, historically black women have experienced a particular form of terrorism from white men. A whole tradition of sexual vulnerability built up during slavery and extended long into the epochs following the Civil War. As slaves, black women had profound difficulties avoiding the sexual predations of white men, and for decades after the end of slavery they had little legal protection against rape and other sexual onslaughts.[5] Historian Peter W. Bardaglio notes that between 1865 and 1899, for example, "only 2 identifiable cases [of rape or attempted rape] involving a white man and a black female could be found" in Southern state court case appeals, and both were successful, partly because "social customs founded in race differences" were admissible as trial evidence.[6] Moreover, as Richard Dyer has argued black women were subject to a continual litany regarding their alleged inferiority to white women in terms of beauty, which amounted to an ideological dimension of their raced as well as gendered vulnerability under white supremacy.[7]

Moreover, the legacy of this vulnerability has continued to the present day. If Dyer, Paul C. Taylor, Charles Mills, and others are correct to maintain that the norm of whiteness's desirability has deeply influenced many black's internal sense of human beauty, even to the point that such beliefs damage their conceptions of themselves and others, then a very strong case may be made for the continuing problem of black women's vulnerability because these standards remain largely in place.[8] Toni Morrison's well-known novel *The Bluest Eye* focuses on several aspects of such psychological damage. In it, the young black girl Pecola expresses the impossible and at the same time perversely "logical" desire to have blue eyes, like the whitest of white girls, because she believes that she will thereby become beautiful and lovable.[9] Philosophers and

---

5. F. James Davis, *Who Is Black?* (University Park: Pennsylvania State University Press, 1991), esp. 38–39, 48–49, 54–55, 62–63, 78, 150–56; Harriet Jacobs, *Incidents in the Life of a Slave Girl* (1861; repr., Cambridge: Harvard University Press, 1987). Frederick Douglass also describes the difficulties his aunt had in resisting their owner's advances and the brutal beatings she took in order to remain true to her husband. See *Narrative of the Life of Frederick Douglass, An American Slave, Written by Himself* (1845; repr., New York: Anchor Books, 1989), 5–6.

6. Peter W. Bardaglio, *Reconstructing the Household: Families, Sex, and the Law in the Nineteenth-Century South* (Chapel Hill: University of North Carolina Press, 1995), 194, 191.

7. Dyer, *White*, esp. 41–142.

8. Paul C. Taylor, "Malcolm's Conk and Danto's Colors; or Four Logical Petitions Concerning Race, Beauty, and Aesthetics," *Journal of Aesthetics and Art Criticism* 57 (1999): 16–20; Mills, *Racial Contract*, 61–62; Dyer, *White*, esp. 41–142; Dawn Perlmutter, "Miss America: Whose Ideal?" *Beauty Matters*, ed. Peg Zeglin Brand (Bloomington: Indiana University Press, 2000), 155–68.

9. Toni Morrison, *The Bluest Eye* (1970; repr., New York: Washington Square Press, 1972), 137.

other critics have noted the wider implications of Morrison's insight. Beliefs about human beauty may deform and distort the ways blacks, particularly black women, think of themselves, thereby opening them to further harm by virtue of their desire to be loved and accepted as beautiful according to a standard against which it is at best difficult for them to measure up. In a world where whiteness is the norm for human physical appeal and attractiveness, such aspirations are far more likely to be cruelly dashed than tenderly fulfilled.[10]

One additional implication of such vulnerability is the effect that these beliefs may have on whom black women might consider as desirable others—partners, lovers, and so on. If deeply influenced enough by ideals of white beauty and desirability, they, like Pecola's mother Pauline, may prefer to love someone who is white over someone who is black. Morrison's novel makes explicit that Pauline lavishes far more love, care, and attention upon the little white daughter of the family she works for than she does on Pecola herself. Pauline also fantasizes about white actresses and tries to emulate their beauty. She dreams of white actors as well, which she observes made it hard to look at her husband afterward because he failed to measure up to their embodiment of white male beauty.[11] Rather than find desirable someone who is like her, Pauline comes to desire who she has been indoctrinated to believe is more beautiful, who meets the dominant standard of beauty, namely, someone who is white. Such perversions of desire are no doubt the main reason Morrison calls the idea of human physical beauty one of "the most destructive ideas in the history of human thought" (97).

As Laurence Thomas has argued, race should not matter when it comes to love and desire for others, but all too often it does.[12] The reason it often does is that the norms of white superiority can work to distort even personal human desire, with particularly disastrous consequences for African Americans, who as members of American culture are constantly bombarded with messages that convey their alleged aesthetic inferiority. For some, like Pecola's mother, it can even fundamentally influence whom they love.

Reflecting the possibility for this kind of perverted preference is, I would argue, why *One False Move* places Lila first with Hurricane, then with the otherwise repulsive thug Ray, who may be a violent, insensitive, psychopathic brute, but at least he's white, and Lila's desire is such that this characteristic in a lover becomes paramount. As the film makes clear and director Carl Franklin underscores in his DVD commentary, Lila is also following in her

10. Taylor, "Malcolm's Conk and Danto's Colors"; George Yancy, "A Foucauldian (Genealogical) Reading of Whiteness: The Production of the Black Body/Self and the Racial Deformation of Pecola Breedlove in Toni Morrison's *The Bluest Eye*," in Yancy, *What White Looks Like*, 107–42; Gary Schwartz, "Toni Morrison at the Movies: Theorizing Race Through *Imitation of Life*," *Existence in Black: An Anthology of Black Existential Philosophy*, ed. Lewis R. Gordon (New York: Routledge, 1997), 111–28; Dyer, *White*, esp. 70–81.

11. Morrison, *Bluest Eye*, 100–101, 97.

12. Laurence M. Thomas, "Split-Level Equality: Mixing Love and Equality," in *Racism and Philosophy*, ed. Susan E. Babbitt and Sue Campbell (Ithaca: Cornell University Press, 1999), 189–201.

own mother's footsteps. Mrs. Walker (Phyllis Kirklin) also had an affair with a married white man, and bore him children he rarely saw or thought about.[13]

The fact that this trait has been passed on from mother to daughter implies that it is part of an ongoing tradition of distorted personal desire. Given that it also fits comfortably with the continuing damage done by the ideal of white beauty as well as other dimensions of the historical vulnerability of black women, I would argue that this perversion of black desire is something about which the narrative seeks to make a point, namely that racism may affect human beings even at the level of who they desire to love.[14]

In presenting this phenomenon critically, the film makes clear that Lila herself has some awareness of how racism has affected her internalized sense of beauty and her romantic preferences. As she caustically tells Hurricane once they finally meet again in the final act of the film, "You figured because I was kind of white, you could fuck me, what the hell. . . . And because I looked kind of black, you could dump me, what the hell." Moreover, she herself points out that she is following in her mother's footsteps by preferring white lovers over black. "Me and my brother's daddy was white, did you know that?" she tells Hurricane. "'Course, we never knew him. He had another family," like her ex-lover, and so never acknowledged Lila or her brother. More generally, Lila expresses the realization that Hurricane, as a socially powerful white man in a small Southern town, took advantage of her at a time when she was a young high-school student who had been caught for shoplifting lipstick and eye shadow not worth ten dollars. Rather than prosecute her, he manipulated her into a sexual relationship because she was close enough to being white that she offered him some allure. In addition, the relationship was something she was willing to accept, given the distortion of her desires by aesthetic ideals skewed toward white beauty and other racialized factors of her experience.

When their liaison resulted in a child, however, Hurricane—at least on the surface—could deny paternity because, given the standard conditions of race relations in America, Lila was black enough so that he did not need to take her seriously as a full-fledged human being and give her the consideration he would extend to a moral equal. Instead, as Mills would note, the ongoing institutional racial hierarchies historically put in place by open white supremacy insulated him from the consequences of his licentious actions.[15] Hurricane could ignore Lila and her predicament of having become an unmarried, pregnant high schooler because his race, combined with his other social advantages, made possible and indeed encouraged such a response from him. He was free and even expected to dump her, given his place in the racialized social hierarchy of the southern United States, because such an action would help to maintain existing social relations rather than disrupt them.

---

13. Carl Franklin, commentary, *One False Move*, DVD, directed by Carl Franklin (1992; Columbia TriStar Home Video, 1998).

14. See also Thomas, "Split-Level Equality," esp. 195–98.

15. Mills, *Racial Contract*, esp. 72–78.

Still, as the film makes clear, Hurricane cannot entirely escape the relationship or its moral consequences, especially in his own mind. Although he
at first tries to deny that the little boy is his, the film has already shown him
looking longingly at Byron (Robert Anthony Bell) twice before, thus indicating
that at some level he acknowledges the child as his son, and as the ex-lovers
talk about why Lila has returned to Star City, she forces him to admit the truth.
A major point of the film, then, is to drive home the idea that Hurricane cannot escape the consequences of his own actions, in particular their racialized
dimensions. In spite of his attempts to use the advantages of whiteness to
avoid the effects of his deeds on Lila, he is ultimately caught up by his own
racialized moral corruption.

As the story develops, *One False Move* sheds its initial guise of *noir* detective thriller to unveil the subtleties of Hurricane's unconscious white privilege.
The film, in the words of its director, "goes from a genre piece to a character
piece" by changing its focus from the investigation of a robbery/murder case
to analyzing Hurricane and Lila's racialized characters.[16] What I wish to underscore here is that the narrative reveals the racial dimensions of Hurricane's
social power to be of a type that blacks must generally be aware of in order to
survive in both the white and black worlds—that is, as a matter of Du Boisian
double consciousness—but whites as a rule are not. Like *Do the Right Thing*,
One False Move may be understood as working to create the first stages of a
racially aware double consciousness in its white viewers by explicitly depicting
and forcefully driving home how Hurricane's racial privilege has damaged Lila
and contributed to her descent into criminality as well as his own moral corruption. In doing so the film seeks to urge its white viewers to reflect on and
critically evaluate the morally and humanly damaging dimensions of white
power and social advantage.

The film achieves these goals partly by first establishing Hurricane as a
sympathetic character while at the same time laying the foundation for revealing his moral decay. In the first part of the film viewers see Hurricane taking
from everyone the petty little perks available to a small-town police chief, such
as neglecting to pay the full bill for meals in the local restaurant ("I'll catch
you next time," he casually tells the waitress when she points out that he has
shorted her) or going behind store counters and helping himself to candy
bars. But eventually viewers realize that this risible small-time corruption
runs far deeper and possesses a racial dimension of which earlier they were
only dimly aware at best. The facts of Hurricane's past sexual relations with
Lila and paternity of a mixed-race child, both of which his "white privilege"
permitted him to ignore, have contributed to Lila's fleeing Star City for the
urban hell of Los Angeles where, failing to achieve her improbable dream of
becoming a movie star, she has drifted into the city's criminal underworld and
participation in the vicious drug-money theft and murders that begin the film.
But now she and her companions are returning to Star City because she wants

16. Franklin, commentary, *One False Move*, DVD.

to see her family, particularly her five-year-old son, most of whose life she has missed. Hurricane's presumption of white advantage thus ultimately anchors the evil that descends upon his hometown because he had earlier used it to seduce a high-school co-ed and father a child with her, then deny any responsibility for his actions.

A further aspect of the damage that Hurricane's use of white advantage produces on Lila concerns her senses of self-respect and self-esteem. As Michele M. Moody-Adams explains, social circumstances can deeply influence our self-perceptions. "The vocabulary in which one learns to give expression to one's self-conception, and even the concepts that initially shape that self-conception" often constitute dimensions of one's social situatedness. These dimensions embody the "normative expectations about emotion, thought, and action" that shape how one generally sees one's self and how one evaluates self-worth.[17] If these normative expectations are circumstantially distorted by hierarchical conceptions of race or class, then those experiencing such distortions will typically find it difficult at best to find resources to resist a corresponding distortion of self-respect and self-esteem. *One False Move* thus offers an illustration of how Lila's respect and esteem for herself have been distorted by her circumstances, and of the role that Hurricane's presumption of white advantage has played in imposing their accompanying degraded normative expectations on her.

At the same time, I would also argue that most white viewers do not take Hurricane's racist behavior seriously until Lila explains their intimate past in the late stages of the film because, in addition to presuming an implicit racial allegiance with his character, many audience members take their cue from McFeely, who likes Hurricane despite seeing him as a rural buffoon with a badge, a "yokel [who] wouldn't last ten minutes" as a policeman in Los Angeles. Rather than become incensed at Hurricane's references to "colored boys" and "niggers," McFeely laughs and does not take them seriously because he does not take Hurricane seriously. Viewers thus relax their concerns over this redneck cop's racist behavior because the main black character feels that Hurricane himself in no way constitutes a significant threat. Instead, viewers see him as an ignorant, laughable country bumpkin whose racism is predictably backward and incidental because that is how McFeely prompts them to see this character, and their alignment in the earlier part of the film is with this black detective from L.A. and his partner, who concurs with McFeely's critical assessment of their redneck colleague.

Such a stance toward Hurricane makes Lila's revelation all that much more shocking. When the narrative shows us that his racial misdeeds have a depth of which we had little or no suspicion, we are stunned, although in retrospect we can see how his past actions toward Lila and his earlier expressions of seemingly harmless, "good ol' boy" racist attitudes are all of a piece. They are

FIG. 15   A visibly constricted shot of Hurricane (Bill Paxton), as fate closes in on him
(*One False Move*, 1992).

two sides of the same coin, the name of which is "white privilege," or perhaps
more appropriately, "white supremacy."[18]

Consistent with many other *noir* films, Hurricane's complicity in this dangerous criminal case also leads to his destruction. As events close in around
him and we learn that Hurricane's involvement is deeper and more compro-
mising, viewers begin to recognize that in many ways this character has set
himself up for a fall because of his own past actions. Like the film's viewers,
and operating narratively here to prompt their insights, Hurricane is forced to
admit that he has had a decisive role in Lila's moral downfall. Yet like other *noir*
protagonists, such as Jeff Bailey (Robert Mitchum) in *Out of the Past* or Jake
Gittes (Jack Nicholson) in *Chinatown*, he is powerless to prevent the events
unfolding around him. As he diligently carries on his police work, he comes
to understand the depth of his own collusion, and with him the viewer comes
to grasp it as well. While he tries to hide knowledge of his role from the other
characters, circumstances are such that he cannot escape liability for his past
misdeeds. As he and the film's viewers progressively grasp, his pivotal role in
the case is too important to be exonerated or remain hidden.

Because of his intimate knowledge of Lila, Hurricane recognizes better
than anyone else clues that reveal she has returned to Star City. But when

18. For fuller arguments regarding why "white supremacy" might be a better term theoretically to describe the phenomenon typically called "white privilege," see Charles W. Mills, "Racial
Exploitation and the Wages of Whiteness," in Yancy, *What White Looks Like*, 25–52, esp. 30–32,
35–36, and Gordon, "Critical Reflections," esp. 173–77. I agree with Mills's and Gordon's arguments that "white supremacy" better captures what is at stake in analyzing such phenomena. In
using the term "white privilege" here and at times elsewhere, I am deferring, perhaps somewhat
meekly, to common usage.

he finally confronts her and tries to arrest this young fugitive from justice, it becomes clear that their secret relationship gives her the upper hand. Because he does not wish to harm her further or to be found out, he promises to let her go free, even though doing so seriously breaches his responsibility as a law enforcement official. Yet his own incompetence interferes with his ability to close the case. He allows himself to be momentarily distracted by Lila when he apprehends her accomplices, the trigger-happy Ray and coldly calculating Pluto (Michael Beach), who have come to pick her up from her Star City hideout. Pluto, whom we know as viewers to be the mastermind behind the savage felonies that opened the film, takes advantage of Hurricane's distraction to pull a knife and stab him. A messy shoot-out ensues, during which Hurricane kills both Ray and Pluto, but in the process Lila also inadvertently catches a stray bullet and dies. After this carnage Hurricane manages to call for backup, but it is clear that he has been seriously, perhaps mortally, wounded.

Helpless and prostrate in the final scene, he at last speaks to his denied son for the first time, who was in the company of the other police officers who answer Hurricane's request for help. In their own attempt to find Lila and because they have discovered that the little boy had been with her the previous evening, they have taken him in their police cruiser to try to find out where she is. Because they are distracted by the necessities of dealing with the crime scene and getting Hurricane medical attention, they forget about Byron in the moments after they reach her hideout. He wanders out of the squad car, approaches his bleeding father lying on the ground, and innocently asks him whether he is dead yet. Hurricane replies weakly, "No, not quite." When the little boy then asks where the lady is whom he had seen the previous evening, Hurricane distracts Byron and asks him to stay with him.

Yet even as he speaks to his denied son for the first time, Hurricane still does not admit paternity. We know from earlier in the film that Lila had pleaded with him to do so, because she did not want her son to grow up never knowing his (white) father, as she did. A phone call interrupts their conversation, however, so its effect on Hurricane is left hanging. In the final scene, instead of telling Byron that he is his father, the young police chief talks about what has happened to him ("I got in a fight"), answers the child's question about his keys, and talks to Byron about how old he is. Although Hurricane is clearly trying to protect the child from the trauma of seeing his mother and her accomplices dead, as well as seeking to establish some sort of conciliatory rapport with him, the narrative withholds the key admission that Lila had begged Hurricane to make to their son.

It is hard not to read Hurricane's reticence here as at least partly racial, even if the film also makes clear that Hurricane has come to understand some of the damaging racialized dimensions of his moral thinking and acting, and seeks to do something to correct them. He has already promised Lila to begin giving her mother money to help care for Byron, and his promise to let Lila go shows that he hopes to make amends for his past racial misdeeds. These acts, we should note, amount to important initial steps in reconciling individuals

FIG. 16   Hurricane (Bill Paxton) speaks to his long-denied son Byron (Robert Anthony
Bell) for the first time (*One False Move*, 1992).

involved in racial difficulties because they begin to address the question of
what is just in such circumstances. However, the narrative withholds the crucial admission that Lila argued would be so important to their child, so that
he could grow up knowing his father and thereby develop better senses of
self-respect and self-esteem than she had. I take this narrative refusal to be
aimed at encouraging the film's audience, particularly its white viewers, to
reflect on the extent to which their ordinary, everyday actions and beliefs may
have devastating consequences for blacks. This sort of cinematic provocation
thus mirrors Hurricane's own realization of how his behavior has devastat-
ingly affected Lila, Byron, himself, and others.

Racism, Tragedy, and Empathy

For white viewers, *One False Move* comes to operate emotionally in ways structurally similar to tragedy, with Hurricane in a role analogous to, but not the
same as, that of a tragic hero. For example, this film character is like such
viewers, just as Aristotle would have it, for Hurricane is neither overly good
nor overly bad, but somewhere in between, with a greater inclination to be
good than bad.[19] I would add, however, that the sense of moral likeness here
includes a racialized dimension that Aristotle would never have anticipated.[20]

19.   Aristotle, *Poetics*, trans. Stephen Halliwell, excerpted in *The Philosophy of Art: Readings
Ancient and Modern*, ed. Alex Neill and Aaron Ridley (Boston: McGraw-Hill, 1995), 498.
20.   Regarding Aristotle's lack of a concept of race, see Julie K. Ward, "*Ethnos* in the *Politics*:
Aristotle and Race," and Paul-A. Hardy, "Medieval Muslim Philosophers on Race," in Ward and
Lott, *Philosophers on Race*, 14–37 and 38–59.

Hurricane also suffers a decisive reversal of fortune. Cole tells him that he is "a lucky guy" because Hurricane's situation lacks many of the drawbacks that often accompany police professionalism: extreme danger and the potential for violence in any situation one might approach, a sense of isolation from one's community and family, lack of trust in others, alcoholism, and so on. The narrative, moreover, goes out of its way to confirm Cole's assessment. Hurricane is indeed a lucky guy. Slightly misunderstanding what this experienced detective is trying to tell him, the young police chief muses that he hardly ever loses a coin toss or a bet, and viewers have witnessed that Hurricane presumes a certain amount of good fortune as his birthright, so to speak, in the reckless way that he acts. He even goes so far as to tell Cole, "My mama used to always tell me that I was born under a lucky star." Hurricane's good fortune could hardly be made more explicit.

With Lila's return to Star City, however, viewers see that Hurricane's luck changes. He falls from "prosperity to affliction," just as Aristotle's model of tragedy would have it (498). His own serious injuries at the conclusion of the film and the inevitable result that his complicity in the case will become public knowledge constitute the retribution he suffers as a consequence of his actions. There is also a sense in which this turn of events is unexpected, "contrary to expectation yet still on account of" the sequence of actions presented (496). Even though the depth of Hurricane's racism is a surprise, it fits consistently with his character and results from a reasonable chain of events. In this way *One False Move* elicits "a sense of wonder" (496), as Aristotle explains the best tragedies do, by being contrary to expectation and at the same time logical.

I would further argue that Hurricane's presumption of his own good fortune amounts to his tragic flaw (498). It is also important to stress here that one crucial dimension of his presumed good fortune is racial; namely, his sense and supposition of whiteness and its advantages, for which he comes to suffer deeply. In addition, Hurricane ultimately recognizes that he has been complicit in Lila's downfall. Like a tragic hero, he changes from ignorance to having insight (497); namely, that he bears a crucial responsibility for her moral decline, as well as for the case ending up in his town. The racial dimensions of this change in self-understanding may be more clearly grasped by means of Mills's concept of the epistemology of ignorance. Hurricane changes from unconsciously thinking and acting by means of his racialized moral psychology to acquiring some knowledge of his racial misdeeds. He comes to see in a way that was invisible to him earlier how his moral actions, decisions, and outlook possess a fundamentally racialized component. In this sense, *One False Move* is actually an aesthetic advance over *Do the Right Thing*, as Hurricane comes to realize the racial dimensions of his moral thinking and acting in a way that Sal never does. Such a realization makes clearer to white viewers the precise nature of this sympathetic racist's mistakes because it offers them the same kind of insight that Hurricane achieves regarding what he has done. There exists far less possibility for misunderstanding this aim of the narrative in Franklin's film than in Lee's.

The film is also unusual in the sense that Hurricane does not escape the consequences of his racism, but suffers real misfortune and injury. This suffering by the protagonist, again in ways similar to a tragic hero, better allows viewers, especially white viewers, to come to realize the racial dimensions of Hurricane's actions by eliciting fear and pity from them, many of whom may recognize themselves in this narrative figure, particularly with respect to their racialized moral thinking. One can see that the explicit link being sought by the filmmakers in connecting unconscious racial advantage to moral harm crystalizes by means of Hurricane's insight into his role in propelling Lila down the path of moral decline. Hurricane's progressive understanding of what he has done thus prompts viewers to grasp this connection in the narrative. It also encourages them to reflect on the role of this connection in their own lives as well. As they view his fate, the severity of which they might arguably perceive as less than completely deserved given the real but attenuated causality his actions play in Lila's downfall, viewers may well feel pity for him, while they may also feel fear because of the realization that he is probably much like them, especially with regard to their unconscious presumption of whiteness's advantages.

Here, then, we might speak of white viewers in particular as having not only sympathy for Hurricane, that is, feeling *for* him in his predicament, but also a certain empathy, a feeling *with* him.[21] However, this feeling of at least congruent sentiments is not likely to make viewers excuse his misdeeds, as they sometimes do for Sal in *Do the Right Thing*, but instead aims back toward viewers themselves in the form of self-questioning and reflection on their own ingrained moral behavior. The empathy felt for Hurricane, as affected by means similar to the structure of tragedy, aims contemplation and reevaluation more squarely back at them, rather than deflecting it, as white viewers sometimes do with Lee's film. It is, then, a critical empathy with Hurricane that also directs criticism at the viewer. Of course, white viewers still have strategies at their disposal to defer or deflect such empathetic calls for reflection, but this narrowing of interpretive possibilities makes *One False Move* arguably a narrative that deploys the character of the sympathetic racist more effectively than *Do the Right Thing*, which leaves more open what stance viewers should take toward Sal.[22]

Borrowing from the structure of tragedy to elicit audience sympathy or empathy, of course, is not unusual in *noir* narratives. One of the most devastating dimensions of films like *Out of the Past* and *Chinatown* is that they offer viewers protagonists whose past actions, done partly in ignorance, come back

21. For more on this difference between sympathy and empathy, see Neill, "Empathy and (Film) Fiction," 175–76.

22. I am not claiming here that *One False Move* is a better film than *Do the Right Thing*, but only that its deployment of the sympathetic racist character type is more effective for white viewers, in the sense that it seems to offer greater potential to be more affecting and leaves fewer possibilities for misinterpretation. I leave open whether those characteristics mean that *One False Move* is a better or worse work of art overall.

to haunt them, but they remain powerless to do anything against the sequence of events unfolding around them. Partly unknowingly they set in motion the wheels of fate that will eventually crush them. Jeff Bailey, for example, believes he has escaped the consequences of his earlier misdeeds when they return from out of the past to ruin his life, in spite of his best efforts to evade them and to develop an improved moral character. Likewise, Jake Gittes's earlier responsibility for many turns of events in *Chinatown,* coupled with his ignorance of the magnitude of evil he confronts, doom him tragically to relive the devastating personal misfortune he had hoped to elude. Similarly in *One False Move,* Hurricane's complicity in facilitating Lila's moral decline sets in motion events that ultimately cause him to suffer deeply, in spite of his other, morally good traits and his efforts to avoid the consequences of his own unthinkingly racialized behavior.

Through the use of *noir* determinism and its borrowings from classical tragedy, director Carl Franklin and his fellow filmmakers thus present to white viewers a deeply troubling aspect of knowledge deriving from African-American double consciousness, namely, that as a social force white advantage may distort black lives in ruinous ways. It can induce them into crime even if they are "good people, Christian people," as Hurricane describes Lila and her family, because it can cause them great moral and psychological harm. Moreover, because whites are typically in a position of social superiority, they need not own up to their responsibility for this devastation. Instead, they may ignore, deflect, or seek to avoid the consequences of their handiwork.

Hurricane's ultimate fate, however, narratively represents the fact that they too may be damaged by their position of advantage, if perhaps not in immediately physical ways like his, then through moral corruption and decay of their souls. A moral rot can set in that may cause them to ignore responsibilities and obligations which they should recognize toward their fellow human beings. In this way the film explores the same set of white supremacist beliefs and actions that Lewis Gordon describes in *Bad Faith and Antiblack Racism* as constituting a misanthropic consciousness into which many people fall by means of such mental postures. Leaving aside for a moment all the damage such an attitude does to others, lurking within it "is the total elimination of the social world,"[23] Gordon informs us, for this way of thinking and perceiving severely truncates whites' ability to achieve connection with others and live fully human lives. Possessing such an attitude profoundly limits whites' humanity and their capacity to fully appreciate its possibilities, making them gravely stunted human beings, to say nothing of the havoc it wreaks on those who come in contact with them.[24] Whole dimensions of human interactions, lifestyles, sensitivity, and even language become off-limits as a condition of acquiescing to this form—in many ways what remains the prevailing norm— of whiteness. Thus one aspect of being white revealed by *One False Move* is that

23. Gordon, *Bad Faith and Antiblack Racism,* 184.
24. Ibid., 182–84.

whiteness typically requires a cognitive, moral, and social amputation of one's full potential for being human, the results of which have disastrous effects for one's self and others, as it does for Hurricane and Lila.

One False Move thus dramatizes an alternative moral vision that directly challenges typical white perceptions of alleged reasons for African-American lawbreaking as well as presenting ways in which racist beliefs can cause grave moral retardation for whites themselves. The highest-ranking representative of justice turns out to be the source of immorality, and his presumption of white superiority lies at the root of his own personal injuries and moral insensitivity. In addition, it has significantly motivated Lila's descent into a life of crime. As she resignedly tells her brother Ronnie (Kevin Hunter) when she first returns to Star City and he explains to her that she cannot visit their home because of the ongoing police investigation, "I already *look* guilty. Looking guilty is being guilty for black people; you know that . . . "

Lila's assertion concurs with many black philosophers' descriptions of whiteness's standard perspective on black human beings: this person is black; therefore this person has committed a crime.[25] By foregrounding and juxtaposing such mundane aspects of the black world with the misanthropic perceptions so typical of white America, *One False Move* means to show that criminality is often not so much a choice as a nearly irresistible, imposed fate for many African Americans because it is drummed into them by so much of their life experience that such a future is their destiny. Messages like this are often difficult to defy, particularly if Moody-Adams is correct in assessing the typical impact of such circumstances on one's self-respect and self-esteem. If one is continually told one is no good, it will be hard not to live down to that expectation.[26]

Moreover, as Gordon argues, the causes of such expectations are phenomena that also harm those who maintain these presumptive perceptions by preventing them from living fully human lives—lives that take advantage of humanity's social dimension in the most complete sense possible.[27] In this sense white superiority prevents human flourishing for whites as well as blacks, a point that Gordon, Laurence Thomas, Martin Luther King Jr., James Baldwin, and others have made again and again.[28] Thus the film urges

25. Fanon, "Lived Experience of the Black," 199; Gordon, *Bad Faith and Antiblack Racism*, 101; Mills, *Racial Contract*, 46–49. As Gordon notes, his description concurs with not only Fanon, but also literary theorist Henry Louis Gates, who argues that, in terms of criminality, race is "downright determinative"; see Gates, "Statistical Stigmata," in *Deconstruction and the Possibility of Justice*, ed. Drucilla Cornell, Michel Rosenfeld, and David Carlson (New York: Routledge, 1992), 333.

26. Moody-Adams, "Social Construction of Self-Respect," esp. 262–63.

27. Gordon, *Bad Faith and Antiblack Racism*, 183–84.

28. Ibid., 182–84; Laurence Thomas, "Moral Flourishing in an Unjust World," *Journal of Moral Education* 22 (1993): 83–96; Thomas, "Self-Respect, Fairness, and Living Morally," in *A Companion to African-American Philosophy*, ed. Tommy L. Lott and John P. Pittman (London: Blackwell, 2002), 293–305; Martin Luther King, Jr., "Letter from Birmingham City Jail" (1963),

its white viewers in particular to reconsider and reexamine what they see as the limits of humanity in order to overcome the truncated consciousness they may currently possess regarding African Americans because of socially embedded racist beliefs and perceptions. Moreover, as Diawara has noted, the film's violent opening sequence serves as a reminder that this moral vision is not confined to a backward rural South populated by ignorant rednecks like Hurricane, but extends to modern urban centers such as Los Angeles, where African Americans typically labor under similar misperceptions and presumptions of guilt.[29]

Alignment, Point of View, and Empathetic Response to Lila

At the same time that *One False Move* urges viewers to develop a kind of critical empathy for Hurricane, it also encourages a rather different sort of critical empathy for Lila, who becomes the focus of the story in the latter third of the film, much like what occurs with respect to the character Judy (Kim Novak) in Alfred Hitchcock's "technicolor *film noir*" *Vertigo* (1958).[30] Audience alignment switches from the investigative team of Hurricane, Cole, and McFeely to Lila, just as Hitchcock's film switches viewer alignment from John "Scottie" Ferguson (James Stewart) to the character played by Novak in the last thirty-six minutes of that film. As a result we come to see the characters involved in vastly different ways.

I take it that this change in audience character alignment is what Franklin means when he says that the film "goes from genre piece to a character piece." The film switches from what Bordwell refers to as "detective narration," where the film encourages audience members to look for information and put it together in order to grasp the story's development, to a more "melodramatic narration," where a wider range of access to characters makes the film more emotionally expressive.[31] In the last third of *One False Move* we have the opportunity to empathize with Lila in ways not offered earlier, for we come to see that her situation was not entirely her choice, but something into which she was seduced by Hurricane and his racialized moral insensitivity, as well as by more general racial expectations in American society. The narrative illuminates her predicament by the way it begins to follow her more closely spatially

---

reprinted in *African-American Philosophy: Selected Readings*, ed. Tommy L. Lott (Upper Saddle River, N.J.: Prentice-Hall, 2002), esp. 247; James Baldwin, *The Fire Next Time* (New York: Dell, 1964), esp. 127–37. (As the references to King and Baldwin should indicate, this view goes back a long way and is not confined merely to professional philosophers.)

29. Diawara, "Noir by Noirs," 275.

30. For the status of *Vertigo* as a *film noir*, see Silver and Ward, *Film Noir: An Encyclopedic Reference*, 392; Spicer, *Film Noir*, 81–83; Kelly Oliver and Benigno Trigo, *Noir Anxiety* (Minneapolis: University of Minnesota Press, 2003), 97–114; and George J. Stack, "*Vertigo* as Existential Film," *Philosophy Today* 30 (1986), 246–64. (The quoted phrase is from 246 of the last article.)

31. Bordwell, *Narration in the Fiction Film*, 64–73.

and temporally, rather than the investigative team of McFeely, Cole, and Hurricane, and through offering greater subjective access to her character.[32] Eventually, the narrative gives her the opportunity to tell us her version of her story, Hurricane's role in it, and how she feels about her fate. These revelations are a decided change from her earlier opacity as one of the mysterious objects of police investigation—"our mystery girl," as McFeely calls her.

Lila's confrontation with Hurricane provides additional subjective access to him as well. We understand both characters better through their interactions and responses, plus we see and hear their expressions of inner feeling. Through this change in alignment to Lila, then, audience members' range of knowledge about her is substantially enhanced. And so are their possible emotional responses, as this change to more melodramatic narration introduces greater opportunities for emotional effects.[33] This change in alignment thus makes possible the critical revelation of the depth of Hurricane's racism as well as a deeper audience connection with Lila. Knowing more of her story obliges us to feel more deeply for her because we come to understand that her moral downward mobility was not entirely her fault, but that she was in many ways propelled into this alternative by Hurricane's presumptions of advantage and ignorance. Audience members feel with her as well as for her because she acquires a more complete humanity and connection with them, which are dimensions she lacked earlier in the film. Lila becomes not simply an opaque and desperate fugitive from justice or the abused lover of coked-up and trigger-happy Ray. By losing her opacity she becomes representative of a full-fledged human being who has been deeply hurt by Hurricane, among others, but who more generally has been damaged by the multiply barbed restrictions of race in America. As someone who has anxiously sought love and approval from others, she has been badly treated by social institutions and individuals acting as their instrument. Her raced and gendered vulnerability becomes a focus of audience scrutiny and as a result raises the possibility of generating a deeper, more thoroughgoing compassion for her, as well as a sense of commonality. Viewers come to realize that, just as they may be hurt by unfair restrictions or the insensitivity of others, so too has Lila.

Although she is the nominal *femme fatale* in *One False Move*, Lila is a character for whom viewers develop a great deal of empathy because they acquire detailed internal access to her predicament. She is more "guilty" of being black and seeking love and approval than she is of freely choosing a path of criminality. By switching focus to her character and aligning viewers with her rather than the investigative team of policemen who pursue her, *One False Move* generates not only a more sympathetic understanding of Lila, but also a more empathetic one. In the last third of the narrative, as viewers gain internal

---

32. For a fuller explanation of spatial-temporal attachment and subjective access as part of character alignment for viewers, see the introduction and Smith, *Engaging Characters*, 83–84, 142–81.

33. Bordwell, *Narration in the Fiction Film*, 73; Smith, *Engaging Characters*, 153.

FIG. 17   Cynda Williams's character pleads with a reluctant Hurricane (Bill Paxton) to tell their son that he is the child's father (*One False Move*, 1992).

access to this narrative figure, the film encourages them to imagine her much more fully from the inside rather than merely objectively—from the outside, as it were.

It is also worth noting that, like Lila, *femmes fatales* in classic American *film noir* have often attempted to use their sexuality and beauty to escape traps of poverty and social confinement. Even some of the worst fatal women, including Phyllis Dietrichson (Barbara Stanwyck) in *Double Indemnity*, Velma Valento (Claire Trevor) in *Murder, My Sweet*, Kitty Collins (Ava Gardner) in *The Killers* (Robert Siodmak, 1946), Coral Chandler (Lizabeth Scott) in *Dead Reckoning* (John Farrow, 1947), and Kathie Moffat (Jane Greer) in *Out of the Past* have backstories that imply a certain depth to their actions because through these details the workings of the *femme fatale* become clearer as desperate efforts to overcome the social disadvantages of class.

In *One False Move* Lila similarly relies on her sexuality and beauty to seek escape from oppressive class origins, with racial dimensions added. But rather than remaining largely opaque, like the standard *femmes fatales* of classic *film noir*, whose subjective depths we typically only glimpse, Lila becomes a much more transparent, understandable character. In a very un-*femme fatale* way, we come to see, she is motivated as a mother, a sister, and a daughter to take the actions she does. She steals Ray and Pluto's money, for example, in order to help care for her son and the other members of her family. The last thing she says to her brother is, "Put the money in the bank." Clearly, she does not intend to return it to her accomplices or use it for her own selfish purposes, since she knows by this time she is a fugitive from justice being sought in Star City itself. Moreover, the whole reason she has traveled there in the first place is because she wants to "see [her] people." Unlike the merely verbal backstories typically given to traditional *femmes fatales,* viewers actually follow Lila on her return home and see her functioning as sister and mother.[34] The last third of *One False Move* is predominantly Lila's in terms of alignment and allegiance. I would argue that this change in perspective helps to deconstruct Lila as a *femme fatale* stereotype, which typically depends on its inscrutability and opacity to work effectively.[35]

Subjective access to Lila also provides further depth that works against her status as a stock "tragic mulatta" figure. Consistent with what literary critic Justus J. Nieland has argued, I would point out that the narrative of *One False Move* provides her with far too much critical depth and agency to remain within the stereotypical version of that concept.[36] To use such categories without acknowledging the ways in which the film critically complicates the figure of Lila is to miss much of this character's point. While it is true that she embodies some of the typical features of this stock narrative figure, as a character she also achieves a subtlety through her detailed depiction that belies a simplistic, cookie-cutter application of such a narrative stereotype. The way in which Franklin and his fellow filmmakers challenge viewers' understanding of this concept—its history, meaning, and the unquestioned presumptions that accompany it, for example—means that Lila reaches far beyond the boundaries of the tragic mulatta idea, and indeed explodes it as ordinarily conceived.

I would further argue that a critical detonation of the concept is a major dimension of what these filmmakers hope to accomplish in the way that they consciously configure this character by offering such extended and detailed access to her in the final part of the film. To use concepts like "tragic mulatta" straightforwardly to understand what the narrative presents may get viewers part of the way in understanding what the film offers, but at the risk of failing to appreciate how it also critically interrogates the idea.[37] Conceptualizing Lila as a tragic mulatta figure does help to pinpoint matters of race mixing and boundary crossing, as Nieland points out, but to recognize this character as only serving those functions is to miss the point of why Franklin and his collaborators give over the last third of the film to Lila in terms of alignment and allegiance, just as it would be a mistake to dismiss the last third of *Vertigo* as unimportant to our understanding of the characters Judy and Scottie. As

34. Martin, *Mean Streets and Raging Bulls,* 141, asserts similarly that Lila "transcends the cinematic archetype of the *femme fatale.*"

35. See, for example, Cimberli Kearns, "Fascinating Knowledge," *Film and Philosophy* 3 (1996): 24–37; Craig N. Bach, "Nietzsche and *The Big Sleep:* Style, Women, and Truth," *Film and Philosophy* 5/6 (2002): 45–59; and Mary Ann Doane, *Femmes Fatales: Feminism, Film Theory, and Psychoanalysis* (London: Routledge, 1991).

36. Justus J. Nieland, "Race-ing *Noir* and Re-placing History: The Mulatta and Memory in *One False Move* and *Devil in a Blue Dress,*" *Velvet Light Trap,* no. 43 (Spring 1999): 63–77.

37. I would argue that this perspective is precisely the mistake of *noir* scholar Foster Hirsch in his assessment of *One False Move.* He argues for an understanding of the film purely from the perspective of its embodiment of stereotypes (*Detours and Lost Highways,* 302).

Nieland argues, Lila's character lays bare historical fictions about such conceptualizations and critically engages ongoing social presumptions that resulted from them.[38] I would underscore in contrast to Nieland's approach, however, that the filmmakers are consciously and critically working toward such goals, not blindly feeling their way toward these insights because of some political unconscious or an irrepressible, deterministic operation of psychological forces stemming from white guilt about race mixing. I do not deny that some of these factors may have had a hand in shaping the film, but I would also argue that to rely solely on such stances unfairly belittles the conscious, active efforts of the film's creators. Given the film's subtle structure, they must have worked consciously toward the goal of eliciting these critical reflections because it is evident in the way the film is put together. Moreover, if we take seriously the thoughtful commentary and interviews Carl Franklin has provided regarding the film, our best option would be to assume the filmmakers' artistry was self-conscious and explicit.[39]

Sympathetic Racists and Audience Allegiance in Black and White

In ways that parallel the explicitly philosophical work of Gordon, Mills, and others, *One False Move* renders much more problematic typical audience allegiances to certain white characters through a critical depiction of one such character's attitude toward race. As in *Do the Right Thing*, such a self-conscious depiction of a white narrative figure encourages audience members to thoughtfully reflect on what it means to be white, as well as what that means for one's self and those with whom one comes into contact. The film also mobilizes audience empathy and understanding for its character Lila, responses that are similarly aimed at encouraging viewers to reflect on dominant beliefs about what it means to be black in America and the implications those beliefs may have for allegiances with African-American characters. Its "epistemological twist" two-thirds of the way through the narrative to humanize and subjectivize its *femme fatale*/tragic mulatta character undermines conventional understandings of such concepts, and in doing so the film turns back onto the viewer the use of such stereotypical conceptualizations.[40] It also aims to raise further questions in the viewer's mind about ordinary white understandings of the interrelations between race, moral action, and what counts as justice. While it remains true that white viewers may resist these calls for reflection and self-examination by means of various readily available strategies, the film

38. Nieland, "Race-ing *Noir* and Re-placing History," 71.

39. Franklin, commentary, *One False Move*, DVD; Beverly Gray, "Triple Threat: Interview with Carl Franklin," *Creative Screenwriting* 4, no. 1 (Spring 1997): esp. 17–18. See also David Orr's interesting analysis of the script, "The Rural Noir of *One False Move*," *Creative Screenwriting* 7, no. 5 (September 2000), 55–59.

40. Wilson, "Film and Epistemology." See also his "Transparency and Twist." Again, I use Wilson's concept to apply to characters, rather than to the narrative itself, as Wilson does.

also substantially reduces the plausibility of employing these strategies that would otherwise help viewers avoid thoughtful mental activity.

This chapter has so far focused almost exclusively on how white viewers typically see the film. I wish also to address briefly how other audiences may perceive its narrative. For example, *One False Move* no doubt reaffirms much of what many black viewers previously believed regarding a sympathetic racist character like Hurricane. Accordingly, they would probably grasp much more quickly than most whites many of the plot turns because their typically deeper knowledge of race would permit them to understand these turns' significance more readily, as well as the meanings of various adumbrations earlier in the narrative. The film would thus offer to black viewers a satisfying affirmation of knowledge they already possessed but that frequently lacked confirmation in the culture at large. In addition, *One False Move* may develop for black viewers a more modest set of insights into sympathetic racist characters as well as the African-American characters around them. For example, black viewers might well ponder once the film is over why an experienced Los Angeles police detective character like John McFeely would fail to take Hurricane's racism seriously. Through reflecting on his actions they might speculate that he does so perhaps as a protective defense mechanism required by working with white folks so much, or perhaps they might see it as another, rather different result of the epistemology of ignorance that takes form in the consciousness of many blacks; namely, that living under regimes of white supremacy can induce nonwhites to accept some dimensions of their alleged inferiority.[41] For black viewers, then, McFeely's character might well prompt contemplation of how racism impairs the psychological workings of its victims.

Such viewers might also gain deeper insight into the more general psychological workings of individuals like Hurricane, who in spite of some good moral qualities is nevertheless unable to acknowledge full humanity in blacks, and what that inability might mean for those who are subject to his actions. In general the epistemological twist of the plot in switching alignment from the police investigative team to Lila would probably be less profound for these viewers as well, but they might still find other cognitive pleasures in watching the film, such as those just mentioned or perhaps others concerning the affirmation of different outlooks and beliefs that seldom arise in mainstream cultural products like film.

In general, *One False Move* offers viewers a crucially important example of how sympathetic racist narrative figures might be used. In particular, it provides a lush illustration of how such a character may provide white viewers deeper insight into the operations of racialized beliefs about blacks in the context of morality and justice. Moreover, it does so in a way that is not unsympathetic to the predicament in which many whites find themselves, namely, that of functioning largely *unconsciously* within practices of thinking and acting according to which they have been raised. The film also presupposes that

41. Mills, *Racial Contract*, 87–88.

when confronted with the contradiction of their unthinking beliefs and actions with principles of justice that they hold dear—such as that all persons should be treated equally—whites can recognize the inconsistency of their actions, revise their behavior, and begin to work at least weakly toward reconciling themselves with those they have harmed.

Such a depiction of a sympathetic racist character, then, seeks to illustrate how whites have a *choice* regarding the acceptance of their own whiteness.[42] In this sense *One False Move* shares a feature with melodrama, namely, that such narratives may be used to make clear to audience members contradictory beliefs commonly held in a particular society, and that there exists a need to choose between them.[43] This *noir* narrative thus offers up the possibility of visualizing how presumptions of white superiority that remain embedded in social practices and beliefs contradict the principle of equality upheld by most white Americans, thereby making clear the need for a change in their belief structures, as well as in their overall outlook and any actions based on these beliefs. While the film does not let whites off the hook regarding their responsibility for racially skewed actions and beliefs, it does allow that these matters may not have been of their own choosing and that there is hope for the possibility of change in their beliefs such that they could think and act in ways that would result in fairer, more equal treatment of blacks, as well as more humanizing social roles for themselves.

---

42. Ibid., esp. 107–9.

43. John G. Cawelti, *Adventure, Mystery, and Romance: Formula Stories as Art and Popular Culture* (Chicago: University of Chicago Press, 1976), 276–80. For the use in an African-American cinematic context of melodrama's capacity to indicate contradictory social beliefs, see my "Race, Rationality, and Melodrama."

[Racism] requires in whites the cultivation of patterns of affect and empathy that are only weakly, if at all, influenced by nonwhite suffering.
—Charles W. Mills, *The Racial Contract*

In this 1995 film about low-level drug-dealers who sell their products 'round the clock (hence the title), Spike Lee uses *noir* conventions to reveal how drug culture may offer deceptively alluring ways out of seemingly hopeless traps of poverty and unemployment for desperate young African Americans. This strategy, in a way, is nothing new for American cinema. The early 1930s gangster films, such as *Little Caesar* (Mervyn LeRoy, 1930), *Public Enemy* (William Wellman, 1931), and *Scarface* (Howard Hawks, 1932), depicted how oppressed "borderline," not-quite-fully white minorities of the Prohibition era—the Italians and the Irish—participated in the illegal drug culture of alcohol to create paths of escape from similar traps of misery and joblessness.[1] Using the strategy here to convey the predicament of more recent ghetto inhabitants, the opening scene of *Clockers* in the flagpole court characterizes drug-dealing's allure as "the most glamorous and remunerative life option for black adolescents," that is, within their severely circumscribed experience.[2] The film illustrates this attractiveness by focusing on the drug trade's tempting promise as a way out from the confinement and desperation saturating these adolescents' existence. In the process, it also depicts the ways in which distorted knowledge and teaching permeate much teenage African-American experience.

The film opens with the credits superimposed over a montage of crime scene photographs depicting half-grown teenagers dead from gunshot wounds intercut with murals dedicated to fallen children and spectators peering curiously over crime scene tape. Then, after some establishing shots, the action begins in the courtyard of a Brooklyn housing project with a group of young teenagers arguing about Chuck D., Tupac Shakur, and whether or not being a hard-core rapper requires committing actual violence. Several members of

---

1. Regarding the ways in which Italian and Irish Americans used Prohibition as a means of social advancement and how early 1930s gangster films used this social fact to encourage sympathy for its protagonists, see Munby, *Public Enemies, Public Heroes*, esp. 39–65. For more about "borderline" whites as not quite fully white and hierarchies within whiteness itself, see Mills, *Racial Contract*, 78–81.

2. Leonard Quart, review of *Clockers*, *Cineaste* 21, no. 4 (1995): 64.

the group vehemently argue is that hard-core gangsta rap appeals to them because it is so bleakly negative, which matches what they see, feel, and experience in their lives. Cornel West has written about this "nihilistic threat" to black America by defining it as a sense of "life without meaning, hope, and love," rather than by the more complicated philosophical meaning given to it by Nietzsche and others.[3] West notes that such feelings have a long history in black America; yet in the past traditional black civic and religious organizations provided a bulwark against such despair for most African Americans. By the early 1990s, however, these traditional institutions were substantially less effective, making this form of nihilism much more widespread. Arguing that nihilism is "a disease of the soul" (18), West contends that its cure requires affirmation of self-worth (19).

In the case of *Clockers,* I argue that Lee helps his viewers to realize that such affirmations of self-worth are precisely what the teenagers in the flagpole court lack. Struggling with societal perceptions imposed on them that they are lesser human beings "naturally" inclined toward violence, sexual predation, immorality, and poverty, many black youth find solace in the simplistically reductive idea that the truest, most "authentic" form of gangsta rap would require that one actually be a gangsta. As black individuals indoctrinated into a society where white superiority is the norm, hard-core gangsta rap, promoted as the "authentic" voice of the "truly disadvantaged" in the form of alleged gangstas who have chosen to rebel against their oppression by commiting actual crimes and living to boast about it in their songs, harmonizes with what these young teenagers have been encouraged to think about being black in America.

While this perspective on gangsta rap clearly has flaws stemming from misconceptions about what counts as "authenticity" in art, such as the idea that its images and metaphors require some sort of direct connection to reality in order to back them up, there is a perverse logic to this perspective that is reminiscent of Pecola's desire for blue eyes. No doubt it appeals to many young teens because when taken literally gangsta rap transparently represents what they have come to believe about themselves and their life prospects. As Michele Moody-Adams has argued, demeaning societal "lessons" can influence black youth to "mistrust themselves" to such an extent that they may "become unable to distinguish self-destructive behavior from behavior that actually promotes one's well-being."[4] A confusion like this would easily reinforce the nihilistic perceptions offered here by these young characters.

Such flawed self-perception may even promote gang membership. As Moody-Adams further argues, many children are drawn into gangs as a way to reaffirm self-respect and to counteract a sense of social isolation. But ironically, she notes, "in viewing his membership in a gang as an affirmation of

---

3. Cornel West, "Nihilism in Black America," in *Race Matters* (Boston: Beacon Press, 1993), 14–15.

4. Moody-Adams, "Social Construction of Self-Respect," 262, 263.

self-respect, the gang member reveals just how completely he has internalized society's effort to marginalize him. For he has come to see himself precisely as he is seen by those who wish to exclude him: as essentially a threatening 'outlaw,' a permanent possibility of danger" (263). Oppressive social circumstances inflicted on young blacks, then, may influence them to feel so negatively about their own self-worth that they embrace perceptions of themselves as "nothing," adopt the thug life of gangsterdom, and express an attraction to hard-core rap as giving voice to their "true" inner feelings as instilled in them by society. It takes no leap of imagination to see this sort of outlook as nihilistic in the everyday sense described by West. More to the point here, viewers may see it depicted by means of the argument Lee constructs for his characters in this sequence that opens the film.[5]

Cultivating Empathy for a Clocker

The film's lead character, Strike (Mekhi Phifer), shows himself to be supremely uninterested in the subtleties of the opening debate just analyzed. He rudely breaks up the argument among his crew members and orders them to get back to work, pointing out that they have to get about their business and make some money, which is their main purpose for being out there, not deliberating the finer points of rapperdom as a reflection of black life. Once everyone returns to their proper place, the narrative offers viewers an example of these young entrepreneurs at work. A customer furtively appears, and one of Strike's crew forces himself off the benches to inquire what he would like to purchase. Like any cost-conscious shopper, the customer asks what the specials are for today ("red caps") before deciding to buy two of them. The crew looks around carefully and after an elaborate exchange of signals to indicate that no one is watching, another crew member fetches the product from a "safe" apartment and deposits it in a trash can for the customer to pick up. Everything is done so that these activities will attract as little attention as possible, and the actual events taking place will escape detection by those who do not have the special knowledge to spot it. This sense of secrecy is emphasized cinematically by shooting the sequence as if from surveillance cameras.[6] As critic Leonard Quart observes, the film's detailed depiction of drug-dealing dynamics clearly shows "how much intelligence is wasted in the elaborate and furtive process of making a sale,"[7] while also implicitly showing how much potential exists in these kids for constructive activity, if only it could be directed into more positive outlets.

5. That the sequence is Lee's inspiration, if not completely his creation, is confirmed by the co-screenwriter Richard Price. See Leonard Quart and Albert Auster, "A Novelist and Screenwriter Eyeballs the Inner City: An Interview with Richard Price," *Cineaste* 22, no. 1 (1996): 15.

6. See cinematographer Malik Hassan Sayeed's remarks on the sequence in Stephen Pizzello, "Between 'Rock' and a Hard Place," in Fuchs, *Spike Lee: Interviews*, 108.

7. Leonard Quart, "Spike Lee's *Clockers:* A Lament for the Urban Ghetto," *Cineaste* 22, no. 1 (1996): 10.

Of course, the hidden knowledge required by these illegal activities is two-sided: it must be both unknown and known, for otherwise such commerce is not possible. The price Strike and his crew must pay for staying in business is serial random raids by the police. Arriving immediately on the heels of this scene but too late to stop any actual transactions, the cops instead harass and humiliate these young entrepreneurs. Strike, for example, must submit to a body cavity search in public, while his mother watches from her apartment window. When the cops come up empty-handed, they turn to insulting and roughing him and the other crew members up. While such harassment typically produces no arrests because those members who are visible have been careful not to carry any drugs themselves, the stress of these encounters has given Strike an ulcer, which he tries in vain to calm with milky soft drinks.

Nor is this the only kind of surveillance to which these adolescents must submit. Strike's boss Rodney Little (Delroy Lindo) cruises the projects like an overseer to make sure that his crews are not goofing off, that they are always working hard to make him money. And if the police are one kind of oppressive presence, Rodney is quite another. Representing himself as the divinely inspired general of his juvenile drug dealer army, this veteran supplier of street product symbolizes the paternal taken to insane extremes. By turns kind and violent, Rodney both sweet-talks and badgers Strike and the other clockers, showing a father's concern at one moment and a pimp's heartlessness the next. He tells Strike that he regards his dealers as his children and Strike in particular as the son who will be his sword and his staff. He gives Strike Mylanta to soothe the younger man's raging ulcer and advises him to see a doctor, self-righteously sermonizing, "You got to take care of yourself."

Yet Rodney also keeps Strike on the benches in the flagpole court supervising middle-schoolers pushing crack to desperate addicts while others work the safe, clean, and easy jobs of selling cocaine to white suburbanites from the order windows of fast-food restaurants. Rodney admits as well to "bloodying" Strike on the murder case around which most of the film focuses. This middle-level distributor of street drugs confesses that he needed "something personal" on Strike, so that his knowledge of the younger man's involvement in a murder would act as insurance that Strike would never turn Rodney in—and always keep Strike working for him. Ever manipulative, Rodney uses knowledge deftly as a weapon. More than once he tells the young clocker, "Don't you know I know everything?" thereby seeking to characterize his knowledge as omniscient and thus an additional tool of confinement.

As one of the few available male role models around the projects who happens to be doing well, Rodney knows Strike looks up to him, so he uses it against the younger man, subverting the latter's admiration for his own personal advantage. He knows, for example, that Strike and the other youths in the area desperately seek a way out of the projects and look to him for answers, so he modulates his pitch for the drug trade in those terms by means of a speech so familiar to Strike he can mouth it from memory whenever he hears Rodney launch into it. The older man lectures the many children who hang out in his candy store that they can buy houses for their mothers and acquire the wealth and status they crave through clocking.

From the outset, then, the film uses a *noirish* thematic determinism to establish a modestly favorable attitude toward Strike by depicting the dangerous and oppressive circumstances under which he must live.[8] The photo stills under the credits as well as the film's early drug-dealing sequences offer audience members a detailed understanding of what he and the other youths must constantly face in order to do business, as well as their likely fate. At the same time, like many classic *noir* films, *Clockers* seeks to articulate some insight into the deceptive allure that criminality might have for these children. Indeed, the narrative clearly aims to achieve these goals: Lee deliberately revised earlier versions of the script in order to develop the psychology of Strike's character more fully and align audiences with this low-level drug dealer. As Lee himself has noted, the film's narrative point of view is Strike's.[9] Regarding Lee's changes in the script from previous versions, film studies scholar Paula Massood has noted that these alterations "expanded audience identification" with Strike and made him "more sympathetic."[10] Understanding that *Clockers* tells its story mainly from Strike's point of view thus becomes crucially important because such a realization allows viewers to grasp that the narrative prompts viewers to see, feel, and comprehend criminal activities from the lawbreaker's perspective, not from the more typical viewpoint of investigating cops. Moreover, given the social circumstances also portrayed early in the narrative, this difference in point of view signifies a racialized perspective that viewers would expect to see explored more extensively as the film proceeds.

Lee accomplishes these goals by exploiting *noir*'s historical development of criminalistic, good-bad characters and its associated strategies. As the narrative unfolds, for example, viewers see more and more deeply into Strike and his point of view because he is a physical participant in most of the film's sequences and the narrative gives us extensive subjective access to what he thinks about them by means of his reactions and comments.[11] I would further enhance Massood's observations, however, with the point that even in the film's early sequences Strike's hardness as a ruthless ghetto entrepreneur is undermined by his pained reactions to his ulcer and the admission that he hasn't "got the stomach for this shit anymore," which speak directly to our allegiance with him. *Clockers* employs *noir* conventions to address the sympathetic construction of a morally ambiguous black character. Lee employs these

---

8. The *noir* dimensions of *Clockers* have also been noted by various critics, including Naremore, *More Than Night*, 246; Guerrero, "Circus of Dreams and Lies," 347; and Martin, *Mean Streets and Raging Bulls*, 59, 82, 137. See also my "Black on White," esp. 98–106.

9. George Khoury, "Big Words: An Interview with Spike Lee"; Delroy Lindo, "Delroy Lindo on Spike Lee," in Fuchs, *Spike Lee: Interviews*, 149, 172.

10. Paula J. Massood, *Black City Cinema: African American Urban Experiences in Film* (Philadelphia: Temple University Press, 2003), 190, 191.

11. As explained in the introduction, these narrative dimensions are just what it means to be aligned with a character. See also Smith, *Engaging Characters*, 83–85, 142–81.

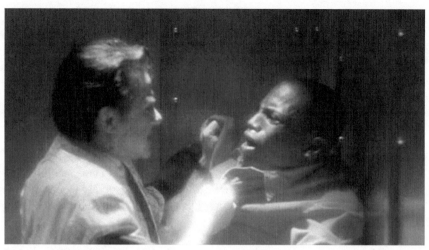

FIG. 18   NYPD homicide detective Rocco Klein (Harvey Keitel) tries to force Strike (Mekhi Phifer) to confess to a crime he did not commit (*Clockers*, 1995).

conventions to create a central narrative figure who appeals to us in marginally sympathetic ways. In the same spirit that classic *noir* sometimes used character entrapment to encourage a modicum of audience sympathy for what were otherwise morally bad characters, such as Alex Sebastian at the conclusion of *Notorious* or Harry Lime (Orson Welles) at the end of *The Third Man* (Carol Reed, 1949), so Lee urges his viewers to minimally sympathize with Strike by showing him as seemingly trapped in a set of oppressive circumstances. In addition, Strike's vulnerability, symbolized by his raging stomach ulcer, reveals his decided ambivalence about (if not a revulsion for) his current occupation, which grows progressively more intense as he draws closer and closer to the fate predicted by the crime scene photos under the opening credits. His physical pain, then, represents a psychic pain that encourages viewers to acknowledge his humanity—a humanity he shares with audience members.[12]

By almost immediately revealing Strike's entrapment and vulnerability in spite of his moral reprehensibility, Lee secures not only a modest possibility for favorably disposing his audience toward this character, but also the possibility to empathetically understanding his predicament. As I noted in Chapter 2, such a strategy is similarly at work in *noir* classics such as *Double Indemnity* and *The Postman Always Rings Twice,* as well as in more gangster and career criminal-oriented *noirs* like *The Asphalt Jungle* and *Night and the City* (Jules Dassin, 1950). Strike's combination of positive and negative characteristics follows a long line of similar *noir* protagonists whose complex mixture of traits often gave viewers grounds for not only sympathizing but empathizing with otherwise blameworthy figures.

12. See also Mulhall, *On Film,* 33–34; Cavell, *Claim of Reason,* 87ff., 429ff., and passim.

These *noir* conventions prove their utility for Lee and his fellow filmmakers by giving them the opportunity to encourage audience members to develop favorable allegiances to characters despite racialized beliefs that might otherwise stand in the way. As *noir* protagonists were often developed to elicit our favor in spite of their criminality or even moral reprehensibility, so Lee develops Strike to urge viewers to ally themselves in minimally positive ways to him and in this manner bypass certain prejudicial beliefs involving race. Rather than presume or reinforce elements of standard audience belief schemata, the narrative calls into action other beliefs about fairness, equality, and humanity in order to overcome many audience members' initial belief structures regarding race—and, for that matter, class. Strike turns out not to be a stereotypical black drug dealer. Instead, he is a morally confused, desperate teenager who possesses painful vulnerabilities, which humanizes him much more clearly for viewers.

As we see more of Strike, we become more firmly allied to him, even if that allegiance remains decidedly ambivalent. Another way Lee accomplishes this goal is by showing us Strike's qualms about murder, a necessary means of advancement in his line of work. When Rodney suggests that fellow drug-dealer Darryl Adams (Steve White) has "got to be got" and Strike seize the opportunity, the young clocker hesitates and asks whether Rodney can find someone else to do the job. Later we see Strike pacing and anxious in front of Darryl's place of employment, unable to generate the nerve required to kill the person who stands in the way of his moving up the ladder to a more secure and estimable position in his chosen profession. His reservations about murder as a form of career advancement also lead him to further procrastinate by entering the bar across the street from the fast-food restaurant where Adams sells drugs. It is there that Strike runs into his older brother, Victor (Isaiah Washington), and fatefully describes Adams's moral evil to his inebriated sibling, as well as the need to do something about such neighborhood problems. Toward the end of the film we hear Strike confess that he "didn't have the heart to do Darryl," an admission that not only reinforces Strike's weakness, but also points to the fact that even though he may be a drug dealer, he cannot bring himself to be a murderer, a moral distinction that indicates some positive core to Strike's values.[13]

As viewers we also see this character's socially attractive traits. First, we should note that actor Mekhi Phifer's physical beauty works in favor of the character he plays.[14] Strike also possesses wit, as illustrated by the ways in which he can come back with cutting humor in response to the needling leveled at him by his prickly crew member Scientific (Sticky Fingaz) or the paternalistic housing project policeman Andre (Keith David). We see Strike's

---

13. Massood, *Black City Cinema*, 191 and 252 n. 29, makes this point as well.

14. Phifer has even been written up in fan magazines for his attractiveness. See, for example, "Mekhi Phifer," *People Weekly*, December 25, 1995, 124, and Evy Sheinkopf, "Who's the Babe? (actor Mekhi Phifer)," *Teen Magazine*, November 1997, 46.

intelligence as well in the careful and detailed ways in which he explains the finer points of drug dealing to his budding protégé, Tyrone (Pee Wee Love). While cultivating the younger boy in this way is clearly horrifying—and is meant to be so—it affords Lee the opportunity to show Strike's more positive side, for as he teaches Tyrone how to hustle, Strike also shows him kindness, generosity, and even a certain measure of benevolence.

Internalized Racism in Teaching and Explanation

Strike's grooming of Tyrone raises a further theme, for passing on knowledge through teaching constitutes another major dimension of the narrative. Like his own substitute father Rodney, Strike hopes to be a teacher and role model to those younger than him. He takes Tyrone under his wing because he wants to pass on what he knows to someone, and craves the admiration that accompanies such a position. Thus he begins tutoring the boy in the ways of drug dealing. "Profit's all in the cut—don't *never* forget that," he commands his new charge. He also lectures him on the proper etiquette of dealing—that is, don't ever use the drugs you sell—and what he sees as the cold, hard economic facts of life: "Any fly shit you want in this world, it costs money. And this is how you get it: hustling. And don't never forget that shit, neither." He quizzes Tyrone on the mathematics of drug sales, asking him to figure out how much profit will be made on the current deal, by way of arguing that Tyrone should stay in school—ironically, in order to be a better dealer. He even gives him a street name ("Shorty") as well as gifts to gain his favor and show the economic power of hustling. Strike's criminalistic instruction is thereby strangely mixed with more innocent qualities, as he seems to honestly enjoy giving the younger boy toys and joking around with him. In addition, viewers get to hear Strike's well-informed lecture about the history of Lionel trains and his prompting about when to say "thank you" for gifts. These interactions with the younger boy offer the opportunity to depict Strike's morally positive characteristics of generosity, intelligence, benevolence, and even, perhaps a bit perversely, courtesy. The narrative exhibition of these traits thus operates to mitigate the older boy's morally negative qualities, such as his willingness to deal drugs and live large from the misery of others.

Strike's tutelage of Tyrone also includes a deadly serious lecture about guns, street violence, and the drug-addicted, psychotic killer, Errol Barnes (Tom Byrd). While proudly showing off his handgun to the younger boy and impressing him with the distinction between fictional "TV-movie violence" and the real-life counterpart that accompanies actual drug-dealing, Strike warns Tyrone to especially watch out for the truly heartless thugs like Errol and brags, "If he ever try to creep up on me, I'm mo' gat his ass, and you best be ready to do the same shit, too," thereby planting in Tyrone instructions that he will tragically follow later in the film. Eventually, Tyrone's mother Iris (Regina Taylor) and Andre pressure Strike to drop Tyrone from his crew. For this Tyrone reproaches him, "You shouldn't have taught me," which reminds the audience of the misguided ways of looking at the world he has already learned from Strike and that he will put to use in the film's final act.

I would also add that, even in rejecting Tyrone, Strike's positive traits are implicated. While he has many self-interested reasons for driving the younger boy away, the narrative offers evidence that Strike does so for altruistic reasons as well. In their scenes together he seems to honestly like Tyrone. His most relaxed and gentle moments are spent tutoring his young protégé in the ways of street life. So late in the film I think it accurate to say that Strike also has Tyrone's best interests in mind when he kicks him out of the crew and drives him away, telling him to go home to his mother because he is too young to be involved in the nasty doings that constitute Strike's drug-dealing life. Because at this point in the narrative Strike himself is beginning to have serious doubts about continuing to clock, it does not make sense that he would want the character to whom he feels closest to take up the mantle that he himself is seeking to throw off. As Strike tries to repel his former pupil, he also begins to call him "Ty" or "Tyrone" rather than by his street name, which I would argue represents the older boy's desire to return his charge to a more innocent state, to a way of thinking before the clocking tutorials began. Sadly, it is already too late. In an errant effort to protect Strike, Tyrone shoots and kills Errol Barnes, who has been instructed by Rodney to assassinate Strike for an imagined betrayal, thus making Tyrone a twelve-year-old murderer and condemning him to take at least the first steps in following the path of his misguided teacher.

It is also worth noting that Lee shows no interest in glamorizing Strike's knowledge of hustling or his way of life. Viewers are not meant to empathize with the young drug dealer too closely, but to have some critical distance on him, so that we may judge the devastation he has brought upon himself and those around him. While Lee takes great pains to make Strike minimally sympathetic and even encourages us to empathetically understand him by means of depicting all the horrific pressures he faces, Strike's shortcomings as a teacher and role model are explicitly pointed out. As Andre tells him angrily as he beats Strike up after discovering the older boy's involvement in Tyrone's downfall, "I'm tired of excuses. You motherfuckers don't know nothing about nothing . . . 'It's not my fault!' Well, I'm not hearing that bullshit no more. It's motherfuckers like you who mugged Rosa Parks." As if to prove his point, Strike responds, "Who the fuck is Rosa Parks?"

Neither is Lee interested in portraying Strike as any sort of role model. Rather, through critically depicting his as well as Rodney's horrifying efforts to pass on what they know, Lee shows that in the absence of other accessible teachers, many black youths will turn to available sources like dealers for knowledge. Because they crave to know about the world around them and dealers are the ones achieving the greatest obvious success out on the streets, such criminals seem in their eyes to be logical sources to which to turn as examples to emulate in their efforts to gain the knowledge, wealth, and power needed to escape the torment of living in the projects. However, Strike and

Rodney's severely limited views of human life choices are shown with all their flaws and inhumanity in order to illustrate the perverse effects that an epistemology of ignorance may have on African Americans living in the crippling entanglements of poverty and ghettoized existence. Like gang members who have accepted the dominant culture's view of themselves as subhuman, Strike and Rodney represent blacks who have at least partly given in to the debased racialized view that they are capable of nothing better and therefore embrace outlaw activities.[15] Yet Lee also portrays this consequence of the epistemology of ignorance as something that can be eliminated through a different sort of teaching and education, which is no doubt why he places such fundamental stress on these matters in the narrative. In this manner, *Clockers* concurs with arguments advanced by Mills regarding the importance of grasping the consequences that racism may have on black psychology itself, in order that this damaging legacy might be better understood and overcome.[16]

Lee's revisions of the narrative in order to stress Strike's point of view thus aims at developing in his viewers, not only a modicum of sympathy for this clocker character, but also a certain empathy. Yet it is an empathy of critical understanding, not close personal identification. Viewers are not meant to imagine themselves as doing what Strike does in the strict identificational sense sometimes meant, but instead to grasp analytically how it might be humanly possible to choose the life path he has while at the same time realizing the error of that choice. Like Carl Franklin's critical use of empathy in *One False Move*, Lee permits both black and white audiences to comprehend what Strike does as well as why, without at the same time endorsing these decisions. As Berys Gaut has argued, this form of empathy as critical understanding may operate in film to help audiences grasp insights of which the narrative characters may not be capable, which I would contend is Lee's aim here.[17]

The film's aim to elicit empathetic critical understanding thus encourages audience members to distinguish between explaining what Strike does and justifying it. Clearly, the film does not *justify* desperate youths' decisions to sell drugs or willingly murder one another, but rather seeks to spur its audience into constructing explanations *why* it might seem plausible to half-grown teens to choose such a life course. The film aims to generate enough audience empathy to elucidate its characters' actions and choices, without validating or excusing them. Such a goal is presumably one reason why Lee and other artists creating this film thought it might put an end to the cycle of black films glamourizing drugs and gang violence. By portraying the impact such choices have on the social fabric of black life and their roots in the very perspectives

---

15. For additional arguments regarding the ways in which African Americans might succumb to prejudicial beliefs about themselves, see Fanon, "Lived Experience of the Black," 184–201, esp. 199; Gordon, *Bad Faith and Antiblack Racism,* 101–2; and many of the essays in *The Underclass Question,* ed. Bill E. Lawson (Philadelphia: Temple University Press, 1992).

16. Mills, *Racial Contract,* 88–89, 118–20.

17. Berys Gaut, "Identification and Emotion in Narrative Film," in Plantinga and Smith, *Passionate Views,* esp. 213–16.

their choosers hope to reject, Lee and others hoped to put an end to the attractiveness of such life choices and the films that glorified them.[18] Although they failed to achieve this goal, thoughtful viewers may appreciate this aim and how it shaped the narrative.

Oppression and Alternative Possibilities

Because Lee hopes to portray the pressures of racialized existence not only on criminals like Strike but also on those who choose a clearly moral course of life, the film shows African-American confinement through vicious social circumstance in a different way through Strike's older brother Victor. As Strike's *noir* double,[19] Victor has chosen the "legitimate" route to try escaping the ghetto. Instead of dealing drugs, he works two jobs, saves all the money he can, and is "never late" to work. As he tells the cops when he turns himself in for killing Darryl Adams, "I'm really trying to move us out of the projects. . . . I'm working, I'm saving, I'm trying to do the best I can . . . [to] provide those ends." Yet Victor, too, is not undamaged by the pressures and confinements that impinge on housing project inhabitants. As the narrative later reveals, he becomes ill when a clocker several years his junior offers him a month's wages every week just so drugs may be sold on the premises of the fast-food restaurant that Victor manages, yet hates. In his second job as a security guard, Victor sees the flash of comparable wads of cash and must endure the contempt of those who would and literally do spit on his determined efforts to work his way honestly out of the projects. As hired "muscle" he must also enforce many of the stereotypes he hopes to escape: as someone who can "speak their language," he is paid to find peaceful ways to turn away black teens who his employer thinks might rob her store.

The overwhelming pressures of these constricting roles and the easy money from the drug trade belittle Victor's tremendous efforts to get his family out of the projects legitimately, driving him to drown his sorrows with Scotch at the local bar. As Quart notes, this inner-city world is one "where violence and desperation are the norm. . . . [L]iving in the projects is like being under constant siege, and escaping it demands an enormous act of will."[20] For Victor, "the very construction of employment, health care, safe housing, raising children, and a great number of the mundane features of 'reasonable' day-to-day

---

18. Lindo, "Delroy Lindo on Spike Lee," 171–72.

19. See screenwriter Richard Price's comment on the good brother / bad brother structure of his story in Quart and Auster, "Novelist and Screenwriter," 17. The "doubling" of characters in *film noir* has been noted as a cinematic exploration of Freudian *doppelgänger* theory, often accomplished by means of mirror reflections, splitting characters into two versions of themselves either literally or metaphorically, or pairing distinct characters off in terms of their similarities and differences. Obvious examples include *The Dark Mirror* (Robert Siodmak, 1946) and *A Double Life* (George Cukor, 1948). See Silver and Ward, *Film Noir: An Encyclopedic Reference*, 83, 94–95.

20. Quart, "Spike Lee's *Clockers*," 9.

living demands extraordinary choices and efforts to be lived mundanely," as Lewis Gordon writes in *Fanon and the Crisis of European Man*.[21] Victor shows the strains of these extraordinary acts of will that he must perform every day by seeking solace in a bottle. He, too, is filled with rage and frustration that he feels compelled to dampen with his drug of choice, an alternative the ineffectiveness of which is reflected by Victor's involvement in Darryl Adams's murder. Thus, even though the film presents Victor as a far more sympathetic character than his younger brother Strike, he nonetheless turns out to be the shooter in the homicide case around which the narrative revolves.[22] Interestingly, Victor turns out to have the strength to kill, unlike his weaker sibling. Yet that strength does him little good, as he too succumbs to the oppressive weight of his racialized social circumstances.

The extended narrative depictions of Strike, Victor, and the racial burden of their social conditions thus offer audiences imaginative access to the ways in which some actions and life choices of black characters might be heavily determined by racialized social forces beyond their control. For white viewers in particular, *Clockers* provides ways to critically understand social phenomena that they might otherwise grasp by means of unquestioned beliefs and background assumptions that presume racist attitudes toward blacks such that choices to, say, deal drugs, would be presumed to result from some form of subhumanity, be it alleged intellectual inferiority, inclination to immorality, laziness, or other forms of human inadequacy. Yet through the use of critical empathy *Clockers* strongly urges its viewers to consider the *full* humanity of these characters who make disastrous life choices for themselves and others, as well as *why* they make such ruinous decisions. In such a fashion it urges its viewers to recognize and acknowledge the full humanity of these characters, while at the same time appreciating their flaws and offering up for consideration the injustice of the social conditions under which they live. The film further seeks to drive home its aims by contrasting these African-American narrative figures with a white character who is a different kind of sympathetic racist, the analysis of which I turn to next.

Rocco Klein as Sympathetic Racist Cop

In concert with its utilization of other typical *noir* features, *Clockers* is also a film about the acquisition, possession, and definition of knowledge. In viewers it further promotes the contemplation of change in one's fundamental systems of belief and action through the way in which Strike, for example, must think about changing his own way of thinking and acting. In doing so, the film links its *noir* epistemological interests to race. These dimensions of the film may thus be profitably understood as black *noirish* extensions of Bordwell's idea of

21. Gordon, *Fanon and the Crisis of European Man*, 42.
22. See also Massood, *Black City Cinema*, 203–4.

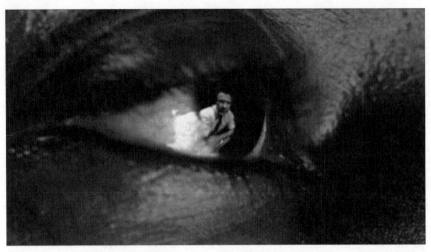

FIG. 19   Rocco (Harvey Keitel) as reflected in Victor Dunham's (Isaiah Washington) eye (*Clockers*, 1995)

detective narration, insofar as the conventions of police investigation become incorporated into an exploration of the epistemology of race. As explained in the analysis of *One False Move,* black filmmakers have devised ways to use *noir* conventions in order to blend detective narration with a more melodramatic form of storytelling so that the interior life of characters can be more fully portrayed. In depicting stories of individuals caught up in the intricacies of race, they have thus created a novel form that exploits the cognitive and emotive capacities of both genres.[23] We have seen some of its emotive, perhaps more "melodramatic" capacities at work in the foregoing analysis of Strike; what I offer in this section takes advantage of black *noir*'s potential for more explicitly cognitive purposes in the form of the parallel story about NYPD homicide detective Rocco Klein (Harvey Keitel), whom the film portrays using a more traditional detective-style narration, a strategy that complements and intertwines with the narrative strand involving Strike.

What characters know and do not know continually arise as objects of desire or investigation in Rocco's thread of the narrative. The homicide detective, as he is reflected in a shot of Victor Dunham's eye, demands, "I want to see what you see," to which Victor wearily closes his eye as if to say, "You can't." Later Rocco tells Strike, "I want to know what you know," but this time Strike profanely explodes, "You don't know a motherfuckin' thing about me. You don't know who I am. You ain't nothing but a racist-assed, nigger-hating cop. You don't know how it is for brothers out here. Shit—and you motherfucking definitely don't know nothing about what's going on out here [in the streets]!"

23. Bordwell, *Narration in the Fiction Film,* 64–73.

After twenty years as an urban police detective Rocco thinks he is capable of knowing and seeing the world through African-American experience. Yet one primary thrust of the film is to show that he does not, that his consciousness of African-American existence is severely truncated. Like Hurricane, his understanding and perceptions are stunted by presumptions of race that prevent him from recognizing and acknowledging the full humanity of black project inhabitants. By virtue of a fundamentally racialized belief structure through which he perceives the world, he is often rendered incapable of grasping the actual truth about those whom he has sworn to investigate, serve, and protect. His experience of looking at murdered African-American children has not broadened his knowledge, but hardened it so that all he can see and think are what his calcified stereotypical prejudices allow. Because of them he is frequently blinded to many truths that are explicitly presented to him.

His implicit assumption, for example—and by implication much of the audience's—is that Victor could not have shot Darryl Adams as he had confessed, for he seems too good a (black) person in Rocco's scheme of things to have committed such a heinous act. Victor is, in other words, an exception to what Rocco sees as the usual iniquity of blacks. In this veteran police detective's view, "something ain't right," so like some *noir* knight errant he refuses to shut the case on the Darryl Adams murder and continues to investigate, against the advice of his partner Mazilli (John Turturro). Rather than Victor, Rocco believes that Strike, the "bad" brother, was the murderer. After pressuring the young drug dealer through much of the film and at the end of his rope in his effort to incriminate him, Rocco finally loses his cool and exclaims, "You're a lowdown, cold-blooded, evil junkyard nigger like I've never seen in my life. . . . I read you like a Marvel fucking Spiderman comic book. . . . I been inside your ball-pea brain since you were born! Twenty fucking years!" Of Victor, on the other hand, Rocco declares, "He's one of the *decent ones,*" one of the extraordinary few "Yos" or "Nubians" (as he and other white police officials typically call African Americans) who seeks to get out of the projects legitimately and make a better life for himself and his family.

Yet Rocco's cognitive blindness, which leads him to this Manichaean conclusion, also causes him to miss crucial features of the case, most particularly Strike's fundamental inability to commit murder and the pressures affecting *everyone* who lives in the projects, even the "decent ones" like Victor. Rocco fails to see, for example, that these pressures could help to explain how the truth is already before him, that Victor was "just sick and tired" of the disrespect shown toward his efforts to move his family out of the projects honestly, the flash of easy money that could be obtained simply by looking the other way, and the lack of recognition he receives from his own community and peers for his heroic labors. Rocco is blind to the possibility that Victor just could not take the pressure and lack of respect anymore, and felt that he had to make somebody "pay" for the misery he felt. One night, after a particularly egregious show of disrespect and a couple belts of Scotch, Victor's anger got the better of him, so he lashed out at the nearest object he could focus his drunken frustrations on: his "competition" at Ahab's restaurant and a drug dealer to boot, Darryl Adams. As Mazilli coldly but accurately explains it, the murder was "like the capper on a bad day" for Victor. But in Rocco's misguided search for a more "reasonable answer"—one that would agree more with his simplistic beliefs about African Americans and their moral capabilities—he is blind to the fact that, as Victor exclaims in frustration after hours of interrogation, "The truth is looking at you, man!" Because of overwhelming pressures arising out of black poverty, lack of recognition, and disrespect, Victor really did shoot Darryl Adams and has confessed to it, yet Rocco cannot recognize this fact until Strike and Victor's mother Gloria (Frances Foster) carefully explains to the detective what happened to her older son the night Darryl was murdered and commands Rocco—and implicitly the audience, "Believe him!"

Because of his simplistic beliefs about blacks and how he acts upon them, there is a way in which Rocco is fundamentally complicit in much of what befalls the African-American characters in the second half of the film, most specifically Rodney's targeting Strike for death and Tyrone's murder of Errol Barnes. If Rocco had not misguidedly pressured Strike to confess to Darryl Adams's murder, events would have played out very differently. It was Rocco who intentionally and calculatedly set Rodney after Strike. It was Rocco who myopically thought that Strike had to have been the murderer in this case, not the saintly Victor. It was Rocco who insecurely refused to let himself to be "played," as he believed—falsely—that Strike and Victor were doing. As a result, Rocco schemed and manipulated to place Strike in a position of danger so that he would have no choice but to confess to a crime—that he did not actually commit. If Rocco had not done or believed as he did, if he had been able to see these African-American characters more accurately, Strike would not have been placed in so much danger, Rodney would not have sent Errol Barnes to kill Strike, and Tyrone would not have felt he had to kill Errol in a misguided attempt to protect his former mentor. Rocco's responsibility in setting these events in motion thus makes him significantly culpable for their having occurred.

Rocco's cognitive inability to think beyond damaging stereotypes about African Americans also points to an epistemological double bind often imposed on such individuals. On the one hand, he does not recognize the truth of Victor's confession; on the other, he does not believe Strike either. As the young clocker puts it, "Black man say he didn't do something, you don't believe him. Black man say he did do something, you still don't believe him." Rocco cannot believe the truth of what African Americans tell him because their statements do not fit into his restricted schema of what the truth should be. As a case-hardened police detective, Rocco thinks that he knows what is going on in the projects and that his task ordinarily consists of coercing the appropriately incriminating statements out of black people in order to show it. Thus he pressures Strike through much of the narrative in order to force his conception of the truth out of the young dealer.

But the truth is far more complicated than Rocco's simplistic conception of it is able to capture. The truth is that even "one of the decent ones," as he calls Victor, even one of the "exceptional" blacks, may be capable of killing someone, so great are the confinements, pressures, and psychological injuries inflicted on people in the projects. The truth is that even drug dealers are capable of companionability, sympathetic fellow-feeling, and concern for others, as Strike shows by enjoying Tyrone's company, being unable to kill Darryl, and trying to help bail Victor out of jail—this last item being an explicit change from the novel.[24] Rocco mouths the usual inanities about how he understands the difficulties facing young African Americans through the history of slavery, racism, no jobs, and so forth. Yet these tired clichés serve as no more than empty platitudes that help to mask his truncated consciousness of African-American experience. Instead of seeing how circumstances could be otherwise and thus produce very different sorts of human beings, a simplistic, Manichaean distinction between good and bad "brothers," both literal and metaphorical, underlayed by a sclerotic view of people of color, frame and direct his search for truth. He is accurate to believe that "something's not right" in this murder investigation, but the fault lies with his own uncomprehending and foreshortened view of his fellow human beings, not with the truth-telling capacities of African Americans or other alleged racially based limitations he presumes they have.

Like most urban-area cops, Rocco probably lives in the suburbs or somewhere equally separated from life in the projects, so he goes there to do a policing job among people with whom he has no association except as victims, suspects, or criminals.[25] His view of them, then, is accordingly limited and unchallenged. Thus he falls easily into thinking about them stereotypically as "Yos" and "Nubians" who rarely tell him anything truthful or intelligent unless he forces them to do it. As revealed by his taunt to a crime scene bystander named Chucky (Spike Lee, making a Hitchcock-like appearance) early in the film who tells Rocco that because he did not witness the murder just committed he could not speak intelligently about it, "I wouldn't want you to not speak *intelligently*," Rocco believes that intelligence is a standard African Americans are all but incapable of achieving. At one point he tells Strike (jokingly, but the narrative intent is serious) that he even has trouble telling black people apart in the daytime, let alone at night; and one reason he begins to suspect Strike in the first place is that he mistakes the young drug dealer's picture for his older brother's at the local bar while checking up on Victor's confession.

When a uniform cop complains at the scene of another murder that "they should blow these projects to Timbuktu," Rocco's partner Mazilli replies, "Why bother? They kill themselves anyway. Like one of those self-cleaning ovens. . . . That's how the Nubians do it, man . . . cycle of shit." Rocco's views are nothing

24. See Richard Price, *Clockers* (New York: Avon Books, 1993).
25. See Price's comments on Jersey City cops like Rocco in Quart and Auster, "Novelist and Screenwriter," 14. In the novel, Rocco lives in a posh Manhattan apartment; see *Clockers*, 45.

out of the ordinary for the people who must police the projects, who consider a child's murder just "another stain on the sidewalk" and taunt their onlooking friends with comments like, "Nothing you ain't seen before, huh fellas?" and "Could be you next." It is true that urban police have enormously difficult jobs and are asked by society to contain problems of profound complexity, but such bigotry and cynicism, while on the one hand perhaps a protective mask that helps them to deal with the unimaginable brutality they see every day, also constitutes an epistemology of racist belief that frequently prevents them from seeing the truth before their eyes, which is, after all, what they are frequently called upon to determine as police officials. This is precisely Rocco's problem. He sees "Justice in Black and White" as the headline for the Nation of Islam newspaper *The Final Call* announces to him at the end of the film; as he looks at it he subtly nods in agreement. For Rocco justice is simple. As he mumbles to a bystander (Spike Lee again) while trudging off to investigate another drug-related murder, "What's so scientific [about it]?"

Yet to be "scientific"—that is, to seek knowledge that could potentially change one's system of belief and to have the capacity to then alter one's beliefs as a consequence of evidence and reasoning—constitutes a major theme of the film, as Rocco's negative example illustrates. His truncated view of African-American humanity, shared by many audience members, represents a typical way of thinking from the perspective of white advantage. It is a form of believing and acting that structurally excludes perception of African Americans as full-fledged human beings. One thing *Clockers* hopes to make clear by means of this character, then, is that such epistemological perspectives are morally bankrupt and inherently unjust, and would require fundamental reconstitution before they could be made fair.

Rocco's racism is relatively explicit throughout the narrative and does not vary until the dénouement, when he grasps that he sees "justice in black and white." His perspective is that blacks are typically inferior human beings whose degraded characters come out in the many crimes he investigates in his capacity as a police detective. What is therefore astonishing is that he also turns out to be, in the eyes of many viewers, "one of the most sympathetic and caring individuals in the film."[26] It is worth considering why viewers might believe him to be so.

While on the one hand Rocco's racism is evident and transparent, on the other, he acts as a moral center, albeit a flawed one, for viewers.[27] Despite his racism, he honestly seeks the truth, works hard to attain it, and steps up to affirm fairness and proper justice by acting morally on behalf of black characters. Surprisingly, it is he who compassionately and unnecessarily goes out

26. See Quart and Auster's questions to Price in "Novelist and Screenwriter," 14.

27. The characters of Andre, the housing authority policeman, and Victor provide some moral centering for viewers as well, but since they are secondary characters as compared to Rocco, who is central and prominently featured in the film's narrative, their influence is less significant. For more on moral centering, see Smith, *Engaging Characters*, 213–16.

FIG. 20   Rocco (Harvey Keitel) guides Tyrone (Pee Wee Love) through his confession of having killed Errol Barnes (Tom Byrd) (*Clockers*, 1995).

of his way to coach Tyrone on how to confess to his murder of Errol Barnes in order to appear as minimally responsible as possible, which I would argue Lee depicts as the appropriate perspective to take regarding Tyrone. Showing an amazing empathy for this young boy's plight that yet fits with his character, Rocco takes Tyrone step by step through what he should say before turning on the tape recorder that will log the boy's official account of guilt. Lee shows this process quite effectively and cleverly by placing Rocco inside Tyrone's flashback to the murder.[28] From this vantage point Rocco carefully narrates each event and painstakingly explains why each one happened in terms that downplay Tyrone's culpability, giving this twelve-year-old boy rather heavy-handed if also largely fitting promptings about his motivations for killing Errol, so that he will have the proper justifications ready to hand when officially confessing.

In spite of Rocco's cognitive blindness to much of what goes on in the projects, he does grasp *some* problems existing there, in particular Tyrone's. I would argue that Rocco's surprising insight accrues partly from the fact that the youngster's predicament is that other projects kids accuse him of being "white," as Rocco notes, because Tyrone tries to do well in school and has sought to stay out of trouble until now. Because of this circumstance Rocco can accurately imagine the boy's situation, since it enables him to think of the child as an exception to his stereotypical image of blacks, in much the same way he thinks of Victor as "one of the decent ones." But instead of misleading him, this possibility enables Rocco to construct an appropriate imaginative bridge between his own experience and the child's, which he uses to help Tyrone tell an official version of the killing in the least incriminating

28. According to Lee, his use of this technique even impressed his producer, Martin Scorsese. See Pizzello, "Between 'Rock' and a Hard Place," 107.

way possible, thereby enabling the boy to avoid a harsher punishment than he might otherwise receive. In this manner Rocco works for a fairer kind of justice than would exist without his efforts.

Another, more modest example of Rocco's caring for justice follows Rodney's destruction of Strike's car. The detective realizes by this point that he was wrong to have misled Rodney into thinking that Strike had betrayed him, so he offers to drop the young, now ex-clocker off at the Port Authority bus terminal. When Strike asks to be taken to Penn Station instead, Rocco responds, "Same difference," showing that his real interest is getting Strike out of harm's way. In this fashion, Rocco seeks to make up for some of the injustice he has heaped on this misguided teenager. It could be argued that Rocco's offer is hardly recompense for all the trouble that he has caused Strike, but the point I wish to make is that Rocco has no reason to help Strike at all, except to make up for the wrongs he did him in the past. Moreover, in doing so he saves Strike's life.

Perhaps most significant of all, however, is the way in which Rocco is moved by and cares about Victor's predicament. Because of what he learns about Strike's older brother and his moral character during the long interrogation following Victor giving himself up, Rocco wants to help this hardworking, church-going, decent young man who was trying to move his family out of the projects honestly. Yet in the process of seeking to help Victor, Rocco sets in motion a chain of events that result in Strike's persecution as well as Tyrone's committing murder to help his friend. For that matter, Rocco also damages his own career by pursuing an investigation after it had been officially closed. In the novel, Rocco's interference causes the case against Victor to be dismissed on the grounds of police misconduct, which I take also to be the case in the film. This outcome would seem to be the only reasonable explanation why Victor is released from jail despite not being able to make bail.[29]

The point I wish to make about Rocco's motivations regarding Victor is that the police detective acts out of a misguided concern attributable to the sympathy he felt for an (otherwise) upstanding young man. Unfortunately, because he has a blinkered view of African Americans his efforts go wildly awry. The compassion he feels for Victor compels him to mistakenly pressure Strike for a confession, in spite of his partner's advice and convincing evidence to the contrary. As Lester Hunt has shown, sometimes our feelings of sympathy—and empathy, for that matter—may profoundly mislead us into doing precisely the wrong thing, which I would argue is what happens to Rocco here.[30] On the other hand, Rocco's motivation to pressure Strike also shows that he has a deep and abiding, if also misconceived, sympathy for Victor that crosses racial lines.

29. Price, *Clockers*, 618–25. It is worth remembering that Gloria rejects Strike's offer of $5,000 to bail Victor out. After explaining to Rocco what actually occurred the night of Darryl Adams's murder, she throws the money in Strike's face. Yet Victor is released anyway. The only way to make narrative sense of this detail is that Victor's release results from Rocco's misconduct on the case, as described in the novel.

30. Lester H. Hunt, "Sentiment and Sympathy," *Journal of Aesthetics and Art Criticism* 62 (2004): esp. 343–48.

Sympathy and How to Do the Right Thing

These actions by a sympathetic racist character serve to encourage viewers to grasp that even those who hold vehemently racist beliefs may sometimes perform morally good actions on behalf of blacks, as well as that in some cases they may establish imaginative connections with them. As deeply flawed a character as Rocco is, he nonetheless provides an example of someone trying to do the right thing, despite his lack of insight into crucial dimensions of African-American social circumstance. What Lee means such a fictional possibility to indicate, I would argue, is that, first, many racists in the actual world may well recognize *some* rights for nonwhites, even if they do not recognize their *full* rights as human beings; and second, that there exists some hope for establishing a more comprehensive sense of these rights even in resolutely racist individuals like Rocco, based on the possibility of extending the recognition that they already grant through developing more fully their already existing imaginative capacities toward African Americans.

The realization of such insights may surprise many viewers, both white and nonwhite. For white viewers, it shows a perhaps astonishing compassion on the part of Spike Lee as the chief storyteller behind this film. In spite of statements he sometimes makes that seem specifically "designed to piss people off," as his white co-screenwriter Richard Price notes, Lee shows an extraordinary consideration for his white characters and their possibilities for improvement, for consciously built into Rocco is the possibility that he could change.[31] This character grasps by the narrative's end some of his own inadequacies regarding his racial outlook, but in addition he possesses at least some of the tools that would be needed in order to revise that outlook, such as the ability to extend in at least some cases sympathy or empathy to others, regardless of considerations of race. Explicitly giving Rocco such depth, I would argue, prompts audience members to grasp that even real individuals like this character might contain within them some of the resources needed for alteration and improvement of their myopic presumptions regarding other human beings.

Lee's compassion even for racist characters like Rocco reflects a subtle understanding of humanity from which many viewers—especially white

---

31. See Price's observations on Lee in Quart and Auster, "Novelist and Screenwriter," 14. It is also worth noting that, not only is Price's assessment of Lee as compassionate toward all his characters consistent with Ebert's observation about *Do the Right Thing*, but also that even Sal reflects a glimmer of this possibility more fully elaborated through Rocco. At the end of *Do the Right Thing*, Sal finds a way of reconciling with Mookie by switching their heated discussion to the neutral topic of the weather, something about which they can both agree—namely, that it will be another hot day. In this way the earlier film introduces the question of how we "are going to live together," which Lee underscores through Mister Señor Love Daddy's explicit statement of it a moment later, during the film's final shot. Presumably, by means of Sal's switching of discussion topic Lee means to indicate that one way to move toward reconciliation is to determine agreed-upon commonalities.

viewers—could greatly benefit, were they to grasp what he is up to in this film. Perhaps for many nonwhite viewers, this insight will be significantly less surprising, since they typically possess greater awareness of such matters already. Still, the idea that individuals like Rocco might be "cured" of their racism may come as a surprise to some nonwhite viewers, too, even if it may also be an outlook with which they disagree.

Overall, I would argue that Rocco is portrayed as a less sympathetic character than Sal or Hurricane, as his fictional personality is presented as a good deal more openly racist. Yet there is a way in which it digs as deeply into racial presumptions as these other fictional characters. Lee again uses many white viewers' presumed racial allegiance to Rocco to prompt insight into their own presumptions about blacks. Namely, Rocco's presumption about the inherent criminality of young black men like Strike operates as a synecdoche for many audience members' beliefs. By exploring how errant and disastrous such a belief may be for Rocco, Lee illustrates how such beliefs typically presumed by those with white advantage can hamper their perceptions of fellow human beings—certainly of criminals like Strike, but even "decent ones" like Victor.

On the other hand, Rocco's different characterological configuration means that he turns out to be a new kind of sympathetic racist character. To use George Wilson's useful concept, there is a different sort of "epistemological twist" to one's understanding resulting from Rocco's ability to empathize with Tyrone. Unlike Sal and Hurricane, who are initially sympathetic narrative figures who also turn out to be racist, Rocco is initially a racist who also turns out to be partly sympathetic, as he perseveres in seeking the truth and ultimately performs morally good acts that benefit blacks in spite of his racism.

Our attitude toward him as audience members is thus deeply complicated by these revelations. On the one hand, he holds calcified prejudicial beliefs that prevent him from recognizing and acknowledging the full humanity of many fellow human beings. On the other, in some limited cases he remains capable of analogizing from his own experience to theirs and performing morally praiseworthy acts on their behalf, which provides optimism that he may be able to overcome his own moral blindness—and that real people like him might be able to do so as well.

Taken together, these conflicting aspects of Rocco provide viewers, particularly white viewers, with insight into a form of racism that may not have previously occurred to them. Namely, Rocco's character shows that racism and sympathy may come in more combinations than many viewers might have imagined. Thus a coherent understanding of Rocco's character may expand many viewers' sense of what racism is by showing them another of its multiplicitous varieties. Full and proper recognition of his character, in the form of coherently integrating the different traits of his fictional personality,[32] would in this manner add depth to what many viewers conceive of as constituting racism.

32. On the importance of integrating different features of a character, see Smith, *Engaging Characters*, 116ff.

Again, this perspective is one argued for by philosophers such as Kwami Anthony Appiah, Charles Mills, and David Theo Goldberg, who contend that the subtlety and variety of racism—or racisms—must be appreciated if the phenomenon is to be eradicated.[33] In this sense the narrative figure of Rocco Klein offers, for white viewers especially, an occasion to gain further knowledge concerning the multifaceted phenomena that constitute racism in its dominant form—what Mills has argued should be called "white supremacy."

To return to the issue of why some viewers would take Rocco to be one of the most sympathetic and caring characters in spite of his explicit racism, we should note that many white viewers initially identify with his beliefs, including those concerning race, justice, and sympathy. Insofar as their allegiance to him is partly racial, it causes these viewers to miss some of the subtleties of how Rocco is misguided by presumptions of white advantage as the narrative constructs him. At the same time, Rocco's quest during the narrative calls to mind the need for truth and justice, which viewers would also typically endorse. In addition, through his efforts of help Victor he tries to be sympathetic toward some African Americans, even if that sympathy is distorted by his racial prejudices.

Because Rocco possesses some attractive or admirable qualities, viewers may overlook this last fault in integrating his character and see him as more fair and equal-minded than the narrative actually depicts him as being. As the flawed moral center of the film, many viewers may tend to move him closer to the ideal center than he actually is, partly because doing so fits better with their existing automatized belief schemata, including its racialized dimensions. Again, rather than answer a call to reflect on their background beliefs, as I think Lee intends, they instead gloss over that call and ignore details of the narrative that do not fit their initial belief configuration, such as the depth of Rocco's inability to acknowledge fully the humanity of all African Americans. The problem, then, of seeing Rocco as the most caring and sympathetic character in the film becomes one of failing to grasp fully the African-American point of view from which it is depicted—from which all human beings deserve full equality and identical human rights. Instead, viewers leave aside Rocco's more egregious racialized flaws and construct him as more fair-minded and sympathetic than he actually is. As with many white viewers' flawed integration of Sal's characteristics in *Do the Right Thing*, they make Rocco more of a moral character than narrative details can support because of their implicitly held background beliefs concerning the presumed greater moral probity of whites.

Rocco's narrative complexity and the film's preoccupation with the pernicious effects of typical presuppositions held by many whites nonetheless show, I would argue, that it aims to prompt in viewers the desire to take on the task of carefully reexamining some of their own presuppositions to the extent that

33. Kwami Anthony Appiah, "Racisms," in *Anatomy of Racism*, ed. David Theo Goldberg (Minneapolis: University of Minnesota Press, 1990), 3–17; Mills, *Racial Contract*, esp. 72–73; Goldberg, *Racist Culture*, esp. 117–47.

they bear similarity to Rocco's. In this sense, *Clockers* is as philosophical a film as *Do the Right Thing*, for it urges its audience members to think deeply and comprehensively about justice, race, and the problems that criminality and lawbreaking represent in communities like the projects fictionally portrayed here. Because *Clockers* refuses to provide easy answers to these profoundly difficult issues, it steers its audience members in the direction of facing that they will have to reflect hard and long on the natures and relations of these problems before they can begin to formulate anything resembling an adequate and just solution to the cluster of dilemmas represented by the film. This prompting to reflect may be why many viewers have expressed distaste for *Clockers*. Perhaps even more starkly than *Do the Right Thing*, it confronts them with specific difficulties regarding race that are profoundly complex and tricky to resolve, and that many viewers would probably rather not think about, much less think through.

On the other hand, it is also important to note that *Clockers* does not leave its viewers exhausted and without hope, but rather explicitly offers up possible avenues for resolution. Because much of *Clockers* is so despairing and unrelenting, Lee felt the need to offer audience members some grounds for optimism at its conclusion.[34] He does this partly through the construction of Rocco's character, but also through the symbolism of trains, which as Diawara, Massood, and others have pointed out represent freedom for African Americans stuck in the urban misery of New York City ghettos.[35] In a breathtaking finale that perhaps aims to address black audience members more directly than white, Strike escapes Rodney's vendetta against him and the burdens of his past life by taking the Santa Fe Limited to an uncertain but clearly brighter future than he would have had in New York. Trading his Lionel trains and the "toy freedom" of drug dealing for the genuine article, we see him in the last scene riding a real train for the first time in his life and looking out at the Southwestern landscape of possibility, a place where whites for the last century and more have found redemption and renewal through the iconography of Westerns—so why not blacks too?[36]

---

34. See Price on the ending of *Clockers* in Quart and Auster, "Novelist and Screenwriter," 17. Spicer, *Film Noir*, 170, also notes black *noir*'s capacity to express "hopes of redemption and reconciliation that 'white' noir conspicuously lacks."

35. Diawara, "*Noir* by *Noirs*," 268–69; Massood, *Black City Cinema*, 199–204.

36. To be fair, the place of blacks in the American West has been noted by many, even through film; see, e.g., *Harlem Rides the Range* (Richard C. Kahn, 1939), the first of several Herbert Jefferies Westerns, and more recently *Posse* (Mario Van Peebles, 1993). My point, however, is that except for occasional appearances by Woody Strode, Sidney Poitier, and very few others, mainstream American cinema has constructed the Western as a space for white possibilities. Perhaps not surprisingly, this practice of iconic exclusion reflects past beliefs in manifest destiny, white supremacy, and their legacies. But as the work of Quintard Taylor and others indicate, there were many significant roles blacks performed in the making of the historical West, such as cowboying, for as Taylor shows, a significant portion of all cowboys were black. See Quintard Taylor, *In Search of the Racial Frontier: African Americans in the American West, 1528–1990* (New York: W. W. Norton, 1998), esp. 156–63.

Strike also becomes "Ronnie" again, finally accepting his given name rather than his street name when it is used to refer to him, thereby symbolically shedding his drug-dealing past—which is another *noir* touch on Lee's part. The once and future name represents this character's new identity as an ex-clocker. He is a different and morally reformed individual, as it has become clear during the film's final half-hour that Strike wants no more to do with hustling. This utilization of different names is similar to the way in which the morally good and bad sides of the main character played by Robert Mitchum in *Out of the Past* were represented by different names—"Jeff Bailey" and "Jeff Markham"—and amounts to a common *noir* strategy to signify differences in a character's identity.[37] Intercut with this sequence we also find out that Victor is freed from jail and rejoins his family in a scene that offers hope that he, like his brother, may similarly find redemption and renewal.

However, there is a deeper purpose to this final admission of hope than to simply make people feel good, for Lee's use of *noir* determinism is also thereby transposed, which invests the idea of *noir* itself with a new set of possibilities regarding audience response. Life in the projects may produce the kind of hopelessness and nihilism that leads to drug abuse or trafficking, as the film's opening sequence depicts, but Lee wishes to stress that it is not inescapable. Strike's flight to New Mexico, Victor's release from jail, even Tyrone's adoption of Strike's model train set in the film's final moments all represent the inspiration that could potentially take people out of the projects and on to better things. The bleak determinism of inner-city life is one imposed on African Americans by white advantage and enforced by institutional forces, such as the police. It includes features like Rocco's cognitive incomprehension of many of the events and people there, as well as presumptions of criminality for its inhabitants on the part of various institutions supporting white power. Yet a crucial dimension of escaping it, Lee hopes to make clear, must come from within through recognizing these institutions for what they are and consciously changing one's life in light of that knowledge—that is, by being scientific, as the film at one point suggests. Through its final sequences, the film directs its audiences to contemplate just such changes in the realm of the moral.

In a turn toward stressing personal responsibility and autonomy, Lee's film implies that part of the task of getting out from under these racially imposed circumstances lies within the capacity of African Americans to generate and implement for themselves. Lee clearly respects Victor's choice to honestly work his way out of the projects, for example, and finds honorable the housing project policeman Andre's attempts to keep children off the streets. Lee also refuses to let Strike off the hook for his hand in facilitating Tyrone's shooting

---

37. Note, for example, the many different names for the character played by Lizabeth Scott in *Dead Reckoning*, as well as those for Claire Trevor's in *Murder, My Sweet* and James Stewart's and Kim Novak's in *Vertigo*. Oliver and Trigo focus on some of the ways in which identity formation and stability lay at the heart of *film noir*. Although I find their psychoanalytic approach overly narrow, they do concentrate on a critically important issue; see *Noir Anxiety*, esp. xiv–xxxv.

of Errol Barnes. This sense of responsibility for one's actions as well as one's community are why the at times intrusive shots of billboards commanding "No More Packing" flash by: Lee aims to impress on those living in the projects that they simply cannot afford to passively wait for white America to make the sort of changes that will improve ghetto circumstances and free its inhabitants of the misery in their lives. Rather, they need to take at least partial responsibility for themselves by consciously recognizing the forces shaping their existence and making choices to alter them. Cries of racism go only so far, as Lee has sometimes noted;[38] after that, people trapped in the projects need to work to understand and counteract these problems themselves because white society as a whole is unlikely to change drastically in the near future and give up its power merely for the sake of fairness. Such a change must be largely motivated by and come from within spaces of the black community, as did civil rights; and it will come, according to the logic of the film, only when those in the projects—in particular, young teenage men—begin to understand and take some responsibility for their own lives through making difficult choices such as choosing more legitimate routes out of the ghetto, walking away from challenges to their manhood, and eschewing violence rather than responding to it in kind or seeking it out.

The intercuts of "No More Packing" billboards, then, signify a crucial step to be taken in order to eliminate these problems and allow young teens to take control of their lives—and perhaps have a greater resonance for many white viewers post-Columbine than they did when the film was originally released in 1995. Young black male rage is not so distant, after all, from its white counterpart, and will likely require similar steps to resolve. Clearly, this option is an arduous path to set before such inexperienced youth, whether black or white, in lieu of other systems of support, but it is a necessary one according to the film that must be taken to counteract such desperate circumstances, regardless of whatever else is done. In particular, young African Americans will need to invent their own ways out from under white supremacism, in much the same way that historically blacks often found it necessary to invent their own ways out from slavery and Jim Crow. Of course, it also implies a responsibility for those who care for and teach these youths to exploit such options to the greatest extent possible. Precisely how that might be done is not made clear, but that uncertainty merely underscores this obligation's urgency and the need to reflect on ways of fulfilling it, which the film directs us as viewers to do.

As I will explain more fully in the next chapter, like a good deal of rap and hip-hop, many black *noirs* previous to *Clockers* used references to law-breaking and criminality to express the desire to escape from the pressures of white power and to create independent spheres in which African Americans could explore new identities and ways of being.[39] *Clockers*, however, pushes

38. For example, Lee made such comments during a CNN interview in April 1996; in addition, Price alludes to similar comments in Quart and Auster, "Novelist and Screenwriter," 16.

39. See also Diawara, "*Noir* by *Noirs*," 273.

the transformation of these conventions even further, as Spike Lee turns *film noir* on its head by showing a way out of criminality and lawbreaking rather than merely a way in. By foregrounding the imposed and racialized nature of the typical housing project, as well as explicitly presenting possibilities for escape, Lee shows how actual project inhabitants may come to see the possibility of creating their own lives independently of that which white power has so often imposed on them—namely, criminality and lawbreaking—and devise new, more liberating forms of African-American existence apart from such determinants.

Liberation, to use Lewis Gordon's explanation of Fanon's view, often depends on people grasping the extraordinary circumstances that have been imposed on them and seeking ways to transform perceptions of those circumstances into a more appropriate form. What are typically taken to be the "ordinary" conditions of African-American existence from a white point of view must therefore be given their proper characterizations as forms of injustice, as impositions that are cognitively abnormal and blatantly misanthropic, before further progress can be made. In addition, this transformation must occur from the bottom up if it is to be fully successful. Closely following Fanon here, Gordon argues that only through the work of those experiencing the oppression themselves—work that truly alters general societal views of these miserable "everyday" conditions from being seen as nothing out of the ordinary to their proper perception as extraordinary injustices—may such conditions be successfully and permanently changed. Without whole-scale transformations rooted in the very conditions to be altered, the changes will not stick.[40] By grasping this aspect of the film's narrative (namely, its implications for real life), viewers may see how the innovative ways in which Lee uses *film noir* conventions to point the way to freedom and liberation, not mere confinement, marginalization, and the sort of nihilistic fatalism that too often results in drug addiction or trafficking.

Aesthetic Response, Race, and Black *Noir*

Taken together, the films analyzed here and in the previous chapter illustrate a remarkable advance in *film noir*. By developing strategies that exploit *noir*'s capacity to favorably present morally good-bad characters as well as borrowing from the repertoire of presenting attractive-bad characters, films like *One False Move* and *Clockers* prompt viewers to think about their racial presumptions and allegiances regarding cinematic viewership and to reflect systematically on their own identities, insofar as they involve unquestioned presumptions of justice, race, knowledge, and morality. These films' self-conscious presentation of sympathetic racist characters, for example, amount to explorations of different versions of white racism and indicate ways to revise and prevent

40. Gordon, *Fanon and the Crisis of European Man*, 62–63.

them. Empathetic black characters, on the other hand, offer the opportunity to identify with narrative figures who might otherwise remain foreign to viewers—white viewers in particular.

In addition, by juxtaposing and contrasting these narrative types, film-makers like Lee and Franklin provide implicit comparisons that aim to benefit black characters in the eyes of many audience members. This technique is not unlike that discussed by Carroll and Smith regarding the moral graduation of characters in films such as *The Wages of Fear* (Henri-Georges Clouzot, 1953). This French film depicts moral lowlifes with whom most of us would never associate in real life. But internally, it presents a moral system within which some characters are less immoral than others, which influences us to side sym-pathetically with the least objectionable ones.[41] In the same spirit, contrasting certain kinds of black characters with sympathetic racists creates a scale of moral gradation that affects greater audience sympathy for the former. Lila and Strike, for example, who by the end of their respective narratives are at least in some respects among the better characters from a moral point of view, ultimately draw audience members to side with them more strongly than with characters who exist even further down the ethical ladder, so to speak, such as Hurricane and Rocco. In ways much like the narrative figures depicted in *The Wages of Fear*, these characters seem preferable by comparison to the less savory racist characters who surround them, thereby inclining viewers by the conclu-sions of their stories to side more readily with these black narrative figures.

The success of this technique is premised on the idea that racism is now more morally objectionable than, say, ninety years ago, when it was still accept-able for whites to be Ku Klux Klan members, participate in lynch mobs, and openly express antiblack racist beliefs. Most people's standard belief schemata differ greatly from what those structures were then, when films like *The Birth of a Nation* (D. W. Griffith, 1915) could attract millions of cheering white view-ers. Filmmakers like Lee and Franklin have realized this change and utilized it to their advantage by presenting black characters with whom whites and oth-ers might not normally identify, in order to encourage them to see some of the ways in which, while we have made great strides in reducing the degree of rac-ist belief and practice in America, we still have some distance to go before we achieve a so-called "end of racism."[42] In these ways such films challenge their audiences, especially their white audiences, to confront, grasp, and overcome a variety of presumed beliefs that otherwise impair their understanding of race.

In this sense black filmmakers and their collaborators have turned *film noir* to philosophical purposes. They have employed conventions of this cinematic art form to urge their viewers to think reflectively on not only the narratives

41. See Smith, *Engaging Characters*, 207–16, and Carroll, "Toward a Theory of Film Sus-pense," 104–5, for discussion of the Clouzot film and this narrative strategy in general.

42. See, for example, Dinesh D'Souza, *The End of Racism: Principles for a Multiracial Society* (New York: Free Press, 1995). For a spirited critique of D'Souza's book, see David Theo Goldberg, *Racial Subjects: Writings on Race in America* (New York: Routledge, 1997), 175–226.

themselves, but also viewers' senses of themselves and others, thereby achieving crucial hallmarks of what it is to be philosophical. As in Lee's success in shaping *Do the Right Thing* by means of *noirish* characterizations and other techniques, *One False Move* and *Clockers* depict for us the complicated, messy entanglement with our day-to-day thinking and acting that we must face, acknowledge, and understand before we may achieve further progress in our battle to eliminate racist phenomena from our lives.

By self-consciously altering matters of allegiance and alignment to the advantage of black points of view, these filmmakers have devised new ways to uncover the unexamined beliefs and practices that constitute racist institutions in America. These institutions not only damage and handicap blacks, but also those who in other ways benefit from them. The films portray unconscious white power and advantage as truncating the moral and social world of whites and as constituting a form of impaired consciousness that prevents them from appreciating or living fuller human lives, condemning them to fall short of any ideal that might include a convincing conception of human flourishing. As in *Do the Right Thing*, such self-conscious depictions of white characters as in *Clockers* and *One False Move* encourages audience members to reflect critically on what it means to be white and the consequences that idea has for actual human beings. By contrast, black characters mobilize increased audience empathy and understanding, responses that analogously encourage viewers to reflect on dominant beliefs about what it means to be black in America and the implications those beliefs may have for allegiances with African-American characters, as well as for actual African-American human beings.

Interestingly, these films also leave open possibilities for reconciliation, such as implied but not really explored at the end of *Do the Right Thing*. Strategies for how we are going to live together are at least broached in broad outline, making these films logical progressions from their 1989 precursor, with its closing statements of at least *prima facie* contradictory moral ideals from Martin Luther King Jr. and Malcolm X. The endings of both *One False Move* and *Clockers* explicitly present more specific possibilities for blacks and whites to accurately understand the intricacies of race and thus work together cooperatively on what Nelson Mandela has called "undoing the continuing effects of the past."[43] By making racism not only accessibly imaginable but understandable, these films enable us to more comprehensively acknowledge its horrific nature and effects, as well as open the possibility for finding ways to move beyond it through devising strategies for common projects that confront it.[44] If those projects are to include achieving greater justice and liberation for all—as they should—then some mechanisms of reconciliation,

43. Nelson Mandela, *Commissioning the Past* (2002), quoted in Adam Morton, *On Evil* (London: Routledge, 2004), 127.

44. For more on the concept of reconciliation and its possibilities, see Morton, *On Evil*, esp. 104–19, 124–35, and Claudia Card, *The Atrocity Paradigm* (New York: Oxford University Press, 2002), esp. 177–80.

social adjustment, and recompense would be required. These mechanisms might create substantial social upheaval or require considerable expense, but as recent philosophers of race such as Bernard Boxill, Howard McGary, and Rodney C. Roberts have argued, these reasons by themselves have never been adequate objections not to work for a just result.[45] Yet before we can embark on such a project, we need a more concrete and detailed understanding of racism as it is, and imaginative works such as those analyzed in the preceding chapters could play a not insignificant role in achieving that understanding.

45. Bernard R. Boxill, "The Morality of Reparations," *Social Theory and Practice* 2 (1972): 113–22; Boxill, "The Morality of Reparations II," in Lott and Pittman, *Companion to African-American Philosophy*, 134–47; Howard McGary, "Justice and Reparations," in *Race and Social Justice* (London: Blackwell, 1999), 93–109; Rodney C. Roberts, "Why Have the Injustices Perpetrated Against Blacks in America Not Been Rectified?" *Journal of Social Philosophy* 32 (2001): 357–73; Roberts, "Justice and Rectification: A Taxonomy of Justice," in *Injustice and Reparations*, ed. Rodney C. Roberts (New York: Peter Lang, 2002), 7–28.

"GUILTY OF BLACKNESS"

> In hip-hop culture . . . crime as a metaphor for resistance is quite influential. . . . The
> point of the rap artist embracing the image of crime is to recode [a] powerful mainstream
> representation.
>
> —Tommy L. Lott, "Marooned in America"

In 1991, black filmmaker and critic Jacquie Jones published "The New Ghetto Aesthetic," an essay that starkly posed divergent possibilities for what was then the emerging cycle of black *noir* films.[1] Noting explicitly that her concerns revolved around "the politics of representation," Jones argued that filmmakers who were part of this movement faced a choice of creating works that either "integrated into the existing protocol of mainstream cinema" or transformed its language and "force[d] it to acknowledge the plurality of American culture" (33). Taking her cue from a similar dichotomy posed by essayist Lett Proctor, Jones contended that such films could either "inspire reflection on the erupting fury in inner cities or merely magnify the grim realities of life for far too many black youths" (37).

Using these alternatives to establish distinct categories of politicized cinematic representation, Jones analyzed several recent releases, aiming her main criticisms at what were then the two most popular black *noir* films, the studio-backed *New Jack City* (Mario Van Peebles, 1991) and *Boyz N the Hood* (John Singleton, 1991). Jones maintained that these films ultimately reinforced rather than challenged racist beliefs about young black men, portrayed black women in stereotypical ways, and offered only a nihilistic outlook for those living in urban misery. Contemptuously dismissing *New Jack City* as "little more than a blackface *Scarface*" (35), she then attacked *Boyz N the Hood* for its even more pronounced Hollywood conventionality. Ironically, this second film's main innovation regarding black cinematic types lay in the way it epitomized a certain simple-minded misogyny that then plagued much of the new black film wave. As Jones noted, "Black women are allowed to occupy two narrow categories in this cinema: that of the bitch and that of the ho" (39).

In contrast, Jones argued that independently financed films such as *Straight Out of Brooklyn* (Matty Rich, 1991) and *Chameleon Street* (Wendell Harris, 1989) embraced the other possibility she outlined. Their narratives compelled viewers to acknowledge the humanity of their characters and the plurality

1. Jones, "New Ghetto Aesthetic," 32–43.

of American existence, and inspired audience reflection on why inner city circumstances might cause inhabitants to seethe with anger (37–38). Clearly hoping to encourage films of this second sort, she noted that while *New Jack City* may have formally introduced a rap sensibility into film by "cinematizing" its aesthetic (34–35), what she saw as rap's most crucial political dimension remained to be properly translated into film narrative.[2] As the epigraph from Tommy Lott makes explicit, for Jones the exposure and recoding of imagery concerning black male criminality constituted rap music's key critical innovation. What amounted to perhaps the most disappointing aspect of *New Jack City* and *Boyz N the Hood* for Jones were their failure to live up to the promise of initial, seemingly politicized images depicting "problems ravaging the Black community" and becoming merely standard romps through the conventions of mainstream Hollywood cinema (34).

Jones's primary concern was clearly the possibility that such "ghettocentric," "homeboy cinema" (36, 33) would reinforce black stereotypes rather than challenge, recode, or transform them. I agree that her concern regarding this film form was and remains real, but would counter that some films aimed partly at mainstream, generally white audiences powerfully actualize the alternative possibility she sketches.[3] As an ideologically ambiguous aesthetic,[4] *noir* may certainly be employed to affirm stereotypic presumptions rather than transform them. Some black *noir* films commit just this sort of unquestioning affirmation, while others attempt to challenge such presumptions but nonetheless leave them in place. Instead of questioning or even bringing racialized presumptions to the surface where they might be critically examined, these films either ultimately take for granted commonly held beliefs about young black men, or their challenges to stereotypic thinking are too weak to alter typical audience belief structures.

On the other hand, certain black *noirs* avoid this trap by more thoroughly humanizing their African-American criminal characters and inviting their audiences to reflect on the causes of criminality in these narrative figures, as the analyses of the previous chapters show. With her discussions of *Chameleon Street*, *Straight Out of Brooklyn*, and other independently financed black films, Jones acknowledges such a possibility, but she casts doubt on this possibility's effectiveness for more mainstream-oriented and financed productions.[5] By contrast, in this chapter I analyze how that possibility has been achieved even in the most unlikely of films, namely some of the "mainstreamed" ghettocentric cinema she criticizes. Through constructing characters using typical *noir* techniques that elicit sympathetic as well as empathetic emotional responses from many audience members, some "new ghetto aesthetic" films humanize their criminal figures in ways that reach across the racial divides that exist in

---

2. See also Watkins, *Representing*, 177ff.
3. For more on the "cross-over" aims of these films, see ibid., 177–95, esp. 187–89.
4. Davis, *City of Quartz*, 41.
5. See, for example, Jones, "New Ghetto Aesthetic," 33–34, 38, 43.

America. Rather than reaffirm or presume stereotypes, these films challenge and recode them to reveal a fuller humanity in the African-American figures that propel their narratives. While these criminal figures perhaps remain unappealing to some, other viewers find in them the sorts of aesthetic features that encourage reconsideration and reformulation of their typical ways of thinking and acting to include a fuller sense of what it is to be human, what it is to be raced, and what sorts of implications such conceptions have for justice and morality.

In a sense, the analyses I offer here build on issues raised in previous chapters, for these investigations necessarily involve description and explanation of cinematic strategies that urge mainstream viewers to favorably ally themselves with morally ambivalent characters and encourage reflection on the alternative perspectives offered. At the same time, these analyses also require a more careful distinguishing between different possible viewer responses than I have provided so far. Acknowledging these differences becomes crucial because for some viewers almost any narrative portraying blacks might well work to confirm their stereotypic thinking, so deeply are their racial beliefs ingrained. Even obviously liberatory and uplifting works like *Eyes on the Prize* or *Roots* might have such an effect in spite of their broad accessibility and clear aim of humanizing African Americans. It must further be admitted that many black *noir* films are politically compromised objects.[6] As Tommy Lott has noted, works that seek to portray blacks in ways that would be readily accessible to mainstream audiences trade in a certain level of conventionality in order to be easily understood.[7] To the extent that they treat race conventionally, they run the risk of falling into racial stereotyping.

Yet in addition, the films I analyze here add something new to the argument offered thus far in the book, insofar as they were among the first relatively mainstream works to focus mainly on African-American characters who were openly criminal—"gangstas," in common parlance. As such, they broke new aesthetic ground regarding how to popularly present audiences with sympathetic African-American male protagonists who at the same time lived outside the law. Thus these films confronted the challenge of how one overcomes the difficulties posed by presenting characters who fit all-too-common stereotypes about such individuals in real life. The point I wish to make in this chapter, then, is that *some* broadly aimed black *noir* films successfully overcame problems of conventionality about race, and to the extent that audience members are open to thinking unconventionally about blacks—that is, to the extent that they are willing to revise their belief schemata to grant full

6. See Watkins, *Representing*. Of course, as explained in the introduction, the concepts of "independent" and "Hollywood" financing used by Jones ultimately break down; see Diawara, "Black American Cinema," and Lott, "Hollywood and Independent Black Cinema," esp. 219–25. Particularly since the mid-1980s, there exists no clear-cut way to distinguish between Hollywood and black independent film.

7. Lott, "Aesthetics and Politics," 288–95.

humanity to black human beings—these films may have a positive effect on viewers' racialized thinking. Such an outcome, of course, depends on receptiveness to the very possibility of such a change in one's fundamental belief structure, which may itself depend on diverse sorts of presumptions and their status at the time of viewing the narrative. A nuanced interest and enthusiasm for certain kinds of politically aware hip-hop or a firm belief in full and universal human equality, for example, may well help to facilitate this process of reexamining one's implicit beliefs about race. Black *noir* narratives such as the ones I analyze here can help to spur that change by deepening one's understanding and enflaming one's sense of righteous indignation over racial injustice.

I should acknowledge here once again that Jones and other critics are correct to mention that market forces were at work in the early 1990s to make possible the real growth of this black *noir* film cycle.[8] The possibility that these films could be made at all was greatly facilitated by a downturn in ticket sales and the need for Hollywood financiers to make some quick money, which they did initially from black audiences who found these films enjoyable. Yet film producers quickly realized that these films had a significant appeal to a secondary audience of whites, which is where the big money was seen to be.[9] My interest here, however, is in how this latter possibility was aesthetically employed, once the market opening blossomed. By exploiting the possibility for "crossover" provided by Hollywood financial need, many black filmmakers realized effective ways to subtly present racial inequities and their genesis in typically presumed beliefs about African Americans—in particular, about young black men—through *film noir* techniques. In doing so, these filmmakers found ways to urge viewers to reconsider their conceptions of humanity, justice, and morality, principally as these ideas pertain to race in America. "The new ghetto aesthetic," then, not only presented possibilities for reaffirming cinematic racial stereotypes for mainstream audiences, but also for trenchantly challenging and critiquing them.

In the discussion that follows, I further develop the theme of sympathetic and empathetic understandings for narrative characters by analyzing several early black *noir* films that aimed to challenge and recode the standard image of young black lawbreakers. By encouraging more compassionate responses and comprehension for characters that viewers might otherwise dismiss as apprentice criminals, gang members, or other underworld figures, these African-American *noir* films encourage substantive reflection on questions focusing around humanity, justice, and race. They delineated and contextualized the alleged predisposition to criminality of young black men and how

8. Jones, "New Ghetto Aesthetic," 33; Watkins, *Representing*, esp. 187–95; Guerrero, *Framing Blackness*, 164–65; Rhines, *Black Film/White Money*, 4, 12–13, 57–78.

9. Watkins, *Representing*, 187–89; Guerrero, *Framing Blackness*, 164; Karen Grigsby Bates, "'They've Gotta Have Us': Hollywood's Black Directors," *New York Times Magazine*, July 14, 1991, 15–19, 38, 40, 44, esp. 18.

this presumption frequently imposes the expectation, both in themselves and others, that such individuals will live degraded forms of human existence. As these films also seek to make clear, such a presumption becomes difficult to escape, given the meager and restricted alternatives typically at these youths' disposal, thereby exposing a form of injustice inherent in this way of thinking.

As in the previous chapter, the perspective found in these films compares favorably with the work of Tommy Lott, Howard McGary, Michele Moody-Adams, and others.[10] By examining the social dimensions of beliefs concerning black criminality, these philosophers argue that negative beliefs imposed on black youths create conditions that in most cases require superhuman acts of patience, fortitude, and will to escape.[11] Many early black *noir* films similarly seek to counteract racialized beliefs about black laziness, immorality, or ineptitude by more fully humanizing their young black male characters and, like some forms of rap, explicitly depicting the harsh and unforgiving conditions under which they live. I thus analyze how these early black *noir* films provide the opportunity to examine conceptions of humanity and race that have impaired real as well as narrative possibilities for young African American males, and how their makers used *noir* strategies and techniques to make these problems striking, accessible, and compelling to viewers, as well as conducive to philosophical reflection.

I begin with analyses of *New Jack City* and *Boyz N the Hood* that partly contest Jones's argument regarding these films, as I believe it worthwhile to present in detail why they hold out some greater initial hope for challenging and recoding racial stereotypes than her essay allows, even if I agree that they ultimately fail. The manner in which these "ghettocentric *noirs*" fall short of their initial promise offer us insight into the direction some later, more successful black *noirs* take.[12]

Flawed *Noir* Narratives: *New Jack City* and *Boyz N the Hood*

Using the distinctive intonations of the gangsta rapper Ice T, *New Jack City*'s opening voiceover proclaims, "You are now about to witness the strength of street knowledge." In this way, the film claims to be an "authentic" account of what it is like for young black men in the racialized inner city. Subsequent music, imagery, and news commentary played over the initial montage reinforce this impression by providing audiences with a catalogue of the difficulties afflicting black urban communities, from unemployment and drugs to

10. Lott, "Marooned in America"; Howard McGary, "The Black Underclass and the Question of Values," in Lawson, *Underclass Question*, 57–70; Moody-Adams, "Social Construction of Self-Respect," 251–66; Armour, *Negrophobia and Reasonable Racism*.

11. See, for example, McGary, "Black Underclass," esp. 63–66.

12. I take the term "ghettocentric *noir*" from Mark Anthony Neal, *Soul Babies: Black Popular Culture and the Post-Soul Aesthetic* (New York: Routledge, 2002), 188.

violence, crime, poverty, entrenched economic inequality, gangs, debt, alcoholism, and homelessness. Thus the film seeks to foster in viewers the expectation, as Jones perceptively noted, that it will confront problems frequently
challenging African Americans, particularly those living in urban distress, by
examining "how these realities breathe life into a sophisticated, entrepreneurial drug culture" (34).

The narrative, however, takes a rather different turn, as it progressively
restricts its focus to misguided black desires for upward economic mobility,
1980s style. By self-consciously comparing the drug culture of crack to the
Prohibition-era drug culture of alcohol, the film accomplishes some of what
Jones would have hoped by presenting its criminals as practicing a brutal,
violent, and unbridled form of capitalism aimed at achieving greater personal
freedom, which the film depicts as directly analogous to the efforts employed
by individuals from earlier oppressed, racialized groups. *New Jack City*'s gangster characters toast their success by exclaiming, "This is the fruit of our hard
work, the belief in the entrepreneurial spirit, the new American Dream!" and
repeatedly measure themselves against another ethnicized cinematic gangster
who viciously clawed his way to the top, Tony Montana (Al Pacino), the Cuban-
American protagonist of Brian De Palma's *Scarface* (1983). At another point
the lead gangster, Nino Brown (Wesley Snipes), compares himself to George
Raft and James Cagney, actors well-known for their portrayals of ethnicized
Prohibition-era gangsters. Like their cinematic outlaw predecessors, nothing
seems to block their quest for instant wealth or efforts to escape the misery of
the ghetto. By depicting how such criminals ruthlessly climb over the backs
of their fellow human beings in order to achieve personal economic success
and what they perceive as individual freedom, the film seeks to make salient
to viewers the logical extremes of unregulated, "free market" capitalism and
rampant individualism.

In this way *New Jack City* exemplifies the drawbacks of unchecked personal
economic advance and the havoc it can wreak on blacks when embodied by
some of its own members, namely, those who have been deluded and made
selfish by brutal circumstance. Through its criminal characters the film exemplifies a kind of false consciousness, an epistemology of ignorance, which beset
many blacks as well as whites who operate under the strictures of racialized
presumption in America.[13] So indoctrinated are these characters by cultural
messages with which they have been bombarded during the late Reagan era,
such as that self-worth and freedom should be measured by material wealth
or that poverty is a sign of laziness, incompetence, or some other intrinsic
inadequacy, they leap at any opportunity to escape the denigrating conditions
in which they find themselves and prove their characters worthy of esteem,
respect, and a perverse form of economic equality. In ways similar to many of
its gangster film precursors, *New Jack City* presents the drug economy of crack
as a sort of unique business opportunity of which some members of the black

13. Mills, *Racial Contract*, esp. 81–88.

community avail themselves in their attempts to escape stereotypical con-
demnations of their racialized moral characters and the lack of freedom these
rebukes entail. By taking advantage of a special, one-time economic prospect,
the criminal narrative figures in *New Jack City* seek to show themselves worthy according to the measures presented to them by mainstream American
culture.[14]

At the same time, the narrative explicitly designates the circumstances in
which these individuals find themselves as imposed from without, as consequences of white power and advantage.[15] Such an implication may be something to which many white audience members in particular may be blind,
which I would argue is one reason why the film opens with the montage and
voiceover statements that it does. The initial sequence operates as a tip-off
that what follows contains information that will be crucial to better understanding problems of poverty and race. As Nino crassly point out during his
trial, "There ain't no Uzis made in Harlem. . . . Not one of us in here owns a
poppy field. . . . This is big business. This is the American Way." By heighten-
ing awareness of such points, *New Jack City* seeks to bring to its audiences'
attention the idea that much urban misery results from forces far beyond the
African-American community's control and much more squarely in the hands
of institutions as well as individuals who do not have the best interests of
blacks uppermost in their minds.

While the film ultimately condemns Nino's behavior, it is not completely
unsympathetic to him or the other criminals portrayed. Significant narrative
details aim to provide grounds for a certain measured positive regard for him
and his fellow gangsters. He tells us, for example, that he "was forced into
this way of life" by having to sell drugs from the age of twelve simply in order
to survive on the streets and recounts some of the horrors through which he
was inducted into gang membership. He also proclaims himself repeatedly to
be his "brother's keeper" to his fellow gang members and shows an affecting
remorse when he is unable to keep that promise.

Consistent with this aim of making its antagonists more sympathetic, like
many classic *noirs* the narrative also portrays the police as little better than
the criminals they oppose.[16] Some of them, such as Lieutenant Stone (Mario
Van Peebles), seem equally vain and status-conscious, whereas others operate using methods little better than those of the lawbreakers they pursue. By
highlighting issues of confinement, criminal humanity, and the similarities
between representatives of good and evil, the narrative uses standard *noir*

14. Jonathan Munby makes a similar point about the protagonists in the cycle of early 1930s
gangster films in relation to what was then the dominant wasp culture. See *Public Enemies, Public
Heroes,* esp. 19–65.

15. See also Diawara, "*Noir* by *Noirs,*" esp. 262–63.

16. See, for example, the discussions of *Brute Force* (Jules Dassin, 1947), *Notorious* (Alfred
Hitchcock, 1946), *Rogue Cop* (Roy Rowland, 1954), *Shield for Murder* (Edmond O'Brien and How-
ard Koch, 1954), and *Where the Sidewalk Ends* (Otto Preminger, 1950) in Silver and Ward, *Film
Noir: An Encyclopedic Reference,* 45–46, 214–15, 245–46, 256, 309–10.

techniques to convey its story and draw attention to larger issues that sur-round problems of race, class, and drugs in America.

The film also explicitly takes on an African-American point of view regard-ing these matters through utilizing such techniques. For example, *New Jack City* from time to time makes explicit the imposed character of circumstance and the position of white power relative to that imposition. There is also at least some hip-hop sensibility that the film expresses cinematically, as Jones noted, such as through its musical track and visual cultural references like actual rappers playing narrative parts, having them wear typical hip-hop cloth-ing or accessories, and by showing clips of Tony Montana from *Scarface*, which represents a cinematic "hip-hop classic" among gangsta rappers.[17]

I would contend that these dimensions of the narrative fulfill expecta-tions raised by its opening montage rather more completely than Jones might wish to admit, for the filmmakers clearly aim to bring out these aspects of the story. As director Mario Van Peebles notes regarding the character Nino, "We wanted to tell the story of a complex villain—someone who is evil but who has feelings, dimension, and a unique identity. We wanted audiences to be drawn to him but not to identify with him."[18] Furthermore, with citations of unemployment statistics and "economic inequality at its worst level since the Great Depression," the opening sequence itself unambiguously reminds us of the many difficulties facing these individuals, while also promising to impart valuable, ground-level wisdom ("street knowledge") regarding their choices of criminality rather than social conformity as a way of life.

There are ways, however, in which the film carries off its aim to achieve these goals less successfully. Contrary to its opening proclamation, the film does not provide adequate "street knowledge" to make Nino's criminality sym-pathetic or understandable to the audience. Life is not sufficiently breathed into his reasons for why big-time drug dealing might hold serious allure, or why his harsh ghetto existence might have compelled him to choose this form of entrepreneurship. In the terminology developed by Smith, Nino becomes neither a good-bad character nor an attractive-bad one, but remains merely an evil narrative figure, as standard audience sympathy elicited for him is not strong enough to move beyond that status. While many ideas in *New Jack City* hold promise of favorably presenting the sort of evil but sympathetic character Van Peebles describes, the film ultimately fails to deliver on that promise for most viewers.

More generally, *New Jack City* does not seriously challenge stereotypical thinking about blacks because it does not create sufficient allegiance to its crim-inals. Nino Brown's backstory, for example, remains exclusively verbal. Thus, like many classic *noir femmes fatales*, he remains evil in a one-dimensional

17. See, for example, *Origins of a Hip-Hop Classic,* directed by Benny Boom, 2003, on *Scar-face*, DVD, directed by Brian De Palma (1983; Universal Studios, 2003).

18. Mario Van Peebles, quoted in "Behind the Scenes" (Production Notes), *New Jack City*, DVD, directed by Mario Van Peebles (1991; Warner Home Video, 1998).

sense because the narrative makes too little effort to dispose viewers favorably to him. We briefly hear that Nino was forced into criminality as a child, that mere matters of survival compelled him to perform cruel acts of brutality. We also see his tearful remorse at having betrayed the trust of his best friend and fellow gangster Gee Money (Allen Payne), but such brief references to Nino's past or compassionate inner life do too little to compel viewers to regard him positively, particularly since these references typically arise in the context of manipulating others for his own benefit, such as during his trial or when he ultimately cons Gee Money into dropping his guard in order to kill him for his gangster incompetence. At best, these narrative details mitigate the evil Nino represents, but I would argue that they do not substantially change most viewers' overall stance toward him. On the contrary, they remain strongly and unfavorably disposed toward him because the narrative so powerfully establishes him as evil by those points in the film. At worst, these narrative details further support in viewers a sense that Nino is willing to say or do anything in order to exploit others and achieve his own selfish goals, thereby making him a still more evil individual.

Moreover, the narrative gives viewers little ground for deciding between different interpretations of who Nino is. Lacking a firm sense of Nino's inner character, his identity remains overly ambiguous throughout the narrative. Features aimed at generating some measured sympathy for Nino make him incoherent as well as incomprehensible. Confident recognition of Nino as a narrative figure remains elusive for most viewers because they are never given sufficient detail to consistently put together his sympathetic attributes with other apparent character traits.[19] Thus Jones is ultimately correct about the film and its failure to fulfill the promise of its initial images, although I would suggest that she underappreciates the potential it expresses for recoding stereotypes of black male criminality. The filmmakers clearly hoped to achieve such a goal, but failed because the character of Nino Brown, as depicted, resists such a possible interpretation.

One way to see this narrative difficulty is through *New Jack City*'s inability to provide a reasonable overall explanation for Nino's evil character. Instead, the film reduces his motivations to mystery and inexplicability. In addition to being generally unsympathetic, his character does not positively affect viewers because it is not presented as fully understandable by human beings. Rather than offer "the strength of street knowledge," *New Jack City* falls back on a tired, hackneyed, and mystifying way of seeing Nino. The film in this sense fails to provide viewers with useful insight into his character and why he does what he does. Nino describes himself as a "demon" when explaining how and why he carried out his initiation requirement so that he would gain membership into his gang of choice: killing a "civilian," who by wild coincidence turns out to have been his police pursuer's mother. Other narrative figures describe him as a "devil"; and the Old Man character (Bill Cobbs), who finally

19. See Smith, *Engaging Characters*, 82–83, 120–21.

assassinates him, declares that Nino is "wanted in Hell" just before dispatching him. In this way the narrative unhelpfully mystifies Nino's reasons for committing evil acts, such as drug dealing and murder. We do not learn from the standpoint of an actual working human psychology why he acts as he does or what specific conditions produced him. Rather, we are told that his choice to do evil is somehow diabolical and therefore unfathomable, inexplicable, the result of mysterious forces beyond human control or understanding.[20] What we witness about him over the course of the narrative, then, remains uninformative with respect to our need to plausibly explain the actual occurrence of such individuals, contrary to the film's opening promise.

Another concern here is that audience alignment with its criminal characters remains weak. The narrative structure stays primarily focused on the police investigative team of Scotty Appleton (Ice T). Rather than explore thoughtfully and thoroughly the whys and wherefores of youth gang criminality, as viewers are led to expect from the initial sequence, *New Jack City* opts mainly for "detective narration,"[21] which ironically cuts viewers off from learning more about the motivations of its antagonists, thus greatly reducing audience opportunity to ally favorably with its lawbreaking characters. There is even a sense in which the narrative is unfocused in terms of point of view. It offers audience members conflicting perspectives on the issues it raises, in particular black youth criminality and willingness to deal drugs, by inadequately coordinating the outlooks of its criminal and detective figures. It seeks to belatedly resolve them by offering too-facile ways of bringing its opposing storylines together, namely the vigilante-style solution provided for the complex difficulties represented by Nino Brown and a final, hectoring plea in its closing on-screen graphic that something must be done about real-life versions of him. If anything, however, the film's opening sequence leads viewers to believe that they would gain valuable insight from the story about how to do precisely that, not be given the task at the end to figure it out on their own, more or less without assistance from the narrative depictions just offered.

Ultimately, viewers may be thrilled by the film's action sequences, but not significantly informed. While many black viewers, for example, may feel reassured by the confirmation of beliefs not usually expressed in mainstream cinema, other black as well as white viewers may feel doubly disappointed because the film promises crucial insights regarding urgent social problems, but fails to keep that promise. Instead it tells the audience that they are on their own in figuring out how to deal with such conundra, even though they probably also sense that something they do not know but had been hinted at by the narrative is absolutely critical to the proper resolution of difficulties

---

20. For a fuller examination and critique of demonic theories of evil, as opposed to ones that help us better understand this moral phenomenon from the point of view of an actually working human psychology, see Morton, *On Evil*, esp. 22–30.

21. Bordwell, *Narration in the Fiction Film*, 64–70. See also Smith, *Engaging Characters*, 152–53.

plaguing inner city life. Cognitive deficits such as these, I would contend, constitute at least part of why the film seems a black *noir* misfire, and why many critics like Jones found it disappointing.

I would also suggest that *Boyz N the Hood* achieves only limited success for related reasons. Its opening prologue similarly offers the promise of insight into difficult choices facing young urban ghetto dwellers and focuses more squarely on the lives of three at-risk teenagers, Tre (Cuba Gooding Jr.), Ricky (Morris Chestnut), and Doughboy (Ice Cube). Beginning with the sounds of sirens and gunshots intermixed with snatches of dialogue concerning an unseen drive-by shooting, the first visual after its title is a graphic of statistics on the shocking mortality rates for African-American men. The film thus pointedly raises audience expectations that it will address important details regarding such matters. But like *New Jack City,* the narrative fails to deliver on that promise. Many viewers feel disappointed, as does Jones, because the film comes up short regarding the expectations it raises to enlighten. While often successful at portraying the complexity of problems facing its protagonists, *Boyz N the Hood* is less successful in its attempts to pose solutions to them. It also indulges significantly in racial stereotyping, thus reinforcing many audience presumptions, particularly on the part of white viewers, that it would have done better to challenge and disrupt.

For example, the narrative attributes Doughboy's ultimately fatal decision to lead a gangster life to the consistent lack of affection his mother Brenda (Tyra Ferrell) shows for him. In the prologue depicting the main characters as preteens, rather than practicing loving, fair, and even-handed parenting, Brenda clearly favors her son Ricky and encourages him to escape the ghetto by developing his skills as a football player, while showering a stream of verbal and emotional abuse on the young Doughboy, telling him that he "ain't shit and never will be shit." Tre, on the other hand, escapes the oppressive difficulties facing other young boys in the neighborhood because he has the disciplined and principled guidance of his father, Furious (Laurence Fishburne), who "teach[es] him how to be a man" and how to make thoughtful choices in his life. Whereas the narrative provides Furious repeated opportunities to present his alleged wisdom and knowledge concerning how African-American men should live, Brenda makes one bad parenting choice after another, continuing to favor Ricky in his clichéd attempt to flee the neighborhood by developing sports skills, scorning Doughboy, and passing on to her sons her emotional immaturity, her impatience, and a desperate if-only-we-could-win-the-lottery mentality. As if to further underscore this contrast, the narrative has Tre's mother, Reva (Angela Bassett), virtually abdicate her parental responsibilities toward her son and portrays other mothers in the neighborhood as crack addicts who allow their toddlers to play in the street and run around in unchanged diapers.

Tre's better decision-making, represented by his willingness to use condoms during sex and his decision to attend college in Atlanta, the narrative simplistically attributes to the presence and guidance of his wise and thoughtful father,

whereas Doughboy's mistakes are laid at the doorstep of his abusive, emotionally immature "welfare queen" of a mother. Fulfilling her abusive prophecy,
Doughboy accordingly spends his time unemployed and sitting on his mother's stoop, drinking 40s, dealing drugs, and shuttling between prison and her
house. While soulfully played by Ice Cube, who injects Doughboy's character
with an affecting vulnerability and depth, this narrative figure does not ultimately help viewers to insightfully understand why young black men might
generally choose criminality as a reasonable way of life. By relying on what
amount to racial stereotypes about black parents, the film offers at best only
specific, conventional, and rather simpleminded explanations for problems
that it so powerfully presents earlier. According to the logic of the film, the
biggest difficulty facing young black men in the ghetto is that they lack strong,
wise, black-nationalistic father figures to show them how to be upstanding
black men, a task that women, especially unemployed, single-parent female
heads of households like Brenda, are allegedly unable to perform. By generalizing these diagnoses to problems ravaging many black communities, the
film, as Jones notes, "comes dangerously close to blaming Black women for
the tragedies currently ransacking Black communities" by advancing an outlook that ominously reiterates the often-criticized and rejected conclusion of
the 1965 Moynihan Report that attributed the ills plaguing African-American
life to the lack of fathers in many families.[22] As a film frequently identified as
a black *noir* and aimed at providing audiences with a better understanding
of the phenomena it depicts,[23] *Boyz N the Hood* fails because, even though it
raises audience expectations that such matters will be helpfully elucidated, it
does not adequately assist viewers in grasping the temptation of criminality
facing its young male characters.

Racial Oppression and Personal Psychology: *Juice*

Films that more successfully examine the brutalization of young black men
include, as Diawara points out, other works from the early 1990s black film
boom, such as Ernest Dickerson's *Juice* (1992).[24] Like S. Craig Watkins and
Paula Massood, I would also add to that list Albert and Allen Hughes's stun-
ning *Menace II Society* (1993), a crucial latecomer in the cycle, and of course
Clockers.[25] Unlike *New Jack City* and *Boyz N the Hood*, these films illustrate
more successfully the hollow triumph of outlaw life by depicting its senseless
cruelty and deterministic nature for many African-American youths while at

22. Jones, "New Ghetto Aesthetic," 41; see also Massood, *Black City Cinema*, 161.

23. Diawara, "*Noir* by *Noirs*," 274; Silver and Ursini, "Appendix E1: Neo-Noir," 412; Jones,
"New Ghetto Aesthetic," 41. As Jones notes, the interpretation that problems facing black com-
munities could be remedied through Moynihan-type solutions was intended by writer/director
Singleton.

24. Diawara, "*Noir* by *Noirs*," 274, 276–77.

25. Massood, *Black City Cinema*, 143–205; Watkins, *Representing*, esp. 199–212, 271 n. 3.

the same time encouraging audience empathy for their characters. Diawara describes *Juice* as a masterpiece "of Black realism as *film noir*" (276), noting its convincing depiction of the main characters' easy descent into criminality. The narrative persuasively represents the escalating transgression and violence engulfing them, until one of the group realizes the vicious cycle in which they are trapped and explicitly rejects the option of settling disputes by means of handguns. *Juice* exemplifies a deterministic *noir* fall from grace while also making clear how few alternatives its character have before them. While this film has something of the after-school special about it—perhaps because the filmmakers were so intent on making certain that their primary audience of disaffected black youth not misunderstand their message—it nonetheless manages sophisticated use of *noir* techniques to convey its themes, which also helps it to become more accessible to its secondary audience of young white viewers.

Films such as *Juice*, then, seek to convey that the sorts of lives imposed on impoverished black teenagers not only produce strong inclinations toward criminality and lawbreaking but are also very hard to escape. In the same way that philosophers of race from Fanon to Gordon and beyond stress how racist conditions generally operate to impose criminality on blacks, these films emphasize ways in which such conditions impinge specifically on young black men and makes that life option exceedingly difficult to resist or elude. Following Fanon, Gordon notes that whites all too often associate criminality and skin color, so one is suspect because one is "guilty of blackness."[26]

Admittedly, alternatives are possible. Through Herculean effort individuals may escape the imposed circumstances that constrict their lives, but it takes extraordinary effort to achieve the goal of living an ordinary life, as Gordon argues and Lee's *Clockers* takes pains to show.[27] At the same time, Gordon's philosophical characterization also implies that such lives as those depicted in *Juice* are more cognitively accessible to others in American society than might be typically thought, especially for those who are not black—and not teenage males. By stressing the quotidian dimension of black life, Gordon intimates that much of this existence shares a crucial commonality with other forms of human life. As Cavell's meditations indicate regarding the ordinary as embodied by actor Fred Astaire's unremarkable dance steps and singing in one of the first scenes from *The Band Wagon* (Vincente Minnelli, 1953), *Juice* emphasizes through its opening sequences an everyday sense of the human with regard to its young African-American characters.[28] By exploiting narrative film's capacity

---

26. Fanon, "Lived Experience of the Black," 199; Gordon, *Bad Faith and Antiblack Racism*, 101–2.

27. Gordon, *Fanon and the Crisis of European Man*, 41–42.

28. Stanley Cavell, "Something Out of the Ordinary," *Proceedings and Addresses of the American Philosophical Association* 71, no. 2 (November 1997): 23–37. In this essay, Cavell also notes in an aside Astaire's "indebtedness for his existence as a dancer—his deepest identity—to the genius of black dancing" (35), an observation that unfortunately cannot be pursued here. For a

FIG. 21   Teenagers give in to temptation and frighten a passerby (*Juice*, 1992).

to make the invisible visible through focusing on details that we might otherwise miss,[29] the film calls viewer attention to how thoroughly human and
like everyone else its young African-American protagonists are. Of course, it
hardly need be said that the invisibility of teenage males' humanity is a characteristic often buried under a mountain of prejudice and presumption about
their alleged characters.

As Diawara notes, *Juice* depicts these teens waking up, showering, getting
dressed, arguing with their parents, and performing other everyday actions that
aim to establish senses of commonality and typicality with its audience (276–
77). Only after affirming this human commonality does the narrative show its
characters being tempted by and descending into transgression and criminality generated by how other people, in particular whites, perceive them. For
example, one day while skipping school as they walk down a street reveling in
their illicit freedom, a white passerby sees them as a gang, walks off the sidewalk and behind a bench as they approach in order to avoid them, and tightly
clutches his briefcase in the belief that they mean to steal it. Tempted by the
substantial social power this perception bestows on them, one of the crew yells
"Boo!" to scare this overly cautious pedestrian. He predictably becomes fright-
ened and walks into a lamppost as he warily eyes these black youths who actually mean him no harm. Prior to this incident, however, the filmmakers have
been sure to establish viewer allegiance with the characters through depicting

compelling analysis of that indebtedness as well as one of *The Band Wagon*'s minstrel-like racial
subtext, see Robert Gooding-Williams, *Look, a Negro! Philosophical Essays on Race, Culture, and
Politics* (New York: Routledge, 2006), 43–67.

29. Cavell, "Something Out of the Ordinary," esp. 25, 36. See also Carroll, "Power of Movies,"
esp. 84–87, and "Film, Emotion, and Genre," 21–47, esp. 27ff.

them performing the mundane actions mentioned above, with which many audience members—especially the black and white male teenagers who particularly at that time were the predominant consumers of rap—might easily identify.[30] In addition to making a connection to these target audiences, these narrative details also serve to encourage favorable responses from other audience members who similarly share or have shared these experiences.

Such analogical bridges to the young black male characters by means of the ordinary become critically important for better grasping why they act as they do. Their actions become more understandable because, as I have argued in earlier chapters, they allow white viewers to develop "a system of mapping that draws correspondences between two person's situation, goals, and emotions" such that they may successfully build cognitive connections between their own experience and those of others.[31] *Juice* thus becomes a crucial vehicle for improving the empathetic understanding of its African-American characters because the details of ordinariness it offers may be used to better comprehend its characters and the choices they make in their lives.

On the other hand, even this narrative unfortunately reverts too far in favor of Hollywood conventionality and ultimately explains the extremes of black youth violence by means of individualistic psychology, rather than oppressive circumstance. *Juice* cops out, as Ed Guerrero observes, by attributing the character Bishop's (Tupac Shakur) deepening criminality to paranoid psychosis, as opposed to the horrid racial and class conditions under which he lives.[32] The narrative depicts Bishop as mentally unstable almost from the start by giving him a catatonic father and having other characters repeatedly describe Bishop himself as crazy, thereby foreshadowing his violent descent into criminality as attributable to inherent mental illness. *Juice* further gives in to Hollywood conventionality by means of alluding to the way in which his criminality might be so explained by showing clips of the *noir* gangster film *White Heat* (Raoul Walsh, 1949), in which the character Cody Jarrett (James Cagney) evinces a similar mental instability that explains his callous lawbreaking and self-destructive behavior.[33] *Juice's* narrative has Bishop enthusiastically cheer Jarrett's every psychotic move. The young teen also comments about Jarrett's self-immolating end, "If you gotta go out, that's how you go out. That motherfucker took his destiny in his *own* hands." Narratively speaking, Bishop's point is that at least Jarrett controlled the circumstances of his death, and this young man admires the Cagney character because he similarly feels that he has little power over his life besides that possibility. So deep are Bishop's senses of unworthiness and lack of self-respect that he would jump at the chance to administer how he dies in order to feel he has something over which he possesses some sort of control.

30. See also Watkins, *Representing*, 187–95, and Massood, *Black City Cinema*, 177.
31. Allison Barnes and Paul Thagard, "Empathy and Analogy," *Dialogue* 36 (1997): 712.
32. Guerrero, *Framing Blackness*, 189.
33. Ibid.

Bishop's association with Cagney's character in *White Heat* thus dilutes the social commentary *Juice* otherwise offers through its carefully constructed verisimilitude to the experience of black youth trapped by poverty and lack of opportunity. Rather than accentuating a *noir* determinism with respect to race, this sequence instead permits audiences to explain away Bishop's descent into violence and murder as a consequence of his unstable personal psychology. The film becomes, in Guerrero's words, a "drama of individual weakness and victimization."[34] By so closely analogizing Bishop with the *White Heat* character, *Juice* dissipates an otherwise powerful indictment of the way that circumstances may often propel black youth into transgression and criminality, even when such individuals seek to resist it, as the film's main character Q (Omar Epps) ultimately does. Such a dilution is precisely what I will argue *Menace II Society* does not back away from, which is a telling reason why so many found it such a disturbing narrative.

Menace II Society and the Meaning of Life

While the Hughes brothers' 1993 debut feature has little sense of public service programming about it, the narrative still possesses a discernable moral point. Told in graphic, documentary-like imagery using voiceover and flashback that recall earlier classics such as *Sunset Boulevard* or *D.O.A.* (Rudolph Maté, 1950), this black *noir* gangster film directly addresses how criminality typically emerges from desperate conditions such as those in the Watts neighborhood of Los Angeles after 1965. By depicting the way in which circumstances slowly but inexorably entrap the main character Caine (Tyrin Turner), *Menace II Society* takes viewers step by step through his progression from innocent child, to teenage, part-time drug dealer ambivalent about more extreme forms of criminality, and finally to murderer and full-time hustler. Taking place mostly at night and suffused with an aura of fatalistic determinism, the film relies on the audience's previous knowledge of *noir* narrative to tell its story of a young African-American male's transformation into a thug.

From the opening scene, in which Caine's best friend O-Dog (Larenz Tate) shoots two liquor store operators over a chance insult, thereby making Caine an accessory to murder and a spontaneous, badly improvised armed robbery, through the main character's steady descent into becoming a vicious and hardened criminal himself, the film consistently uses *noir* conventions and themes to highlight both the circumstances that made Caine a criminal as well as their unjust, imposed nature. As Allen Hughes has commented, the point he and his fellow filmmakers sought to convey was "how these kids can become . . . criminals out of desperate conditions."[35] From a philosophical perspective,

---

34. Ibid.

35. Allen Hughes, interview in *The Hughes Brothers Talk About "Menace II Society,"* no director listed (1994), on *Menace II Society*, DVD, directed by Albert Hughes and Allen Hughes (1993; New Line Home Video, 1997).

FIG. 22   O-Dog (Larenz Tate) takes offense at a remark about his mother by a frustrated liquor store operator (*Menace II Society*, 1993).

then, we might reformulate Hughes's point to say that the film addresses the Kantian-style question, "How is it possible for criminals to result from the typically miserable living conditions under which so many impoverished and socially disadvantaged young black men live?"[36] Like many of its predecessors in the ghettocentric *noir* cycle, the film aims to provide practical "street knowledge" that would help audiences better understand black youth criminality. Yet by adapting *noir* techniques in more effective ways, it conveys its insights much more forcefully. In particular, it more successfully encourages favorable emotive as well as cognitive audience responses to its young black criminal characters by more thoroughly humanizing them than many other films have.

Like numerous classic and neo-*noirs* before it, *Menace II Society* goes out of its way to make its main character sympathetic. In addition to his participation in frequent criminal activity, early on the narrative explicitly depicts how Caine loves and respects his grandparents, who raised him. After his last day of high school, for example, they proudly and affectionately greet him at home, telling him how joyful they are at his having earned a diploma. His affectionate response makes obvious that he basks in their love. Of course, in other ways he finds their outlook on life incomprehensible and his grandfather's (Arnold Johnson) advice particularly irrelevant and riddled with meaningless platitudes, even if Caine nevertheless treats him with respect. Early in the narrative, as they sit watching television the film offers us the young man and his family exemplifying fundamentally divergent responses to the Christmas classic *It's a Wonderful Life* (Frank Capra, 1946). Caine's grandmother (Marilyn

36. See, for example, Immanuel Kant, *Prolegomena to Any Future Metaphysics*, trans. Lewis White Beck (New York: Liberal Arts Press, 1950), 3.

Coleman) smiles happily at the story being presented to her, while his grandfather nods satisfied approval. Caine, on the other hand, can only wrinkle his
brow in incredulous puzzlement over the source of their cinematic pleasure.

A moment later Caine's friend O-Dog shows up for a visit, and Caine's
grandfather launches into a lecture for the two young men about how they
should find solace and guidance in the Bible. As his grandson complains in
voiceover, "My grandpa was always coming at us with that religion. And every
time, it would go in one ear and out the other," illustrating a sentiment often
felt by teenagers about parental (or grandparental) advice. Even when these
characters do listen, they still fundamentally disagree with the older man's
position. When O-Dog actually does pay attention to the grandfather's pontifi-
cating for a moment, he respectfully argues back by offering an intuitive statement of the problem of evil against the existence of an all-good, all-powerful
Christian God. "Sir, I don't think that God really cares too much about us, or
he wouldn't have put us here." Referring to the squalor and wretchedness of
the housing project in which they live, O-Dog continues, "Look at where we
stay at. . . . It's messed up around here."[37] Caine's grandfather sadly responds,
"You don't have any belief, boy," thus showing him to be on the opposite side
of the fence concerning the relation between faith and evidence in embracing
a typically formulated Christian God's existence. But the point I wish to indicate here is that the exchange takes place on respectful grounds, in particular on the part of Caine and O-Dog, in spite of their differences with Caine's
grandfather—and their ongoing, active participation in crime and brutality
outside the family circle.

Once the grandfather has completed his homily, he asks in exasperation,
"Caine, do you care whether you live or die?" The young man ponders for
a moment, in order to genuinely consider his grandfather's question, and
answers, "I don't know." By regarding his grandfather so sincerely here, Caine
shows his respect and concern for him, in spite of the vast experiential and
generational divides between them, as well as showing an initial consideration
for what will become the central question in Caine's life from this point on in
the narrative.

Finally, when his grandparents find themselves at the end of their rope and
decide to kick their delinquent grandchild out of the house, he is devastated.
The prospect of being cut off from their love and affection brings tears to
Caine's eyes, as his grandparents represent absolutely critical foundations for
his young emotional life. His response, which I would point out is not primarily one of anger but of heartbreak and shock, shows the depth of attachment
he has for them, in spite of his otherwise brutalized life. After weakly arguing against their decision he accepts their resolve to not allow him to spend
another night under their roof, which shows a deference to his grandparents
that may strike some viewers as anomalous but is nevertheless consistent with

---

37. It is perhaps worth noting that Doughboy expresses similar objections to a Christian
God's benevolence in *Boyz N the Hood*.

his moral character as the narrative has presented it. While a young hoodlum who has by this point in the film dealt drugs, robbed, stolen, assaulted, and even murdered, the film has also shown us that he cares deeply enough about his grandparents to defer to them out of respect, even when he thinks they are wrong. Given his clearly depicted loving attachment, Caine's deference makes sense, even if it also may come as a surprising insight to some audience members that a young black gangsta might be capable of such emotional depth. This character's response to his grandparents, I would argue, urges viewers to not only sympathize but to empathize with him in spite of his criminality, as his filial deference serves to humanize him and invest him with a positive moral trait that most audience members would admire and hope to emulate (at least sometimes), despite other vicious aspects of his personality.

In addition, the narrative shows viewers how Caine helps out Ronnie (Jada Pinkett), ex-girlfriend of his substitute father Pernell (Glenn Plummer), and their son Anthony (Jullian Roy Doster). He frequently stops by their house to give her money and the child toys. Plus, Ronnie makes clear that she sees something of value in Caine, in spite of his trajectory down a path toward life imprisonment or death, which encourages viewers to search for what it is that she finds worthwhile in his character as well. Caine himself even tries to escape the doom that is fast closing in around him and actively reflects on how the many temptations to brutality have done him no good. For example, when he is beaten by the police, after being racially profiled as a likely criminal for being a young black man with a nice car, and is forced to recover in the hospital, we see him thinking long and hard about the effects the desperate conditions of the street have had on him and what is truly of value and meaningful to him in his life. After some hesitation he accepts Ronnie's invitation to move to Atlanta with her. In his voiceover Caine tells us that life "was starting to look differently to me" because his care and concern about Ronnie and Anthony have helped him realize that there are things in life that make it worth living. A final visit to Pernell, who is serving life without parole for the many crimes he has committed, seals his decision to change his ways. The older gangster tells his surrogate son that he should go with Ronnie to Atlanta and asks him to "take care of my son. I can't do shit for him in here. You teach him better than I taught you, man. Teach him the way we grew up was bullshit."

The point of Pernell's speech is to provide the perspective of a wiser, more experienced character who has realized too late the error of his ways. With little to do besides lift weights and read every book in the library, as Ronnie puts it, Pernell has had time in prison to reflect on what matters in his life and has realized that actively caring for other people—namely Caine, Ronnie, and Anthony—for their own sake would have given his life meaning in a manner that would have influenced him to change his ways, if only he had understood the importance of caring in time. Unfortunately, from prison Pernell has no way to act on his love and concern for Caine, Ronnie, and Anthony other than severing his ties with them. This affirmation of Caine's reflections about life's meaning from the older gangster thus confirm his suspicions about the need to change his life and begin anew, even if, as Caine also realizes, Atlanta is still in America and he will still be "just another nigger from the ghetto," as he complains to Ronnie. On the other hand, Caine also grasps that by traveling to a new city, he can at least start over without all the baggage he carries in his neighborhood and away from the temptations represented by his current circle of friends, namely, O-Dog and others intimately connected to crime.

Unfortunately, fate catches up to Caine before he can escape. As he and his friends pack up the final boxes for his departure and after Caine and Ronnie have decided to visit his grandparents one last time in order to say good-bye, another brutalized youth seeks revenge for a savage beating Caine had given him. Organizing a drive-by shooting, this individual rains a shower of bullets on Caine and his friends at the moment when his escape seems imminent. Caine is hit several times, but his final act is one of compassion: he shields Ronnie's son Anthony from the gunfire with his own body. As he expires on the sidewalk from the fatal consequences of his own actions, he reviews the salient events in his life and realizes that his death is a sort of retribution for all the pain and suffering he has caused. As the accompanying summary montage makes clear, the entire film has been a flashback at the moment of his death. In order to underscore what we have seen, his final voiceover tells viewers that, having thought long and hard about his grandfather's question ("Caine, do you care whether you live or die?"), the young man has decided that he does, but "now it's too late."

As audience members we see him die, in spite of the fact that he has come to the realization that life is indeed worth living, that it does possess meaning and value, because the circumstances that produced Caine also consume him. The same desperate conditions that shaped this protagonist have also forged his killer, a character so minor he does not even rate a name, only a description, "Ilena's cousin" (Samuel Monroe Jr.). As the Hughes brothers themselves have indicated, by taking away a character with whom audience members have come to identify, the narrative compels them to feel his loss much more acutely than they would have otherwise.[38] The emptiness viewers feel at seeing killed a protagonist about whom they have come to care and empathize aims to make them think about why he had to die, what brought him to this undesired end. By aligning viewers so closely with Caine over the course of the narrative and giving them so much subjective access to him by thoroughly presenting his actions, his words, and even his reflective thoughts by means of the voiceover narrative, the filmmakers have worked to ally audience members keenly with the protagonist. Exploiting the opportunity afforded by *noir* techniques to narratively follow this character so intimately, the film has operated to create a solid, if limited, favorable attachment with Caine, so that audience members will have the opportunity to understand him cognitively, critically, as well as empathetically, which make clearer the circumstances that led him to

---

38. Allen Hughes, interview in *The Hughes Brothers Talk About "Menace II Society,"* on *Menace II Society,* DVD.

act as he did, and why such conditions might explain his misguided life as well as his death, in spite of his ultimate decision that he would rather live.

Black *Noir*, Nihilism, and Film as Philosophy

By focusing so clearly and precisely on "how a kid comes to be a gangster, or a hustler," as Allen Hughes puts it,[39] *Menace II Society* raises itself to the level of being film as philosophy, in the sense that it strong-arms its viewers to reflect on the events depicted and their meaning. Like *Do the Right Thing* and other works previously discussed, this film urges viewers to address epistemological questions such as that formulated in the previous section; that is, how it is possible for criminals to result from the typically miserable living conditions under which so many impoverished and socially disadvantaged young black men live. The film goes beyond being mere sociology by virtue of urging viewers not only to focus on the particulars of the specific social situation but also to reflect on the beliefs and presumptions that make such conditions possible, namely those involving race and class, and how those beliefs might play themselves out in viewers' own actions. Fulfilling Jones's condition that the new ghetto aesthetic should "inspire reflection on the erupting fury of inner cities,"[40] the narrative offers a vividly harrowing yet compassionate illustration of how a child may grow up to be a hustler, given certain desperate conditions made possible by entrenched ideas about the differential value of human beings based on their skin color and wealth. In addition, it underscores how even despite thoughtful effort and resolve these conditions may remain too powerful to elude. Caine's failure to escape these conditions, symbolized by his loss to the audience, thus serve to emphasize their power and perniciousness, which the Hughes brothers stress as real by having the story take place in an actual housing project in Watts, Jordan Downs, and by creating an affecting verisimilitude to the arbitrary and violent life on the streets of a racialized inner city.

It is also worth remembering that the question Caine ponders so long and hard over much of the film is a fundamentally philosophical question, "the most urgent of questions," as Albert Camus described it in "The Myth of Sisyphus,"[41] and one that finds expression in the Western philosophical tradition from the ancient era to the present day.[42] The question of whether life has any real meaning, given the horrendous, cruel, but immanently changeable

39. Ibid.

40. Jones, "New Ghetto Aesthetic," 37.

41. Albert Camus, "The Myth of Sisyphus," in *The Myth of Sisyphus and Other Essays*, trans. Justin O'Brien (1955; repr., New York: Vintage, 1991), 4.

42. See, for example, *The Meaning of Life*, ed. E. D. Klemke (New York: Oxford University Press, 1981); John Cottingham, *On the Meaning of Life* (London: Routledge, 2003); Richard Norman, *On Humanism* (London: Routledge, 2004), 132–59; and Julian Baggini, *What's It All About? Philosophy and the Meaning of Life* (2004; repr., New York: Oxford University Press, 2005).

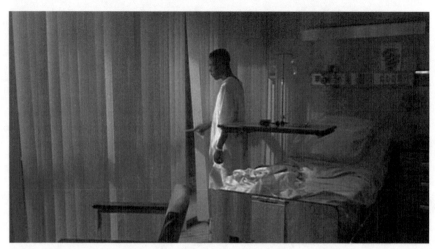

FIG. 23   Caine (Tyrin Turner) thinking about the meaning of life while recovering in
a hospital (*Menace II Society,* 1993)

circumstances under which many individuals live—in particular, young black
men caught in a web of presumption and prejudice about their alleged natures
and what they might be capable of—becomes the fundamental question of
Menace II Society.[43] As the film repeatedly emphasizes, this question lies at
the base of Caine's narrative trajectory. From his grandfather posing the question of whether Caine cares if he lives or dies twenty minutes into the feature
and Mr. Butler's (Charles S. Dutton) lecture about the difficulties of being a
black man in America and how Caine "has to think about [his] life," to the
character's own thinking about the question as he recovers in the hospital and
during his final moments before he expires, the narrative returns again and
again to the issue of what makes a human life worth living, what might count
as valuable enough that one would wish to continue one's existence rather
than dying, in spite of racism, poverty, lack of opportunity, and other forms of
oppression.

43. Grant Farred, "No Way Out of the *Menaced* Society: Loyalty Within the Boundaries of
Race," *Camera Obscura,* no. 35 (May 1995), argues that "overdetermination . . . is the central trope
of this movie" (13). Yet while I would agree that determinism is indeed centrally important to
Menace II Society, his argument fails to appreciate the narrative's focus on the value and meaning of human life, as well as the film's overall positive response to it. In addition, Farred's essay
is riddled with inaccuracies: according to it, the film is set in Compton (e.g., 9–12), the character
Stacy (Ryan Williams) dies in the final shootout (14), and A-Wax (MC Eiht) fights with Caine over
Ronnie and subsequently mails the surveillance tape from the opening liquor store robbery to the
police in order to exact revenge on Caine (17–18). However, the story is clearly set in Watts, Stacy
survives the shootout—in fact, he isn't even hit because he is inside the house when it occurs—
and it is Chauncy (Clifton Powell) who fights with Caine over Ronnie and mails the tape to the
police, not A-Wax. These errors substantially weaken Farred's overall argument, as they constitute
crucial claims in support of his argument for overdetermination being the film's central trope.

While skeptical about traditional, religiously based responses to this question, as expressed by O-Dog's objection to the grandfather's religious position, the film does not reject them outright. As Mr. Butler tells Caine about his own "ex-knucklehead" son Sharif (Vonte Sweet) and how he has found guidance out of his budding gangsterdom through the Nation of Islam, "If Allah helps make him a better man than Jesus can, then I'm all for it." I take it that these narrative details represent a certain pragmatic outlook on the part of the Hughes brothers regarding the possibility that religion might offer meaningful answers to the dilemmas faced by young black men. If it works effectively to turn one's life around and gives it meaning, then it is acceptable to use, even as the filmmakers remain dubious of its literal truth.[44] On the other hand, these expressions of religious skepticism only serve to emphasize further the film's unifying theme, the question of whether human life has meaning, whether one should care if one lives or dies. What makes this question especially urgent for Caine is that his classed and racialized circumstances make answering the question markedly more important than it might be otherwise, as his determinations will likely have very immediate consequences in his life—or death.

I would argue, then, that the narrative details provided in this film induce viewers to think seriously and systematically about the meaning and value of black human life "in just the ways that philosophers do," as Stephen Mulhall describes the conditions for films to philosophize in his book *On Film*.[45] In other words, the narrative in *Menace II Society* shows a sophistication and self-awareness about its subject matter such that it directly confronts viewers with the challenge of reconsidering their preconceived ideas about the human value of young black men, the meanings connected to these presumptions, and how such individuals might become criminals as a result of them. What the filmmakers have in mind, I would argue, is to oblige viewers to reformulate and recode their presumptions about race, humanity, and justice. By consistently working to humanize its protagonist and create a certain measured positive viewer attachment to him, the film aims to make its audience

44. Farred, "No Way Out of the *Menaced* Society," argues that Mr. Butler as well as the film's outlook on religion are "cynical," pessimistic, and "desperate" (10, 13, 14). But again, these characterizations do not take full account of the nuanced presentation of Mr. Butler's lecture to Caine. The teacher clearly states his ambivalence about the Nation of Islam: he agrees "with *some* of the things they say regarding black people," but he is also willing to accept the usefulness of a religious position with which he fundamentally disagrees, for as he states emphatically at the outset of his assessment of his son's religious choice, "I'm no Muslim." Mr. Butler accepts NOI for the practical good it does his son and others, not for its religious truth, which he does not accept. I would add that I think the Hughes brothers convey a general ambivalence about religious solutions here and elsewhere in the narrative to express their belief that while some individuals like Sharif may find life meaningful through them, such answers do not speak to the *general* problems that young black men typically face which compel them to feel that their lives are meaningless. It is my impression that the filmmakers believe a different sort of answer would be needed, one that would be, broadly speaking, secular in nature.

45. Mulhall, *On Film*, 2.

members feel the urgency of this challenge, as it pointedly indicates that complacent or unquestioning reliance on these internalized presuppositions contributes heavily to the dire circumstances in which many young black men find themselves, and specifically to the feeling they often have that their lives are meaningless and without value. Of course, as noted in previous chapters, this narratively imposed obligation to philosophize may be one from which some viewers recoil, but my point is that *Menace II Society* clearly throws the gauntlet down in an emotionally devastating way by mobilizing significant viewer empathy for its criminal protagonist, then killing him off. Naturally, it is another matter whether viewers pick the glove up.

Through employing a socially critical *noir* aesthetic, the Hughes brothers and their fellow artists lay bare the everyday injustices and unfairness that contribute to black criminality, as well as call our attention to the presumptions that underlie these inequities. They further show how difficult it can be for young men to resist the force of these presumptions, especially given circumstances that work to limit their experiences and subsequent worldviews. As already noted, these thematic considerations elaborate on assertions made by philosophers at least since Fanon that the ordinarily presumed guilt of blacks on the part of many whites often imposes on blacks a way of life that they can see as no good, but that they find extreme difficulty in resisting or escaping, given the alternatives that are ready to hand for them.[46]

Ultimately, I would contend that *Menace II Society* elaborates and embellishes on arguments such as those advanced by many recent philosophers focusing on race by delineating how this presumed guilt of blacks and related conditions may compel them into a way of thinking as well as life choices that not only degrade them but that they find difficult to avoid. For example, the film performs this service for Gordon's Fanonian explanation of presumptions that link criminality and skin color in dominant white consciousness. The film also illustrates how these beliefs may deeply racialize the life possibilities many individuals feel they have before them, confining them to misery-ridden alternatives and severely limiting their consciousness of opportunities for resistance or escape, particularly if Moody-Adams is correct in her diagnosis regarding the effects of such beliefs on the psyches of young African Americans themselves.[47]

Told in a nearly classic *noir* manner, *Menace II Society* works to bring these matters to its viewers' attention by exploiting possibilities of alignment and allegiance with its protagonist while at the same time using its *noir* techniques to foreground the misery and unfairness of racialized poverty. By detailing the nuanced particulars of Caine's existence, the film portrays him as a morally

---

46. Fanon, "Lived Experience of the Black," 184–201. It might also be worth noting here that the Hughes brothers characterize themselves as "thinkers." See Henry Louis Gates, "Blood Brothers: Albert and Allen Hughes in the belly of the Hollywood beast," *Transitions*, no. 63 (1994): 170.

47. Gordon, *Bad Faith and Antiblack Racism*, 101–2; Gordon, *Fanon and the Crisis of European Man*, 58–66; Moody-Adams, "Social Construction of Self-Respect."

complex, good-bad *noir* character who curries a measured positive audience allegiance despite his criminality. Even as viewers watch him do horrible things, they ultimately remain tied to him favorably because they have seen and understood what motivates him to commit such atrocities, thereby giving audience members a critical empathetic understanding of his reasons for acting. They come to see "from the inside" why he does what he does, without losing their critical perspective on his heinous actions. In this manner they see that he is not solely at fault for his actions, but that certain conditions have strongly influenced (although not absolutely forced) him to act as he does. The film also repeatedly exposes audience members to other, more positive dimensions of his character, such as his affection for his grandparents and his attempts to reflect on his life. By carefully modulating audience sympathy, empathy, and antipathy for this character, the film constructs a narrative figure through which many viewers—in particular, white viewers—might better grasp the implications of their own presumptions regarding young black men and how these beliefs could potentially play themselves out in the lives of such individuals.

The film also makes clear how these circumstances are entirely contingent, yet fail to move most whites, even as it produces "America's nightmare," namely vicious psychopaths like O-Dog, who in the words of Caine's voiceover is so because he is "young, black, and didn't give a fuck." On the other hand, even here the narrative of *Menace II Society* complicates audience response. Intended to act as an internal yardstick for the main character, O-Dog helps audience members to further ally with Caine by showing comparatively how much better this protagonist is than his more conscience-free best friend.[48] More exactly, O-Dog constitutes a variation on attractive-bad characters as described and explained by Murray Smith.[49] Not only does actor Larenz Tate bring the socially attractive traits of charisma and physical beauty to the role, but the character itself is also humorous in a grotesque, macabre sort of way.

Much like Hitchcock characters analyzed by Richard Allen, O-Dog's ability to make us laugh despite our better moral judgment draws viewers to him even in the face of his otherwise psychopathic character.[50] When he shoots a desperate crack addict over a perceived insult to his own rather straitlaced heterosexuality, for example, he picks up his victim's bag of cheeseburgers that he had earlier refused as payment for drugs and guilelessly offers them to his friends. When they refuse his offer in sickened revulsion, O-Dog is mystified: he does not understand why they might find his murderous actions something that might emotionally taint the food he is offering them, for free

---

48. Albert Hughes and Allen Hughes, interview in *The Hughes Brothers Talk about "Menace II Society,"* on *Menace II Society,* DVD. As noted in previous chapters, this function of comparing morally bad characters within a narrative has been described and explained by Noël Carroll and Murray Smith; see Carroll, "Toward a Theory of Film Suspense," 104–5, and Smith, *Engaging Characters,* 207–16.

49. Smith, "Gangsters, Cannibals, Aesthetes," 217–38, esp. 223–28.

50. Allen, "Hitchcock and Narrative Suspense," 163–82.

no less. During the opening murder-robbery, his anger over his victim having only "six motherfucking dollars" in the cash register is such that he brutally kicks the already dead proprietor lying on the floor next to him. Finally, when O-Dog visits with Caine after he has returned home from the hospital and is still recovering from his nearly fatal gunshot wound, O-Dog complains to his friend, "We still mad at you for dropping all that blood on us." Again and again O-Dog's behavior is ghoulishly inappropriate, but its very ghastliness often provokes grotesque laughter from the viewer, despite knowing at another level that such laughter is inappropriate, particularly from the audience's standard moral perspective.

Although audience members remain ambivalently disposed toward O-Dog pretty much throughout the film, his attractive-bad character points to a further, related effect the film encourages, namely, that of finding these characters' gangster lifestyle in some ways seductively alluring.[51] This aesthetic effect is similar to what Matthew Kieran has described as "the challenge of immoralism" provided by some fictional works.[52] Immoral art offers us no explicit moral guide with regard to how we should view the immorality it portrays and requires us to exercise moral judgments that we would "properly consider to be problematic or defective" (60). We exercise in our imaginations aesthetically "fitting" emotional responses "while nonetheless . . . recogni[zing] them to be, in actuality, morally defective" (61). The imaginative exercise of such morally defective judgments, however, "can afford us knowledge. We can come to understand better how and why people think or feel differently by engaging works we deem immoral" (62). Thus, as Kieran argues, the value of an artwork may sometimes depend on its compelling depiction of immoral perspectives that require the audience to "traffic in, and take up, immoral responses and attitudes" (72), even as they recognize such things to be immoral. While properly appreciating this value requires "certain background capacities and experiences" in moral judgment (73), given those abilities we may find value in some works of immoral art because the morally problematic experience they offer permits us to acquire a better grasp of the worlds they represent, particularly ones in which there is a great "amount of suffering, morally problematic experiences and evil actions" (73), such as those depicted by *Menace II Society*.

Kieran bases his argument partly on the Hughes brothers' admitted model for their film, *Goodfellas* (Martin Scorsese, 1991),[53] which he judges to be a work of immoral, but nonetheless aesthetically valuable, art because it enhances our understanding of a certain morally defective way of thinking, namely that practiced by its low-level Mafiosi characters (see 58–61). Although I would

51. Albert Hughes and Allen Hughes, interview in *The Hughes Brothers Talk About "Menace II Society,"* on *Menace II Society*, DVD.

52. Matthew Kieran, "Forbidden Knowledge: The Challenge of Immoralism," in *Art and Morality*, ed. Jose Bermudez and Sebastian Gardner (London: Routledge, 2003), 56–73.

53. Albert Hughes and Allen Hughes, interview in *The Hughes Brothers Talk About "Menace II Society,"* on *Menace II Society*, DVD.

not claim that *Menace II Society* is itself an immoral work of art—in fact, I claim the opposite—its narrative success nonetheless requires that the film effectively portray the powerful seductiveness of its characters' nihilism and their choices to commit criminal acts. In order to draw viewers into intimately understanding such a way of thinking and its consequences, the film strongly encourages them to imaginatively exercise "fitting" judgments about its characters' criminal activities, such as Caine's act of vengeance for his cousin Harold's (Saafir) death or O-Dog's many grotesque responses to the horrific conditions around him. The intimate depiction of characters like Caine and O-Dog thus serve to give viewers greater insight along the lines described by Kieran's essay into the evils of oppressive circumstances and the consequent attitudes often produced. Namely, if such conditions can comprehensibly produce individuals like these characters, then there is a strong argument to be made that they are fundamentally pernicious and should be eliminated, given the typical audience's background capacities and experiences in moral judgment.[54]

One influence that *Menace II Society* aims to have on its viewers, then, is to show them the powerful seductiveness of nihilism in the lives of these young men, for without grasping the forceful attraction of this outlook, those seeking solutions to the problems it poses will not be able to take proper account of its strength and allure. They will be, as Kieran might point out, at an epistemic disadvantage (72–73). Yet by imaginatively "slumming it," as Murray Smith refers to this aesthetic strategy, viewers may indulge in a kind of "knowing, self-conscious, imaginative play with the morally undesirable in the domain of fiction" so that greater knowledge of nihilism's attraction might be obtained.[55] On the other hand, by presenting how strongly this way of seeing the world permeates the lives of many young black men and making its power of temptation accessible to viewers, the film may mislead some audience members who lack the requisite background in moral judgment into believing that nihilism is a powerful and effective way to look at life. This possibility leads, I believe, to the many accusations of nihilism that *Menace II Society* has generated.[56]

Here, however, we also need to distinguish between different kinds of nihilism, their moral purpose, and the relationship they have to *film noir*. Even though many critics have criticized *Menace II Society* as nihilistic and hopeless, it is neither. It clearly depicts a way out for Caine, as well as holding out the hope that the conditions and background assumptions that make them

---

54. I am perhaps glossing over precisely what these background capacities and experiences in moral judgment might be. Suffice it to say that they would minimally have to include a solid commitment to *full* equality and justice for *all* human beings and a willingness to revise one's background assumptions concerning race.

55. Smith, "Gangsters, Cannibals, Aesthetes," 225.

56. See, for example, Todd Boyd, *Am I Black Enough for You? Popular Culture From the 'Hood and Beyond* (Bloomington: Indiana University Press, 1997), 82–104. Watkins, *Representing*, 196ff., and Massood, *Black City Cinema*, 169–74, contest accusations like Boyd's by arguing in ways similar to what I offer that the cinematic representation of such nihilism may have positive dimensions. However, I base my argument on different claims.

possible could be overcome. In terms of analysis suggested by Kevin Stoehr, this *noir* film is actively nihilistic, as opposed to being passively so.[57] Drawing on a distinction made by Nietzsche, Stoehr contends that nihilism affords the possibility for "creativity or life-affirmation to forge new values" (119 n. 6), in addition to merely rejecting old ones.

Building on Stoehr's insight,[58] I would argue that *Menace II Society* exploits just such an active nihilistic possibility. By depicting Caine's decisive turn from not caring whether he lives or dies to embracing the idea that caring about others gives his life meaning, the film holds out the possibility that new values may be forged even in light of rejecting traditional old ones, such as those embodied by oppressive racist institutions or the religious perspectives about which O-Dog and the narrative itself express skepticism. Any new values may well incorporate aspects of the old, but taken as is, these values do not speak effectively to how the world ought to be, which is the nihilist's core insight (see 112–13).

Jacqueline Scott has argued in analogous fashion for the utility of Nietzsche's views with regard to matters of race.[59] While the mere overthrow of old values can leave us bereft regarding where to turn or what to do, Scott points out that a Nietzschean revaluation of race would also afford opportunities to reconceptualize the idea of race and its role in cultural institutions that shape our lives. In addition, Nietzsche's attack on decadence indicates that affirming life is worth living not only can, but should be employed to counteract the passive variety of nihilism articulated by Stoehr.[60] Thus nihilism, as sometimes embodied in *noir*,[61] may play an active, positive role in human life as well as a passive, negative one. Moreover, recognizing these alternatives is consistent with Mike Davis's observation that *noir* is an ideologically ambiguous aesthetic because this artistic form may be employed, as he notes, in politically divergent ways.[62] As a corollary, I would also point out that *noir* may be used in morally divergent ways as well. Consistent with this line of thinking, Caine's decision to change his ways and affirm life as worth living embraces a similar perspective regarding *noir*'s employment in *Menace II Society*.

The Hughes brothers do not downplay the difficulties confronting those who would seek to exploit such affirmative *noir* possibilities, which is presumably one reason why they felt it necessary to kill off their protagonist. But the

57. Kevin Stoehr, "Nihilism and *Noir*," *Film and Philosophy* 8 (2004): 112–21.

58. Stoehr actually condemns *film noir* in general as "fundamentally" passively nihilist (e.g., 119), as some of it admittedly is, although he also recognizes the possibility that it could be used subversively (ibid., 121 n. 15)—that is, in the service of a more positive, active nihilism, particularly with regard to black *noir*, as I argue here.

59. Jacqueline Scott, "'The Price of the Ticket': A Genealogy and Revaluation of Race," in *Critical Affinities: Nietzsche and African American Thought*, ed. Jacqueline Scott and A. Todd Franklin (Albany: SUNY Press, 2006), 149–74.

60. Ibid. See also Jacqueline Scott, "Nietzsche and Decadence: The Revaluation of Morality," *Continental Philosophy Review* 31 (1998): esp. 66.

61. I should point out that Stoehr is not alone in arguing for *noir*'s nihilism. Porfirio, "No Way Out," 77–93, esp. 80, 89, does so implicitly, and Tuska, *Dark Cinema*, xvi–xxi, does so explicitly.

62. Davis, *City of Quartz*, 41.

sense of his loss that viewers feel at the end of the film also serves to under-score the randomness of violence under these conditions as well as the urgency and weight of the task ahead, for without grasping the full dimensions of the dilemma posed by nihilism and the factors contributing to it, there is little hope of successfully resolving them. As a fictional cinematic narrative aim-ing to show how young black men may become gangsters, *Menace II Society* exploits the empathy viewers feel for its main character in order to bring home the full impact of racial unfairness compounded by class disadvantage, as well as the consequent feelings of nihilism that frequently result from them.

Of course, the theme of nihilism may be consistently found in many black *noirs*. As noted earlier Doughboy's mother tells her son when he is a child that he "ain't shit and never will be shit," and his actions in *Boyz N the Hood* conform to a belief in those denigrations. In *Juice,* on the other hand, Bishop clearly expresses a deep, destructive passive nihilism. He claims to care about no one, not even himself. "I ain't shit. I ain't never gonna be shit," he tells the main character Q. He also remarks to his friends, "We ain't shit." As the previ-ous chapter noted, *Clockers* begins by foregrounding this feeling in its young African-American characters. Exposing such a problematic outlook in young black men even goes back to *Do the Right Thing*. As Spike Lee wrote about his own character's outlook on life, "Mookie—like many Black youths—has no vision. . . . The future might be too scary for kids like Mookie, so they don't think about it. They live for the present moment, because there is nothing they feel they can do about the future. What I'm really talking about is a feeling of helplessness, powerlessness, that who you are and what effect you can have on things is absolutely nil, zero, jack shit, *nada*."[63] This feeling is also what Cornel West had in mind in his essay "Nihilism in Black America."[64]

I agree with Massood that *Menace II Society* is "the culmination" of the ghet-tocentric *noir* film cycle, but not exactly for the reasons she gives.[65] As perhaps the epitome of these nihilistic black *noir* films, *Menace II Society* nonetheless refuses to indulge in some of the simpler (and more simple-minded) solutions to nihilism portrayed by other films in the cycle, as well as more recent black *noirs* like *Belly* (Hype Williams, 1998). This refusal makes *Menace II Society* a much harder film to watch, as it calls on viewers who take it seriously to do much more difficult cognitive and emotional work. Its narrative confronts them with a profoundly complex social problem, an evil of existing circumstance that admits no easy solution. They are then asked to think hard and reflect on their own complicity in it, namely through their personal presuppositions concern-ing race and class, and to seek ways to go beyond them. It further urges viewers to take seriously the immorality of its characters, to the point that it calls for viewers to make "fitting" immoral judgments that they know to be morally defective, even if the film also ultimately rejects its characters' immoral views.

---

63. Lee and Jones, *Do the Right Thing: A Spike Lee Joint,* 63–64.
64. West, "Nihilism in Black America," 11–20.
65. Massood, *Black City Cinema,* 143; see also 145–74.

   Yet the benefit of the difficult cognitive and emotional work called for by the film is that, following Kieran and Smith, viewers achieve a greater understanding of the world around them than they would have had otherwise, and thus have some hope of successfully going beyond the same old tired solutions ordinarily proffered regarding racism. Specifically, if appreciated properly, viewers acquire a better comprehension of some of the ordinary evils collected under the term "racism," and with that knowledge in hand, they may step forward to address the task of revaluating what race is, its consequences, and reconceiving its role in the cultural institutions that shape our lives.

   The need to explain comprehensibly the evil actions and beliefs that comprise racism rather than understanding it in ways that mystify the phenomena is important here because, as philosophers from Hannah Arendt to Adam Morton have sought to make clear, evil in human life is most frequently done by ordinary individuals disturbingly like ourselves, not psychopathic demons such as that proposed by *New Jack City*, or mentally ill individuals such as in *Juice*.[66] If we are to demystify racism, then we must acquire a thorough sense of how gangstas might often—perhaps even typically—be ordinary human beings forced to make choices under extraordinarily oppressive circumstances. Their evil actions may be largely explained by the pressures exerted on them by conditions created because of social institutions that maintain perceived differences between human beings with respect to skin color, physiognomy, and so on, as well as their integration with presumed differences of class. Reciprocally, racism may become more clearly something in which ordinary individuals indulge as part of their everyday lives. These sorts of demystifying elucidations are what I would argue *Menace II Society* aims to generate in its viewers. In demonstrating to them how a relatively ordinary individual can become a gangsta, the film seeks to make transparent racism's banality of evil.

   Given this interpretation of *Menace II Society*, it becomes clearer how *Clockers* may be understood as a further exploration of racism's banality. As noted in the previous chapter, Strike's choice to be a 'round-the-clock drug dealer represents the consequences of a young black male coming to believe in his own alleged subhumanity. As someone bombarded with such "ordinary" assertions both explicitly and implicitly by the culture surrounding him, Strike has decided, in a "perversely logical" way that parallels Pecola's wish for blue eyes, that given his circumstances, his best life option would be to do what we find him doing at the beginning of the film. One idea its narrative presumes as more or less established by means of these earlier films, then, is the nihilism that forms the "ordinary" background for Strike's decision to deal drugs in the first place. *Menace II Society* and its ghettocentric *noir* predecessors thus lay a foundation for Lee and his collaborators' exploration of Strike's evolution from a drug-dealing crew chief to someone who rejects such a life. Expressed another way, like *Clockers* the films discussed in this chapter analyze

---

   66. Hannah Arendt, *Eichmann in Jerusalem: A Report on the Banality of Evil* (1963; repr., New York: Penguin Books, 1994); Morton, *On Evil*, esp. 2–9, 79–81, 87–90.

and examine the "humanity of racism" and its consequences, which Jacquie Jones identified as a crucial dimension of *Do the Right Thing,* and which I take here to represent another dimension of Arendt's conception of evil's banality and its permeation through much of our mundane and ordinary lives.[67]

At the same time, a drawback in seeking to make this form of nihilism vivid and its appeal understandable for viewers is that of shading off into excess when depicting its component parts, namely, its misogyny, homophobia, and brutality. These components of the black nihilistic outlook are well documented in the form of the hard-core rap music that forms the backdrop to these films.[68] Cinematic narrative unfortunately allows for the expression of such beliefs all too easily by means of Hollywood conventionality. This ready availability in the music and easy access to cinematic convention makes it difficult, when portraying these elements, to avoid falling into a trap of passively integrating into the protocols of mainstream cinema as outlined by Jones and elaborated at the beginning of this chapter. Many of the films in this cycle do precisely that in regard to these sorts of beliefs, including *Menace II Society.* As such, these works are at least morally flawed from the perspective of advocating the recognition and acknowledgment of full humanity for *all* human beings, if not aesthetically flawed in this regard as well. On the other hand, as Tommy Lott argues, these sorts of flaws are the unfortunate legacy of black film's simultaneous reliance on and struggle for independence from mainstream cinema.[69]

The ghettocentric *noir* cycle focuses powerfully on making young black male criminals sympathetic as well as empathetic because the epistemology of ignorance regarding them has proven particularly difficult to break through and has affected many whites' as well as blacks' abilities to recognize and acknowledge their full humanity. These unusually recalcitrant presumptions about the alleged nature and capacities of black human beings greatly hamper a better understanding of the unique problems such individuals face in the real world. These films have also received a good deal of attention on account of their violence, brutality, and downbeat narratives. Of course, these were the complaints lodged against classic American *film noir* itself when French critics first named it, too.[70]

The point that I wish to underscore here, however, is that despite their imperfections these black *noir* films provide fertile grounds for constructing analogical bridges to the experiences of others whose lives may be separated from viewers by beliefs regarding race, class, and other presuppositions concerning alleged differences between human beings. As such, I would also

67. Jones, "In Sal's Country," 34; Arendt, *Eichmann in Jerusalem.*

68. See, for example, Lott, "Marooned in America," 122–25.

69. Lott, "Aesthetics and Politics," esp. 284–91; Lott, "A No-theory Theory of Contemporary Black Cinema."

70. Jean-Pierre Chartier, "Americans Are Also Making *Noir* Films" (1946), trans. Alain Silver, in Silver and Ursini, *Film Noir Reader 2,* 21–23.

suggest that the best of them, namely *Menace II Society* and *Clockers*, fulfill at least some of the crucial conditions for black film as a sort of politically informed, imperfect "Third Cinema" as outlined by Tommy Lott and Clyde Taylor.[71] By speaking polyvocally in both independent and mainstream voices, they offer viewers the opportunity to "read through" their own conventionality and grasp a more subtle, subversive message regarding the presuppositions surrounding black humanity, particularly as it shapes the circumstances of young African American men, and how those circumstances often produce in them a destructive form of passive nihilism. In speaking thusly, not only have these films promoted rich grounds for sympathy, empathy, and critical understanding for young black men, but as I will argue in subsequent chapters, black *noir* offers the potential for developing still more general pathways for understanding individuals not only young, black, poor, and male, but facing other forms of oppression.

71. Lott, "Aesthetics and Politics"; Lott, "Hollywood and Independent Black Cinema"; Taylor, *Mask of Art*, esp. 254–73.

All I wanted was to be a man among other men.

—Frantz Fanon, "The Lived Experience of the Black"

Fanon's insistence that he be treated as a man resonates powerfully for African Americans. Frederick Douglass used the concept of manhood to differentiate between having the mentality of a slave and aspiring to be free and treated as a full-fledged human being.[1] Similarly, civil rights protesters after World War II often wore signs proclaiming "I AM A MAN" in order convey their full humanity and demand respect.[2] British abolitionists used the idea as early as the 1780s, from which it found its way into American antislavery literature.[3] One finds it in black art, too, as when Ralph Ellison wryly declares in *Invisible Man*, "I am not a spook . . . I am a man of substance, of flesh and bone, fiber and liquids—and might even be said to possess a mind," or when Muddy Waters belts out, "I'm a man / I spell M, A child, N / that represents man," in "Mannish Boy."[4] While not wishing to downplay the deeply gendered assumptions inherent in this ultimatum,[5] I do want to note that it possesses a rhetorical strength for African Americans of which not even whites can legitimately claim to be ignorant. It should come as no surprise, then, that such humanistic conceptualizations arise in black *noir* films as well.

To better focus on late twentieth-century expressions of this frequent African-American demand, in this chapter I examine black *noirs* that lie close to but nonetheless outside the "ghettocentric *noir*" cycle discussed in the previous two chapters. In contrast to stories that revolve crucially around black youth, gangs, and drugs, the narratives of *Deep Cover, The Glass Shield,* and *Devil in a Blue Dress* go a modest step further to examine a more generalized sense of racialized humanity that deforms black existence. These works redirect the focus of black *noirs* by concentrating viewer attention on how even morally good adult men may be drawn into evil and criminality by means of racial oppression and presumed expectation. By working to encourage positive

1. Douglass, *Narrative of the Life of Frederick Douglass*, e.g., 66, 68, 74ff., 98.
2. Steven S. Estes, *I Am a Man! Race, Manhood, and the Civil Rights Movement* (Chapel Hill: University of North Carolina Press, 2005).
3. Noted in ibid., 2–3.
4. Ralph Ellison, *Invisible Man* ([1952]; repr., New York: Modern Library, n. d.), 3; Muddy Waters, "Mannish Boy," written by Bo Diddley, adapted by Muddy Waters, *Hard Again* (Blue Sky, 1977).
5. For an analysis of this demand's gendered assumptions, see Estes, *I Am a Man!*

audience engagement with such characters, these films urge viewers to reflect in more nuanced ways on being black in America. They seek to make more glaringly evident the moral obligation to reflect on such affected ways of thinking and acting by offering, not only grounds for thinking that would help to bridge the gaps between perceived differences in humanity, but also by sometimes explicitly calling for reflection on the part of the viewer. In this fashion *Deep Cover, The Glass Shield,* and *Devil in a Blue Dress* aim to chip away at more deeply embedded foundations of institutionalized racist belief. Ed Guerrero has observed that "black people have honed and perfected a wicked, penetrating vision of America's noir world that can only be described as the funkier side of noir."[6] The films analyzed here exemplify that vision in striking ways that expand its horizons and appeal.

Working for "the Man": *Deep Cover*

One work frequently linked to the ghettocentric *noir* cycle is director Bill Duke's 1992 film *Deep Cover.*[7] Through its employment of cinematic rap allusions, such as referencing Brian De Palma's *Scarface,* employing rappers in secondary roles, and filling out its narrative with a hip-hop soundtrack, the film clearly associates itself with the black *noirs* discussed in the previous two chapters. Yet *Deep Cover* also distinguishes itself from these films, particularly by the way that it focuses on an adult protagonist, rather than a youth coming of age. As such, its narrative takes a decidedly different trajectory, namely that of being a *noir* character study of an adult black male.

Its protagonist (played by Laurence Fishburne), like many figures depicted in classic *noir* films, possesses multiple names. These multiple names represent a fractured, fragmented identity that fits appropriately with the conflicted and contradictory circumstances of "twoness" that African Americans face generally, as W. E. B. Du Bois described more than a century ago in his famous discussion of "double consciousness."[8] This duality of identity becomes a narrative theme in *Deep Cover,* as Fishburne's character often thinks of himself as acting either as Russell Stevens Jr., police officer, on the one hand, or John Q. Hull, drug dealer, on the other, depending on the situation in which he finds himself.[9] In addition, when he expresses a desire to acquire ethnic African masks about one-third of the way through the film, after meeting his drug operation's money launderer, the art dealer Betty (Victoria Dillard), he does so literally from behind the mask he wishes to buy. This use of masks calls to

6. Guerrero, "Circus of Dreams and Lies," 346. As noted in the introduction, Guerrero's argument about black *noir* divides these films in a different way from that which I propose in this book. Still, I do not see our perspectives as being in complete disagreement.

7. See, for example, Diawara, "*Noir* by *Noirs*," 266, 274, 276.

8. Du Bois, *The Souls of Black Folk,* 45.

9. I want to thank Mitch Avila for bringing the themes of masks and double consciousness in *Deep Cover* more fully to my attention.

FIG. 24   The film's protagonist (Laurence Fishburne) holding an African mask (*Deep Cover*, 1992).

mind Du Bois's metaphor of the "veil" with which he argues African Americans are born; that is, the way in which they are compelled to look at themselves not only from an internal perspective but "through the eyes of others."[10] The film literalizes this image by having the main character hold the mask up to his face when responding to Betty's pointed inquiries, as she, a black woman, reflects this veiled status back by donning sunglasses while posing her questions.

Such narrative interplay with "veils" reminds viewers of how African Americans often find it difficult to unify their sense of identity, given the conflicting pressures exerted on them by contradictory views of themselves. While perhaps not impossible to reconcile, these tensions, arising from differences between black and white perspectives on racialized humanity, make their conjunction in one person quite likely to result in a divided sense of who one is. On the other hand, the familiar *noir* technique of multiple naming eloquently conveys the impression of fragmentation that typically accompanies African-American existence.

Moreover, unlike the black *noir* protagonists discussed in Chapters 4 and 5 *Deep Cover*'s main character already knows what he wants from the outset: "to be of some use, to make a difference" to his community, as he tells his future Drug Enforcement Administration (DEA) boss Jerry Carver (Charles Martin Smith). His main quest over the course of the narrative is thus not to discover *what* he should aim for in his life, as the characters must typically determine

10. Du Bois, *The Souls of Black Folk*, 44, 45.

in the ghettocentric *noir* films discussed previously, but *how* he might best achieve that goal. From the outset this narrative figure understands himself as having a life that possesses meaning and value, even if he remains unclear about how best to express them. As Aristotle indicated long ago, this difference in how one understands one's life amounts to the first step toward integrating one's actions and goals with those of others, so that some sort of reasonable human flourishing might occur. Understanding one's life as having meaning and value is, in other words, crucial to the acquisition of *phronesis,* or practical wisdom,[11] which places *Deep Cover's* protagonist in a situation distinctly different from those of the characters discussed earlier.

This narrative figure initially believes that being a street cop will be the optimal means by which to express a "politics of caring about the Black community," as Diawara describes it,[12] but Carver persuades him that being an undercover agent will more fully realize what he sees as important and meaningful in his life. By arguing that Stevens would be of far more benefit to the black community working as "a scumbag for the right side" in order to bring down big-time, illegal drug suppliers, Carver convinces him that working in deep cover as a drug-dealing "snitch" would more optimally achieve his moral goal of making a positive difference for his community. Ironically enough, Carver's success here means that a white bureaucrat lures this African-American character into the *noir* underworld.

To his dismay, our protagonist discovers that, by working for the DEA, instead of being "a cop pretending to be a drug dealer, I ain't nothing but a drug dealer pretending to be a cop." Rather than making a meaningful difference to members of the black community, he realizes, "I sold drugs. I watched people die and I didn't do nothing. I killed people"—people "who looked like me, whose mother and father looked like my mother and father," the very people to whom he wanted to be of some use. But as a "scumbag for the right side"—in his DEA-approved identity of John Q. Hull, drug dealer—he finds himself powerless to make any sort of positive moral difference. Being a servant in the thrall of institutions that maintain existing power relations forces him to perform the same actions as any other scumbag. Thus, Carver's introduction of a *noir* underworld into this character's life gulls him into selling "drugs to kids and pregnant women," as he ruefully observes in his voiceover, stand by as black people are murdered, and even kill African Americans himself in the course of maintaining his "mask" as a drug dealer for the DEA. He realizes as well that this induced confusion over his identity has brought out a seductive darker side, a capacity for evil. As he narrates his story he observes,

11. Aristotle, *Nicomachean Ethics,* esp. 89–90, 91–93, 96–99. See also John M. Cooper, *Reason and Human Good in Aristotle* (1975; repr., Indianapolis: Hackett, 1986), esp. 91–115. I use the older translation of *phronesis* here as "practical wisdom," rather than Irwin's "prudence."

12. Diawara, "Black American Cinema," 24. I disagree with Diawara about the main character discovering this politics of caring over the course of the narrative. As the film makes clear, the protagonist already possesses such a politics from the first scene in which we see him as an adult, even if he remains unsure how to best implement it.

"I was good at it [dealing drugs]. Being a cop was never this easy." Later, he confesses, "It was fun. I liked being a big shot. Wouldn't you?"

Noir scholars Alain Silver and James Ursini remark that *Deep Cover* puts "a new spin on the *noir* hero" by offering viewers a protagonist caught in "a system that has manipulated him since childhood" and his gradual realization of its ubiquity,[13] its reach even inside himself, to the point that he has again and again unknowingly acted in complicity with it. Moreover, through questions directed explicitly at the viewer, the film implicates audience members in this manipulative system as well. By addressing the viewer openly with pointed questions through the protagonist's voiceover, *Deep Cover* challenges its audience members to reflect on the degree to which they, too, would like being "a big shot," if faced with the option of indulging in the pleasures of power, money, and freedom made possible by working for institutions that maintain white advantage. The narrative underscores this seduction through having the protagonist's crime partner, David Jason (Jeff Goldblum), tempt him with the claim that money will solve all difficulties posed by race. "Five hundred million dollars and no more 'nigger,'" Jason argues in trying to convince the undercover policeman to remain a drug dealer once the latter reveals his other identity. Of course, this "whitening" power of money is specious. As George Yancy points out, "Within the eyes of whiteness, [even] Oprah [Winfrey], despite her talent and financial success ($1.1 billion), is still inferior because she is black."[14] The protagonist of *Deep Cover* seems to know this intuitively—or at least he acts consistently with this knowledge, for he rejects Jason's offer, but the seductive, allegedly de-racializing power of money is nonetheless highlighted. In addition, by pointedly returning to a call for reflection at its conclusion, the film challenges viewers to think about the degree to which they, too, may already be implicated in the oppressive system of power relations depicted by the narrative and what they might do if they took seriously the matter of changing it.

Deep Cover aims to bring audience members to a new level of understanding regarding corrupt but invisible dimensions of the status quo and how these might be implicated in matters of identity, race, and class. It seeks to accomplish this goal by offering viewers the story of its *noir* protagonist's gradual discovery of truths about these matters both for and about himself. Through exploiting the voiceover technique's capacity to directly and intimately address viewers— particularly about the moral dimensions of the story being presented—the film explicitly calls for them to reflect on what they have learned over the course of the narrative, as well as what they should do about it. In this manner, the film spurs what I have described earlier as a "Socratic impulse" in viewers to reflect critically à la Socrates about themselves in light of what its narrative presents.

By means of engaging audience members firmly in its black protagonist's trajectory of realization, the film's *noirish* narrative also operates to align them

---

13. Silver and Ursini, "Appendix E1: Neo-Noir," 406.

14. George Yancy, "Introduction: Fragments of an Ontology of Whiteness," in Yancy, *What White Looks Like*, 7.

closely with him. The film's point of view is very much his: not only is he in nearly every scene, so that we see his reactions to the situations around him as well as hear what he says, but the subjective access afforded by his voiceover provides us with further considered thoughts and reflections regarding the events depicted as he tells his story from some point after their occurrence.

Such close alignment with the main character helps to give viewers ample reason to feel a favorable allegiance toward him. As a narrative voice constructed as reliable,[15] he acquaints audience members with his positive moral attributes and ideals, even if they also witness how oppressive influences temporarily seduce or confuse him. On the other hand, viewers see that he typically exhibits admirable traits and seeks to uphold his moral goals. He shows compassion toward secondary characters like his neighbor's neglected son James (Joseph Ferro), the young woman who is stoned into oblivion and in thrall to Eddie (Roger Guenveur Smith), the drug dealer he quickly replaces ("You need to take this girl off the fire, man; she's done," he tells the incompetent hustler), and the nameless twelve- or thirteen-year-old dealer he sees shot in the back for selling drugs on the wrong street corner. Viewers also witness how he agonizes over the terrible things he must do in the service of the DEA, such as killing his drug-dealing competition, or selling drugs to the weak and vulnerable. These sequences illustrate his sense of conscience over seeing inflicted or himself inflicting pain and suffering on other human beings, no matter how good or bad they are. Overall these actions encourage us to sympathize with the protagonist, to look favorably on his character as he confronts the details of his dilemma, because we see as viewers that on balance he possesses moral and other attributes that we admire.

The extensive access viewers have to this character also helps them to empathize with him, for they come to see in him traits and ideals that they would typically like to think of themselves as having. These traits and ideals include the wish to make a positive difference to their community, a deep and abiding compassion for others, and a humanity that encompasses both admirable strengths as well as crippling weaknesses. By means of *noir* techniques developed for encouraging not only sympathy but also empathy for morally complex lawbreakers, this film depicts its protagonist's feelings and sentiments as *fully* and routinely human, rather than as something less than that, and therefore raced as black according to common social presumptions—that is, raced as inferior.[16] Rather than emphasize differences between human beings, the narrative stresses their commonalities regardless of race, such as possessing similar responses to pain and suffering, thereby making possible the building of empathetic bridges between audience and character.[17] The film

15. For a more thorough discussion of narrative reliability, see George M. Wilson, "*Le Grand Imagier* Steps Out: The Primitive Basis of Film Narration," *Philosophical Topics* 25 (1997): 295–317.

16. Diawara, "*Noir* by *Noirs*," 271, makes a related point about *noir* and identification.

17. Mulhall, *On Film*, 33–34; Jones, "Impairment of Empathy," 71ff.; Barnes and Thagard, "Empathy and Analogy."

depicts the main character's seduction by power and evil not as difficulties that exclusively (or even probably) tend to befall blacks, but rather as utterly *human* dilemmas. *Deep Cover* portrays the kind of coldhearted selfishness and sense of dominion to which he temporarily succumbs in ways that foreground their human universality—that is, their potential to seduce virtually anyone, regardless of race.

Here, as in other films I discuss, the peculiar lure of criminality developed in earlier *noir* films works in favor of showing that blacks are no different from other human beings. The filmmakers of *Deep Cover*—as well as many other black *noir* films—deploy the determinist tendency to break the law often found in classic *noir* narratives, but frequently attributed to dimensions of class oppression,[18] as indifferent to considerations of race. There is a sense, then, in which *noir* determinism operates as a form of "equal-opportunity" oppression in these narratives, as a way to characterize *human* problems, rather than being employed to depict problems specific to raced human beings.

Admittedly, such determinism may pose more of a seductive possibility for some than for others, depending on the historical particulars of their circumstances. But these particulars are not marked as *inherently* raced in *Deep Cover* or many other black *noir* films, but rather as *contingently* imposed consequences of poverty, lack of opportunity, social inequality, racialized presumptions about human "others," and so on. These circumstances, in other words, could easily have been otherwise if certain different historical events had occurred—for example, if the Founding Fathers had outlawed slavery at the Constitutional Convention in 1787. This dimension of contingency *Deep Cover* explicitly depicts by underscoring the full-fledged humanity of its African-American protagonist and conveying that sense of humanity to viewers through strategies that encourage strong favorable empathetic as well as sympathetic allegiances. By employing such strategies, cinematic narratives like *Deep Cover* may offer up the circumstances depicted as lacking inherently racialized aspects because, not only are such conditions portrayed as contingent, as possibly being otherwise, but the main characters to whom viewers find themselves becoming attached clearly constitute individuals who merely happen to be raced, rather than as inherently raced human beings.

This foregrounded contingency is one thing that makes these films so interesting and worth our consideration, not only as viewers, but as philosophical thinkers. By providing alternative ways to perceive and think of racialized social conditions, these narratives offer up, as well as human beings, unconventional visions of race and its consequences for serious consideration. In doing so, these visions implicitly challenge standard presumptions that often cloud a better sense of what race is, such as that it is "those people's" nature, family structure, etc. Films like *Deep Cover* thus encourage viewers to think

18. See the entries for *The Damned Don't Cry* (Vincent Sherman, 1950), *Raw Deal* (Anthony Mann, 1948), *Too Late for Tears* (Byron Haskin, 1949), and *Try and Get Me* (Cy Enfield, 1950) in Silver and Ward, *Film Noir: An Encyclopedic Reference*, 78–79, 238–39, 292–93, 295–96.

about the contrast between racial stereotypes and how they attach to human beings on the one hand, and the possibilities offered by strategies embodied in their narratives to circumvent such stereotypes on the other.

In order to see how such reflection might be encouraged, let us examine *Deep Cover's* attempts to invoke it. We know from the very beginning, for example, that the protagonist is dead set against being seduced by evil and has resolved to avoid the pitfalls of becoming a criminal. It happens to him anyway, though, because of presumptions by others about black male humanity and manipulation by a system that has stage-managed his thoughts, feelings, and actions since childhood. People find it easy to think of him as a drug dealer, so it is a relatively uncomplicated matter for him to slip into the role that his DEA boss proposes: working as a scumbag for the right side. Even though Russell Stevens Jr. has resolved to himself as a ten-year-old that "it wasn't gonna happen to me" regarding his father's junkiedom and descent into criminality, the character finds to his dismay that that is precisely what happens to him.

These and other forms of presumptive, institutional manipulation are made explicit through the film's narrative. At one point the main character becomes so successful at buying cocaine that the amount he acquires far exceeds the budget that Carver has for the undercover operation. When this employee of the federal government asks what he should do with all the drugs he now has, his DEA boss callously responds, "You're a drug dealer—deal drugs." Thus he ends up doing just the opposite of what he had hoped to accomplish. Rather than being of some use and benefit to the black community, he finds himself selling crack to the naïve and vulnerable—"kids and pregnant women," as he tells us—in order to finance the undercover operation of which he is a part. Later he finds himself living the lavish, profligate lifestyle of the successful drug dealer, which again Carver explicitly orders him to take up so that the operation will remain covert. As already noted, the main character finds it easy and fun to act out this "mask" that societal institutions and presumptions have made for him. Carver's manipulation of his operative thus underscores that a cognitive slot already exists in many people's thinking—including his own—for him to become a generic black drug dealer, so his posing as one merely fulfills expectations they already had. In the terms provided by Murray Smith, his pose fits neatly into their preexisting, automatized belief-schemata, their co-text, for understanding cinematic representations—and, for that matter, the world.[19]

Deep Cover draws our attention to how the main character is compelled to fulfill these expectations by the machinations of social institutions serving white advantage. Ironically, Carver's orders that he act out the role of a drug dealer to the hilt demonstrate how such criminal identities may be efficiently imposed on African-American men by institutions serving existing power relations. Carver's undercover operative, the straight-arrow cop Russell Stevens Jr., who has resolutely stayed away from drugs and alcohol all his life, need do little besides stop shaving, get his ear pierced, and act in ways that do

19. Smith, *Engaging Characters*, 194.

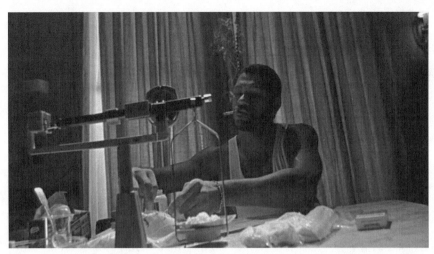

FIG. 25   The undercover policeman Russell Stevens Jr. (Laurence Fishburne) becomes drug dealer John Hull (*Deep Cover*, 1992).

not contradict societal expectations about black men in order to slip into the social role of John Q. Hull, street hustler, because such a role fits so harmoniously with common presumptions about being a black male in America.[20]

In contrast to the main character's fate, his white DEA boss Carver notes that he "went to Princeton to avoid all that shit" and thus may coolly operate as a crude moral utilitarian regarding such matters. Rather than having to deal with the sticky details of day-to-day illicit drug deals or the sad, enervating circumstances of desperate individuals looking for a score, his social distance means he can blithely propose that his employee sacrifice his current clientele to whom he sells drugs in order to catch the main West Coast suppliers of cocaine, thus saving future potential victims from damage and devastation. Personally unaffected by the human cost of his decisions, Carver is much freer to think about how the operation's success may boost his career and help him climb the bureaucratic ladder at the DEA. Thus he tells his operative that it would be great if they could take down the main supplier "by the end of the month, [because] it'll go into the report for this quarter," impress the members of Congress who approve funding for the operation, and "make us look efficient," which would greatly increase Carver's career opportunities, regardless of the undertaking's cost in human life and suffering.

This DEA functionary's sense of the undercover drug operation shouldered by the protagonist is predominantly administrative and detached. Thus

20. See, for example, Levin, "Responses to Race Differences in Crime," and *Why Race Matters*, where this philosopher argues in favor of such stereotypes based on a crude form of Bayesianism. For critical responses to Levin's argument regarding how these presumptions should operate in people's thinking, see Armour, *Negrophobia and Reasonable Racism*, esp. 36–60, and O'Connor, *Oppression and Responsibility*, esp. 111–34.

his insensitivity and self-interest may achieve much freer rein than the main character's, as he rarely faces its dispiriting human expenditures, except when forced to do so. Even then his detachment typically allows him to evade it, as he does when his operative confesses to being troubled by seeing a young dealer shot in the back. Murder, drug addiction, and the tragic waste of human potential are mere stepping-stones to Carver's job advancement. Rather than being firmly committed to morally benefiting others, as the main character is, the film portrays Carver as cynically committed to selfish career goals.

Narrative Voice and Epistemic Authority

Like other black *noirs* such as *Clockers* and *Menace II Society, Deep Cover* aims to convey knowledge as well as insight, making it "one of the most didactic Black films," as Diawara notes.[21] Rather than being a disadvantage, this characteristic becomes an asset because typical *noir* narrative techniques that foreground these aims (particularly by means of voiceover) also heighten our dramatic interest. Told in retrospect and with careful reflection on the story depicted, the extradiegetic narration adds a dimension of critical perspective to the events, which gives the protagonist's storytelling an air of considered moral judgment about what he has experienced.

His voiceover further adopts the cadences and vocabulary of black speech, which convey a distinctively African-American perspective. For example, his initial address to the audience is, "So gather 'round as I run it down, and unravel my pedigree."[22] Viewers' first impression of the protagonist and the story he tells thus blend together the strands of blackness, *film noir,* and didacticism. The film explicitly foregrounds its stance as a cautionary *noir* tale, a streetwise lecture about what the main character has come to know about being African American, which he conveys by means of recounting his experiences as an undercover cop working in the service of the DEA.

In the opening flashback depicting events from the main character's childhood, his father tells him, "You better know what you want. Else, how you expect to get what you want, if you don't know what the hell you want?" This exchange between father and son indicates from the outset the importance placed on knowing what one wants in life, and it is underscored by the fact that the flashback depicts the father, Russell Stevens Sr. (Glynn Turman), as knowing by contrast that he has already wasted his own life. "Don't you ever be like me! Don't be like me!" he angrily tells his son as he whacks him with his hat. We know from the context that the father's anger stems far more from his own frustration and disappointment in himself than anything he sees in

21. Diawara, "Black American Cinema," 23.

22. As I explain more fully below, this statement quotes the traditional black vernacular poem "The Fall"; see Dennis Wepman, Ronald B. Neuman, and Murray B. Binderman, *The Life: The Lore and Folk Poetry of the Black Hustler* (Philadelphia: University of Pennsylvania Press, 1976), 79.

his ten-year-old son, as his hotheaded reaction is far in excess of the child's lackluster response to the command that he never take drugs in order to avoid the pitfalls of a junkie parent.

Of course, the son *does* know what he wants, as his adult voiceover tells us after we see his father gunned down by the liquor store operator his desperate dad had just robbed: *not* to be a junkie like his father, *not* to fall into the trap of criminality posed for black men by generalized social presumption, and (a few moments later, we find out) to make some sort of positive difference to the black community. As the narrative makes clear, however, the main character's quest to achieve these noble moral goals becomes perverted by the overwhelming institutional pressures bearing down on him, so that he ends up serving their purposes rather than his own.

The film also returns repeatedly to the main character's racialized circumstances by referencing African-American oppression through quoting and paraphrasing a "toast" (a black vernacular folk poem).[23] With its affinity to rap and ability to express analogous sentiments about racial injustice and oppression, use of this poetic form becomes an especially poignant way of expressing the predicament in which the main character finds himself as a result of his manipulation by a system that has controlled him since childhood. When he is driven to the deepest depths of despair by the social pressures that threaten to crush him, he describes what he feels these forces have turned him into by reciting from the traditional jailhouse poem "The Fall of Jezebel." As we see him finally give in to social expectation and snort his first noseful of cocaine late in the film, he rhapsodizes in his voiceover from this work, which inmates have recited since at least the 1960s:

You know that the jungle creed say that the strongest feed
On any prey it can,
And I was branded beast at every feast
Before I ever became a man.[24]

Given common social presumptions regarding the allegedly inherent animalistic, immoral, not-quite-fully-human nature of black men, this short stanza effectively portrays how the protagonist feels he has been seen since long before he became an adult, serving to confirm Silver and Ursini's insight regarding his manipulation by a system from childhood.

Elsewhere, when describing the cruel, Hobbesian circumstances in which he operates on the streets, he again recites from the poem. In the opening sequence he references the poem twice: first, when he initially addresses his audience to "gather 'round as I run it down, and unravel my pedigree," and

---

23. Ibid., 1–2, 9–12.

24. Laurence Fishburne, commentary, *Once in the Life*, DVD, directed by Laurence Fishburne (2000; TriMark Home Video, 2001). The poem itself is a variation of "The Fall," which Wepman, Neuman, and Binderman recorded in 1963; see *The Life*, 79–88, esp. 79–80.

second, when he describes how his father "found his grave in the snow," as he watches him die from a gunshot wound received after committing a robbery. Later still in the film, to describe the brutal existential conditions of drug-dealing, the main character tellingly quotes this stanza:

> Where junkies prowl, where tigers growl,
> In search of that much-needed blow,
> Where winos cringe on a canned-heat binge,
> And find their graves in the snow.[25]

In many ways these poetic phrases establish a baseline from which this character must operate. Like the rap songs and haunting underscore the narrative also utilizes,[26] references to this jailhouse poem enhance *Deep Cover's* narrative by adding emotional weight and a sense of considered experience to the protagonist's storytelling voice, giving it a depth it would otherwise lack. Quoting from "The Fall of Jezebel" ultimately offers viewers a better sense of the main character's circumstances, authority, and humanity, his complex mixture of compassion, cunning, and cruelty that has been bred within him by life on the streets. This toast helps to enhance the audience's sense of the main character's knowledge of another kind of existence of which many viewers know little or nothing, doing so in ways that shock, surprise, and delight by virtue of the poem's twisted beauty,[27] which reflects the character's own.

Recitation from the poem also lends an air of moral regret to the main character's narration, as "The Fall of Jezebel" tells a similar story of sin and remorse, of human life wasted and insight gained too late to do its protagonist any good. Paralleling what literary critics Alan Wald and Paula Rabinowitz have identified as "Marxist *noir*" poetry,[28] this black vernacular toast projects a sense of fatalistic authority on the main character as a source of knowledge regarding his street saga of duplicity, manipulation, and the struggle to remain nonetheless human, giving his account undertones informed by sorrow, foreboding, and abiding humanity. These thematic leitmotifs thus serve to reinforce to viewers that the main character's chronicle possesses a kind of reliability—a street credibility, a sense that he knows what he is talking about and therefore

25. Wepman, Neuman, and Binderman, *The Life*, 79–80. Lawrence Fishburne remarks that he used "The Fall of Jezebel" as an audition piece for years before contributing bits and pieces of it to *Deep Cover*. In addition, one of his motivations for writing his play *Riff Raff* (titled *Once In the Life* when made into a film) was to provide a fuller venue for the poem (Fishburne, commentary, *Once In the Life*, DVD).

26. Silver and Ursini, "Appendix E1," 406.

27. Wepman, Neuman, and Binderman, *The Life*, 79; Jerry H. Bryant, *"Born in a Mighty Bad Land": The Violent Man in African American Folklore and Fiction* (Bloomington: Indiana University Press, 2003), 97–98.

28. Alan Wald, in Graham Barnfield, "'The Urban Landscape of Marxist *Noir*': An Interview with Alan Wald," *Crime Time*, June 26, 2002, http://www.crimetime.co.uk/features/marxistnoir.html (accessed March 24, 2006); Rabinowitz, *Black and White and Noir*, 6–8.

may have something significant to say about the pitfalls of working for institutions that support and maintain white advantage. As cautionary *noir* tale, then, *Deep Cover*'s narrative voice is substantially enhanced by recitation from this poem. It adds an air of sad wisdom to the knowledge the protagonist conveys about his misadventures within white power structures.[29]

Learning from the Logic of White Power

Elsewhere in the narrative, equipped with knowledge acquired on the streets, the main character seems to be working toward achieving his moral goals, albeit in a roundabout manner. As a "scumbag for the right side" he climbs the drug-dealing ladder and insinuates himself into meeting the main supplier of crack cocaine on the West Coast, Anton Gallegos (Arthur Mendoza), whose pretensions the protagonist quickly deflates by describing him as "a creep in a black cape." The prospect of finally arresting this purveyor of mass evil excites the hardworking undercover cop. But then Carver tells him that Gallegos can no longer be taken down because the State Department wishes to protect Gallegos's uncle, the powerful and influential Latin American diplomat Hector Guzman (René Assa), and does not want him smeared by having his nephew arrested on drug charges, as they had earlier. "We like [the uncle] now. We want him to run for president down there or something," Carver feebly tells his operative.

This manipulation of the "war on drugs" for the purposes of foreign policy shows the main character that problems ravaging African-American communities play a strictly secondary role to other dilemmas those in power see as higher priorities, such as "fighting Communism" and having business-friendly but despotic leaders in Latin American countries so that (mainly white-controlled) American corporations may operate more easily. Accordingly, the main character sardonically refers to Gallegos as "the new Noriega," Panama's erstwhile dictator whose corrupt and drug-dealing presence U.S. officials long tolerated because he pledged fealty to American foreign policy; and at another point Hull's crime partner David mentions that Gallegos's uncle goes fishing with George (Herbert Walker) Bush, then U.S. president.

This subordination of problems that African Americans often face to other concerns shows the main character that there are, as Mills argues in *The Racial Contract*, "norm[s] of far greater value of *white* life, and the corresponding crystallization of feelings of vastly differential outrage over white and nonwhite death, white and nonwhite suffering" (101). Such a sacrifice, according to this logic, would not be tolerated if the lives in question were white, but since they are merely those of "niggers and Spics," as our protagonist bitterly remarks,

---

29. There is a sense in which Fishburne's star persona and buttery-smooth, seductive voice enhance *Deep Cover*'s narration as well, but I mention these factors only in passing, even though they deserve more thoughtful analysis.

the sacrifice is acceptable. By virtue of the State Department's orchestration and complicity in these dealings, the main character has illustrated for him (and implicitly, so does the audience) how government institutional bodies may maintain and support *de facto* racist rankings even to the point of their causing disproportionate violence, suffering, and death to nonwhites, a sad fact that Mills also notes in *The Racial Contract* (82–83).

These revelations as experienced by the protagonist provide viewers with an invitation to consider the validity of similar connections that might be made outside the fictional world of *Deep Cover*. By mixing its imagined elements with real-life aspects of U.S. governmental policy, the film seeks to confront its viewer with the possibility that such outrageous and cold-hearted manipulations may not be confined to the fictional world depicted through the *noir* story of John Q. Hull, undercover agent for the DEA, but may well arise elsewhere—namely, in real life and actual U.S. foreign policy.

According to the logic of white power laid out by the film, then, Gallagos and his uncle must go free in spite of their direct hand in facilitating—and profiting greatly from—the death and deformation of huge numbers of blacks and others to whom their agents sell crack. By being held back in this way the main character realizes that he "can get more clout and more money on the street" than through the white power structures offered to him by his DEA boss. He still wishes to make a difference, rather than be cynically content with the "spoils of war," as Carver is. Paradoxically, the main character realizes that he can do more good for the black community by being an outlaw drug dealer who quits pretending to be a cop than by being a cop pretending to be a drug dealer, as Carver had guided him to be. Realizing that he has been duped, manipulated, and "turned out like a two-dollar 'ho," he quits Carver's undercover drug operation.

Refusing the bureaucrat's offer to follow him to Washington and merely work in the interest of selfish career goals, the main character strikes out on his own. This decision requires him to use his position and knowledge as a drug dealer to create change independently, rather than working through the protocols and channels of white policing structures. Thinking now as a streetwise African American working to help his community rather than a cop pretending to be a drug dealer, he kills Gallegos and entraps the uncle, who under the misguided aegis of white power possesses diplomatic immunity. The main character tricks Guzman into agreeing, on videotape, to finance the manufacture of a new designer drug that would further ravage those stuck in poverty and disadvantage. In acting positively for his community and eliminating not only the main supplier of drugs on the West Coast but also his corrupt, seemingly untouchable diplomat of an uncle, *Deep Cover*'s protagonist must reject the protocols of white power, breaking its laws and procedures in order to construct his own point of view and means. Hull uses African-American sensibilities and street smarts to subvert the established order and change the typical ways of thinking and acting that racially skew the so-called war on drugs. By managing to kill Gallegos and smear the uncle anyway, in spite of his boss's explicit instructions not to do so, he achieves far more good for the black community than any route that service to Carver and the DEA might offer.

Jerry Carver, Pimp for White Power

It is worthwhile at this juncture to make more explicit the narrative intertwining of *Deep Cover*'s protagonist with his DEA boss, and the latter's hand in transforming his employee into "a scumbag for the right side," as it provides further insight concerning the film's perspective on race, criminality, and social presumption. During their first meeting this white bureaucrat points out to Stevens that in spite of being a policeman, his psychological profile is almost exactly that of a criminal's, with analogous scores for anger, repressed violence, and resentment of authority.[30] The protagonist is, in other words, already psychologically an outlaw, a trait that he hides behind a badge. Yet even with this mental profile, he still wishes to do good for his fellow African Americans. By manipulating his desire to be of service to the black community and seducing him into thinking that he will achieve a greater human good, Carver persuades his future servant to believe that "under cover all your faults will become virtues . . . [there] you *will* be of use; you *will* make a difference." Under Carver's influence, he takes the offered assignment to go into deep cover and pose as a drug dealer, even though he also has the feeling, in typical *noir* fashion, that to do so "would be the biggest mistake of my life." He has a premonition that becoming a scumbag for the right side will do him far more damage than good, but the DEA functionary coaxes him into believing the opposite, in spite of his misgivings. Much of the film, then, depicts its protagonist's struggle to make narrative sense of how that mistaken decision to work for a governmental structure like the DEA confused his sense of self,

---

30. Kenneth Chan, "The Construction of Black Male Identity in Black Action Films of the Nineties," *Cinema Journal* 37 (1998): 35–48, argues that the protagonist of *Deep Cover* "internalizes the stereotypes and the labels that the white police establishment places on him" (39). But Chan's argument misses the point of these narrative details. As the film portrays him, the main character really *is* angry and filled with repressed violence. But these dimensions of his personality are due to frustrations over injustice and racism, not the imposition of racial stereotypes from the white police establishment. Rather than being merely *constructed* by Carver as angry and repressedly violent, he actually *is* these things long before he meets Carver, but for clearly understandable reasons. He is righteously indignant over injustices perpetrated against African Americans and consciously seeks to do something about them, even if he is unsure what the best means might be to accomplish that goal. Diawara, for example, underscores that the film is about black rage against racial injustice ("*Noir* by *Noirs*," 266). Moreover, as my analysis should make evident, *Deep Cover*'s story is about how the protagonist comes to fill out the "rigid moral code with no underlying system of values" and "insufficiently developed sense of self" that his psychological profile reveals he lacks at the film's beginning. By the narrative's end, these previously lacking dimensions of his character have developed into solid and abiding aspects of his identity. Those developments, one might say, constitute his "character arc."

separated him from the concerns of other African Americans, and perverted his moral goal of making a positive difference to the black community.

On the other hand, there is a sense in which Carver might seem to function as something like a borderline sympathetic racist character—or more precisely, a racist character who has a few sympathetic moments, similar to Rocco in *Clockers*. I do not think that audiences generally find themselves being lured into an allegiance with him for much of the narrative, only to suddenly find out that he is also racist through a clear epistemological twist, as with Sal in *Do the Right Thing* or Hurricane in *One False Move*. Yet I would also argue that he should not even be seen as a racist who turns out to be marginally sympathetic in the way that Rocco does. Rather, there is no real twist in our knowledge of Carver's character over the course of the narrative, no revelation that tells us he is not quite what he had seemed. While our allegiance to him varies, he remains a generally unsympathetic character throughout, depicted primarily by morally negative traits, even if he does have some minor sympathetic moments. Still, the subtleties in our allegiance to him are crucial to understand, as he ranges from out-of-touch, racist bureaucrat, to office functionary with *some* heart and possibly *some* racial awareness, to soulless careerist whose heart has been burned out of him by the calculating inhumanity of the institutions to which he has dedicated his life.

One additional element regarding audience sympathy for Carver is how it may be affected by white racial allegiance. Initially, I would argue that the film can lead some white viewers to believe that he is overall a minimally good, if also rather pompous and self-important, narrative figure. For example, some viewers may believe that Carver generally seems to have had the best interests of the black community in mind when recruiting agents to help rid it of one of its worst problems, namely the epidemic of illegal drugs ravaging many of its parts in the early 1990s, even if such a crusade would also simultaneously advance his career at the DEA. He seems genuinely committed to eliminating drugs like crack from the streets. He also has a strategy for how one might best go about doing so: by going after the big-time suppliers rather than street dealers, who may be easily replaced.

Moreover, late in the narrative when his operative confronts Carver about setting up Gallegos for arrest and finds that option off-limits, the DEA functionary expresses shame and regret at having deceived his agent about the goals and possibilities for their operation. He even confesses that he did not originally get into his position for the money and power that he now craves, but because of the manipulations and deceptions of those above him, he feels powerless to achieve the moral goals he once had and has come to believe that the "spoils of war" are all that remain available to him. "That's all there is," he pleads while taking a pull from his flask to blur the twinges of conscience he feels. Even though the narrative shows that Carver has given up on working in the interest of his moral ideals or the black community by this point, it also shows that he possesses a decided ambivalence in having made that choice. By meeting his operative carrying a pocket flask, Carver is represented as clearly unhappy over his own self-betrayal and powerlessness, as well as the betrayal of his employee. His apologetic tone further elicits viewer compassion about his guilt over having deceived someone who trusted him.

Yet even as these claims are true within the narrative, Carver exhibits other traits that should give even white viewers who understand him as generally sympathetic pause—make them think that this positive dimension to his character may not be dominant in depicting who he is. Carver also performs actions and harbors traits indicating that he does not have the full equality of blacks uppermost in his mind. In his initial appearance on-screen, for example, viewers hear Carver asking the African-American candidates for his undercover operation a Zen-like query. As Guerrero observes, Carver's question is impossible for them to answer properly because, like a *koan*, it could have either no correct response or innumerable ones for African Americans, who "must confront or negotiate this question every day of their lives."[31] In order to test his applicants' ability to respond under pressure, Carver begins his interviews by posing the inflammatory, racist question, "Do you know the difference between a black man and a nigger?" By using such a provocative, insulting term as a white official addressing black men, Carver seeks to rankle his prospective job candidates at their core, in order to test their "cool," as Guerrero puts it (ibid.).

The first candidate, completely taken aback at such an openly bigoted question from a potential white superior, tries to brush it off with a forced laugh and the confession that, at the moment, he cannot think of a way to explain the difference. In response Carver smiles maliciously and observes, "Most niggers don't," and asks for the next candidate, for this applicant's inability to respond immediately and resourcefully to such an outrageous and insulting question means that he is of no use to Carver. It is worth noting, however, that the film briefly acknowledges this first candidate's offended response to Carver's insinuation, which I understand to mean that, combined with his malicious smile in making it, illustrates the narrative as siding *against* Carver rather than *with* him, and encourages the viewer to do so as well. His employment of such an inappropriate question to screen his applicants is not presented as something of which we should approve, but rather disapprove. Such disapproval is reinforced when the second applicant for the undercover position lunges over the desk, grabs Carver by the lapels, pulls him out of his chair and into the air, and demands to know, "Who the fuck do you think you're talking to?" To this Carver timidly concedes, "Right. Thanks for coming in."

While played partially for laughs at Carver's expense, these vignettes also establish him as a white character who provokes rather different responses from different viewers, as his use of this racially offensive question speaks to viewers in racially divergent ways. While aimed at putting typical black viewers

31. Guerrero, *Framing Blackness*, 208. Clearly, the way in which I interpret Carver makes him out to be something more than just "a slimy Washington bureaucrat" (ibid.), although what I have to say does not completely contradict Guerrero's assessment.

on their guard regarding his behavior in the future, Carver's behavior also provokes a sense of racial allegiance in some white viewers. These audience members pick up on this mean-spirited question at black's expense, even if they also
acknowledge its racial offensiveness, by virtue of the way in which it plays off
typical white presumptions about African Americans. In the background of
many white viewers' thinking is the old racist proverb "There are good niggers
and there are bad niggers," as well as the belief that all stereotypes allegedly
have some element of truth to them.[32] Thus, while playing off Carver's oblivi-
ousness to how offensive he really is to his black applicants, this sequence also
offers some white viewers a sort of in-joke about the general way in which they
think they should know about and categorize African Americans.

Many white viewers may well be as truly offended by Carver's question as
are typical blacks, even if they may not appreciate its insult at the level that
most blacks do. But the point I wish to make here is that the term evokes
different responses in viewers, divided according to how they experientially
understand this word, because its function as an insult impinges on them in
divergent ways. The term plays off different presumptions in different people
regarding the human beings it allegedly describes, and those differences will
be significantly rooted in how they have experienced the use of the word. For
some, it will be a stinging personal insult; for others, it will merely be a derogatory term that one should no longer use in describing actual human beings.
Such an experiential difference will matter critically regarding the degree to
which the character of Jerry Carver curries favorable viewer allegiance.

It should also be noted that Carver gives white viewers more generally
a character with whom they might partly identify early in the film's narrative simply because he embodies the human ideal in standard Hollywood
cinema—that is, a white man.[33] Even for white viewers for whom Carver's use
of the term may be insulting because they have accurately imagined for themselves what it must be like to be black and insulted by being called a "nigger,"
he might still offer this link through which they might ally to him. In addition,
he provides a further spark of allegiance, at least for some viewers, by acting
out his whiteness through a privileged use of the word. As a white male official
sitting on the authoritative side of a desk, he is the least likely type of person
to have been harmed by this term's offensiveness. While not impossible, the
circumstances under which someone would describe him as a "nigger" and
mean it as a hurtful insult would be quite unusual.[34] Carver's use of the term
thus functions without a real knowledge of the harm in might cause personally, an epistemological position that at least some white viewers will share.

32. For a more detailed description and analysis of white uses of the word "nigger," see
Randall Kennedy, *Nigger: The Strange Career of a Troublesome Word* (New York: Pantheon, 2002),
esp. 3–34. Carver's use of the term corresponds to what Kennedy refers to as "nigger-as-insult."

33. See Dyer, *White*.

34. Kennedy, *Nigger*, 25–34. Of course, as Kennedy notes, an individual such as Carver could
be insulted by being called a "nigger lover" (25–27), but that term has a different impact as insult
when contrasted with "nigger," which Kennedy argues is more personally damaging.

To reach back to an old distinction made by Bertrand Russell, he has at best knowledge by description of the term, but not knowledge by acquaintance.[35] That is, Carver may have had the term's sense of insult described for him by others, but he probably does not know from personal experience what it is like. He also seems an unlikely candidate for having imagined its significance as an insult for himself. Insofar as some viewers may share this limited knowledge of the term, they may be susceptible to allying with him on that basis.

By the film's end, however, the film means for even white viewers who may initially identify with Carver not to do so, for by that point in the narrative he has taken on the very traits of duplicity and coercive manipulation that he had earlier regretted in his superiors. This change in Carver's character over the course of the narrative aims to bring even somewhat racially resistant white viewers closer to the main character in terms of allegiance because, unlike Carver, this DEA operative's positive moral traits remain much more constant throughout the narrative, even if he seems to temporarily lose his way, his sense of moral direction, for some of the story. His compassion for others, for example, finds repeated expression, and his hope to be of some use remains consistent. Carver, on the other hand, has simply given up. This stronger moral centering emanating from the main character in comparison to Carver urges audiences to ally more strongly with him than with his erstwhile boss, especially in the final portion of the narrative. I understand this late character divergence as being aimed to motivate even resistant viewers to consider the film's African-American protagonist more favorably.

At the same time, during these two characters' initial meeting viewers see something of a different Jerry Carver. When police officer Russell Stevens Jr. is the first one to respond to the DEA recruiter's potentially incendiary question satisfactorily, "his face a cool, dissembling mask," as Guerrero notes,[36] Carver smiles and enthusiastically begins to brief the street cop on the requirements of successful undercover work. He passionately expresses a wish to do good by taking down big-time drug dealers and ridding the black community of one of its worst problems. He also tells his potential recruit that, because of his criminalistic psychological profile, "You'll be a star there. . . . You'll do a lot more good [under cover] than you ever would have in [a police] uniform. You *will* be of use, you *will* make a difference" to the black community. Because he seems so dedicated to doing good when viewers first hear Carver talk about undercover work, he seems to be a character who might well elicit some minimal positive allegiance from many viewers, particularly white ones, even if he also seems to be oblivious to the more offensive dimensions of his use of the word "nigger."

Thus, the first impression Carver gives is complex, ambiguous, and different for different viewers. To some white viewers he may appear to be someone

35. Bertrand Russell, *The Problems of Philosophy* (1912; repr., New York: Oxford University Press, 1959), 46–59.

36. Guerrero, *Framing Blackness*, 208.

who wants to help the black community by ridding it of the dangerous drugs destroying it from the inside. We later see this kind of initial impression of Carver confirmed as he reminds his operative why he is working under cover, at a time when this policeman posing as a drug dealer asks his superior "What am I doing here?" and seems to have lost his moral compass. The Washington bureaucrat sensitively if also manipulatively recounts what were then thought to be the horrific details of a "crack baby's" first few hours of life as well as its dismal prospects for the future, in order to remind his operative of what he is doing and why.

On the other hand, viewers also see more and more of Carver's manipulativeness in his interactions with his employee. He repeatedly refers to his knowledge of the undercover cop's life as God-like and directs him to proceed with the operation as quickly as possible, presumably because that would be best for Carver's own career at the DEA. This manipulation continues until the scene in which he finally admits that even though he got into the project of supervising undercover DEA agents in order to do some good, he no longer sees that as possible, given the overwhelming pressures of institutional power bearing down on him. Rather than continuing to seek ways to provide service to the black community, Carver has surrendered to these forces and contented himself with the self-interested goals of enhancing his own personal position—grabbing the "spoils of war" that he recommends his operative acquire as well. Through these details the filmmakers urge viewers to see that Carver, in spite of at one time having had the goal of eliminating drugs from the black community, has caved in to the institutional pressures of existing power relations and opted to garner satisfaction exclusively from selfish achievements like moving up the bureaucratic ladder. At the same time, the narrative portrays Carver as similarly a victim of existing power structures maintaining white supremacy, for he, too, has been thwarted in achieving his moral goals by them.

In the film's final sequences, however, Carver is more at ease with his decision to merely enhance his career and even seeks to coerce his former agent into doing his bidding in an effort to achieve additional personal advancement. Whatever his earlier ambivalence about snookering his operative, Carver has ultimately embraced the institutional position into which he had earlier been pressured. He thus becomes a character willing to go along with existing racial relations, a narrative figure who, in spite of earlier sympathetic moments and real if at times clueless concern for African Americans, ultimately ends up being not only a racist, but a callous bureaucrat to boot.

This change is well adumbrated over the course of the narrative, so this final version of Carver's character should appear logical to viewers because it fits consistently with his character as it has been presented earlier in the film. In noting the forces of moral purpose, careerism, and manipulation working at odds in Carver's character, viewers finally come to see that thirst for advancement and power have won out. Thus, even resistant white viewers should be able to discern by the film's final scenes that Carver is no character with whom one should wish to ally.

It is also worth noting that even in being thwarted in his efforts to achieve the moral goal of helping blacks, Carver is simultaneously a beneficiary of that denial, as failing to fulfill his moral ideals nonetheless helps him to advance his career. This result illustrates the asymmetrical effects that racially biased institutions may have on whites and blacks who work in their service. While Carver may survive relatively untouched from his personal failure to achieve his moral goals, his operative, as a member of the black community committed to its betterment, is not so lucky. Like Carver, the character played by Fishburne could forgo his moral ideals, content himself with the "spoils of war," and concentrate on enhancing his career in Washington. But such a choice would come at a far greater price than it would for his white boss. Carver's failure matters less to him because he is less intimately connected to the black community. As an outsider, his failure may weigh heavily on his soul, so to speak, but it does not do so materially, as it would his operative, who is a member of the group he seeks to help. The protagonist's failure would require him to write off a group of which he had considered himself an integral part, so its loss would require much more fundamental changes in his sense of identity than such a loss would mean to Carver. Following Carver's example here would thus have a far more profound and deleterious effect on the main character than such a decision would have on his former boss.

Making a Difference Epistemologically

By the film's final act, *Deep Cover*'s protagonist has become much more savvy about negotiating obstacles placed in his way by institutional functionaries like Carver. By showing the videotape of Guzman agreeing to finance the new designer drug and distributing copies to the press, he outsmarts his old DEA boss in the penultimate sequence, in which he testifies before a congressional subcommittee hearing concerning his role in the undercover operation. He incriminates the Latin American diplomat, in spite of Carver's best efforts to protect someone he had once described as "a self-promoting, duplicitous greaseball." In this way the main character illustrates how he has learned to overcome certain institutional barriers placed in his path, thus demonstrating a new level of understanding that the film goads the viewer to emulate as well. The protagonist even manages to "flip" Carver's insulting question from the original interview. When the DEA functionary angrily demands to know how much money his former operative skimmed off the top of his final deal on behalf of the DEA, the former state-sponsored drug dealer responds by quoting Carver's *koan* back to him: "Jerry, what's the difference between a black man and a nigger?" When Carver expresses his confusion, the main character finally expresses his anger at having such an insulting question asked of him by sucker-punching his former boss and paraphrasing his original answer:

"The nigger's the one that would even think about telling you." In turning the use of this insulting term back to a meaning more in line with one of its many black vernacular uses, he reclaims the term for himself as well as the black community,[37] which once again shows him acting in accordance with his oft-stated moral goal "to be of some use, to make a difference somehow."

Here the film offers us an opportunity to see not only how criminality may be imposed on African Americans, but also how they seek to make such impositions their own through creative subversion and interpretation, thereby redirecting them to their own purposes.[38] *Deep Cover*'s main character manages to forge a new and more fully formed sense of identity not only by using elements of street-savvy blackness, but also by subverting conceptions of black criminality forced on him, and turning them in his favor, as he does Carver's racist question. By reinventing himself as John Hull, outlaw with a moral purpose, the main character is able to find a way out of the drug-dealing life imposed on him by the DEA while at the same time reclaiming pieces of his old straight-arrow self, the cop Russell Stevens Jr. He overcomes—in part at least—the fragmented sense of identity that the white world would presume to force on him and fills out a more coherent sense of who he is by keeping his eyes on his ultimate moral goal—trying to be of some use, making a positive difference in the lives of his fellow human beings—an advance that Aristotle would point out is an advance in "practical wisdom."

Some might see Hull's escape from the clutches of the DEA at the end of the film as a facile endorsement of lawbreaking, yet as he soliloquizes in his voiceover during the story's final moments, "It's an impossible choice. But in a way, we all have to make it." Particularly in situations where African Americans find themselves in circumstances that have been imposed on them, they may be forced to choose between being criminals or fools, between transgressing white power or dumbly serving it. Given such an outrageous moral dilemma, the film implies, self-reflectively choosing criminality, as defined and imposed by white power, may sometimes constitute the better choice. At least it affirms one's independence and freedom, and through one's self-conscious disruption of existing power structures perhaps it might yield some good as well, unlike the other possibility. If one manages to subvert these institutional obstacles for the sake of higher moral goals, as the main character does by the film's end, one may be able to forge a new sense of self that will be more autonomous from presumptions of white supremacy and create new possibilities for more fully human lives.

In this way *Deep Cover* offers viewers a detailed internal perspective on the motivations for and reasoning behind black rejection of the white status quo, an empathetic look, in other words, at what Mills describes as the overlapping parallel universe of African-American experience, which is rendered

37. For a description of black vernacular uses of the term, see Kennedy, *Nigger,* 34–55, 172–75.

38. Diawara, "*Noir* by *Noirs,*" 274.

virtually invisible by the epistemology of ignorance imposed on whites by the racial contract. As Mills explains, the institutionalized beliefs that comprise the category of whiteness require that its members remain blind to their own position of power and advantage, and to the consequences that position has for persons not counted as white. Moreover, they will often be unable to recognize the immorality of their own racialized actions because institutionalized beliefs guide them to think that what they have done is right.[39] Similarly, *Deep Cover* critiques constructions of race and the institutions supporting them by explicitly depicting their injustices and iniquity; that is, by clearly portraying the deformation and distortion that such structures inflict upon the lives of many African Americans, in direct contrast with typical white ways of seeing these matters. It also gestures toward ways in which African Americans might negotiate these obstacles such that they could more effectively unify their senses of self.

Moreover, through its open-ended final question ("What would you do?"), the film explicitly urges viewers to reconsider their own ways of thinking about these matters and contemplate changing their lives in light of the new knowledge it has presented to them. In the format of a cautionary *noir* tale, the film calls on its viewers to reflect thoughtfully on—that is, to think philosophically about—the perspective on white power and attendant problems of class it has presented, as well as how such factors may play a role in their own thinking and acting. By openly summoning its viewers to think about presuppositions that underlie viewers' sense of self as well as the social world around them, *Deep Cover* represents especially well how *film noir* conventions constitute a set of techniques and themes that may be used to present and elicit philosophical consideration of matters concerning justice, humanity, and race through film.

Against Self-Interest: *The Glass Shield*

Another work closely linked to but distinct from the ghettocentric *noir* cycle is Charles Burnett's 1995 film about the Los Angeles County sheriff's department. Described by *noir* scholar James Naremore as one of the "most impressive African American movies about crime" because it tends "to refigure or transform the familiar patterns of noir,"[40] the film portrays how a young black deputy finds that his seemingly innocent "white" lie, promised impulsively to help a fellow officer in a jam, forces him to support views and actions that dehumanize all African Americans, thus compelling him to actively maintain the very oppressions he hopes to battle against and escape himself.

In his enthusiastic desire to fit into cop culture, John "J.J." Johnson (Michael Boatman) puts up with humiliation and presumptive stereotyping from the

---

39. Mills, *Racial Contract*, 18–19, 94–95.
40. Naremore, *More Than Night*, 246.

beginning, and in some cases tries to take on those prejudices himself. His first day on the job, for example, as he drives into a spot reserved for deputies he is automatically assumed to be a lawbreaker by the veteran white officer who sees him parking there. He must then explain to the skeptical deputy that—in spite of his black skin—he is a new co-worker rather than a jail trustee. The veteran officer reacts to this unexpected piece of information with a look of shock and dismay. Later other fellow deputies momentarily hesitate to shake his hand when they meet him, initially resisting the obligation to touch black flesh in partnership, and afterward whisper their offended disbelief to each other at being forced to let him join their ranks. His boss, Chief Massey (Richard Anderson), bluntly insults his writing abilities. "I've seen three-year-olds who spell and use grammar better than that," he tells his new charge about the first arrest report he files. This white station head rides J.J. again and again for minor errors in his incident and arrest reports, such as misspelling "Sepulveda."[41] J.J. must therefore work hard to turn in flawless paperwork, knowing full well that he is being held to an outrageously high standard that few if any of his fellow white officers could meet. Trying nearly every strategy he can think of to assimilate, he even attempts to bond with the other male deputies in the department by taking on their prejudiced beliefs about women and Jews, which they direct primarily toward the other new employee "making history," Fields (Lori Petty), the only female—and Jewish—deputy at Edgemar Sheriff's Station.

J.J. yearns to join the closed society of cops, that institution dedicated to serving and protecting (white) power, and whose stated clubhouse mottoes are, as he is explicitly told, "Don't trust anybody" and "Talk to no one." Initially J.J. puts up with racist presumptions and unfair double standards because he knows that those attitudes accompany being the first black person to break the color line at places like the Edgemar Sheriff's Station. As was the case for Jackie Robinson, perhaps the most formidable hurdle in "making history" does not involve having the talents to do the job well, but having the psychological toughness to put up with the continual shower of racist insults, slights, abuses, and unfair forms of measurement that require far more of one's self than any standard applied to whites in such positions.[42]

J.J. finds that in order to gain access to the closed order of policemen, the costs are even higher than he anticipated, for he must sacrifice virtually all commitment to other African Americans. As a fellow officer derisively warns him, "Now, you're one of us—not a *brother.*" Thus, when one of his white colleagues follows standard departmental procedure by stopping a young man in a nice-looking car simply because he is black and is so blasé about the

---

41. Not to be pedantic or anything, but "Sepulveda" does not even occur in the *OED.* See the *Oxford English Dictionary Online,* http://dictionary.oed.com (accessed July 26, 2005). It is, of course, the name of a street in Los Angeles.

42. See, for example, Scott Simon, *Jackie Robinson and the Integration of Baseball* (Hoboken, N.J.: John Wiley and Sons, 2002).

practice that he admits it to the assistant district attorney during a pretrial preparation, J.J. agrees to back the other officer up and later commits perjury regarding the facts surrounding the case because he wants so much to be inscribed within the "thin blue line." To make legitimate the search and arrest that uncovered a handgun apparently used in a murder, J.J. takes on the other officer's racist presumption of guilt for this suspect and falsely swears under oath that the defendant made an illegal left turn, which then serves as the pretext, from a legal standpoint, for stopping him and eventually searching his car for the gun.

After testifying, J.J. puts together various pieces of evidence and realizes that the weapon he found in this suspect's car was *not* used in the murder for which he is being tried, and that the serial number for the gun had been changed—ironically enough, with "white-out"—on the arrest report J.J. filed about the incident. The young man he helped to arrest, Teddy Woods, played appropriately enough by gangsta rapper Ice Cube, has been framed by J.J.'s fellow officers because his image fits the crime. In other words, he is framed because he is black, a detail of the film that concurs, as we have seen, not only with presumptions made evident by many other black *noirs*, but also with Lewis Gordon's observation that, from a typical white perspective, an African American's "color is the evidence. He is guilty of blackness."[43] *The Glass Shield* reinforces this idea by having the Woods character observe, "It's like the song says: my skin is my sin," a rap-like observation that paraphrases not only Gordon, but also Fanon.[44]

In working to reveal the truth about this victim of racial injustice, J.J. finds that "there's no one to tell" about such corruption, as one of his few honest colleagues, Foster (Linden Chiles), tells him. The ubiquity of institutional structures supporting such racist presumptions reach horizontally as well as vertically all the way to the city council, some of whose members owe hidden debts to the sheriff's department for covered-up crimes of the past. But J.J. persists, and with the help of Fields and Foster, who become his allies, he exposes these white injustices and makes possible Woods's escape from conviction for a crime he did not commit.

Although its protagonist is close in age to the ghettocentric *noirs* discussed in the previous two chapters, *The Glass Shield* clearly distinguishes J.J. as being slightly older and possessing additional maturity. Thus the narrative is less a coming-of-age story than one of adult realization, a quality it shares with *Deep Cover*. The audience's first impression of the main character is just after he has graduated from the Sheriff's Academy and is being called to duty at the Edgemar Sheriff's Station, thereby "making history" as the first black deputy to serve there, as the intercom announcement of his appointment notes. J.J. has a clear life plan—being a policeman—and positive, if also vague, moral goals in mind for how he wishes to live his life. He clearly aims to help

43. Gordon, *Bad Faith and Antiblack Racism*, 102.
44. Fanon, "Lived Experience of the Black," 199.

his community be a better place to live and honestly hopes to do some good through his actions, traits that help audience members ally positively with him in spite of his naïve participation in the injustice that propels much of the narrative. Although the film depicts the naïveté of J.J.'s desires as directly comparable to the comic book images that play under the opening credits, his positive moral traits place him much closer to *Deep Cover*'s protagonist than to those in, say, *Menace II Society* or *Clockers*. Unlike ghettocentric *noir* characters, he knows what he wishes to do with his life and where he wants it to go. He has a sense of what is valuable and good in human life, so he has no need to perform the basic sort of search for meaning in one's existence that preoccupies these other protagonists for much of their cinematic stories.

On the other hand, even after having sorted these questions out and being in one sense prepared to become the Los Angeles Sheriff's Department equivalent to Jackie Robinson, J.J. remains ill-equipped to deal with both the level of resistance and bigotry he encounters and his own internalized complicity with it. *The Glass Shield* takes pains to depict the depth of these racialized beliefs in both its main character and others. Moreover, for their roles in revealing the corruption of their fellow officers, J.J., Foster, and Fields must pay dearly. Foster must admit to committing perjury in an earlier trial, during which he helped to cover up the excessive brutality of his peers, thereby humiliating himself, endangering his career, and risking imprisonment. His whistleblowing also further excludes him from the community of cops through which he had presumably found much of his sense of identity, since he has broken the code of silence that forbids members from breaking ranks with the thin blue line. Fields, on the other hand, is severely beaten by "unknown assailants" and while recovering in the hospital decides to leave the force. Despite liking the work, she can see that the Los Angeles County Sheriff's Department remains too sexist, racist, and unjust for her to be a true member. For his part in blowing the whistle, J.J. must not only abandon his life's dream of becoming a policeman, he must also pay for his white lie by being prosecuted for perjury. To heighten the racial injustice of this consequence, by contrast the narrative notes that the stupid and racist white deputy he helped out by lying, the aptly named Bono (Don Harvey), is granted immunity for giving J.J. up.

As he tells his girlfriend Barbara (Victoria Dillard), "I thought I was doing right" by giving in to his colleagues' racist prejudices—and as far as a typical cop's mentality about race would recommend what he should do, he was.[45] Acting like a crude act-utilitarian weighing what amounts to the best kind of justice achievable on the streets, J.J. felt he was serving "the greater good" overall by lying to the jury and thereby getting another presumed killer off the streets. Similar to *Deep Cover*, this narrative shows that presumption's frequent roots in racialized beliefs about African Americans, something that J.J.

45. See David Barstow and David Kocieniewski, "Records Show New Jersey Police Withheld Data on Race Profiling," *New York Times*, October 12, 2000, p. 1+, and Feagin, Vera, and Batur, *White Racism*, esp. 142–47.

eventually realizes exists at a background level not only among his fellow cops, but in himself as well.

By exposing the corruption and racism that are woven into the everyday functioning of the Sheriff's Department, the young deputy comes to grasp that police work as it currently exists in Los Angeles embodies an institutional set of beliefs that operate powerfully against the interests of African Americans such as himself. Like *Deep Cover*'s protagonist, J.J. comes to see that his own self-deception and the ubiquity of the moral corruption around him have made him blind to certain forms of racism because these features of his existence have become like water to fish for him.[46] He no longer sees them because he has been completely submerged in them, a way of thinking out of which he was shaken only by his personal immoral involvement and their consequences during the Teddy Woods case. The overall aims of the narrative, then, involve showing that J.J.'s naïve dreams of being a cop and "doing right" impose on him an alienation from the African-American community the cost of which becomes too high for him to bear. Being one of them and not a brother requires him to enforce presumptive stereotypes that he ultimately finds himself unable to administer and to lie in order to protect blatantly racist cops who callously impose crimes on those who fit the image regardless of their actual guilt or innocence.

In constructing this story about the Los Angeles Sheriff's Department, Burnett and his collaborators reverse "the police procedural by centering on an idealistic young black cop who is assigned to a corrupt division" rather than the crime itself,[47] and having him find that the depth of moral corruption runs far wider and deeper than he had ever imagined. But in another sense, this narrative strategy is not a completely unfamiliar *noir* trope, for it also uses the "rogue-cop formula" in the manner that it is employed by the neo-noir *Serpico* (Sidney Lumet, 1973). As Naremore point out, *The Glass Shield* exploits a familiar *noir* technique to depict the level of institutionalized racism in the rogue police unit that J.J. joins.[48] Through this use of *noir,* the audience is aligned with the protagonist as it follows him while he uncovers stereotypic beliefs in most of his fellow officers as well as himself. Thus, as the character discovers these truths within the narrative, so do we. J.J. and his friends' desire for true justice further aims to mirror similar presumed sentiments in the audience, making close positive allegiance with them much more likely than with their racist antagonists. J.J.'s later realization that he himself has held and practiced some of these racist beliefs therefore models for viewers what the narrative hopes to encourage them to do: think about the degree to which such beliefs may be internalized. The film focuses the effects that the epistemology of ignorance may have on not only whites, but blacks themselves—how their own beliefs and consciousness may be colonized by conceptions detrimental

---

46. Mills, *Racial Contract,* 76.
47. Spicer, *Film Noir,* 169.
48. Naremore, *More Than Night,* 246–47.

to themselves and their community, a point that philosophers of race have been arguing at least since Fanon.[49] By showing viewers how even a basically good and sympathetic character like J.J. may become caught up in presuming black guilt, the film means to convey that such background beliefs may infiltrate even those we would not otherwise suspect of harboring such beliefs, even viewers themselves.

More generally, the film makes clear how the established racial order in Los Angeles as standardly administered by the police oppresses African Americans. Such a portrayal is meant to confer to viewers a dissatisfaction with that system of justice's state, to dissolve any complacency that might exist regarding the fairness of Los Angeles's constabularies regarding race, and to instill a desire that the existing "social contract" in such places be changed for the better in a way that incorporates the alternative moral perceptions and ideals depicted. In this way the film transforms into narrative arguments advanced by Mills in *The Racial Contract* as well as David Theo Goldberg in *Racist Culture:* namely, that social orders such as one may find in urban centers like Los Angeles are fundamentally racialized. Demarcations of race not only signify alleged differences in kinds of human beings, but also demarcate differences in moral treatment because of alleged differences in morality. People "of color," so the assumption goes, are more prone to indulge the animal side of human nature, more prone to violence, more prone to criminal activity. The reasons may vary; such unfortunate behavior may be attributed to genetic differences, cultural idiosyncrasies, lack of education, or economic disadvantage. The end result, however, remains constant: these people must be kept separate from those who allegedly resist such temptations more successfully and abide by the law. Policing institutions merely enforce beliefs implicit in the standard sensibilities of white advantage by working to keep these people "in their place" and treating them differently from the way in which the allegedly more law-abiding white citizenry is treated.[50] By deftly illustrating such assertions, *The Glass Shield* also incorporates Mills's and Goldberg's claims that such conditions are morally intolerable, require immediate change, and yet remain invisible to most whites.

A set of onscreen graphics at the film's conclusion links its fictional depictions to the real world by testifying to the ongoing struggles, at least as of the mid-1990s, that the black community of L.A. had to face vis-à-vis the policing institutions of its neighborhoods, thereby historicizing the events depicted and stressing their alarming "normality" from the cognitive stance of typical whiteness. In addition, these historicizing graphics will probably now remind

---

49. See Fanon, "Lived Experience of the Black," and Gordon, *Fanon and the Crisis of European Man.*

50. Mills, *Racial Contract,* 46–49, 84–85; Goldberg, *Racist Culture,* 204–5. See also Charles W. Mills, *From Race to Class: Essays in White Marxism and Black Radicalism* (Lanham, Md.: Rowman and Littlefield, 2003), esp. 147–218, and David Theo Goldberg, *The Racial State* (London: Blackwell, 2002).

many contemporary viewers of how *The Glass Shield* presages LAPD's Rampart Division scandal in 1999, as well as many other systemic problems that have plagued that city's law enforcement bodies for decades.[51] Last, by noting that the film is based on a true story, these graphics make explicit the direct connection between its fictional world and the all-too-real one it aims to mirror.

As the film's opening images show, J.J. simplistically thinks that his life will involve the sorts of dangers and rewards that one might find in comic books, rather than the real-life institutionalized racial prejudices of the L.A. police force. Yet through audience alignment with him viewers come to realize that cartoonish forms of mayhem and violence are hardly the greatest dangers J.J. must face. Rather, institutionally embedded racial beliefs constitute a far greater threat than any injury the character might receive in tracking down or apprehending criminals. As a sworn officer of justice, J.J. represents someone who ought to administer that ideal in the fairest and most even-handed way possible. When that possibility becomes endangered or is subverted by ideas of race, the film implies, a far greater menace faces society: that of having a justice system which is *itself* unjust and thus fails to guarantee basic rights to society members. That possibility is a far worse danger than having criminals running loose and causing mayhem, as the problem with justice becomes a fundamental part of the system rather than incidental, thus more comprehensive and difficult to fix. By alluding to the actual history of such systemic injustice and its disproportionate impact on adult black men, *The Glass Shield* urges viewers to consider the ingrained nature of its presumptions in many people's belief structures as well as in the institutions nominally designated to protect them, thereby invoking once again the "Socratic impulse" characteristic of many black *noirs*.

Race and the *Noir* Lessons of History: *Devil in a Blue Dress*

Rather than portray contemporary events and the existing social order, Carl Franklin's alluring retro-*noir* explicitly moves away from these concerns in order to examine their historical antecedents. This 1995 film recreates a 1940s-era detective story set in postwar Los Angeles, complete with voiceover, convoluted plot, and passages into a criminal underworld where the main character, Ezekiel "Easy" Rawlins (Denzel Washington), must obtain information essential to his case. In many ways, the film is the most obviously recognizable and straightforward of black *noirs*, with its careful period detail and self-conscious use of classic *noir* themes and techniques. As such, it has been the focus of

51. See Davis, *City of Quartz*, esp. 250–316, and Feagin, Vera, and Batur, *White Racism*, 147–51, regarding the Los Angeles police force's ongoing policies toward African Americans and other minorities. For similar cases of racial profiling by police forces in New York, Maryland, New Jersey, Illinois, Florida, and elsewhere, see Alton Fitzgerald White, "Ragtime, My Time," and David Cole, "The Color of Justice," *Nation*, October 11, 1999, 11–12 and 12–15.

FIG. 26   Easy Rawlins (Denzel Washington), looking very much the *noir* detective
(*Devil in a Blue Dress*, 1995)

considerable scholarly attention.[52] In addition, writer/director Carl Franklin
has admitted that while making the film he thought of it as similar to *The Big
Sleep*, no doubt because of its convoluted plot and jaundiced view of those in
power. Plus, the film was marketed as a "black *Chinatown*."[53]

I also wish to note that it represents a further move away from the cycle of
films discussed in the previous two chapters, as Easy, like many classic *noir*
protagonists, is a war veteran, a full-grown adult, and possesses a life invested
with meaning and value. He has taken advantage of the GI Bill, for example,
and bought himself a small house, which the film makes clear he dearly loves.
He also values having a regular job over its illegal alternatives. As Franklin
notes in his commentary, these elements aim to portray how Easy believes
that the "American Dream" is possible for him.[54] These traits serve to distinguish him from the kinds of protagonists found in the ghettocentric *noir* cycle,
which makes *Devil in a Blue Dress* a different kind of film, even without the
additional differences in historical setting and a blues-oriented rather than a
hip-hop soundtrack. As Ed Guerrero has argued, this film represents perhaps
more completely "the potential for a fully developed black cinema" because its

52. See, for example, Guerrero, "Circus of Dreams and Lies," 346–49; Naremore, *More
Than Night*, 249–53; Wager, *Dangerous Dames*, 125–27; Oliver and Trigo, *Noir Anxiety*, 163–88;
Hirsch, *Detours and Lost Highways*, 302–4; Mark L. Berrettini, "Private Knowledge, Public Space:
Investigation and Navigation in *Devil in a Blue Dress*," *Cinema Journal* 39 (1999): 74–89; and
Nieland, "Race-ing *Noir* and Re-placing History," esp. 71–75.

53. Carl Franklin, commentary, *Devil in a Blue Dress*, DVD, directed by Carl Franklin (1995;
Columbia Tristar Home Video, 1998). See also Naremore, *More Than Night*, 249, and Nieland,
"Race-ing *Noir* and Re-placing History," 72.

54. Franklin, commentary, *Devil in a Blue Dress*, DVD.

narrative illustrates how African-American filmmaking may "struggle against, represent, and mediate the fundamental condition of black people in America."[55] Even a scholar of classic *noir* like Hirsch grudgingly admits that "the film rewrites some noir genre conventions."[56]

Set primarily in Los Angeles's black community, the film depicts the everyday oppression and harm done to African Americans trying to live unexceptional lives in the years after World War II. The background of *Devil in a Blue Dress* bustles with the activities and locations of a bygone era, but inflects them with a raced perspective. Rather than show viewers the Los Angeles of Hollywood and Vine or Schwab's Drug Store, its focus is Central Avenue and the streets of Watts; and the activities depicted are the day-to-day matters of black Americans, which were mostly absent from the classic *noir* films of that era.[57] In this manner the film embroiders into its narrative elements of Lewis Gordon's Fanonian description of racist oppression: "the imposition of extraordinary conditions of the ordinary upon individuals in the course of their effort to live 'ordinary' lives."[58]

Having followed Horace Greeley's advice and gone West to evade the poverty and crime-ridden life of Houston's Fifth Ward, Easy finds to his dismay that California promises the same miseries for African Americans. At first escape to a life that aspired to the "American Dream" no doubt seemed attainable: Easy had secured a job at one of Los Angeles's many aircraft plants, bought his small house, and settled comfortably into the working-class neighborhood of Watts. But Easy's voiceover tells us in the film's opening sequence, "It was summer 1948 and I needed money." He had been fired three weeks earlier for refusing to work overtime at his job (in contrast to his white co-workers, who the film makes clear were permitted to refuse overtime) and has no idea how he will pay his mortgage, already nearly two months overdue. To make his payments, he reluctantly takes a detecting job from a sleazy white "businessman" named Albright (Tom Sizemore), who does "favors for friends."

From the start we are aligned narratively with the film's protagonist and given virtually exclusive access through him to the film's story, as we follow his actions and his voiceover narration tells us what we are to make of the situations in which he finds himself. The film also quickly establishes for viewers traits in Easy with which most could easily identify: needing an income, looking for a job, and wariness about Albright and his offer of seemingly too-easy money. As viewers see more of the film, it also presents them with strong evidence that, in contrast to many white *noir* heroes, Easy makes enormous efforts to escape lawbreaking and live a respectable, morally principled life. Unlike the ambivalent *noir* characters noted by Borde and Chaumeton and other critics,[59] "Easy's always trying to do better," as his friend, the bar owner

55. Guerrero, "Circus of Dreams and Lies," 329, 351.

56. Hirsch, *Detours and Lost Highways*, 303.

57. Naremore, *More Than Night*, 233–42.

58. Gordon, *Fanon and the Crisis of European Man*, 41.

59. Borde and Chaumeton, *Panorama of American Film Noir*, 7–9; Naremore, *More Than Night*, 20. See also Chapter 2.

Joppy (Mel Winkler), observes. In order to overcome his rough background, which we see briefly in flashback, Easy has moved away from the bad influence of criminal friends and the easy descent into lawbreaking they represent. He finds, however—and audience members are meant to realize along with him—that the color of his skin forces him back into crime's hidden economy. His *noir* fate is to be sucked into a life he does not want to live, that he has explicitly rejected, because he is consistently restricted to illicit social spaces and denied access to others that would permit him to practice better moral behavior, such as that of unremarkably working at a factory and puttering with the fruit trees around his house. At first desperate for money to live and pay his mortgage, and later a suspect in two murders, he has little choice but to help Albright find Daphne Monet (Jennifer Beals), even though Easy senses his employer is a gangster and would prefer to see Daphne go her own way.

Eventually, in angry, despairing response to being pushed around and beaten up by the cops, Albright, and various others, he calls for help on his old friend Mouse (Don Cheadle), a trigger-happy career criminal and murderer who is one of the many evil influences Easy had hoped to escape by moving from Houston to Los Angeles. Together they find Daphne and resolve Easy's dilemma with Albright and the police, although Easy must restrain Mouse every step of the way from acting out Easy's rage and shooting anyone who even slightly crosses either one of them. This *noir* doubling, as Guerrero has pointed out, works "Easy and Mouse in psychological counterpoint,"[60] but rather than serving to indicate Easy's darker side it points to his humanity, restraint, and desire to escape the rage lurking in his heart. Mouse's psychotic behavior shows by contrast Easy's more principled and thoughtful actions, which further prompts audience members to side with him emotionally. In this way, *Devil* contrasts with many other *films noirs*, illustrating Easy's conscious and determined efforts to "do better" rather than succumb to a fatalistic *noir* determinism about the inevitability of human evil, as frequently evidenced in, say, Fritz Lang's work.

Devil in a Blue Dress means to present its viewers with the general validity of the idea that even when African-American adult men try to escape the criminalistic *noir* underworld, it often pulls them back into its influence. Yet this idea's power here, as the film takes pains to point out, is not due to the inherent evil of raced human beings, but to a thoroughly corrupt and corrupting racial order imposed by presumptions of white advantage. As Guerrero notes, Easy's actions underscore how for many African Americans crime is perceived as a matter of "survival," as opposed to "the act of a deviant individual." Such a depiction urges viewers to see "crime more in a socioeconomic context," namely, as "the informal resistance of a subject people against a racially unjust system."[61] Easy's descent into crime thus symbolizes a common African-

---

60. Ed Guerrero, review of *Devil in a Blue Dress*, *Cineaste* 22, no. 1 (1996): 40. Guerrero later incorporated much of this review into "Circus of Dreams and Lies," 346–49.

61. Guerrero, "Circus of Dreams and Lies," 346.

FIG. 27   Mouse (Don Cheadle) and Easy (Denzel Washington) in visual counterpoint (*Devil in a Blue Dress,* 1995)

American perspective regarding such activities, one that highlights their quality of being unfair impositions often forced on black Americans.

The fate of Daphne Monet, the film's *femme fatale,* reinforces this point. Literally the "devil in a blue dress" of the title, she is so not because she is bad or evil, but because she is Creole and has taken advantage of being light-skinned enough to "pass" for white. Initially engaged to Todd Carter (Terry Kinney), a white character I analyzed briefly at the beginning of Chapter 3, she finds herself being blackmailed by a politician who knows her secret and opposes Carter in the mayoral race. In order to thwart this blackmail and keep her secret hidden, she purchases photographs showing her fiancé's political rival to be a pederast who molests young boys. It is this political rival who has actually hired Albright to find Daphne, obtain the photos, and probably kill her. Daphne's racial transgression thus motivates the film's main criminal acts. Moreover, once Easy makes certain that her secret will remain unknown to others, she believes that Carter will marry her, as they had originally planned, because she thinks that all that matters between them is their love for each other and desire for personal happiness. Thus she is devastated when he refuses to go through with his proposal because she is not white. She, too, remains confined to the spaces reserved for people of color in 1948 because, for her fiancé, not even love can overcome the "one-drop rule" that condemns anyone with a trace of black ancestry to the status of blackness.[62] After Carter rejects her, she drifts back into the *noir* underworld of crime with her knife-wielding gangster of a brother, Frank Green (Joseph Latimore).

62. See Davis, *Who Is Black?* and Ian F. Haney Lopez, *White by Law: The Legal Construction of Race* (New York: New York University Press, 1996).

FIG. 28   Daphne Monet (Jennifer Beals) is tortured by Albright (Tom Sizemore, off-camera) (*Devil in a Blue Dress*, 1995).

Daphne has motivated all the film's killing and criminality not from inherent evil, but through her efforts to cross an unjust social barrier and escape the confinements imposed on her by race. As numerous critics have pointed out, the filmmakers' use of Daphne's character illustrates how the figure of the *noir femme fatale* may be revised through that of the mulatta.[63] The film clearly flags for viewers the unfairness of Daphne's racial position, thus altering the traditional figure of the mulatta itself, but this representation of unfairness also serves to change the valence of Daphne's status as a *femme fatale*. She is a "fatal woman" because she has acted to escape the unjust confines of race, not because she is motivated by greed, selfishness, hatred, or other evil motivating forces typically at work in *noir femmes fatales*.

The ending of the film, several critics have argued, is optimistic. Rather than the downbeat or fatalistic conclusion that often serves as the signature of more classic *noirs*, they contend that *Devil in a Blue Dress* ends on a relatively happy note for Easy.[64] It shows his neighborhood as a place of camaraderie and contentment, where he may interact with friends and forget about all his recent past troubles by playing dominoes, talking, and drinking whiskey. While not wishing to dispute the existence of these narrative elements, I would also point out that this final sequence also contains less sanguine details that mean to indicate for the viewer trouble on the horizon for Easy as well as the black community. For one thing, there is the restrictive surveillance implied by the policemen cruising slowly by Easy's house, not only indicating that the cops

---

63. Naremore, *More Than Night*, 251; Nieland, "Race-ing *Noir* and Re-placing History," 63, 71–75; Berrettini, "Private Knowledge, Public Space."

64. See, for example, Spicer, *Film Noir*, 170, and Naremore, *More Than Night*, 253.

will be keeping their eye on him as a troublemaker and a suspect, but also fore-shadowing more oppressive forms of police surveillance in store for the neighborhood's real-life correspondent in a few decades. Then there is Easy's acceptance of "private investigating" as an occupation that Albright and racialized circumstances had earlier imposed on him. He tells his friend Odell (Albert Hall) that he "ain't studying no job," but has decided to set up his own business doing the very thing he had initially resisted doing for the sleazy white gangster and was later forced by circumstances to take up with a vengeance.

Easy also paraphrases Albright when he defends himself from Odell's doubts about such a profession being a positive life choice. "You get into trouble doing that," his friend warns him. Easy responds, "Yeah, well, like a man [namely, Albright] told me once, you step out your door in the morning you already in trouble. Just a matter of whether you're mixed up at the top of that trouble or not, that's all." I would argue that this paraphrasing indicates a certain Hobbesian, dog-eat-dog mentality that Easy has taken on from the white gangster. It is true that Easy implies he will make it his own by "going into business for [him]self," but a certain amount of cynicism about the world that Albright originally conveyed through his comment remains in Easy's paraphrase of it.

There is also the troubling implication that Mouse remains a significant part of Easy's life, in spite of the evil he represents to the main character. He asks Odell, a churchgoing man, whether you should keep as a friend someone who does "bad things—I mean *real* bad things," even when you come to know that fact about him. Perhaps not fully appreciating the seriousness of Easy's question, Odell responds with a slightly too-pat answer by saying, "All you got is your friends." There is also the character of the Woodcutter (Barry Shabaka Henley), whose presence over the course of the narrative has foreshadowed trouble for Easy time and again. He appears here once more, seeking to cut down trees, an act he believes will reduce the bad luck around the neighborhood. It is also worth noting that the music played over these final moments is not some simplistic "Don't Worry—Be Happy" tune, but an orchestral piece that suffuses the sequence with a certain sadness that represents not only a nostalgic yearning for this lost time and place, but also casts over Easy and the neighborhood's future a certain ominous mood. Its significant featuring of minor chord arrangements thus mean to shade the viewer's emotions partly toward something less than a completely positive response to the narrative's conclusion.

As for our *noir* protagonist himself, Easy seems to have come to a reconciliation with his fate of being someone who lives outside the law. His partial acceptance of Albright's outlook on life, for example, represents a certain hardening of Easy's heart as a result of his experiences with this white gangster, Daphne Monet, Todd Carter, and the several murders that revolved around maintaining the color line. Easy has become tougher and more wary over the course of the narrative, a change that represents a loss of innocence. Even though the knowledge he has obtained about the color line's subtleties will no doubt help him survive, there is also a more melancholy aspect to his acquisition of this knowledge, for Easy's new awareness of the world's harsh conditions regarding race and his human possibilities in it mean that Easy himself has become a more distrustful and suspicious individual. Already wary about matters of race at the film's outset, circumstances have forced him to become still more guarded.

This change actually makes him less sympathetic than he was earlier in the narrative, even if it is possible to explain this change for legitimate reasons. Easy has been forced to become both less open and more scornful of the actual human possibilities open to African Americans by the end of the film. While these insights may amount to a form of "practical wisdom" about race relations in America, they also represent a certain strangulation of hope in Easy's character. His personal optimism about the human spirit, already slightly shriveled, has suffered a further reduction, making him a sadder, if wiser figure.

This wisdom Easy acquires, as in the other black *noirs* discussed in this chapter, serves to urge audience members to come to similar insights about the actual status of race in their own world, which is neither the easiest nor the most pleasant task one might face at the end of a film. Finally, there is the extradiegetic matter of most viewers being aware of the tragic destruction of the real-world version of Easy's neighborhood just seventeen years later. Even though the last few seconds of the film depict Easy's contented visage looking out at children playing, people simply living their ordinary lives, and his brief soliloquy to friendship, the film's conclusion also means to convey a distinct undertone of sadness and foreboding, as well as what I would argue is a sense of responsibility to reflect on the state of race in America. The troubling melancholy of the film's conclusion means to spur viewers into thinking about how such a decent neighborhood could have sunk so low in less than two decades—although admittedly, this narrative prompt will have differential impacts on different viewers, depending significantly on whether they see the ending as optimistic or more downbeat.

The differences in perception here will be to some extent racially skewed. African Americans, for example, seem more likely to notice the more downbeat elements than whites because these symbols of ongoing oppression will no doubt mean more to them and thus be more salient in their viewings of cinematic narratives, to say nothing of their greater likelihood of knowing *what* they mean. As symbols, these narrative features will resonate more deeply with their automatized belief schemata through which they view the film. Whites, in contrast, will no doubt seem generally more inclined to dismiss these factors and focus on the more upbeat dimensions of this ending because such features harmonize better with their typically more rosy picture of race relations in America. Of course, some whites may sensitively detect the less sanguine features of this final sequence, too, but my point here is that such a response seems likely to be less than typical.

More broadly, the film's setting in post–World War II Los Angeles provides previously uninformed viewers with critical background information concerning more recent events, namely, various riots in Los Angeles, by underscoring the historical depth of their causes, including the imposition of extraordinary

conditions like criminality on African-American men and their frequent confinement to crime-ridden social spaces. In this way *Devil in a Blue Dress* seeks
to reveal to viewers the hidden underside of white supremacy and challenge
them to rethink their place in its moral institutions as well as their view of
its commonly accepted presumptions, history, and consequences. As in *The
Glass Shield*, the narrative presents these matters and implicitly urges its viewers to reflect on them, thereby illustrating Mills and Goldberg's claim that
ideas of race fundamentally affect typical thinking about not only morality
but space. As Mills writes, "Part of the purpose of the color bar / the color
line / apartheid / jim crow is to maintain [racialized] spaces . . . to have the
checkerboard of virtue and vice, light and dark space, *ours* and *theirs,* clearly
demarcated."[65] Similarly, Goldberg argues that "racisms become institutionally normalized in and through spatial configuration . . . being conceived and
defined in racial terms."[66] Through its vivid portrayal of spatial and moral
demarcations by means of imposed conceptions about race, *Devil in a Blue
Dress* serves to illustrate and enliven the same territory of white supremacy's
unfairness and injustice as that indicated by these thinkers.

In particular, Easy's character works to obscure the moral boundaries set
out for him by race and show their artificiality by contrasting his principled
and restrained responses with those of Mouse. Whereas Mouse embraces
criminality with comically maniacal relish, Easy resists these pressures and
responds with horror to Mouse's many evil deeds, such as his killing of Joppy.
Even though this ex-boxer turned bartender is responsible for Coretta's (Lisa
Nicole Carson) death as well as getting Easy into this whole mess in the first
place, Easy is still saddened to the point of grief upon discovering that he has
been choked to death by the psychotic Mouse.

Of course, numerous critics have remarked on the film's careful delineation of various spatial boundaries by race.[67] From Albright's intrusion into Joppy's bar at the very beginning of the film through Easy's uncomfortable visits
to the Santa Monica pier, the "whites only" section of the Ambassador Hotel to
first meet Daphne, his subsequent drive with her into the white neighborhood
where McGee lives, and other racialized incursions, the film reminds viewers
that where one goes often bears the mark of social boundaries defined by presuppositions concerning this vexing concept. As viewers become more closely
allied with Easy, they are urged to begin seeing more clearly white supremacy's
unfairness—its moral bankruptcy, its unfair imposition of rigid boundaries
on African Americans and the places where they can safely be, its fundamental immorality, its continued and long-standing injustices. Such an implicitly
corrupt and corrupting social order, the film encourages filmgoers to grasp,
calls for a committed moral dedication to its improvement, to the eradication

65. Mills, *Racial Contract,* 48.

66. Goldberg, *Racist Culture,* 185.

67. See, for example, Nieland, "Race-ing *Noir* and Re-placing History," 72–73, and Berrettini,
"Private Knowledge, Public Space."

of its damaging, unjust advantage and power, so that something better may actually be possible for those whose lives it affects (namely, everybody), just as Mills, Goldberg, and other philosophical theorists of race urge on the basis of analogous reasoning.

Black *Noir* Moves Beyond the Gangsta

With a change in focus from black youth to adult male characters, there is a corresponding change in what kind of knowledge these films seek to convey to their viewers. Rather than center around realizations about one's self and what gives one's own life meaning and value, *Deep Cover, The Glass Shield,* and *Devil in a Blue Dress* urge audience members to think more about the social world at large and one's place in it. By demonstrating how even morally good adult male characters may be coerced into criminality through oppressive circumstances connected to race, these films seek to instruct viewers in additional subtleties of racist presumptions and the unconscious ways in which they operate in the mundane lives of all Americans. By following these films' characters in their discovery of such truths for themselves and making explicit links to real-life events, these narratives further aim to spur their viewers into thinking about the implications of such matters not merely in the fictional worlds depicted, but also in the very real one in which we live.

This difference from youth-centered black *noirs* represents a modest step forward aesthetically, as it develops black *noir*'s potential for more perspicuously representing problems of race that have previously escaped attention in most mainstream cinema. By focusing on morally good adult black men, these films offer slightly more generalized grounds for bridging the gap between black and white American experience that often prevents greater understanding of differently racialized forms of human existence. As such, the step forward represented by these films means that black *noir,* as an aesthetic style, may be employed to represent a broader range of human potentialities, as well as become a stronger means to spur reflection in viewers regarding their typical presumptions concerning race. These films thus expand black *noir*'s potential for triggering a "Socratic impulse" in viewers as well as its potential for depicting fuller conceptions of the human.

Another way to grasp this step forward in cinematic aesthetics is to realize that while these works aim to entertain and engage mainstream audiences even more broadly than their ghettocentric *noir* counterparts, they also attain conditions set out by earlier critics for subverting traditional Hollywood conventions and allowing for the expression of human liberatory sentiments. In other words, Tommy Lott's and Clyde Taylor's goal for black cinema to "imperfectly" achieve positive human potentials is more nearly attained.[68] The radical

---

68. Lott, "Aesthetics and Politics"; Lott, "Hollywood and Independent Black Cinema"; Taylor, *Mask of Art,* esp. 255–73.

political aspirations outlined by late 1960s Latin American critics and film-makers for Third or Imperfect Cinema are thus closer to being made real, as these films more effectively resist mainstream stereotypical images and advance the political interests of oppressed peoples.[69] By utilizing *noir* techniques to provide viewers with detailed representations of racialized adult men from an African-American perspective, *Deep Cover, The Glass Shield,* and *Devil in a Blue Dress* constitute black film as imperfect cinema, with a *noir* twist. As we will see in the next two chapters, other works extend black *noir*'s range even further, making it a still more supple and subtle collection of artistic narrative techniques for conveying difficulties revolving around conceptions of race, identity, humanity, and justice.

69. For more on Third or Imperfect Cinema, see Fernando Solanas and Octavio Gettino, "Towards a Third Cinema," and Julio Garcia Espinosa, "For an Imperfect Cinema," in *Film and Theory: An Anthology,* ed. Robert Stam and Toby Miller (Oxford: Blackwell, 2000), 265–86, 287–97, and *Questions of Third Cinema,* ed. Jim Pines and Paul Willemen (London: BFI Publishing, 1989).

The flourishing of any given person's humanity requires its acknowledgement by her others.
—Stephen Mulhall, *On Film*

By presenting still more striking, innovative occasions for viewers to consider what it means to fully acknowledge another, African-American and other film-makers have pushed black *noir* into new regions of aesthetic advance, for these innovations have incorporated into the film form an interrogation of presuppositions concerning additional forms of social disadvantage that operate in concert with race. Accordingly, I argue that the films I examine in this chapter illustrate Mulhall's link between acknowledgment and flourishing, and the relation of these ideas to justice, for where injustice exists, these components of a decent human life will be distorted or absent as well.[1] For example, female gothic *noir* characteristics structure Kasi Lemmons's *Eve's Bayou* (1997), thereby bringing into focus concerns of African-American women, something often absent from earlier black *noirs*. Its narrative calls for viewers to reflect on conceptions of memory, reality, and self from a raced as well as a gendered perspective, thus bringing into view a whole range of humanity that is inadequately understood by many viewers. Likewise, *noir*-influenced films such as the film version of Walter Mosley's *Always Outnumbered, Always Outgunned* (1998), Antoine Fuqua's *Training Day* (2001), and Lemmons's second feature film, *The Caveman's Valentine* (2001), prompt extended audience reflection about the humanity of otherwise negatively stereotyped black figures, namely, ex-cons, corrupt cops, and mentally ill homeless persons, thereby formally expanding black *noir*'s range to the consideration of presumptions regarding other types of socially oppressed human beings besides black youth and adult men.

A crucial point I wish to make in this chapter and the next is that African-American *film noir* has not only continued to progress and develop but matured as a set of techniques for appealing to audiences to think reflectively about the troubling interdependencies of morality, justice, and social oppression. Its ongoing development may be attributed to how black *noir* possesses capacities to depict and dissect evolving forms of the racial contract as well as the diverse and bacteria-like forms of social domination in general. Like its *noir* predecessors, these black *noirs* trouble us about injustices and moral inequities long after the film stock (or its equivalent) has stopped rolling by utilizing *noir*'s

---

1. Mulhall, *On Film*, 35.

special aptitudes for critically representing social oppression and eliciting seri-ous reflective thought concerning previously hidden presuppositions about human beings and the moral relations between them.

These films accomplish much of what I analyze here by extending *noir*'s potential for encouraging sympathetic and empathetic understanding for other types of Cavellian individualities—that is, kinds of characters that certain people are, such that we could imagine ourselves having met them or meeting them in other circumstances—thereby expanding viewers' imaginations regarding what a full-fledged sense of humanity involves.[2] To elicit acknowledgment and recognition of normally stereotypical characters as the fictional equivalent of full-fledged human beings, these films exploit *noir*'s capacity to prompt such responses, particularly by means of empathetic understanding. Taking as my point of departure Mulhall's argument concerning how *Blade Runner* encour-ages empathetic responses to its replicant characters, I maintain that, by depict-ing vulnerability, pain, or suffering as peculiarly human, these *noir* films moti-vate viewers to incorporate previously "othered" individualities into their sense of the human, prompting a growth in moral imagination.[3] But prior to address-ing this issue, I consider another dimension of viewer asymmetry with regard to race, namely what it might mean for a film to be "universally accessible."

Eve's Bayou and Its Critical Reception

When writer/director Kasi Lemmons released her first feature film, critic Andrew Sarris wrote, "To hail Ms. Lemmons' *Eve's Bayou* as the best African-American film ever, as one may be understandably inclined to do, would be to understate its universal accessibility to anyone on the planet with the slightest involvement in the painful experience of family life."[4] Other crit-ics praised the film in similar ways.[5] While in one sense surely appreciated, in another this form of backhanded praise was bizarre, for as film studies scholar Mia L. Mask notes, such remarks betray a real reluctance to describe and admire a film as an outstanding work of art by and about African Ameri-cans.[6] I would further argue that this form of praise is particularly odd, given that *Eve's Bayou* tells a story that contains *only* African-American characters. Thus it would seem to border on the perverse to downplay or ignore the fact that the film takes place entirely within the milieu of an all-black enclave in the United States—specifically, in a town that "was named after a slave" and

2. Cavell, *World Viewed*, 29, 33, 35.

3. Mulhall, *On Film*, 33–51.

4. Andrew Sarris, "A 10-Year-Old Murderer Propels a Nervy Debut Film" (review of *Eve's Bayou*), *New York Observer*, November 17, 1997, 37.

5. See, for example, Cynthia Joyce, "Eve Gets Even," *Salon*, November 7, 1997, http://archive.salon.com/ent/movies/1997/11/07eve.html, and Louis B. Parks, "Jackson Takes a Detour to the 'Bayou,'" *Houston Chronicle*, November 8, 1997, Houston Section, p. 1.

6. Mia L. Mask, "*Eve's Bayou*: Too Good to Be a 'Black' Film?" *Cineaste* 23, no. 4 (1998): 27.

whose residents are that slave's descendants, as the film tells us. In reflecting on how she set the stage for her narrative as an African-American saga, Lemmons remarks, "This beginning is kind of a history lesson."[7] The film explicitly presents its fictional history about the town's founding matriarch as a framing device, stressing its racial dimensions and underlining their critical importance for a proper understanding of the characters. The narrative moreover returns to these matters at its conclusion by reiterating this racial history, to further stress its importance.

Lemmons's goal as well as her reasoning for providing a "history lesson" harmonize with Charles Mills's assertion that a detailed awareness of the nation's past is crucial for a proper understanding of race. "The exposure of misrepresentations" and "excavations of histories concealed"—setting the record straight, so to speak—regarding the actual events that occurred between whites and blacks in the history of the United States are vital to an accurate grasp of the concept's current importance.[8] Accordingly, as Lemmons makes clear, her story presumes a conscious knowledge of the history and consequences of race relations in the United States and how those dimensions of black experience operate as background assumptions, as co-text, to the story, which the prologue quickly sketches for the viewer. It is for these reasons that I find bizarre that many critics would forget or ignore the specific racial identity of the characters and treat them as if mentioning their racial history would constitute an admission that the film lacked "universal accessibility."

On the other hand, part of this film's interest from the perspective of recent philosophical theorizing about race is that viewers often do not see Lemmons's narrative as having racialized dimensions, or hesitate to admit it, in spite of her explicit efforts both at the beginning and end of the film to emphasize that these characters are descendants of an African slave. Rather, many viewers see the film as entirely untouched by matters of race, as if that dimension of the story were merely an accidental feature that did not matter. Such understandings of the film mean that these viewers presuppose the concept of "universal accessibility" to be defined in terms of whiteness, as Dyer has argued in *White* and I have explored in previous chapters. Perhaps too, as Mask argues, this preconception remains in place partly because the main characters in the film, the members of the Batiste family, hold many recognizably middle-class American values that make them seem "just like" whites (27).

At the same time, as Mask further remarks, because it is a story of affluent middle-class, French- and English-speaking blacks, the film also challenges essentialist notions of blackness (ibid.). Never for a moment does it ask us to indulge in film historian Donald Bogle's damning litany of stereotypes—toms, coons, mulattoes, mammies, or bucks—or their contemporary counterparts.[9]

---

7. Kasi Lemmons, commentary, *Eve's Bayou*, DVD, directed by Kasi Lemmons (1997; Trimark Pictures, 1998).

8. Mills, *Racial Contract*, 119.

9. Donald Bogle, *Toms, Coons, Mulattoes, Mammies, and Bucks: An Interpretive History of Blacks in American Films*, 4th ed. (New York: Continuum, 2001).

Eve's Bayou focuses on a form of blackness not usually acknowledged, albeit one closer to typical white sensibilities than those usually depicted in black *noirs*. Yet this *African-American* dimension of the narrative seems to have been ignored or misunderstood by many viewers in favor of the belief that these characters' accessibility is due to their being "just like" whites. The accidental propinquity of human individualities here means that, ironically, many white viewers have an easier time identifying with these black characters than they do with characters such as the empathetic gangsters and others described in previous chapters. To put it another way, to many white viewers the characters of *Eve's Bayou* seem much more "white" than those typically portrayed in black *noirs*, rather than black in another way.

This dimension of the film further elucidates why it was so highly praised by critics who nonetheless did not want to label it an African-American film. What it implies, of course, is that being a black film would put off mainstream viewers who have been conditioned to view films from a white point of view. While in one sense this form of praise might be seen as "telling it like it is" and recognizing some brute fact about Western cinematic viewership and its implicit racism, it is also important to note that these comments operate to reinforce such myopic normative standards, even though many critics would presumably have hoped to have moved beyond them in their personal film viewing.

Such a way of looking at this film further hints at the idea that a black film that lacks any representations of whites permits audience members trained to perceive fictional film narrative through whiteness to "forget" that they are viewing a story about African Americans. As events taking place in Louisiana, a state that considered anyone with one drop of black blood, any "trace of black ancestry," to be African American,[10] and at a time (the early 1960s) when people across the South were being beaten, jailed, or murdered for integrating public places, registering black voters, or protesting that African Americans were not permitted to practice the full equality guaranteed them by the U.S. Constitution, the absence of whites and interactions with them in *Eve's Bayou* allows many viewers to "forget" or overlook the violence, immorality, and injustices of race in American history.[11] If *Eve's Bayou* had included a scene in which one of its characters had been forced to deal with whites — even some act as ordinary as buying food, clothes, or medicine for their children from a white salesperson — could this façade of universal accessibility have been preserved? The likely ugliness of such a scene would have made that illusion difficult, if not impossible, to maintain, for it would have reminded white viewers in particular of their privileged status in contrast to the film's characters, thus destroying their fantasy that these individuals were "just like" them in terms of social equality. White superiority would have been inscribed into

---

10. Cited in Davis, *Who Is Black?* 9.

11. See, for example, Denise Dennis, *Black History for Beginners* (New York: Writers and Readers Publishing, 1995), esp. 171–73.

the narrative in a way that would have rendered impossible the impression that these characters were "just like" viewers in ways that made race irrelevant. It would rather have reminded them of what segregates African Americans in general, and thereby what institutional forces maintain white advantage. Such reminders would no doubt have proved inimical to viewers' sense that the film presents characters who are in no important ways socially different from whites.

The presentation of this alternative narrative scenario is in no way meant as a criticism of *Eve's Bayou*. I present it only to highlight the fact that such a scene would have made difficult, if not impossible, a certain misunderstanding of the narrative, one that viewers should not have had anyway, had they been paying proper attention. If nothing else, the framing story should have reminded viewers that the story being told was one in which race played a crucial role, even if that factor remains one that the narrative implicitly addresses as something that can and should be overcome. It is also probable that the moral ugliness of such a scene would have alienated many viewers, regardless of their racial identity. In all likelihood it would have constituted an aesthetic flaw in the film because it would have amounted to an unnecessary deviation from the film's central focus.

Film Noir and Female Gothic Melodrama

Unlike many critics, I consider *Eve's Bayou* a female gothic melodrama that, by virtue of its narrative content and style, also functions as a *film noir*. As such, I argue that it is similar to classic *noir* films like *Shadow of a Doubt* (Alfred Hitchcock, 1944), *Undercurrent* (Vincente Minnelli, 1946), *Sleep, My Love* (Douglas Sirk, 1948), *Secret Beyond the Door* (Fritz Lang, 1948), and *Caught* (Max Ophuls, 1949), which were created as female gothic melodramas and at the same time ended up in the *noir* canon. This aspect of *film noir* has received far less critical attention than its indebtedness to male-oriented hard-boiled and pulp fiction. Still, as film studies scholars like Steve Neale, Murray Smith, Elizabeth Cowie, Thomas Schatz, Andrea Walsh, and others have pointed out, many female gothic films of the 1940s used the same narrative and stylistic techniques as *film noir*—low-key lighting, unbalanced compositions, voiceover narration, flashbacks, detective-like investigation by the protagonist of a sexual other who somehow threatens the main character, and so on.[12] The only evident difference between many of these female gothic melodramas and

---

12. Neale, *Genre and Hollywood*, 161–64; Murray Smith, "*Film Noir*, the Female Gothic, and Deception," *Wide Angle* 10 (1988): 62–75, esp. 63–65; Elizabeth Cowie, "*Film Noir* and Women," in *Shades of Noir*, ed. Joan Copjec (London: Verso, 1993), esp. 130–37; Thomas Schatz, *Boom and Bust: The American Cinema in the 1940s* (New York: Charles Scribner's Sons, 1997), 232–39; Andrea S. Walsh, *Women's Film and Female Experience, 1940–1950* (Westport, Conn.: Praeger 1984), esp. 168–70, 190–91; Spicer, *Film Noir*, 10–11.

films noirs seems to have been the gender of the intended audience and the narrative's main characters.[13]

Actually, this apparent dissimilarity is a distinction without a difference, as philosophers would say, because the overlap between these two kinds of films is such that many female gothic melodramas were actually classified as *films noirs* according to classic accounts like Silver and Ward.[14] It is not as if the gender difference in characters and audience kept many viewers and critics from thinking of such female-oriented films as *noirs* as well.[15] There seems to be no reason, then, to maintain a categorical distinction between many examples of these two kinds of films, for as Neale has remarked, "Any absolute division between *noir* and the gothic woman's film is unsustainable."[16] Thus Neale, Cowie, Schatz, and others have argued that many female gothic films are *films noirs* as well, as instances of the two forms often share precisely the same stylistic as well as narrative characteristics, with some films thus falling into both categories at the same time. Like other forms of *noir*, critics have noted that this vein has additionally carried over into neo-*noir*. Cowie notes Kathryn Bigelow's *Blue Steel* (1990) as one such example, but Curtis Hanson's *Jagged Edge* (1987) would qualify as well, as would Mary Lamb's *Siesta* (1987), Lizzie Borden's *Love Crimes* (1991), and Tamra Davis's remake *Guncrazy* (1993).[17]

In discussing the "family resemblance" between 1940s female gothic melodramas and hard-boiled *noir* detective films, Schatz notes that their shared characteristics derive from shared "basic structure, thematic and gender-related concerns, and deployment of *noir* stylistics." He goes on to describe their overlap in terms of common concerns regarding "gender difference, sexual identity, and the 'gender stress,'" such as that exerted by the *femme fatale*, which has been a focus of *noir* scholarship since its inception. Both film forms typically involve "an essentially good although flawed and vulnerable protagonist at odds with a mysterious and menacing sexual other." Their social milieus are often "crass, duplicitous, and amoral," and the audience's point of view and knowledge are generally aligned with the protagonist as he or she investigates this sexual other. Both kinds of films typically build to a resolution of their mysteries as well. As Schatz notes, "In both forms, however, the resolution rarely marks a return to complete stability or moral equilibrium." Consequently, doubts and tensions linger.[18]

Of course, there are also differences between female gothic melodrama and typical *film noir*. For example, in female gothic narratives the "heroine

---

13. Regarding this kind of alleged partition between the two types of films, see in particular Smith, "*Film Noir*, the Female Gothic, and *Deception*," 63.

14. See the entries for the films just mentioned in Silver and Ward, *Film Noir: An Encyclopedic Reference*, 52–54, 253–54, 257–58, 299–300, and 386.

15. See especially Cowie, "*Film Noir* and Women," 136, and Neale, *Genre and Hollywood*, 161–64.

16. Neale, *Genre and Hollywood*, 164.

17. Cowie, "*Film Noir* and Women," 159–60; Spicer, *Film Noir*, 165–68.

18. Schatz, *Boom and Bust*, 236–37.

not only tends to survive but to attain a new awareness of herself and her world. . . . The resolution of the female gothic involves a redemption of sorts." Still, in what Schatz sees as the best of the female gothic *noirs*, this redemption may be ironic to the point of being "positively Brechtian." He cites Hitchcock's *Shadow of a Doubt* as such an example, at the end of which young Charlie (Teresa Wright) becomes a character whose world "can never be the same" because she has seen into its corrupt and fetid core by discovering the truth about her beloved Uncle Charlie (Joseph Cotten), who turns out to have been a serial killer in spite of all the filial love she and other characters direct toward him. At the very heart of her "average" American family lay a form of corruption that, until its revelation, young Charlie could never have imagined. Ultimately, her knowledge of this reality not only damages her psychologically, but forever changes the parameters of her world.[19] Put in more standard philosophical terms, she has grasped an instance of the "banality of evil"—the idea that evil actions might be possible for almost anyone—that she could not have understood prior to her *noir* experiences.[20]

In many female gothic melodramas that also fall into the category of classic *noir*, a place of comfort and safety, such as the family, is transformed into a place of mystery and danger by means of horrific revelations about one or more of the group's members. These revelations often concern sexual desire or perversion, as in *Caught, Sleep, My Love*, and *Secret Beyond the Door*. At times there are overtones of the supernatural, carried over from nineteenth-century gothic romances. Settings may include an old castle or a family mansion where scenes of foreboding creepiness may unfold.[21]

Naturally, 1940s women's gothic *noirs* share a good deal in common with other gothic melodramas aimed at women as such narratives had developed to that point in twentieth-century cinema.[22] As in Hitchcock's *Rebecca* (1940) and *Suspicion* (1941) and George Cukor's *Gaslight* (1944), the affluent female protagonists in these films are often tormented by husbands who apparently either wish to kill them or drive them mad. By means of their narrative and style, these films, many critics have more recently argued, are actually within the overlap with *film noir* as well.[23] And, of course, there are the films that far more classicist *noir* critics unproblematically placed in the *noir* camp, even though they were made and understood at the time as female gothic melodramas.

Regarding more recent critics' arguments in favor of *film noir*'s overlap with female gothic melodrama, it is noteworthy that Lemmons herself refers to *Eve's Bayou* as a melodrama.[24] This reference should not be surprising, as

19. Ibid., 238–39.

20. Arendt, *Eichmann in Jerusalem*.

21. For more on the typical features of female gothic *noirs*, see Neale, *Genre and Hollywood*, 164; Spicer, *Film Noir*, 10–11; and Cowie, "*Film Noir* and Women," 154.

22. Tania Modleski, *Loving with a Vengeance: Mass Produced Fantasies for Women* (New York: Methuen, 1984), 21; Guy Barefoot, *Gaslight Melodrama: From Victorian London to 1940s Hollywood* (New York: Continuum, 2001), 20–23, 39–40.

23. Noted in Cowie, "*Film Noir* and Women," 129–30.

24. Lemmons, commentary, *Eve's Bayou*, DVD.

critics of the 1940s often understood *noir* films as melodramas.[25] Moreover, Lemmons's understanding of her film in no way precludes the possibility that it falls into the overlap between female gothic melodrama and *film noir*. Thus I will argue that *Eve's Bayou* fits conditions which place it within the common space that makes it a *film noir* as well as a female gothic melodrama, even if this characterization was not specifically Lemmons's first-order intention for her film, just as it was not for makers of 1940s gothic melodramas. I would further argue that the film may be insightfully analyzed as a black *film noir*, for doing so reveals a depth to the film as well as a flexibility in the idea of black *noir* that might otherwise go unnoticed.

Eve's Gothic *Noir* World

Eve's Bayou focuses on the story of ten-year-old Eve Batiste's (Jurnee Smollett) perception of events leading up to her father's death. Told entirely by means of the familiar *noir* technique of flashback and bracketed by a voiceover narration that troublingly reflects on these events from more than three decades after their occurrence, Eve discovers what she sees as an enormous danger to her family at its very heart. Similar to the threat found by young Charlie in *Shadow of a Doubt*, Eve comes to understand that the stability of her family is imperiled by her beloved father, Louis's (Samuel L. Jackson) uncontrolled philandering. We later find out that the danger posed by Louis may go even deeper. The narrative offers the possibility that Eve's fourteen-year-old sister Cisely (Meagan Good), Louis's favorite, might also be the object of incestuous attentions.

Louis himself admits to being unable to control his womanizing. Aside from seeing it time and again in his actions and hearing about it repeatedly in what other characters say of him, late in the narrative we hear a letter being read that Louis has written to his sister Mozelle (Debbi Morgan), where he confesses "to a certain kind of woman I am a hero. I *need* to be a hero sometimes. That is my weakness. That much is true." Eve's task, then, as the female *noir* protagonist in this film, is to investigate her father and verify the existence of the danger he poses, then try to find some way to do something about it and restore her family to its condition of stability, safety, and comfort. As in many *noir* narratives, her attempts to achieve these goals do not go quite as she had planned and have psychological repercussions that deeply trouble her. In fact, as the film makes clear, more than thirty years after these events have taken place, their memory continues to reverberate and resist being fully sorted out for her character.

25. Cowie, "*Film Noir* and Women," esp. 129–30; Steve Neale, "Melo Talk: On the Meaning and Use of the Term 'Melodrama' in the American Trade Press," *Velvet Light Trap* 32 (1993): 66–89; Higham and Greenberg, *Hollywood in the Forties*, 19–50. It is in fact startling to note the degree to which Higham and Greenberg, writing in the late 1960s, classify female gothic melodramas as *noirs* and what we now recognize as classical *films noirs* as melodramas.

To better see how this female gothic melodrama also coincides with elements of *film noir,* it is useful to take a close look at its opening sequence. As David Bordwell has argued, the "primacy effect" of film openings typically frame our expectations of the story we will be told.[26] In *Eve's Bayou,* after the soundtrack begins with a series of eerie, haunting, and confusing sounds aimed at disorienting the viewer and putting her on her guard, the opening shots depict in black and white a montage of extreme close-up, slow-motion, off-kilter images accompanied by not-quite distinguishable sounds that we slowly realize are those of a couple passionately making love. Momentarily we will find this suspicion verified by means of their first clear depiction in the reflection of an eye that witnesses them. Just prior to that shot, however, we see both of this character's eyes in a reaction shot to the initial images as the first words of the film are offered in the form of Eve's adult voiceover narration (spoken by Tamara Tunie). Through the juxtaposition of this image of her eyes and her words, we are introduced to Eve.

Reflecting on the confusing impressions the film has just presented, the adult Eve remarks, "Memory is a selection of images: some elusive, others printed indelibly on the brain." The images of the opening montage obviously number among the latter for Eve, in whose eye they are then clearly reflected, and who still struggles to determine their appropriate meaning decades after they have occurred. The film thus mimics these images' indelibility by showing them to the viewer as images reflected in Eve's pupil, as if she literally could not get them out of her sight. Later we will find out that the individuals involved are her father Louis and Matty Mereaux (Lisa Nicole Carson), the wife of his best friend. In the opening sequence, however, we do not know who these people are, nor even who has witnessed them.

As with standard Hollywood narrative, the film raises these questions in the minds of viewers in order to address them later in the narrative. But we should note that this opening sequence, placed among the initial credits of the film, also establishes a set of generic expectations in the viewer. By mobilizing *noir* techniques such as voiceover, flashback, an air of mystery or investigation, and even the black-and-white photography and unbalanced composition of these initial shots that are reminiscent of classical *films noirs* of the 1940s, the film suggests that the story will concern itself with trying to make sense of these images in ways that coincide with typical conventions of *noir.* Moreover, by depicting a world from the perspective of a female black protagonist, the film shows us something that has hitherto been largely absent from recent black *noirs*—namely, the employment of *noir* techniques for the purposes of centrally portraying concerns and outlooks of African-American women.

Consistent with other female gothic *noirs,* as the narrative fills in the background to the opening images we realize that the person who witnessed the couple making love was ten-year-old Eve, the protagonist of the film. We also come to understand that the incident completely unsettles her and that she

26. Bordwell, *Narration in the Fiction Film,* 38.

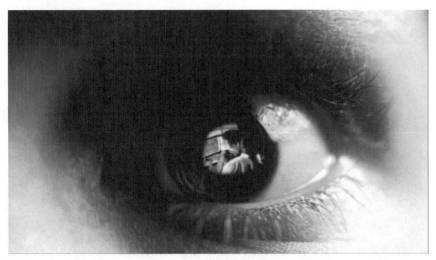

FIG. 29   Matty Mereaux (Lisa Nicole Carson) and Louis Batiste (Samuel L. Jackson) in erotic embrace, as reflected in Eve's (Jurnee Smollett) eye (*Eve's Bayou*, 1997)

sees it as a threat to her family. As the narrative shortly reveals, one night as her parents hosted a party, Eve awakened from a late-evening nap to see her father and Matty passionately embracing and "rubbing," as Eve obliquely describes it. The sight frightens the young girl and she cries out in horror. Louis, shocked and appalled that his daughter would see him in the act of having adulterous sex, moves to comfort his child and take her mind off what she has just witnessed.

But Eve does not forget what she has seen, and later breaks into tears when she tells her older sister Cisely what she saw. As her father's favorite child, Cisely immediately defends him and insists on reinterpreting what Eve has witnessed. Cisely takes her younger sibling step-by-step through the events in a way that makes what Eve saw seem like a harmless act of drunken clumsiness, brought on by one of their father's funny jokes and Matty's inebriation. We are shown this reinterpretation literally in the film, with Cisely and Eve sitting in the foreground while in the background their father and Matty go through the motions of a rather different scene from the one we initially saw from Eve's perspective. After Cisely's reinterpretation, Eve questions, "You sure?" to which Cisely answers with that absolute confidence we only seem to have as fourteen-year-olds, "I'm certain." As Eve looks skeptically at her older sister, she clearly shows that she is not convinced by Cisely's reconstruction of these events, yet this recasting strongly appeals to her because of its soothing conformity to what she wants to believe about her father. Eve is deeply conflicted about the images she has witnessed and what they mean because she is pulled in different directions by what she believes she saw on the one hand and how she wants to feel toward her father on the other. Viewers are similarly torn, as the film ties our point of view and knowledge closely to Eve's, so that at this

FIG. 30   Louis, appalled that his daughter has seen him having adulterous sex (*Eve's Bayou*, 1997)

point in the narrative we, too, have witnessed Louis's kindness and his charm as well as his sexual transgression.

As in many other female gothic *noirs,* then, the film focuses around Eve's attempts to make sense of what these images of another family member's sexuality mean and what she should do about them. This quest drives the narrative for the viewer as well. What is the proper meaning of Louis's interactions with his best friend's wife? What do Louis's adulterous actions mean for Eve and the rest of the family? How far do Louis's desires extend? What other events will they cause in their wake? Of course, none of these questions is immediately apparent from the opening images, but as the narrative unfolds such concerns are urged onto Eve as well as the viewer, for the incidents depicted continually circle back to these opening images and the ambiguities surrounding Louis's character. Thus the film mobilizes familiar *noir* expectations about the need to investigate a mysterious sexual other, in this case the protagonist's father, the threat that sexual other may pose, and the challenge of how to reestablish comfort and stability within the social unit of the family.

In addition, we should note that after the film's opening images have appeared and the much older Eve makes her voiceover declaration about the memory of images, she continues to frame the story we are about to see in a chillingly *noir* fashion:

> The summer I killed my father I was ten years old. My brother Poe was nine, and my sister Cisely had just turned fourteen. The town we lived in was named after a slave. It's said that when General Jean-Paul Batiste was stricken with cholera, his life was saved by the powerful medicine of an African slave woman called Eve. In return for his life,

he freed her and gave her this piece of land by the bayou. Perhaps in gratitude, she bore him sixteen children. We are the descendants of Eve and Jean-Paul Batiste. I was named for her.

This voiceover narration further invokes *noir* expectations by raising the question of how and why the ten-year-old Eve could possibly have killed her father. It also places Eve firmly in the context of her family and her place of birth, thereby invoking the main characters' racial background as a crucial narrative element, as noted earlier. Eve's voiceover intertwines the mystery and otherworldliness of the Louisiana bayou with her family's history, and the images we see as Eve explains her filial origins explicitly reference this element, showing us fields of sugarcane, trees overgrown with Spanish moss, and waterways that seem to have few if any distinguishing navigational features, as well as offering us the unearthly sounds of the swamp and long-ago slave chants. We are likewise told of how the original Eve's saved her master's life by using "powerful medicine" in a tone that evokes the supernatural, a clear echo of the magical elements so common to gothic romance and often found in female-oriented *noirs*. But here they are played in an African-American key. These distinctive *noir* features thus combine with the expectations that matters of race will play a crucial role in how the narrative proceeds and how the questions raised by the opening sequence will be resolved.

The stress placed here in the initial framing story on the family's troubled racial ancestry also implies that their difficulties may be partly attributed to that history—but not in the way that might typically be thought by white viewers. *Eve's Bayou* works hard to rule out the usual interpretation of blackness's relation to sexuality, namely, by means of ideas centering around excessive black carnality. For all his character's sexual voracity and self-centeredness, Samuel L. Jackson portrays Louis very sympathetically—even charismatically. The narrative also emphasizes that he is a caring, thoughtful, and beloved father, and other characters repeatedly comment on his substantial skills as a doctor. On the other hand, we find out that he is perfectly willing to send his children outside to play while he dallies with one of his pretty female patients. Louis is thus both attractive and repellant as a character, an ambiguous alloy of morally good and bad characteristics in Smith's terminology. Perhaps, then, we might describe him as a "sympathetic philanderer," in terms analogous to those developed in Chapter 1. In understanding him thusly, we should note that audience members' responses mimic those of the main female characters, particularly Eve, who also finds Louis lovable and good as well as menacing. His overdeveloped sexuality clearly troubles his younger daughter while at the same time he dotes on her and her siblings. Having such an ambiguous, morally complex character as the focus of investigation would seem a particularly good way to convey the *noir* threat of the female gothic.

Louis's complex characterization also enables the film to present his troubling sexuality as fully explicable in strictly *human* terms, without the usual stereotypical references to outsized black sexuality. Indeed, like African-

American film pioneer Oscar Micheaux's *Within Our Gates* (1920) more than seventy years before, *Eve's Bayou* suggests that Louis's sexual appetites arise not from black desire but from white, as white men have historically possessed far greater opportunity to consummate such cravings through racially inflected laws and social sanctions.[27] Thus if Louis's troubling sexual appetites arise from anywhere, given the opening sequence's "history lesson" it would seem that they are inherited from the white side of the family, for General Jean-Paul Batiste appears to be the origin of exaggerated sexual desire, rather than the family's original Eve. As our narrator, the adult Eve, subtly expresses through her tone, there is some skepticism to be articulated regarding the stated reason (gratitude for her freedom) that her female ancestor had sixteen children with Jean-Paul. Given the racialized customs during the time at which Eve's freedom would have occurred, somewhere between the French settling of Louisana and outbreak of the American Civil War, it seems far more likely that the original Eve's freedom as a manumitted slave would have been conditioned and restricted by her need for a white protector, which she could have secured through sexual favors to her former master.[28] The reference to sixteen children thus implies a sexual voracity more on the part of Jean-Paul than the original Eve. As a result, Louis's carnal appetites would appear to be more due to the white side of the family than the black.

In using the conventions of the female gothic *noir*, *Eve's Bayou* foregrounds the threat Louis's promiscuity poses to the family and others around him. Yet in using these techniques the film also takes care to portray his sexuality in explicitly *human* form, rather than in ways that would mobilize racialized allusions to black carnal prowess. The film normalizes Louis's sexuality by ruling out the explanatory possibility of Louis's actions being due to blacks' stereotypical portrayal as oversexed human beings, an idea that dominated many earlier efforts to explain black carnality. The film even underscores this point about Louis's humanity. When his wife, Roz (Angela Bassett), explains her disappointment in him to Mozelle, she states explicitly that he is "just a man," which alludes to a theme explored at length in the previous chapter. Thus Lemmons's efforts parallel Micheaux's to provide a nonracialized explanation for why certain immoral black characters act in the way that they do. In this fashion Lemmons also works within the framework of a black philosophical tradition forged by thinkers such as Frederick Douglass, Ida B. Wells, Frantz Fanon, Angela Davis, Tommy Lott, and Joy James, who all argue forcefully against the idea of blacks (especially black men) as oversexed human beings.[29]

27. Jane Gaines, *Fire and Desire: Mixed-Race Movies in the Silent Era* (Chicago: University of Chicago Press, 2001), esp. 185–95.

28. See Davis, *Who Is Black?* 36–40, and Bardaglio, *Reconstructing the Household*.

29. Frederick Douglass, "Introduction," and Ida B. Wells, "Lynch Law," in Wells et al., *The Reason Why*, 7–16, 29–43 (see preface, n. 1); Frantz Fanon, *Black Skin, White Masks*, trans. Charles Lam Markmann (New York: Grove Press, 1967), esp. 163–66; Angela Davis, "Rape, Racism, and the Myth of the Black Rapist," in *Women, Race, and Class* (New York: Random House, 1981), 172–201; Lott, *Invention of Race*, 27–46; Joy James, *Resisting State Violence* (Minneapolis:

In *Eve's Bayou* there is nothing racially coded as black about Louis's philandering. His weakness is portrayed as a *human* weakness, not one stemming from his being raced as black. If anything, his dalliances are subtly raced as a proclivity inherited from his *white* ancestor, by means of the initial story concerning Jean-Paul Batiste and the implication that he desired extraordinarily frequent couplings with the original Eve.

The narrative also poses further questions to the viewer that serve to link it to female gothic *noirs*. Did Louis have incestuous desires toward his favorite daughter Cisely? Did Eve have a hand in her father's death? These questions trouble the story recounted by Eve as she sifts through her memories more than thirty years later, trying to make sense of their meaning and significance. Moreover, as events that take place entirely within the context of an all-black parish set in the bayous of southern Louisiana, the story acquires a sensibility that dramatically alters its import. Elements of the mystical and inexplicable permeate the film, complementing its presumption that in some cases truth is indeterminable. Eve is not certain about the precise degree of complicity she had in her father's death; nor is the narrative clear about what happened between Cisely and their father. Viewers see both Cisely's and Louis's versions of what occurred, and the film explicitly withholds grounds for deciding which one is more accurate.

Lemmons has remarked that she intended the film to be a meditation on memory, reality, and identity. She meant, for instance, for there to be ambiguity with respect to what really happened between Cisely and her father. The writer/director explains:

> I wanted to ask questions—the question of the nature of reality, the interaction between the real world and the metaphysical world, and the nature of memory. . . . And I wanted to ask the question, what is more important, your point of view, or what actually happened? The creative rewriting of our personal history—that really interested me—how your point of view can become everything, and so the question became more important than the answer. . . . I feel that maybe something happened between [Cisely's and Louis's] two stories. Maybe there's reality to be found between . . . their stories. But the main thing that is certain is that something happened that horrified both Cisely and her father. And they retreated behind their interpretation of what had happened . . . probably to protect themselves. And also I wanted people to make their own decision at different points in the movie. I'm not trying to be cagey, but . . . it's interesting to me [when people understand movies differently.] Some people think that Cisely is lying and some think that Louis is lying—and that's really interesting to me. And that was my intention.[30]

University of Minnesota Press, 1996), 133–53; James, *Transcending the Talented Tenth* (New York: Routledge, 1997), 61–81.
30. Lemmons, commentary, *Eve's Bayou*, DVD.

Rather than strongly determine what her viewers should think, Lemmons consciously chose to compel them to actively reflect on what might have taken place and what that ambiguity means in the larger context of someone's life. If we are forced to make major decisions in our lives based on events whose meaning may only be unstably established, then what does that mean about the certainty we might secure for our identities, our senses of reality, and our lives in general? I take it that Lemmons urges her viewers here to step back and reflect on the role that ambiguity, memory, and what we narratively make of our lives have in determining the paths we choose to take and the shape we give our identities.

Given what Lemmons offers here regarding her intentions and the ways in which they are clearly detectable in the narrative, it is also clear that she has made a philosophical film in the sense that Cavell and Mulhall use that term. Cinematic works may be philosophical in a strong sense by being sophisticated and self-aware of the issues on which they focus, by making real contributions to the intellectual debates about these issues, and by thoughtfully reflecting on and evaluating views and arguments regarding such issues. In virtue of fulfilling these conditions, *Eve's Bayou* is a film that philosophizes, for it compels viewers to think seriously about ambiguity, memory, narrative, and reality, "in the way that philosophers do," as Mulhall argues in *On Film* (2). Indeed, if these questions are not classically philosophical ones, it is difficult to imagine what questions might be.

In addition, the film subtly guides its viewers to think in new ways about these matters, which is another hallmark of the philosophical.[31] *Eve's Bayou* directs its viewers to think about these matters by stressing that sometimes what amounts to the truth cannot be absolutely determined, even when life-and-death choices hang upon that determination. In this fashion the film advances a point about truth not unlike that argued for by William James in "The Will to Believe."[32] Sometimes we must make a choice, even when ambiguity and uncertainty are necessarily part of that on which we base our decisions. Thus the adult Eve's closing voiceover narration recalls and reformulates her opening one:

> The summer my father said good night I was ten years old. My brother Poe was nine and my sister Cisely had just turned fourteen. We are the descendants of Eve and Jean-Paul Batiste. I was named for her. . . . Like others before me, I have the gift of sight [that is, the supernatural ability to see what she has not witnessed], but the truth changes color, depending on the light. And tomorrow can be clearer than yesterday. Memory is a selection of images: some elusive, others printed indelibly on the brain. Each image is like a thread, each thread woven together to make a tapestry of intricate texture, and the tapestry tells a story, and the story is our past.

31. Mulhall, "Ways of Thinking."

32. William James, "The Will to Believe," in *The Will to Believe* (1897; repr., New York: Dover, 1956), esp. 17–22.

By film's end, Eve's world returns to something resembling stasis, but that return is decidedly ambivalent and ironic. Her father is dead, which is something that Eve wished for and acted to bring about, yet the reason she wanted him dead may not have been accurate. Even her sister Cisely does not know whether their father acted upon—or even had—incestuous desire toward her. Given that Eve narrates the film from more than thirty years after its events occurred, it is clear that these images, events, and their meaning continue to trouble her, for their implications are not fixed, but shift depending on which details she stresses or foregrounds.

This narrative instability is another aspect of female gothic *noir* exploited by the film. Protagonists are often morally shaken or uncertain of the redemption offered by the narrative's resolution. As Schatz explains regarding *Shadow of a Doubt,* such endings may be deeply ironic because the female protagonist's world will never be the same. Thus for Eve, the sense of security she had previously vanishes with Louis's death, even though he was the source of the family's endangerment as well. In addition, she can never know if what she so fervently wished for and had a hand in causing rested on a sound epistemological basis. Her world is beset with uncertainty and irresolution, as was young Charlie's at the conclusion of *Shadow of a Doubt.* Moreover, these difficulties have followed Eve into her adult life. It is true that in her concluding voiceover the adult Eve expresses some guarded optimism that clarity and reconciliation with the past may be possible. Yet, as she notes, what counts as the past is hardly stable, but changes, depending on the differing weight and significance we attach to the images and ideas that we weave together to make up our personal histories.

By broadening such considerations to the general human condition, Lemmons implicates the viewer as well. The narrative urges audience members to think reflectively not only on how its characters are affected by these philosophical considerations, but also on how they play themselves out in viewers' lives. The film stresses that the difficulties facing Eve are not unique to her, but permeate the lives of human beings in general as creatures who construct their own pasts and thereby have a major role in determining their own identities. One of the narrative elements that makes *Eve's Bayou* involving for viewers, then, is that many of its most interesting features are not merely idle curiosities, but are strongly implicated as crucial to the meaning of their everyday lives. These considerations are philosophical ones because they compel us to focus intimately, intensely, and systematically on what it is to be human. Eve's questions about the metaphysics of identity, memory, and reality are ours as well.

Noir, Empathy, and African-American Female Characters

These correlations between the narrative of *Eve's Bayou* and the human condition raise once more the issue of viewer empathy. By focusing on such matters *Eve's Bayou* offers its white viewers potential analogues for a successful mapping from their experience to that of black characters—a way of overcoming empathetic impairment while not ignoring the racialized dimensions of Lemmons's narrative figures. *Eve's Bayou* offers access across racialized divisions by showing viewers universalistic aspects of its black characters' lives without losing sight of their historical specificities. In this way Lemmons provides her white viewers with possible ways across social divides without at the same time ignoring them, as critics like Sarris seem to have done. Lemmons not only builds on female gothic *noir* conventions, but uses them to expand and extend black *noir* narrative to include a greater voice for black women as well. Specifically, she uses the possibilities offered by a blending of female gothic *noir* and black *noir* to cultivate empathetic understanding of her narrative figures. In so doing, she extends this imaginative capacity in the service of expanding one's sense of humanity.

The film thus offers details that help its viewers—especially its white viewers—to build bridges across specious racial divides that unfairly separate human beings from one another. It encourages its white viewers to see African Americans, and African-American women in particular, as fellow human beings, but does so in a way that incorporates differences rather than ignoring them. It is for this reason that I would deem *Eve's Bayou* an epistemological triumph as well as an aesthetic one, for it offers ways to reorient white cinematic sensibilities by expanding white viewers' horizon of possibility for what it is to be human, and it does so by making cognitive space for black reality alongside white, rather than ignoring their divergences. While these effects are no doubt achievable by other cinematic forms, female gothic *noir* may well be especially conducive to conveying them for black female characters.

What Is It Like to Be a Caveman?

In *Eve's Bayou*, Lemmons uses *noir* strategies to encourage audience alignment and allegiance with female characters, thereby offering viewers the opportunity to develop positive, empathetic responses to Eve and other women in the film. At the same time, she offers viewers an external but still not unsympathetic outlook regarding Louis's moral complexity. Because *noir* provides strategies and techniques for positively presenting morally good-bad characters who range from mostly good with some morally negative traits to clearly bad characters who possess few redeeming features, Louis's moral ambiguity fits easily within its range. From this perspective it is worth observing that Lemmon's second feature, *The Caveman's Valentine* (2001), more centrally investigates the humanity of an outright negatively stereotyped black character, namely, that of a mentally ill homeless man.

In this film Lemmons provides a chance for viewers to see such a narrative figure from the inside, for the narrative encourages viewer sympathy as well as empathy for its main character, Romulus Ledbetter (Samuel L. Jackson again), a delusional, paranoid schizophrenic who lives in a cave in New York City's

Inwood Park. Beset by deranged visions of others trying to control his thoughts and steal his ideas, within the narrative Romulus also functions, after a fashion, as the detective for a murder that no one but he believes has occurred. Like a psychotic Philip Marlowe, Romulus continues to investigate even after he is warned off the case by authorities and beaten up by criminals who want to discourage him from continuing his work. Again like Marlowe and similar *noir* figures, he finds clues or details that others have missed or overlooked as unimportant and poses previously unasked questions that uncover critical pieces of information. For these efforts, his muse, the hallucinated figure of his ex-wife Sheila (Tamara Tunie), needles him by calling him "a psycho Sherlock Holmes." As a socially marginalized character who fights both real and imagined oppressions and frequently alienates those around him because of his pathological phobias and distrust of others, Romulus is a narrative figure who takes many *noir* character attributes to their logical limit—for example, fear, paranoia, social marginalization, resentment toward those at the top of power structures, and an ability to operate in a *noirish* underworld—by grafting them onto real-world correlatives. In *The Caveman's Valentine* these *noir* traits not only represent estrangement and disaffection from a corrupt status quo, as they did in many classic *noir* films, but constitute real dimensions of Romulus's psychosis.

Based on a mystery novel by George Dawes Green,[33] the film mobilizes familiar *noir* strategies and techniques for presenting good-bad characters to humanize a well-known cultural stereotype. For example, having a sense of humor is one of this character's socially agreeable traits that helps audiences ally with him. When asked by a police detective what programs he receives on the broken, disconnected television that sits in his cave, Romulus wryly replies, "All of them. The whole heady broth of American culture." While talking to himself about the possibility of successfully masquerading as a sane person in order to gather crucial information, he observes that his chances of pulling the ruse off are "about zero." And when the dog of one of the people he must deceive in his masquerade growls at him, he acknowledges the dog's superior detecting skills by telling her, "Hey, dog. You think I'm running a con, don't you? You think I'm the [dirty, battered] shoes and not the [clean, borrowed] suit. . . . You're right." Romulus's sense of humor comes through in spite of his insanity. Moreover, for all the character's psychosis actor Samuel L. Jackson portrays him as someone with some personal charm.

In spite of his homelessness, paranoia, and apparently incurable state of delusion, Romulus does not represent a "throwaway person," in Jackson's words, "but someone with strong emotional ties to his daughter and flashes of musical genius";[34] in other words, someone of value, a human being who

---

33. George Dawes Green, *The Caveman's Valentine* (1994; repr., New York: Warner Books, 1995). Green also wrote the film's screenplay, which closely follows the novel. See *The Caveman's Valentine*, DVD, directed by Kasi Lemmons (2001; Universal Studios, 2001).

34. Samuel L. Jackson, cited in the production notes, *The Caveman's Valentine*, DVD.

is—albeit tenuously—connected to the rest of humanity. Neither does the film shy away from the racialized dimensions of this character's situation, but implies that they have contributed to his difficulties, for Romulus's mental illness and circumstances betray overtones of the asymmetrical social pressures exerted on black men, even while it acknowledges that his illness is real. Integrated into his many tirades, for example, are allusions to injustices against blacks by various civil authorities. According to Romulus "tax collectors, police brutality, drug wars, and backed-up toilets" embody the dreaded Y-rays that he believes emanate from the imagined master manipulator Stuyvesant's lair atop the Chrysler Building. Romulus believes Stuyvesant uses these Y-rays to exert mind-control over everyone else, so the homeless man zealously guards himself against them. One of the reasons he is homeless, lives in a cave, and subsists on the margins of society is that he believes such strategies allow him to remain "free" from the domination that Stuyvesant allegedly exerts.

Romulus also integrates recent specific miscarriages of racial justice, such as those involving Abner Luima and Amadou Diallo,[35] into his invectives against the forces tormenting him. The narrative makes clear that he has some reason to be distrustful of the forces arrayed against him, although it also makes clear that his mental illness dominates the reactions he has to them. While Romulus is perhaps a more problematically engaging character than most *noir* protagonists, *The Caveman's Valentine* works to humanize a deeply flawed and morally complex character whom viewers would probably in actual circumstances dismiss with hardly a thought. In this way the narrative works against certain elements of typical viewers' background beliefs in order to bring those presumptions into the foreground and throw them into question.

For all his paranoidal delusions and inability to respond reasonably to the many challenges life throws before him, Romulus and the many voices inside his head are conscientious seekers of the truth. As he tells another character, "Swarms of moth-seraphs howl in my skull. Lies vex them." These moth-seraphs, represented as angels in Romulus's visions by naked, African-American athletes, are the rulers of his psyche and rise into action when he composes music as well as when he senses injustice. Although not terribly reliable guides to appropriate behavior, they nonetheless drive Romulus on his quest to right what he perceives as the wrong done to the young homeless man he found early one Valentine's Day frozen to death in a tree outside his cave. Doggedly and in spite of his psychological limitations, he pursues his investigation in order to find out what really happened. Romulus even shows flashes of detective insight, such as when he realizes that a particular scar (a brand) supposed to be on the murder victim, but missing from the autopsy report and photographs of the victim's body, is the key to the mystery. Like some finely tuned but wildly unreliable truth detector, Romulus can sense some things that his fellow characters overlook, partly because they do not trouble to think

35. For more information on these individuals, see Feagin, Vera, and Batur, *White Racism*, 145–47.

deeply enough or carefully enough about the case because of presumptions about the homeless, junkies, and others living at the margins of society.

Romulus also turns some of his weaknesses into advantages, such as his ability to go into the *noir* underworld of New York City homeless persons to gather evidence and investigate possibilities that other individuals either could not or could not be bothered to pursue. His indifference to the socially accept-able—another trait he shares with *noir* detectives like Philip Marlowe—and skills as a street person also come in handy. Breaking into locked rooms and trespassing are matters of utter indifference to him. Not having a job further gives Romulus plenty of time with which to pursue his leads and intuitions. At the same time, viewers see him in thrall to debilitating delusions, fits of panic, and seemingly uncontrollable tirades against all the forces that he feels tyran-nize him. Beset with what he calls "brain-typhoons," Romulus is a *noir* detec-tive who at the same time literalizes many of the difficulties that frequently trouble more standard *noir* characters at subtler levels.

Cinematically, *The Caveman's Valentine* looks and sounds much like *Eve's Bayou*, particularly in its *noirish* opening sequence, which uses distorted black-and-white imagery and sounds to make the audience feel anxious and uncertain.[36] As in the earlier film this technique puts the audience on their guard by notifying them that the narrative will incorporate suspense and mys-tery, urges them to desire the disambiguation of these images, and wonder what will happen next. The film returns to this sort of sequence in portray-ing Romulus's flashbacks and visions throughout the narrative, in order to characterize his memories, madness, and delusion as of a piece with the sus-pense, anxiousness, and uncertainty that the narrative more generally offers the viewer. Romulus's wildly unreliable behavior and thinking thus become additional sources of suspense for viewers. His characterological ambiguity encompasses not only moral dimensions, but his sanity and actions. Given his mental illness, the prospects for a successful resolution of the film's mys-tery are even far less likely that they would be otherwise.

By humanizing Romulus, the film encourages a certain empathetic under-standing for this very marginalized character and thereby extends the uses of black *noir* to include a still wider scope of application. Namely, through Romu-lus it prompts viewers to try to imagine the situation, views, and emotions of a crazy homeless black man. *The Caveman's Valentine* gives us detailed and intimate representations of what it is to be such a person "from the inside," and encourages us to stretch our imaginations to include such individuals within the scope of envisionable humanity. In both this film and *Eve's Bayou*, then, Lemmons employs narrative fiction's capacities to prompt audience members into thinking critically and reflectively about the perspectives of

36. This similarity is no doubt due to the fact that *Eve's Bayou* and *The Caveman's Valentine* share many of the same filmmaking personnel—specifically, director (Lemmons), director of pho-tography (Amelia Vincent), editor (Terilyn Shropshire), musical composer (Terence Blanchard), sound designer, and actors, particularly Samuel L. Jackson and Tamara Tunie.

others that they might otherwise think of—unconsciously or not—as beyond the range of ordinary humanistic understanding. By using *noir* strategies and techniques in her films, she helps viewers, particularly white viewers, to begin figuring out ways to build bridges across categories of race and other divisions of difference by eliciting acknowledgment and recognition of her characters as representations of full-fledged fellow human beings, as envisionable human individualities, rather than pejoratively charged cultural stereotypes.

The Injustice of the Everyday: *Always Outnumbered, Always Outgunned*

Subtleties of *noir* characterization and its role in expanding audience appreciation of others may also be discerned in the film version of Walter Mosley's *Always Outnumbered, Always Outgunned* (1998), directed by Michael Apted and starring Laurence Fishburne.[37] Based on a collection of short stories partly inspired by Plato's dialogues and told using the voiceover of a character who, as in Billy Wilder's 1950 *noir* classic *Sunset Boulevard,* viewers realize by the film's end is already dead, the film chronicles the story of Socrates Fortlow (Laurence Fishburne), a middle-aged African-American ex-con who seeks to go straight and make a decent life for himself.[38] The film introduces viewers to this character by means of a black-and-white montage of images that represent Socrates' nightmare, which we soon realize is a flashback to the double murder and rape that landed him in an Indiana prison for almost twenty years. Once freed, he took off for the anonymity of Los Angeles, where he believed he would have a better chance to start over. The narrator, whom we eventually come to know as the protagonist's best friend, Right Burke (Bill Cobbs), summarizes, "Socrates was a violent man. He'd come up hard, and gave as good as he got. The rage he carried brought him to prison. But the Indiana Correctional Authority wasn't able to stem his anger."

As the narrative unfolds, we see that many of the things that make Socrates angry are the numerous forms of injustice that he sees happening around him every day. In particular, the quotidian injustices of racism and classism are sore spots for the former convict. Experiencing life as a member of the black underclass has rubbed him raw with the continual litany of slights, injuries, and unfairnesses that such an existence so disproportionately inflicts on its members. These inequities rankle him and keep his anger at just below a boil. As the narrative fills out his character, we see that even little incidents easily

---

37. Walter Mosley first wrote *Always Outnumbered, Always Outgunned* as a series of short stories that appeared in an assortment of venues. They were later published together as a collection, on which Mosley based his screenplay for the film. Picked up by HBO and released on cable television, Mosley and lead actor Fishburne executive-produced the film, and white Briton Apted directed.

38. For *Always Outnumbered, Always Outgunned*'s inspiration stemming partly from Plato's dialogues, see Charles E. Wilson Jr., *Walter Mosley: A Critical Companion* (Westport, Conn.: Greenwood Press, 2003), 26.

push him to act out his rage. As Burke observes, "He'd lived close to the edge for so long that you knew he was bound to get cut."

This connection between black underclass experience and anger has not escaped the attention of philosophers. Both Frantz Fanon and Cornel West have written about how "the lived experience of the black" creates frustration and rage in its victims.[39] In a similar vein Howard McGary has examined the presumed requirements for escaping urban poverty. He argues that by presupposing personal effort to be the sole avenue for escape to which poor blacks should aspire, many people expect them to meet an unfair standard of exceptionality in order to overcome the racial and class disadvantages that are their lot. The adversities facing the black underclass are such that, in the absence of strokes of good fortune, only extraordinary motivation and superhuman effort could lift one out of such circumstances. However, McGary cautions, "We must draw a line between what people are required to do as a matter of moral duty and supererogatory acts."[40] Given the overwhelming institutionalized racial and class-based injustices of American society, he reasons that pulling one's self out of the urban underclass solely through these means constitutes an action above and beyond the call of duty. Small wonder, then, that the temper of a character such as Socrates Fortlow might simmer at a barely controlled rage. The dice are loaded against him, and he knows it—and the filmmakers want us to know it, too. Much of the narrative focuses on Socrates' attempts to control his anger in the face of so much injustice and general indifference to it.

Furthermore, the resolution of such injustices, even at a personal, individual level, call for extraordinary amounts of patience, which Socrates all too obviously lacks. As Bill Lawson wryly notes, "It is true that if one tries hard enough and has the patience of Job, one may make it out of poverty. However, if it takes Herculean effort to overcome some social adversities, one should not be held in moral contempt if one does not try."[41] In contrast, *Always Outnumbered, Always Outgunned* offers us a main character who is willing to go to extraordinary lengths—and distances—to find a job, but he lacks the patience of Job to await their successful fruition, as his anger time and again derails his attempts to long-sufferingly expect the eventuality of justice and its triumph over the personal iniquities committed against him. As McGary and Lawson would be quick to point out, given Socrates' circumstances he should not completely shoulder the blame or condemnation for his inability to control his anger. In fact, the responsibility lays largely elsewhere, which makes his anger to some extent justified—a point that again the filmmakers want their viewers to grasp. Socrates' anger is a righteous anger, not the result of some pathological tendency or genetic predisposition. Moreover, as

39. Fanon, "Lived Experience of the Black," 184–201; Cornel West, "Malcolm X and Black Rage," in *Race Matters*, 95–105.
40. McGary, "Black Underclass," 65.
41. Bill E. Lawson, "Mediations on Integration," in Lawson, *Underclass Question*, 8.

FIG. 31   Socrates Fortlow (Laurence Fishburne), confined by bars that represent his
black underclass confinement (*Always Outnumbered, Always Outgunned*, 1998)

Aristotle argued, sometimes it is appropriate to be angry and righteously act
from it.[42] In addition, given the extraordinary and ridiculously unfair circumstances under which Socrates must operate, he is in many ways already being
supererogatory just to get through one of his days without losing his temper
each time he faces a moral decision. Of course, Socrates' character is clearly a
work in progress. The narrative shows he is trying to develop patience in the
face of overwhelming injustice—because, in a way, he has no choice. Nothing
else will help him get through the trials and tribulations of his day.

    Burke also tells viewers in his voiceover that Socrates "was a solitary man,
who kept his own counsel," thus further establishing him, like many other *noir*
characters, as isolated and alienated. Socrates also similarly lives by his own
rigid moral code. "Every night Socrates gave himself a grade," Right informs
us. "He'd once made a promise, a dark oath. He swore he'd never hurt another
person except to do good. Any time he wrote down failure, someone had been
hurt but no good had been accomplished." Like many white *noir* characters,
such as Spade or Marlowe, despite his alienation from society Socrates has
his own vision of proper human conduct. Indifferent to many standard legal
and moralistic principles, his view of how one should act toward others is

42. Aristotle, *Nicomachean Ethics*, 62; Aristotle, *Rhetoric*, trans. Lane Cooper (1932; repr., New
York: Appleton-Century-Crofts, 1960), 123–27.

nonetheless intimately connected to what it means to live a decent human life. "If you don't know when you done wrong," Socrates tells a young delinquent he befriends, "well, life ain't worth a damn." Good actions thus fundamentally undergird a worthwhile life for Socrates. One of the ways in which he tries to keep his simmering anger in check, then, is by constantly measuring his actions against a rigorous moral standard and an overall moral goal—a procedure that would put him in good stead with his namesake, as well as with the likes of Aristotle, Kant, Mill, and Rawls.

Always Outnumbered, Always Outgunned is therefore about much more than Socrates' *noir* characterization, as it also takes pains to depict the day-to-day struggles many African Americans must face in what Lewis Gordon calls "an anti-black world."[43] The film presents the ordinary difficulties of being a member of the black underclass in excruciating detail. The daily grind of getting through the day with at least a shred of one's dignity intact are laid out for the thoughtful consideration of viewers. Commonplace tasks—having enough money to eat for the day, getting a job, and not letting one's anger and frustration eat one alive—require enormous effort, because of racial and class-based domination. Small wonder, then, that by the end of the day members of the underclass often have so little energy left for anything else, such as working for the political rectification of social injustices. *Always Outnumbered, Always Outgunned* offers viewers the opportunity to reflect on these unfairnesses and their interrelations through positive engagement with Socrates' character. By eliciting sympathy as well as empathy and acknowledgment for his humanity, the film seeks to create a better understanding of him as well as those confined to similar straits.

To better grasp the film's intended effect on viewers, we might consider what a few representative philosophers of the everyday have written about the topic. Regarding the largely unconscious actions we perform in living our ordinary lives, Henry David Thoreau began *Walden* by urging Americans to seriously consider them and reflect upon how they possess an extraordinary element of the uncanny, of the bizarre. As Cavell has shown, Thoreau's strategy in the early pages of *Walden* is to defamiliarize his readers with their ordinary lives in order to compel them to reconsider the circumstances under which they live.[44] We "labor under a mistake," Thoreau tells us (3),[45] by passing our existence as if we had no alternative but the common mode of living (5). For, rather than work to acquire what would make us better human beings, we instead seek "treasures that moth and rust will corrupt and thieves break through and steal" (3). By challenging and seeking to distance us from our perceptions of ordinary life, Thoreau aims to influence us to see differently, to

43. Gordon, *Bad Faith and Antiblack Racism*, e.g., 96; Gordon, *Fanon and the Crisis of European Man*, 11–12, 25, 34.

44. Stanley Cavell, *In Quest of the Ordinary* (1988; repr., Chicago: University of Chicago Press, 1994), esp. 9–25.

45. Henry David Thoreau, *Walden; or, Life in the Woods* (1854; repr., New York: Dover, 1995).

redirect our vision in order to help us understand how our lives are devoted to false necessities that coarsen and blind us to the moral poverty of our ordinary circumstances. Through this technique of defamiliarization, Thoreau hopes to help his readers envision alternative ways of living that would improve their lives ethically rather than just materially.

French social theorist Michel de Certeau, on the other hand, directs our attention to the particular details of ordinary life. He writes, "What I really wish to work out is *a science of singularity;* that is to say, a science of the relationship that links everyday pursuits to particular circumstances."[46] De Certeau envisions this science of singularity as a prerequisite for any attempt to resist "official" knowledge's overwhelming dominance in how we understand day-to-day experience. He asserts that within an attentive and intimate knowledge of the everyday's actual details—its habits, procedures, techniques, and so on—lie untapped possibilities for freedom, creativity, and improved social relations (xxiii–xxiv). Actualizing these possibilities, however, depends upon a completely reconfigured sense of the everyday because its liberatory elements escape detection by standard forms of knowledge. De Certeau thus argues that a reconfigured sense of the normative ways of acting could serve us well in the project of separating modes of dominant knowledge from actual modes of day-to-day living. In addition, they would facilitate improved senses of autonomy, creativity, and social harmony for ordinary human beings (xi–xii).

In distinctly similar ways, philosophical theorists of race have engaged in an investigative critique of the everyday. Like Thoreau and de Certeau, they urge their readers to reconsider the structures of our everyday sensibilities and reflect upon how their details involve something quite extraordinary. Specifically, they argue for the necessity of grasping particularities in order to improve human life morally—to open new possibilities for human freedom, creativity, and social relations, especially with regard to race. Yet the prospect of such social change predictably threatens those who are members of dominant American culture—even many "goodwill whites," as Janine Jones has called them. This sense of threat seems to occur in spite of the fact that the cognitive and moral reconfigurations proposed would agree with fundamental principles that most of these individuals profess to hold.

As noted earlier, these philosophical theorists of race further argue that everyday life in America presupposes the systematic oppression of entire groups of human beings, from whose domination whites have long benefited, *and* from whose circumstances they continue to benefit. The everyday life of persons counted as white presupposes a system of dominance such that, when examined in its actual, specific details, excludes from consideration nonwhites as being fully human, racializes social orders and space, and makes the pursuit by nonwhites of ordinary goals such as employment, health care, safe housing,

46. Michel de Certeau, *The Practice of Everyday Life,* trans. Steven Rendall (Berkeley and Los Angeles: University of California Press, 1984), ix.

childcare, and the other benefits of full-fledged humanity extraordinarily difficult to attain. In particular, these theorists contend that one overlooked aspect
of white supremacy is how it permeates our everyday perceptions and sensibilities; that is, our ordinary ways of thinking, believing, and acting.

These theorists aim to bring the epistemological misperception of everyday details to our attention, so that we may reformulate and redirect our moral
vision in a way that would allow us to see more accurately the unjust and
unfair circumstances that constitute many people's ordinary lives, rather than
sweeping our "white gaze" over them obliviously. In many ways, then, these
theorists' efforts reflect the use of a defamiliarization technique on the epistemological level similar to that argued for by Thoreau and de Certeau, who
both sought to bring to our attention details that had been there all along,
but which habit and custom rendered invisible. It need hardly be said that
this technique is an exemplary philosophical move: questioning familiar and
accepted presuppositions has been a fundamental part of philosophy's repertoire since before Socrates.

A noticeably similar strategy for putting ordinary presumptions into question is deployed in *Always Outnumbered, Always Outgunned*. The title itself is a
reference to underclass status à la de Certeau; in other words, of always operating under the thumb of power. Yet the film urges us to see its details in a different way—to perceive them as extraordinarily unfair rather than simply "the
way things are" for many underclass individuals. One way the film encourages this altered way of seeing is through documenting not only the everyday despair and humiliation but also the hope of recovery and survival that
successful living under white supremacism requires of African Americans.
Socrates' quest for a regularly paying job frames much of the narrative and in
this manner depicts the perverse degrees to which African Americans must
often go merely in order to secure "ordinary" employment. Socrates finds that
his skin color, past and present occupations (serving time in prison and col-
lecting bottles and cans for recycling), and street address in Watts mark him
as unemployable, so he ranges ever further from his home in hopes of finding
employers who will not stigmatize him for his neighborhood, his blackness,
his past, or his present, but rather recognize him for the individual he really
is: someone who more than anything else wishes to live a self-reliant, morally
righteous, worthwhile life.

The film also foregrounds how each one of Socrates' decisions and actions
requires a careful moral choice, from deciding how to deal with a young boy
who kills a neighbor's chicken for fun, through weighing what to do about the
everyday insults and humiliations that constitute the powerlessness brought
on by racism and poverty, to pondering the meager alternatives brought on by
his best friend's impending death. The narrative depicts Socrates' life as by no
means easy, and made all that much harder by the rage he feels at the injustices
and inequities that shape his and others' circumstances. Echoing Thoreau's
dictum that "our whole lives are startlingly moral" (141), *Always Outnumbered,*

Always Outgunned is a deliberate, reflective film that portrays each one of its main character's actions as carrying astonishing moral weight.[47]

By depicting the small successes as well as the failures that make up Socrates' life. however, Apted, Mosley, and Fishburne have managed to fashion from techniques and themes developed through earlier African-American *noir* films a tale of not only despair, but also of hope and survival. In doing so, they leave aside the spectacular violence that so often portrays the urban inner city in film and develop possibilities for carrying on and even flourishing. One way in which they accomplish this advance is by focusing on moral decision-making as requiring creative improvisation; that is, they portray moral evaluation on the model of African-American classical music—in other words, as jazz. Such a description of moral decision-making as jazz-like improvisation arises in Lewis Gordon's work:

> Wouldn't it be wonderful if we could live the folkways and mores of our society in the form of a jazz performance? Imagine what would happen if the laws and economic structures were opportunities for freedom instead of constraints upon it. Each generation of our society could recognize and interpret what had been handed down—without slipping into epistemological conundra—and simultaneously recognize its active role in the constitution of its meaning and where it was going. And the task of every generation? To live in a way that brought out the best possibilities of their society's ongoing composition of itself.[48]

The filmmakers here have taken this reflection one step further and shown how it might work in real life, for *Always Outnumbered, Always Outgunned* seeks to portray the idea that in one's day-to-day existence, as in jazz, "one had to, has to, go forward."[49] Socrates must improvise moral solutions using the materials and possibilities at hand. Like a jazz musician he must find his balance of duty, freedom, tradition, and responsibility in the novel transposition of the moral choices available.

The film, then, may be seen as consisting of a series of moral questions that Socrates must face in his day-to-day life. What do you do when no one will hire you? What do you do when you discover someone has culpability for the murder of another? What do you do when a local youth, now a crack addict, terrorizes the neighborhood? What do you do when your best friend faces a slow, agonizing death and asks for your help to end it? The film moreover underscores that these questions are deeply complicated by their surrounding circumstances. For example, prospective white employers find you

---

47. Tom Tunney notes many of these features in his review of the film in *Sight and Sound* 8, no. 11 (November 1998): 66–67.

48. Lewis R. Gordon, *Her Majesty's Other Children: Sketches of Racism from a Neocolonial Age* (Lanham, Md.: Rowman and Littlefield, 1997), 223.

49. Ibid.

intimidating and frightening, because of their stereotypical beliefs about economically disadvantaged black men. The individual complicit in murder is a boy of no more than twelve. The crack addict in question is black and would be treated unfairly in the current justice system far out of proportion even to his crimes. Because of the holes in America's social "safety net," your best friend lacks adequate insurance coverage to pay for either the treatment or the pain relievers he needs, which is why he asks you to buy him a gun so he can shoot himself.

These extraordinary difficulties call for extraordinary responses, ones not straightforwardly dictated by rules deriving from utilitarian, Kantian, or other standard codes of morality. Blind application of moral decision procedures, for example, is not possible, since the most complicating factor, the systematic maltreatment of human beings because of their skin color, fails to constitute a morally relevant feature under the normal application of these ways of thinking.[50] The alternative posed in the film, by contrast, is one of improvising solutions from the materials and possibilities at hand, of interpreting past traditions and rules, considering the options and freedoms that one might achieve, and trying to best accommodate everyone involved. In this sense, Socrates' actions are true to those of his namesake, for they aim to be consistent with providing a good life for all.

Socrates' alternative procedure for finding the proper action, then, requires thoughtful engagement and reflection. *Always Outnumbered, Always Outgunned* depicts a further necessary component by showing the community's crucial involvement in deciding the crack addict's fate and in working out how to rear an orphaned boy befriended by Socrates. Proper resolution of such matters depends on grasping that they cannot be determined through one individual's mechanical application of rules deriving from traditional moral perspectives. Rather, one must be ready to create resolutions not previously envisioned through implementing jazz-like moral improvisations that work through different possibilities and recognize the freedom and facticity of all those involved.

Such moral improvisation as suggested in *Always Outnumbered, Always Outgunned* is, I would conjecture, piecemeal, noncomprehensive, and probably could not be codified by universalistic procedures or rules. Rather, moral decision-making will in a sense be situational by virtue of being constituted through and directed at specific circumstances that may not present themselves elsewhere. It is, in short, a program of what some philosophers have

---

50. Whether these matters could be worked into such standardized ways of thinking is a hotly contested issue. Thomas Hill and Bernard Boxill, for example, argue that while currently not a part of such procedures and principles, considerations of race could be straightforwardly incorporated. Others, such as Charles Mills and Robert Bernasconi, are much more dubious that such easy reconfigurations are possible. See Hill and Boxill, "Kant and Race," 448–71; Charles W. Mills, "Dark Ontologies: Blacks, Jews, and White Supremacy," in *Blackness Visible: Essays on Philosophy and Race* (Ithaca: Cornell University Press, 1998), 67–95; and Bernasconi, "Kant as an Unfamiliar Source of Racism," 145–66.

described as moral realism, for this film presents particularistic jazz-like solutions to pressing moral difficulties even as they fail to produce universalistic moral principles from which one could then operate mechanistically.[51]

The moral improvisations depicted in the film represent a de Certeauvian "art of the weak"—that is, maneuvers performed in plain sight of the enemy.[52] Because this film seeks to offer moral provocations in the context of popular cinema—that is, in the context of a mass art that must find extensive common ground with the culture it criticizes, thereby lacking fundamental aesthetic, economic, and ideological autonomy—it may provide less than a full-scale revolutionary rejection of the morally objectionable conditions imposed by late capitalism. Such an artwork must, rather, operate in the face of presumptions that embrace all the allegedly wonderful benefits provided by our current economic system. Despite this limitation *Always Outnumbered, Always Outgunned* manages to advance deeply troubling claims about the terms and conditions of racialized everyday life as it exists in urban America during the late twentieth and early twenty-first centuries.

As Janine Jones has argued, many whites feel threatened by such challenges to their everyday sensibilities and ordinary perceptions. Yet it is really little different from Thoreau's assertion in *Walden* that his readers live "a fool's life," "labor under a mistake," and lead "lives of quiet desperation" (3–4). Thoreau hoped to characterize the materialistic culture of mid-nineteenth-century America as a system of oppression that makes human beings morally worse rather than better. It coarsens and punishes us, he writes in those early pages of *Walden,* making it impossible for us to appreciate the moral import of even ordinary decisions in our lives. His project in writing *Walden* was to transform our perception of everyday life, so that we might overcome the blindness from which we suffer regarding our penurious moral condition.

Similarly, philosophical theorists of race hope to characterize the currently existing liberal democracy in America as an oppressive system that, when examined in detail, will be exposed as distorting and damaging those who live under it, and in particular blacks, while making whites normatively blind to the unfairness and immorality that underpin their everyday lives. These theorists, too, wish to transform our perceptions so that we may better see the oppressive system from which whites still largely unknowingly benefit. Most accepted philosophical justifications of liberalism characterize racism as an unfortunate aberration, a marginal if also harmful anomaly that does not affect the moral categories that broadly underlie the system. Thus for John Rawls in *A Theory of Justice,* race may safely be ignored from behind the veil of ignorance because it allegedly does not substantially affect the decisions made from that

---

51. See, for example, John McDowell, "Virtue and Reason," *Monist* 62 (1979): 331–50; Sabina Lovibond, *Realism and Imagination in Ethics* (Minneapolis: University of Minnesota Press, 1984); David McNaughton, *Moral Vision* (Oxford: Blackwell, 1988); and Jonathan Dancy, *Moral Reasons* (London: Blackwell, 1993), esp. 55ff.

52. De Certeau, *Practice of Everyday Life,* esp. 36–37.

perspective. Among the standard presuppositions of liberalism are that one has an unencumbered freedom to choose and work toward desired goals in one's life, that one may determine one's own character and self-definition, and that differences from others may be universally transcended.[53] Racism, as an aberration, may sometimes contingently interfere with the implementation of these presuppositions, but it does not alter their overall soundness.

In response, many philosophical theorists of race argue that such characterizations may well be fundamentally flawed. Rather than see racism as a marginal anomaly, they seek to illustrate its place at the center of much standard liberal theory by showing how the two have worked and continue to work hand-in-glove. Racism is not an add-on, some accessory wrongfully attached to the pristine doctrine of liberalism after the theory itself was worked out. Rather, racism, racial hierarchy, and white supremacy constitute the conditions under which liberalism itself was theorized and continues to be theorized.[54] Kant, for instance, may be seen simultaneously as the father of modern moral theory and the language of rights as well as the father of modern racism.[55] Similarly, John Stuart Mill advocated the right to individual liberty while at the same time denying it to Asian Indians, the Irish, and many others.[56] White moral blindness to these matters, as Mills argues in *The Racial Contract,* stems from an epistemology of ignorance that render details of the link between liberalism and racism cognitively undetectable. To counteract this blindness, specific elements of everyday life need to be brought to our attention—de Certeau's science of singularity must be directed at quotidian American life, so that we might better see the workings of white advantage, separate "official" knowledge's normative dominance from our actual day-to-day existence, and explore alternative ways of resolving problems of racism and classism.

As elements of everyday life, the particularities of white advantage demand our attention—in our philosophizing as well as our day-to-day lives—and philosophical theories of race, augmented by careful viewings of films like *Always Outnumbered, Always Outgunned,* offer us not only a critique of the current everyday epistemology of whites in America, but also a sense of possibility regarding what might be done to revise this troubling element of American life through cognitive and moral transformation. Like his namesake, Socrates goads us to reflect on moral, racial, and economic dimensions of our lives, and how they are imbricated into the very fiber of our existence, such that we take seriously *all* the decisions we face and think about the myriad ways in which they affect our fellow human beings.

---

53. Rawls, *Theory of Justice,* esp. 201ff.

54. Regarding this point, see especially Charles W. Mills, "White Right: The Idea of a *Herrenvolk* Ethics," in *Blackness Visible,* 139–66.

55. Charles W. Mills, "Kant's *Untermenschen,*" in *Race and Racism in Modern Philosophy,* ed. Andrew Valls (Ithaca: Cornell University Press, 2005), 169–93.

56. Goldberg, *Racial State,* 63–72; Georgios Varouxakis, "John Stuart Mill on Race," *Utilitas* 10 (1998): esp. 30–32.

Training Day, Empathy, and Moral Corruption

Black *noir's* capacity to expand audience sensibilities of what it is to be human may also be illuminated by examining Alonzo Harris, the character played by Denzel Washington in *Training Day* (Antoine Fuqua, 2001). Although viewers' allegiance to Alonzo varies substantially over the course of the film, generally they proceed through its early sequences feeling at least minimally favorable toward him, partly because of Washington's empathetic star persona, partly because they have been told that he is the respected head of a successful under-cover police squad, and partly because of some of the apparently sensible things this character says about the difficult decisions that must be made in order to maintain justice on the streets of a sprawling city like Los Angeles. However, as the narrative develops—particularly in its latter half—positive audience regard for Alonzo fades. In spite of occasional flashes of moral goodness, at least in his words, we come to understand that Alonzo does not have morally appropriate reasons for the brutal and heinous acts he commits. Rather than working from the crude utilitarian sense of street justice that he professes, his actions ultimately stem from selfishness and a desire for personal gain. We see that his declarations of maintaining a sort of it-all-works-out-in-the-end justice of the streets are mostly window dressing for self-interested goals. Like Orson Welles's character Hank Quinlan in *Touch of Evil*, Alonzo talks of the need to help justice along by violating the human rights of suspects when jus-tice cannot otherwise be obtained. In working so frequently from this brand of crude utilitarian morality, where the ultimate goal is the happiness and safety of society and human rights are only important relative to that goal, Alonzo has lost his way and justice for him has degenerated into personal whim.

This malevolent self-righteousness is the negative side of many *noir* char-acters' personal moral code. If such a narrative figure possesses some sort of power, like that which accompanies being a police officer, the dangers of a personalized moral system become those of arbitrarily and capriciously met-ing out whatever the character feels is right, with nothing to hold such dangers in check. This moral difficulty was recognized by artists from early on and has fueled many of its stories.[57] Like Quinlan and similar *noir* characters,[58] Alonzo's sense of what is just has broken down into self-centered acts and conviction statistics. As he declares repeatedly to distinguish the lofty values of ideal jus-tice from what he alleges is his own more pragmatic, down-to-earth version, "It's not what you know; it's what you can prove." Unfortunately, all too often Alonzo is no more seeking justice than the criminals with whom he deals. His actions are driven more by the goals of inducing fear and intimidation in his

57. For example, Dashiell Hammett's 1924 story "The Golden Horseshoe," reprinted in *The Continental Op*, ed. Steven Marcus (New York: Vintage, 1975), 43–90.

58. This negative side of *noir* characters' personal moral code was explored in many films of the later classical *noir* period; for example, *Where the Sidewalk Ends* (Otto Preminger, 1950), *On Dangerous Ground* (Nicholas Ray, 1952), and *Shield for Murder* (Edmond O'Brien and Howard Koch, 1954).

opponents, attaining career objectives, or achieving greater personal gain than by what is fair and morally appropriate.

From what he and other characters say, viewers get the sense that at one time Alonzo desired true justice and adherence to the law—as his former mentor, Roger (Scott Glenn), puts it, Alonzo's ambition was "saving the goddamn world"—but that time is long past. Corrupted by the vast riches and the pervasive moral decay around him, Alonzo has become a lawbreaker himself—only in this case, one protected by a badge. Compelled to step over the line of violating human rights again and again in the belief that such actions merely help justice along, assist him in doing his job, and provide him opportunities for promotion and advancement, Alonzo has stopped caring how far he steps any more, just so long as it cannot be detected, fattens his conviction record, advances his career, and supports him in achieving his self-centered personal aims, which he nevertheless persists in believing are, in the grand scheme of things, just.

Despite Alonzo's profound moral corruption, viewers do not completely lose their empathy for and allegiance to him. One of the film's producers remarks that "[Denzel Washington] always plays someone with whom the audience has a great deal of empathy. This is a movie that challenges that empathy."[59] One goal of the narrative is to get its viewers to understand a twisted and confused human being, without at the same time justifying his actions, partly by using Washington's empathetic charisma to draw them into this character's moral world and show them how he thinks, what he sees, and why he acts the way that he does. In addition to things explicitly said or done in the narrative, the film utilizes the socially agreeable traits of charm, sexiness, intelligence, and beauty that Denzel Washington can project into a role to seduce its viewers into finding Alonzo's morality understandable, alluring, and worthy of consideration.[60]

The narrative does not, however, seek to have its viewers simply embrace or approve of Alonzo's judgments and actions, but urges them to maintain a critical distance on him and his iniquitous deeds. The film provides a way to achieve this critical distance through offering viewers the character of Alonzo's trainee, Jake Hoyt (Ethan Hawke), a young policeman who is powerfully attracted to but ultimately rejects Alonzo's arguments that what he does is just. By focusing on Jake's responses to Alonzo's deeds and framing this veteran undercover cop's story by means of his trainee's, the film urges viewers to take their cue from this character who, like much of the audience, is new to Alonzo's world. Jake thus serves as a moral center from which audiences may understand Alonzo. At the same time, *Training Day* powerfully shows us the appeal of Alonzo's brand of morality—its *prima facie* allure and

59. Jeffery Silver, interview, in *The Making of Training Day: Crossing the Line,* directed by Stephen J. Morrison (2001), on *Training Day,* DVD, directed by Antoine Fuqua (2001; Warners Brothers Home Video, 2001).

60. This, in any case, is the director's view. See Antoine Fuqua, commentary, *Training Day,* DVD.

appropriateness in *some* of the circumstances under which these events take place, and compounds its audience's initial approval of such actions by means of Washington's empathetic persona, his socially agreeable characteristics as an actor, and the sincerity he projects into the role.

Training Day tells a morally complex story about the sense of street justice held by a morally ambiguous character. It attractively shows audience members the temptation that such a code and character provide, while nevertheless offering a more critical moral orientation toward him in its final half. Ultimately, Jake's judgments are meant to prompt the audience's negative moral judgment about Alonzo because his assessments appeal more strongly to viewers' accepted norms for justice and morality than Alonzo's. On the other hand, this attractive-bad character's form of rough justice appeals impressively to audience members' desires for some protection from the chaos on the street by means of competing moral norms. For a good portion of its narrative, then, the film balances Jake's critical perceptions with Alonzo's allure, and keeps the audience anxiously uncertain which it prefers, appealing to them first one way, then another regarding which character's morality they prefer. This *noir* suspense regarding morality thus drives much of the narrative.

The film, however, ultimately prompts its viewers to side with Jake. It presents Alonzo's justifications for why his actions should be seen as just, given the circumstances under which they are committed, as unsatisfactory because, as Jake stubbornly points out, they fail to exonerate how much Alonzo lacks respect for other human beings and their rights. His actions remain murder, armed robbery, assault, battery, and coercion. Appealing to a "real world" sense of street justice that may not be achieved except by means of these acts does not adequately support their necessity because, as Jake would point out, there *do* exist alternatives that nonetheless respect human rights. These alternatives, even if they take longer to implement, remain better for all of society because they protect the innocent, more properly identify the guilty, and apportion out punishment and reward more fairly. In this sense, the narrative ultimately favors Jake's sense of the sanctity of human beings and their rights over Alonzo's crude utilitarian stance.

Still, when assassins finally kill Alonzo near the end of the film, viewers do not simply feel that he has gotten what he deserves. As Fuqua describes him, Alonzo has become pitiful at this point, after Jake has defeated him and taken as evidence of his corruption the stolen one million dollars that would have saved him. "The system's failed him as well," Fuqua explains, "the guy has nothing left."[61] Alonzo is thus made humanly vulnerable because Jake has taken away his last chance for surviving the moral decay of which he has become so much a part. There is a sense, then, in which he too is a victim and worthy of our compassion. At one time apparently a decent cop who wanted to do some good, the pervasive evil that exists above as well as below him has seduced Alonzo. As Fuqua argues, this brand of iniquity "is everywhere," and

61. Fuqua, commentary, *Training Day*, DVD.

officials who condone actions like Alonzo's—represented here by "the three wise men" (Tom Berenger, Harris Yulin, and Raymond J. Barry), the police officials who give him permission to act as he does, as long as they receive a cut of the take—bear ultimate responsibility for the moral decay that pervades life on the streets, for their moral laziness and indifference permit as well as encourage it. Add to these factors the residual empathy and allegiance for Alonzo generated earlier in the film through Washington's characterization, and one can see why Alonzo's death is one about which the audience may have some ambivalence. The film ends with the voiceover of an anonymous news-caster briefly summarizing the story of Alonzo's death in a way that entirely elides the corruption of which he was a part, thereby telling audiences that neither his loss nor Jake's preservation of justice in this one particular instance has had any substantial impact on the system as a whole.

Given this sense of overwhelming moral corruption through *noir* charac-terization, *Training Day* alludes to *films noirs* such as *The Set-Up* and *China-town*, where such corruption may be criticized or rejected by characters but remains largely unaffected by a single individual's actions. Instead, the film offers a sort of resignation that isolated individual actions will do little beyond preserving one's personal integrity in relation to the moral decay that pervades many cities. However, the film leaves open the possibility that collective action might have an effect on such corruption and thereby alter the way in which typical urban administrations operate.

In order to portray such a perspective, Alonzo functions as an attractive-bad *noir* character, someone with whom we partially ally positively in spite of significant moral drawbacks. Although charming, sexy, intelligent, and physi-cally attractive, his evil and eagerness to spread corruption to others eventu-ally become clear. In this regard, Alonzo is not unlike African-American film pioneer Oscar Micheaux's main character Isiaah T. Jenkins (Paul Robeson) in *Body and Soul* (1925). Like the earlier film, *Training Day* offers viewers an evil black character whose badness is due to negative *human* qualities rather than racial ones, and whose character is offered for audience consideration by the filmmakers in order to get them to think about why that character is bad from a *human* perspective, why racialized explanations of him would be inad-equate, and what they would need to do in order to protect themselves from such characters and prevent their existence in the future. One may see these dimensions of Alonzo and his human corruption particularly when the neigh-borhood members of "the Jungle" support Jake in his struggle against his cor-rupt superior, rather than backing Alonzo out of some twisted sense of racial loyalty. These characters express that they can see the differences between the morally upstanding Jake and the crooked Alonzo, and they consciously choose as a group to help the better moral being.[62]

I would further argue that this similarity between Alonzo and Micheaux's character reflects the fact that it has taken mainstream audiences three-quarters

62. Ibid.

of a century to catch up with Micheaux—in other words, what Micheaux sought to present in 1925 for black audiences, who as silent film scholar Charles Musser has argued were themselves not quite ready for such characterizations, it has taken mainstream audiences until 2001 for a significant portion of them to be at least arguably prepared to see such a character as human rather than as pathologically racial.[63] On the other hand, such characterological presentations remain contested territory, as many viewers no doubt continue to see Alonzo through the stereotypical lens of the black criminal rather than seeing him as a flawed human being.[64] However, one hopeful implication of this ongoing contestation is that it raises certain racialized beliefs to a level where they might be openly debated and perhaps changed.

In constructing Alonzo so that viewers will understand in detail a morally horrible human being, then, the filmmakers draw them imaginatively into Alonzo's world partly via Washington's star persona and show them "from the inside" how the character thinks, what he sees every day, and why he acts in the way that he does; and in so doing they urge viewers to think about what it takes to maintain a modicum of justice on the streets and what should be required of policing officials who do so. In this sense, the film offers us a kind of "challenge of immorality" as was discussed in connection with *Menace II Society*. Although not in Kieran's sense an immoral work,[65] like the earlier film *Training Day* nonetheless devotes significant portions of its narrative to presenting Alonzo's seductive immorality in an appealing light. By providing such a powerful rendition, the film offers viewers an opportunity to imaginatively "slum it," morally speaking, and learn something about that world because the narrative compels them to consider critically the intimate workings of this character's depravity.[66]

As in Kieran's example of *Goodfellas* (Martin Scorsese, 1991), Alonzo's character requires us "to imagine certain propositions and commitments as holding," though we do not in fact believe them to hold and we know at some level that they are immoral (60). *Training Day* moreover helps us to gain knowledge by virtue of compelling us "to understand better how and why [immoral] people think or feel differently" (62). As Kieran explains, "The immoral character of the imaginative experience afforded by a work may directly deepen our understanding" (63). By virtue of powerful, alluring, and empathetic portrayals of characters like Alonzo, a work such as *Training Day* may be aesthetically valuable, even though its main character is immoral, because the knowledge we gain about the world by thinking about the film's seductively evil antagonist is inseparable from its immoral dimensions. Of course, on the whole the film remains a moral work because it provides us with Jake as a guide and

63. Musser, "To Redream the Dream," 97–131.

64. Anecdotally at least, I have found this perspective to be the case with many white viewers.

65. Kieran, "Forbidden Knowledge," 62.

66. Smith, "Gangsters, Cannibals, Aesthetes," esp. 223–25.

through him prompts us to orient ourselves critically with regard to Alonzo and his actions. However, it would not have the emotional and cognitive intensity it does if it did not rub our noses in the sweet smell of moral corruption and dare us to indulge in its pleasures.

By challenging us critically regarding Alonzo's evil character, *Training Day* urges us to consider the consequences of his actions toward those under his sway, namely, criminals, suspects, bystanders, and anyone else who might happen to be in his way. The film asks us to reflect on whether one has to break a few eggs to make an omelet, as some might argue about the ethics of street justice. In addition, it prompts us to consider the question, how many eggs are too many? Here the film encourages viewers to step into the murky waters of black marketeer Harry Lime (Orson Welles), the eponymous third man in Carol Reed's famous British *noir, The Third Man* (1949). As they ride to the highest point on the huge Ferris wheel of the Prater amusement park in post–World War II Vienna, Harry attempts to justify his actions, which have killed many and injured more, by asking his friend Holly Martens (Joseph Cotten) to consider the people far below them: "Look down there. Would you really feel any pity if one of those dots stopped moving forever? If I offered you twenty thousand pounds for every dot that stopped, would you really . . . tell me to keep my money— or would you calculate how many dots you could afford to spare?" In similarly seductive ways, both Harry and Alonzo tempt viewers to seriously consider denying acknowledgment to those around them, and in so doing test the strength of viewers' integrity as well as their willingness to back it up with action. Viewers are thus encouraged to imaginatively check their moral mettle against what these corrupt characters offer as an alternative.

Training Day adds to these considerations the matter of race, in the sense that most of those under Alonzo's thumb are African American, and their race provides a further complicating factor to the injustices Alonzo so blithely heaps upon them. Harry and Alonzo's challenge to viewers' morality and their strength of character in acting on it nevertheless remain much the same. Just as Harry tests the audience's resolve concerning what they think of as moral and what they would do to stand up for it, so does Alonzo with his arguments about the difficulties of maintaining a modicum of street justice, given the forces arrayed against such a possibility. In both films, the seductiveness of immorality significantly challenges their viewers, even if they both also provide moral guides as well, albeit significantly flawed ones, through the characters of Holly Martens and Jake Hoyt.

The strength of these moral challenges, I would argue, indicate something about a more general need to reflect on justice and how we might best achieve it. It is not something about which we can afford to become complacent. Rather, our vigilance is required in ways that we may well have inadequately appreciated. *Training Day* reminds us of the additional complications race may create in thinking well about such matters, but like *The Third Man* it underscores our need to actively contemplate the ongoing commitment to treating others fairly and equitably in our everyday lives. This is not something that we may let sink to the level of background presumption regarding how it is being carried out.

Taken together, the four films analyzed in this chapter provide striking examples of how *noir* techniques may be developed to expand audience senses of humanity. By taking on more challenging forms of individualities and devising ways to encourage viewers to sympathize, empathize, and acknowledge them, these films mark further stages of black *noir*'s aesthetic growth. In the process they also advance the interests of antiracism, justice, and overall human flourishing. But such advances are hardly the furthest extension of black *noir,* as the films to which I turn next employ its components in still more liberatory ways.

I want people to think about the power of images . . . how imagery is used and what sort of social impact it has—how it influences how we talk, how we think, how we view one another.
                                                                    —Spike Lee, interview

The films analyzed in previous chapters encourage various forms of sympathy, empathy, and acknowledgment for their characters, and do so in ways that extend the application of *noir* characterization to narrative types not centrally addressed by earlier films. In this chapter I argue that black *noir* has not only continued building on these advances, but broadened further still by contributing to the development of more generalized ways to incite audience contemplation about racialized life. Here the focus comes to be not only on blackness, class, gender, or their interrelations, but also on whiteness, other ethnicities, refugee status, and the African diaspora.

In particular, the films I analyze in the final third of this chapter sharpen *noir*'s critical capacities to expose not merely new versions of the constantly evolving racial contract in America, but social oppression worldwide. Such films demonstrate that black *noir* has contributed to establishing what might be called a *"noir* Atlantic," capable of influencing audience members to scrutinize the dilemmas of not just African Americans but other disadvantaged populations. In one way this development merely reaffirms *noir*'s internationalism, as *noir* has always been a transnational phenomenon anyway, even if it also remains, perhaps somewhat paradoxically, an apparently "American style."[1] Such innovations depend crucially on black *noir*'s revitalization of the possibility for focusing audience attention on matters of social disadvantage. In ways similar to Paul Gilroy's conception of a "black Atlantic," which details the predicaments of modernity and its racial dimensions in particular, black *noir* may evoke a level of analytic and reflective possibility such that it and other *noir* elements may now be directed to examining circumstances of

---

1. See, for example, Naremore, *More Than Night*, 11–39; Munby, *Public Enemies, Public Heroes*, 186–220; and David Desser, "Global Noir: Genre Film in the Age of Transnationalism," in Grant, *Film Genre Reader III*, 516–36. I contend that *noir* remains an *apparently* "American style," as for example Alain Silver has argued in his introduction to Silver and Ursini, *Film Noir Reader*, esp. 3–10, because most of its paradigmatic examples derive from Hollywood or other forms of American filmmaking, as well as the common perception that it is quintessentially American in origin—which is, of course, debatable, but nonetheless remains the standard view.

oppressively challenged populations generally.[2] Just as the European Enlightenment and black responses to it provide a toolbox full of ways to deal with difficulties posed by the modern world, so black *noir* offers inspiration for how to generate reflective thinking in regard to global problems of race and other forms of social unfairness.

I begin by examining two black *noir* films that direct viewer attention to some of the peculiarities of white racialized moral psychology in the United States and how its configuration reflects deeper problems linked to ways in which whites generally regard matters of difference itself. I then link this aesthetic innovation to other cinematic attempts in black *noir* to catalog the continually evolving versions of racialized thinking that persist in American contexts. Finally, I analyze several films that reflect the inspiration and example of black *noir*, and that I argue have led to the creation of a *noir* Atlantic cinema.

White Fears of the Other: *Summer of Sam*

Spike Lee's 1999 film takes the thematic developments analyzed in Chapter 7 one step further in order to offer a subtle form of racial analysis. On the surface, *Summer of Sam* may not seem to be about race at all. Yet I would argue that by focusing on how suspicion and fear of difference cause violent tensions in an Italian-American neighborhood of New York City during the hot summer of 1977, the film crucially addresses matters of race as well. Using *noir* techniques that at times tacitly quote from Jules Dassin's classic *The Naked City*, particularly in the framing story narrated by Jimmy Breslin, which mimics producer Mark Hellinger's voiceover in the older film, Lee depicts how several young men who grew up together begin to suspect an old friend of the serial murders taking place in their neighborhood, after he returns from living in Manhattan with ideas and an outward appearance totally foreign to them. Afraid of the unfamiliar and unable to assimilate their old companion into the simple-minded stereotypes with which they were raised, these young men reflexively treat him with suspicion, distance themselves from him, and ultimately refuse to acknowledge him because they presume his guilt based on their own unexamined phobias of those not like them.

Lee also introduces broader allusions to race in order to thematize these suspicions of difference and transform this Bronx tale into a parable about racial lynching. With scenes of white neighborhood gangs roving the streets with baseball bats looking to beat up anyone who might not "belong" there and individuals who look different being refused service at diners while police officials collude with vigilantism and mob hysteria, the allusions to America's historical involvement with antiblack racism and lynching are striking. In

2. Paul Gilroy, *The Black Atlantic: Modernity and Double Consciousness* (Cambridge: Harvard University Press, 1993).

addition, similar to white criticisms of black somatic aesthetics,[3] most of the characters repeatedly criticize the anomalous physical appearance that their old friend Ritchie (Adrien Brody) has taken on. With his hair spiked and his body adorned with the regalia of punk rock, Ritchie embodies a look they cannot assimilate. At first, they seek to fit him into readymade outsider categories by calling him a "freak," a "vampire," and a "fag," in spite of those categories' obvious inappropriateness. Later they tell Ritchie outright that he is no longer welcome in the neighborhood because the way he looks upsets them. Eventually they settle on thinking of him as a satanic cult member because his appearance is so foreign to their way of thinking that they can find no other place for it. They put him at the top of the list of suspects who they believe might be the killer who roamed the streets of New York City that hot summer, the Son of Sam, even though the narrative makes clear this suspicion has no basis in fact. Ritchie is then persecuted by these self-appointed vigilantes on the basis of groundless suspicion and fear, his only real crime being that he does not look, think, or act like these other young men.

Tellingly, Lee and his fellow filmmakers portray Ritchie as the most sensitive, caring, and thoughtful of this neighborhood gang. He openly objects to their violent actions against those weaker or different from them, sees people for who they are instead of by means of myopic stereotypical categories, and thoughtfully listens to his friends' problems, rather than using their admissions as the basis for mean-spirited games of ridicule and one-upmanship. In his second scene in the film Ritchie defends the neighborhood junkie Woodstock (Saverio Guerra), whose appeal for charity has incurred the abusive wrath of the gang. "You ain't Bruce Lee," he tells one of them, "Stop kicking Woodstock." Ritchie recognizes that their old neighbor is still a person, even though he has become a drug addict and is clearly going through the early stages of an unintended withdrawal, making him more appropriately an object of pity than abuse.

Later in the same scene, he responds warmly and openly to Ruby (Jennifer Esposito), whom the other young men—including her brother—denigrate as a "skank." Ritchie, however, sees her as someone who is similarly dissatisfied with the confining restrictions of neighborhood life and beliefs. He and Ruby interact in ways noticeably different from the defensive posturings and sadistic abuse practiced by those around them. A few moments later Ritchie's old best friend Vinny (John Leguizamo) takes the young punk for a ride in his car so that he may confess the numerous kinky sexual escapades he has had behind his wife's back. As Vinny reveals, he seeks these adventures outside his marriage in the bizarre belief that a man should not have any but the most puritanical sex with his wife. To do anything else, Vinny argues, would be "a fucking sin." Ritchie carefully listens to his friend's catalog of misdeeds and

---

3. For an analysis of such criticisms, see Taylor, "Malcolm's Conk and Danto's Colors," 16–20.

outrageous rationalizations and, after a little gentle teasing, offers the best advice he can think of in response. Ritchie's reaction to Vinny's problems and worries is in stark contrast to those of gang members Anthony (Al Palagonia) and Brian (Ken Garito), who use Vinny's earlier show of vulnerability as a way to ridicule and manipulate him.

On the other hand, Ritchie is also a deeply complex *noir* character, especially for mainstream audiences. While he is explicitly thoughtful, kind, and considerate toward others in the sequence described above and elsewhere, he secretly makes his money by doing strip shows for lonely gay men and servicing their illicit desires in a room over the theater where he works. The film also portrays Ritchie as sexually confused. Of course, being a punk does not exactly endear him to the hearts of many mainstream audience members, either. There is a great deal of moral ambivalence for them about Ritchie—just as Borde and Chaumeton argue there was for Humphrey Bogart's *noir* characters more than half a century ago.[4] But this ambivalence only adds to Ritchie's complexity and ambiguity, drawing audiences to desire a clearer sense of who he is and what he will do as the narrative proceeds.

Similarly, the film portrays Vinny in morally complex ways. While he is clearly presented as the second-most sensitive member of the old neighborhood gang (after Ritchie) and does not indulge in the vicious tormenting of others practiced by his friends, Vinny is even more confused and unable to make sense of his own life. He moreover lacks both the analytic skills and the desire to figure these matters out. The film manifests Vinny's confusion in his numerous frantic erotic couplings and his progressively worsening drug abuse. Rather than seek clarity, self-understanding, and self-improvement, Vinny craves kinky sex, Quaaludes, and cocaine. To compound these difficulties, Vinny is psychologically weak, insecure, and easily swayed by others. Again and again he asks members of the old neighborhood gang how he looks and gives in to their assessment rather than thinking for himself or trying to practice accurate self-perception.

Ritchie says more than once that, not only does Vinny not listen to attempts at thoughtful self-reflection, he all too willingly goes along with what others say they believe. One night after the two old friends have been kicked out of a diner because other customers do not like Ritchie's look and Vinny expresses sympathy for their prejudices, in particular their revulsion at Ritchie's wearing a spiked dog collar, the young punk tries to explain to his friend why he has chosen that form of neck accessory: "We're *all* wearing dog collars!" he exclaims. "You're wearing a dog collar! You're a fucking dog of society, man. You're on a leash to a certain way of thinking." Ritchie wants his old best friend to understand why the dog collar is an expression of his view regarding how most people—including Vinny—think, how it rudely projects his rejection of that mode of conformism, and why he struggles to break free from the conventional ideas with which they have been raised. When Vinny confesses

---

4. Borde and Chaumeton, *Panorama of American Film Noir,* 7–9.

that he has no idea what Ritchie is talking about, his old friend mutters in resignation, "What else is new?" Vinny's combination of being easily swayed, his inclination to avoid self-reflection or thoughtful understanding, and desire to conform thus make him relatively easy prey for those who strongly express their beliefs, such as Joey T. (Michael Rispoli), Anthony, and Brian, who ultimately browbeat Vinny into betraying Ritchie. By means of such character traits Vinny becomes an example of someone who does unjust things in spite of having better instincts.

Summer of Sam also builds considerations of casual white racism into its narrative. In Ritchie's first scene, when he asks his mother to lend him some money, his stepfather, Eddie (Mike Starr), hotly objects, "Hey, Ritchie—how about *working* for a living? Only the colored and Spanish live off of welfare." A little later in the film, when New York City police detectives appeal to the neighborhood Mafia boss and his cronies for assistance, they have a racially charged exchange over who was the best major league baseball player in their city during the 1950s, Willie Mays or Mickey Mantle. The exchange makes clear that the white Mafiosi believe that Mays was at most the second-best player because he was black. They claim that his famous "basket catch" in the 1954 World Series, for example, was just luck. To underline the outrageousness of this claim, Lee and his collaborators show us documentary footage of Mays making that amazing catch as one of the Mafiosi advances this ridiculous assertion. The filmmakers place these references to casual white racism into the narrative in order to prepare viewers to see how the events that unfold later possess distinctive parallels to such unconscious prejudices, and to build their case that viewers should reflect on how these beliefs need to be brought to the surface and critically examined.

The narrative thus configures Vinny's traits into those of a figure who might be called a "sympathetic bigot," a character toward whom viewers generally respond favorably in spite of holding prejudiced beliefs or acting toward others in bigoted ways based on alleged differences. In *Summer of Sam* Vinny is someone who engages in immoral acts against others because of the phobic beliefs that have been drummed into him and in spite of his better instincts. Although not as racist a character as, say, Vito or even Sal in *Do the Right Thing*, he nevertheless thinks and acts in ways that many racists do.

Here Lee and his collaborators are interested in exploring how characters like Vinny come to think and act as they do. Vinny gives in to group thinking and goes along with beliefs and actions that in other ways he knows are wrong because he is weak-willed, unreflective, and wants to fit in. He has never understood how and why he should think for himself and is disinclined to learn. Furthermore, he is so self-absorbed with his own problems that he seems unable to think of much else, as his inability to listen, frenzied couplings, drug use, and querulous worrying portray. Instead, he allows the other young neighborhood men to browbeat him into betrayal with taunts such as "killer, fag, pimp, punk rocker . . . queer, pervert, degenerate, whatever the fuck it is. I mean, c'mon—who wants something like that around here anyway?" And it works—Vinny does indeed betray his old best friend and stands idly by as others beat him senseless at the end of the film, despite also acting in ways that show he knows what he is doing is morally wrong. Like many whites who went along with mob actions in spite of knowing better, Vinny's weaknesses, ignorance, and unwillingness to reflect lead him to act in ways that acquiesce in the brutalization of other human beings based on what amount to superficial, meaningless differences.

Through these elements Lee and his collaborators transform *Summer of Sam* into a *film noir* about how hysterical "othering" can lead to lynching. In order to further assist this transformation, they use the *noir* themes of confinement and determinism. Fate slowly closes in on Ritchie as his progressive marginalization culminates in a merciless beating, and his best friend Vinny inexorably succumbs to the dictates of the dominant "white gaze" by giving in to the assertions of other neighborhood gang members to see Ritchie as someone punishable for merely being different.[5]

Characters in the narrative also specifically reference the theme of lynching. When Ritchie first discovers that Vinny has betrayed him and as a result has led a group bent on violence to one of his hangouts, he says to his old best friend, "So you [brought] a vigilante lynch mob down here to string me up." In this instance Ritchie escapes, because of the ineptitude of his would-be assailants, but out of frustration they viciously beat another young punk who crosses their path and provocatively claims to be a Boston Red Sox supporter to these staunch New York Yankee fans. Near the end of the film, the news reporter John Jefferies (Spike Lee) excitedly describes the crowd awaiting the arrival of the person who was later proved to be the real Son of Sam, David Berkowitz (Michael Badalucco). Jefferies refers to this roiling mass outside the police station as a "potential lynch mob" full of "rage and vengeance." While he goes on to describe them as "going crazy" at Berkowitz's arrival and giving in to "pandemonium . . . hysteria . . . [and] chaos," we hear the crowd screaming "Kill him!" "Burn him!" and "Lynch him!" while on the soundtrack The Who's ironic "Won't Get Fooled Again" comments extradiagetically on the intercut screen images of not just one, but two hysterical groups bent on extralegal retribution. One is the crowd outside the police station, nearly out of control and demanding the summary execution and burning of someone who has yet to be tried for the actions of which he stands accused. The other is the neighborhood gang including Vinny that, ignorant of the events being televised, has finally caught up with Ritchie and beats him into unconsciousness, despite his innocence of the crimes of which his assailants accuse him. Such allusions to lynching, of course, have a special meaning for blacks, who were long the victims of such actions. Ritchie's differential otherness functions here to broaden these concerns to fearful reactions regarding otherness itself and

5. Again, for use of the term "white gaze," see Fanon, "Lived Experience of the Black," 185ff.

FIG. 32   Anthony (Al Palagonia) and Joey T. (Michael Rispoli) drag a beaten and bloodied Ritchie (Adrian Brody) off to see the neighborhood Mafia captain, as former best friend Vinny (John Leguizamo), holding guitar, looks on passively (*Summer of Sam*, 1999).

urges audience members to reflect on the ethics of "othering," its causes, and how easily these might go awry.

The film also subtly emphasizes how such mentalities embrace virtually all whites: male and female, adults and children, gay and straight—even junkies—so long as they are able to gain acceptance by means of some semblance of normalcy, a normalcy that is subtly raced as white. Both men and women, young and old, scream for the death of a suspect whose guilt has yet to be determined, demanding that he be strung up and burned before any evidence against him may be presented. Similarly, young children are shown to have already learned to fear physical difference. When Ritchie gently bends down to speak with one of the children in his old neighborhood, she bursts into tears and screams for her father to pick her up and protect her from this awful representative of human variation. In addition, even those whites who are normally marginalized in the community, such as the junkie Woodstock and the cross-dressing Bobby del Fiore (Brian Tarantina), become part of the vigilante gang seeking violence against Ritchie.

White solidarity here trumps other forms of social difference. For example, the status of white womanhood's commonality with white masculinity is emphasized through Dionna's (Mira Sorvino) refusal to go into the famous punk nightclub CBGB's because of all the strange-looking people in attendance. One patron even speaks to her (and the audience's) fears by addressing the camera as it represents Dionna's point of view. "You scared?" the young female punk sneers. Later in the film Dionna ironically calls attention to white womanhood's alleged need of white male protection in the face of black male sexuality during the cemetery scene, in which she and her husband Vinny have a verbally abusive argument over his many infidelities. After Vinny jealously accuses her of enjoying the sex orgy that they have just attended (at the ironically named "Plato's Retreat," a legendary 1970s private club), Dionna explodes in anger over his hypocrisy and sarcastically invites any black men within earshot to take advantage of her alleged sexual vulnerability in the face of Vinny's threat to abandon her. These scenes and others depict how age, gender, clothing choice, and even illegal drug preferences do not matter as much as Ritchie's rejection of looking and acting like "normal people," conceptions that are plainly raced as white. Such narrative elements thus draw further attention to the theme of lynching by highlighting not-so-subtly raced solidarities and phobias surrounding perceived differences from the standard norm of whiteness.

The film also returns again and again to the matter of Ritchie's punked-out hair as a marker of anomaly, and how upsetting it is to those who believe others should have the sort of hair "normal people"—that is, typical white people—possess. Vinny, for example, repeatedly comments on how he cannot get used to Ritchie's spiked and later Mohawked hair, as if his old friend's choice of coiffure amounted to his primary social offense. This rejection of nonstandard hair uncomfortably alludes to dominant white rejections of typical black hair and hairstyles on alleged aesthetic grounds, as well perhaps to its erstwhile souvenir value as evidence of lynchings.[6] Acceptable-looking hair must be the sort that fits within the parameters of whiteness, which Ritchie's punked-out hair, like typical black hair, does not do.

Finally, when the television reporter played by Lee goes to the African-American neighborhood of Bedford-Stuyvesant to obtain what he describes as "a darker perspective" on these serial murders, one of his respondents tells him: "I am going to give you your darker perspective. The darker perspective is . . . I thank God that it is a *white* man who kills all of those *white* people, because if it were a *black* man who kills all of those *white* people, there would be the biggest race riot right here in New York City." This observation reveals one of the ways in which the city's community is riven with racial tensions that could easily result in mob hysteria and lynching. Such commentary by black New York City residents enlists them as a sort of Greek chorus whose remarks illuminate the panic and paranoia felt by whites in the city, who perhaps for the first time begin to acquire a sense of the fear and stress that is inextricably linked to the normal lives of persons of color in America. The specter of violence or abuse is latent, but palpable, visceral. Virtually any individual could be a potential carrier because there is simply no way to tell from looking at them who will be a threat and who will not. Nor will past experience help all that much, as it might still not clarify of whom to be wary. Similarly, white city residents cannot tell who the Son of Sam is, or whether he might

---

6. Regarding the former point, see Taylor, "Malcolm's Conk and Danto's Colors," 17–18; regarding the latter, see Allen et al., *Without Sanctuary*, esp. Plates 31 and 32.

even be someone they know. In this fashion *Summer of Sam* alludes to black sensibilities regarding racism and how it can permeate one's everyday life.

In a brief discussion of racial lynching in *Bad Faith and Antiblack Racism,* Lewis Gordon observes that "the victim is anonymous except insofar as he can be identified as a member of a hated *group.*"[7] Consistent with this idea, characters in *Summer of Sam* repeatedly tell Ritchie, "I don't know you," even though they have known him all their lives and in Vinny's case have been best friends. Instead they repeatedly place him in some misunderstood, marginalized outsider group by which they feel threatened (freak, vampire, cult member, punk rocker, degenerate), in an effort to distance themselves from him. In this manner they remove Ritchie's human individuality, making him the nameless member of some hated category. Similar to Gordon, in summarizing the views of Frederick Douglass and Ida B. Wells-Barnett on the topic, Tommy Lott notes that conceptually "lynch law applies to people who are considered beyond the pale of human sympathy."[8] As Cavell would argue, they cease to be acknowledged or recognized as human and are at best distinguished through some stereotypical category.[9] Gordon points out that the *racial* dimension of this human diminution reveals itself through the ways in which the power relations of such symbolic persecutions mimic those of white advantage. The anonymous member of an outsider group moves into the subject position of being black, while the enraged mob as an instrument of retribution becomes empowered as white (115). The punishment becomes a punitive action by those with power, who act out their symbolic whiteness by imposing it on an individual for being different, who is thereby treated as if he or she were stereotypically black.

Bernard Boxill extends these observations by noting that "the symbolic meaning of a lynching is that its victims, and those like them to whom it is meant as a warning, have no rights." Conversely, its perpetrators "admit no wrong." Rather, they hold "themselves up for approval and [declare] their righteousness." As such, "the effectiveness of lynching as an insult lies in the especial vehemence and perverse eloquence with which it makes its point."[10] Persecutions of this sort are not meant merely to harm the individual involved, but rather are meant as warnings to *all* those in the group to which the individual belongs who would even hint at challenging the status quo. This will happen to you, too, if you so much as dare to question your place in how things are.

Like some members of the black community, punks like Ritchie openly challenged how power relations stood, doing so in ways that ranged from emulating contrary hairstyles, clothes, bodily adornments, and music to violating notions of respectability and propriety—in other words, from personal aesthetics and etiquette to politics. Ritchie's persecution, then, parallels that of

7. Gordon, *Bad Faith and Antiblack Racism,* 114–15.

8. Lott, *Invention of Race,* 39.

9. See Cavell, *World Viewed,* 33–34.

10. Bernard Boxill, *Blacks and Social Justice,* rev. ed. (Lanham, Md.: Rowman and Littlefield, 1992), 139.

blacks who rebel against the power relations confining them in the sense that the neighborhood gang punishes him symbolically for the same reason—that is, for daring to think, act, and look differently. When so viewed, the persecution of one individual stands in for the persecution of all in his or her marginalized group, for it is meant as a warning—a threat—by those in power against issuing challenges against them. Such punishment also underscores the power of refusing to acknowledge others as fully human, as it shows what is possible as a result of dehumanizing individuals through their reduction to a stereotypical category. *Summer of Sam* works to expose the poverty of such symbolic persecutions by revealing their ultimate foundation in ignorance, fear, xenophobia, or weakness.

Other *noirs* have explored the issue of lynching, but without directly indicating its racialized dimensions. As briefly noted in the introduction, *Try and Get Me* explicitly condemns this extralegal practice. But oddly, all its characters are white. This narrative choice seems strange because the history of lynching in America would lead one to believe that the lead characters who suffer this fate would be black.[11] Yet white actors Lloyd Bridges and Frank Lovejoy play these roles, and no references to race are made in the narrative. Similarly, director Fritz Lang's American debut *Fury* (1936) powerfully advances an antilynching theme, and its narrative character is such that it merits an entry in Silver and Ward as "one of the earliest of *film noir*."[12] What makes *Fury* particularly interesting in this context are its parallels with a racial lynching just a few years earlier. On August 7, 1930, a crowd of thousands stormed the county courthouse in Marion, Indiana, and lynched two young black men suspected of involvement in the murder of a white man and the alleged rape of his girlfriend. Photographers extensively documented the proceedings.[13] One of these photographs became "one of America's most famous lynching photographs," as thousands of copies were sold as souvenirs of the event for fifty cents apiece.[14] The Indiana attorney general's office attempted to prosecute various mob participants for this double lynching, but witnesses, including law enforcement officers who were in the courthouse at the time, refused to identify fellow townspeople who participated.[15]

In *Fury*, the narrative similarly takes place in a Middle American small town, and witnesses, including law enforcement officers, similarly refuse to

---

11. See, for example, Dray, *At the Hand of Persons Unknown*, and Allen et al., *Without Sanctuary*. Silver and Ward, *Film Noir: An Encyclopedic Reference*, 294, notes a "factual basis" for *Try and Get Me*'s story in a 1933 incident without mentioning the lynching victims' race, which probably means that they were white. I would still argue, however, that it is noteworthy that the filmmakers chose to portray the characters who were lynched as white, presumably in order not to offend their primary audience's racial allegiances.

12. Silver and Ward, *Film Noir: An Encyclopedic Reference*, 110.

13. James H. Madison, *A Lynching in the Heartland: Race and Memory in America* (2001; repr., New York: Palgrave Macmillan, 2003), 5–11.

14. Ibid., 115; Allen et al., *Without Sanctuary*, 176.

15. Madison, *Lynching in the Heartland*, esp. 81–85.

identify who participated in the lynching. But in the fictional case newsreel footage is used to incriminate members of the lynch mob. The state's attorney freeze-frames parts of the footage to show specific townspeople's participation in the attempt to murder the suspect. Some African-American newspapers of the era argued for just this strategy of using the many photos of the Indiana incident as documentary evidence against mob participants, but this possibility was not pursued.[16] *Fury*, however, does, and several mob participants are found guilty, based mainly on the evidence provided by raw newsreel footage. But again, the narrative makes no direct references to race and its relation to lynching (although Lang does insert a few incidental shots of African Americans elsewhere).[17] It is not too difficult to think of historical explanations why direct racial references might have been absent from these two films, but the point I want to make here is that even socially critical *noirs* of the classic era and earlier did not address the issue of race while condemning the emotionally charged issue of lynching, which makes *Summer of Sam*'s *noir*-influenced commitment to exploring racialized lynching (in 1999!) all that much more striking.

Another race-based connection *Summer of Sam* raises is the issue of how vigilantism and lynching have often symbiotically coexisted with white officialdom. Early in the narrative, two police detectives appeal to the neighborhood *capo*, Don Luigi (Ben Gazzara), to help them catch the serial killer. Interspersed with the racially charged argument mentioned earlier over who was the best New York City baseball player of the 1950s, Don Luigi discusses the problem as a community leader and agrees to assist the police. Later, after realizing that the task force working to solve the murders is stumped, he tells his cronies, "We gotta get this rat bastard. We gotta do it. Because they [the police] can't do it." With officialdom's blessing he forms roving gangs armed with baseball bats to "protect" the neighborhood, institutes blockades on the bridges allowing access to his community, and tells his soldiers to compile lists of suspicious individuals, who are inevitably those whose appearance or actions somehow do not fit into a strictly policed conception of what it is to be "normal"—or as the film makes clear, what it is to be normally white. These lists quickly degenerate into catalogs of those whom Luigi's minions do not like and reach such proportions that even people with "weirdo eyes" and those against whom the Mafiosi carry a grudge are added to it. The name of a local priest, Father Cadilli (Bill Raymond), is added to the list because he used to beat some of the gang members when they were schoolchildren. The priest is duly stopped and searched by Luigi's men on the suspicion of being the Son of Sam, even while the gang simultaneously asks him for a blessing for their actions. In doing so he ironically and exasperatedly quotes from scripture (Luke 23:34), "Forgive them, Father, for they know not what they do."

16. Ibid., 115.
17. Could Lang or his fellow filmmakers have consciously worked in allusions to the Marion, Indiana, incident? It is certainly possible, although I have no direct evidence that they did.

Charles Mills has interpreted the collusion between white officialdom and vigilantism as part of the physically violent aspect of coercion that enforces artificial racial differentiation.[18] Lynching operates as a form of "massively disproportionate retaliatory violence" that is intended to force nonwhites to remain obediently in their subaltern positions by stressing the violence's difference in scale and ferocity (86). As a technically illegal activity, lynching is something that may regularly occur—particularly with its intended force—only through the collusion and at times encouragement of those in power. Lynching also helps to enforce the cognitive dimensions of racial differentiation, which include for nonwhites learning to see one's self as undeserving of the advantages whites receive by providing a strong physical incentive to believe that the dominant position's formulations are accurate (87–88). Mills likens this second form of coercion, which is ideological as well as cognitive, to the intellectual equivalent of "seasoning," or slave breaking. He notes Frederick Douglass's description of this process as a darkening of one's "moral and mental vision" and an annihilation of one's power of reason, which are necessary degradations if nonwhites are to see themselves as appropriately subordinated by this sort of racial differentiation.[19] Such cognitive miseducation is greatly facilitated by white officialdom's open and willful blindness to violent racial acts such as lynchings.

A separate though related aspect of the film's racially inflected exploration of themes surrounding lynching is its calling to viewer attention a disproportionate horror at the death of whites, as opposed to those of nonwhites. This disproportionality is due to the existence of a "norm of far greater value of *white* life," as Mills notes in *The Racial Contract* (101). The ugliness of such disproportionate valuing is gauchely pointed out by Don Luigi, who when initially requested by the police to assist in catching the Son of Sam, responds defensively, "I'm asking you. This guy—how many people did he kill? Three, four, five? And with no disrespect, Detective [gesturing to the black police officer played by Roger Guenveur Smith], in Harlem last night, your people, the coloreds—how many of each other did they kill? Seven, eight?" One of Luigi's lieutenants interjects, "Eight, nine, at least, and on Saturday, twenty—if we're lucky." Luigi then continues his argument, "So, why don't you ask me who killed *them*? Not enough press in it for you? Not enough *Post* or *Daily News* headlines?"

These offensive comments make brutally explicit the differential valuing to which Mills refers. Institutions of power such as the police or mass media reflect a far greater concern for the loss of white lives than they do for black lives. Legal theorist Jody David Armour notes that this differential norm has been firmly established in U.S. court deliberations as well. Punishments, for example, are clearly allotted on the basis of race by juries, with blacks receiving far more severe punishments than whites for the same offense.[20] He also

18. Mills, *Racial Contract*, 81–87.
19. Douglass, *Narrative of the Life of Frederick Douglass*, 98; cited in Mills, *Racial Contract*, 88.
20. Armour, *Negrophobia and Reasonable Racism*, 59–60.

notes that "the lives of minority victims are valued less highly than White victims" in death penalty decisions (59). Sadly, as Mills would note, this disproportionality is a consequence of the differential valuation of human beings built into our racialized social epistemology.

Another dimension of *Summer of Sam*'s narrative we should briefly note here is how it also highlights other kinds of fears of difference and their links to "normalcy."[21] Variations regarding gender and sexuality, for example, figure significantly in the ways that the characters relate to one another. The restrictive policing of masculinity plays a fundamental role in how the neighborhood gang of young men responds to each other as well as to Ritchie. Their taunts and ridicule draw strict lines around what counts as acceptable male behavior and what does not. Perhaps not too surprisingly, their policing efforts revolve mainly around rather straitlaced notions of heterosexuality and male privilege. In fact, one of the pieces of "evidence" that they use for thinking of Ritchie as the Son of Sam is that he has found employment as a dancer at the gay strip club "Male World" and has made a pornographic film in order to buy a guitar. The obvious irrelevance of Ritchie's manner of employment and presumed sexuality to the likelihood of his being a serial killer is even pointed out by Vinny, who initially tries to defend his friend by arguing that these matters have no relation to one another. Of course, being Vinny, he crumbles in the face of his opponents' vehement refusal to recognize the absurdity of the logical connections they have made.

The neighborhood gang's treatment of the cross-dressing Bobby del Fiore, on the other hand, makes clear that his behavior is highly unacceptable until it becomes convenient for them to provisionally allow him to associate with their group. They also make clear the lines to be drawn between allegedly acceptable and unacceptable sexuality for women as well as men. Ruby's brother Brian and his friends crudely and harshly criticize her desire for female sexual pleasure, for instance, even though it makes possible the sort of male sexuality prized by these men; and the hypocrisy of male sexual freedom versus female modesty is further made clear during Vinny and Dionna's argument after the sex orgy at Plato's Retreat. When Vinny angrily calls his wife a "whore" for participating, even though it was at his urging, and daring to derive pleasure from it while high on cocaine, Dionna responds by calling him a whore as well, to which Vinny primly responds, "I *can't* be a fucking whore because I'm a *man!*" Of course, as the narrative has made clear by this point, if anyone deserves to be called a whore, it is Vinny.

These other dimensions of xenophobia and their links to a strict policing of what counts as "normal" parallel as well as complement the ways in which the film underscores fear of racial differences. By illustrating that the punitive maintenance of racial "normalcy" possesses crucial connections to other

21. I want to thank members of my Spring 2005 Philosophy and Film class for bringing this dimension of *Summer of Sam* to my attention, particularly Tim Oakberg, Emily Robins, J. R. Logan, and Sheena Rice.

forms of what is typically thought to be normal, *Summer of Sam* broadens its critical perspective on standard responses to difference itself.

If we view *Summer of Sam* with sensitivity concerning how it explores attitudes about race and otherness, its narrative brings out how viewers—particularly, white viewers—need to attend to unquestioned assumptions regarding these matters in ordinary life. As such, this film joins forces with other black *noirs*, in spite of its focus on whites, by exposing how a distorted social epistemology undergirds whiteness. Such attempts to broaden critiques of race as one finds in *Summer of Sam*, I might add, show a conscious effort on Lee's part to come to terms with problems of difference in general, very much in line with the efforts of philosophers who critically theorize race. Perhaps, too, it is a response to critics such as bell hooks and Douglas Kellner, who have argued that one weakness of Lee's earlier productions was that his racial critiques were too confined to single-issue or identity politics, and that he needed to incorporate a politics of otherness.[22] *Summer of Sam* bespeaks an effort to convey a broader understanding of the human condition, rather than one that rests content in a parochial perspective, as the narrative recognizes that there exist similarities between problems facing many different marginalized groups. Goals and efforts aimed at greater fairness and liberation may thus be shared as well. This broadened perspective is essential if problems of race, and for that matter difference, are to be fully understood and eradicated. Thus, although *Summer of Sam* predominantly focuses on whites, it highlights not only racial attitudes but their underlying presumptions of difference, in order to criticize and provide the hope of changing them.

Viewer reflection spurred by this film can accordingly bring to the surface beliefs regarding previously unquestioned aspects of everyday life that betray a raced sense of knowledge and cognition. When contemplated through the lens of offering a racial critique, a film like this one can help viewers, especially white viewers, see what the relevant moral facts are regarding racial injustice, to use Hill and Boxill's phrasing.[23] Such films may also fulfill more generally at least some of the conditions that Adrian M.S. Piper describes as the cognitively transformative possibilities possessed by contemporary works of art. For sympathetic viewers and under the proper conditions, such as having a conscious sensitivity to matters of race and an openness to the possibility of receiving race-based criticisms, black *noirs* like *Summer of Sam* have the capacity to challenge viewers in ways that force them to identify and confront their own racist beliefs.[24] Such artworks may furthermore assist in convincing viewers to learn to listen or observe sympathetically those who may be somehow subordinate to them, so that they might acquire a better sense of

22. bell hooks, *Yearning: Race, Gender, and Cultural Politics* (Boston: South End Press, 1990), esp. 183–84; Kellner, "Aesthetics, Ethics, and Politics," 73–106, esp. 98–99.

23. Hill and Boxill, "Kant and Race," 470.

24. Adrian M.S. Piper, "Two Kinds of Discrimination," in Boxill, *Race and Racism*, esp. 231–37.

moral relevance. Laurence Thomas has explained this sympathetic listening as "moral deference," a kind of humility in the face of radically different and cognitively challenging moral experience.[25] Such humility is indispensable if those who are socially advantaged are to know, understand, and do something to correct the social injustice to which they are otherwise insensitive.

Summer of Sam intentionally troubles viewers. It makes them uncomfortable about forms of social injustice based in fear of difference and how easily individuals might ignore, approve, or participate in them. The complexity of its characters urges viewers to think about the actions the film depicts and ask, "How can these characters act like this?" thereby encouraging further reflection after the film is over and the house lights come up. Moreover, the sheer construction of its narrative by viewers induces them to ponder the roles that ideas of race and other forms of difference play in the creation of its characters. By responding thoughtfully to such troubling provocations, audience members might better grasp relations between epistemology, morality, and social oppression because they are being asked to directly confront the roles such things play in their understanding of the story presented. In this sense *Summer of Sam* illustrates a real advance in the development in the reflective and analytic power of black *noir* because its narrative prompts us to think about even broader considerations regarding the operation of institutionalized social disadvantage.

Transcending Human Differences in *8 Mile*

A striking if perhaps surprising companion piece to *Summer of Sam*'s analysis of otherness is a rather different depiction of whiteness in the biopic *8 Mile* (Curtis Hanson, 2002). Loosely based on the life of popular white rapper Eminem, the film offers as its centerpiece the serious portrayal of what is commonly known as a "wigger"; that is, a white person who acts like a black person.[26] Crispin Sartwell has analyzed this concept in order to foreground its positive critical capacity, which he takes to be its ability to analyze whiteness all the way "down to the level of gestures: it is a completely specific attack on everything it means at a given moment to be white." In part, he argues, this is a matter of "self-critique: part of what most wiggers are attacking is . . . the inscription of white culture on their own bodies and expressions" (43). At their best, then, wiggers "perform" their criticisms by means of "an aesthetic repertoire that pits itself against the aesthetic canons of whiteness" (36), both as it exists as parts of themselves and as it exists institutionally. Not content to target merely their own whiteness, Sartwell observes, "they are criticizing in ruthless detail their own parents and communities. They are expressing

25. Laurence Thomas, "Moral Deference," *Philosophical Forum* 24 (1992–93): 233–50.
26. For this preliminary definition of "wigger," see Crispin Sartwell, "'Wigger,'" in *White on White/Black on Black*, ed. George Yancy (Lanham, Md.: Rowman and Littlefield, 2005), 35.

hatred for their lily-white suburbs, their excellent lawns, their good manners, their careers, their lockstep obedience to social conventions" (43). Even more powerfully than punks like Ritchie in *Summer of Sam,* wiggers represent a rejection of white aesthetic standards, which are criticized through an appropriation of black aesthetic sensibilities.

To some extent, Sartwell admits, wiggerism fits into a tradition of romantic distortions of blackness, but one with distinct strategic advantages concerning human liberation. While in many ways it remains a form of experiential "slumming" for whites (38), it also creates the possibility for developing a form of white double consciousness, an understanding of "white culture simultaneously from inside and outside" (45). As first argued by Linda Martín Alcoff and taken up elsewhere in this book, developing such a sense of one's race for whites is crucial for any sort of progressive social change. Wiggerism thus allows for self-conscious criticism of whiteness itself (44), insofar as it may be acted out in the wigger's performance of blackness. Crucial to the possibility of such a performance is hip-hop music and culture, "the wigger's instruction manual" (43). Particularly in the form of gangster rap, hip-hop offers a catalog of "self-expression as defiance" (as Tommy Lott noted more than a decade ago), as well as a studied self-consciousness in presenting it (41).

In this context, a narrative loosely based on Eminem's life provides an opportunity for representing cinematically wiggerism's possibilities for critiquing whiteness, as it provides a lucid illustration of how to be a race traitor for white youth. *8 Mile*'s main character, B-Rabbit (played, of course, by Eminem), is "Detroit white trash" like him (45), as well as someone who seeks to make his mark in rap. The film thus explores what it is like to be white in a black world and be accepted there because one has become competent at performing its inhabitants' behaviors visually, aurally, and culturally, and in some sense made them one's own. *8 Mile* thus depicts someone who knowingly exists simultaneously inside and outside white culture, and for this reason may forward a compelling analysis of its racial dimensions. In this fashion the film provides an example of someone who has partially transcended the racial gap between blacks and whites, and whose existence hints at the possibility of further transcendences, in spite of the problem that some romanticization of blackness has taken place as well.[27] But as long as the latter can be held in abeyance and itself critiqued, additional insights and advances may be possible because its positive critical dimensions can then be fostered. *8 Mile* offers these features as embodied in its main character for our consideration, which viewers may thoughtfully take up by means of reflecting on their potential for further transcending human differences.

I would also maintain, perhaps a little surprisingly, that *8 Mile* might at least arguably be considered a black *noir* because it fits many of the conditions for such films outlined in the introduction. Most important, it offers a criticism of whiteness's antiblack racism by means of *noir* techniques. As a gritty

27. See also Sartwell's brief discussion of Eminem, in ibid., 44–46.

"urban drama" that takes place mostly at night and in darkness,[28] its grainy cinematic look, its references to social determinism regarding both class and race, and its focus on a vulnerable, good-bad protagonist whose anger, frustration, and oppressive circumstances might well prove to be his undoing, the work fits easily alongside many other black *noirs* of the last two decades, such as *Juice, Clockers,* or *Menace II Society.* Moreover, it conforms to Tommy Lott's conditions for a work to be a black film by focusing on the aim to foster social change regarding antiblack racism and incorporating values consistent with African Americans' engagement in a protracted struggle to achieve full social equality.[29] It further provides striking new "ways to think" about whiteness à la Cavell and Mulhall, particularly by means of its careful and serious presentation of a wigger figure for viewer consideration. With characteristics like these, there seems little reason to exclude *8 Mile* from the category of black *noir.* In conjunction with *Summer of Sam, One False Move,* and *Clockers,* it offers much food for thought regarding the deconstruction of whiteness and possibilities for developing white double consciousness. By providing a viable alternative to standard whiteness, *8 Mile* signifies on the wigger figure in ways that demonstrate how whites might live and still reject many of the norms inscribed on their bodies—and minds.

The Evolving Racial Contract: *Out of Time* and *Never Die Alone*

Even as films like *Summer of Sam* and *8 Mile* show a potential for generalizing the critical capacities of black *noir,* the film form remains a viable means through which to examine continuing problems of antiblack racism and ways in which their associated conceptions constantly adapt and change to meet existing conditions. Carl Franklin's *Out of Time* (2003), Ernest Dickerson's *Never Die Alone* (2004), and Spike Lee's *Bamboozled* (2000) address more recent versions of race relations in America than these directors' earlier work. Even in the more conciliatory narratives of Franklin's and Dickerson's films, however, there continue to be telling references to antiblack sentiments, while Lee's 2000 film compels us to confront whether new forms of racialized thinking and acting really are that different from earlier versions.

Out of Time's main character, Mathias Whitlock (Denzel Washington again), is police chief of the quiet city of Banyan Key, off the coast of southern Florida, where he supervises three other officers. The work pace is such that he even has time to remind the school crossing guard to be on time. Through a combination of personal flaws, misjudgments, and a deceptive plan put over on him by others, he becomes enmeshed in circumstances that indicate his guilt in a combination of murder, arson, and theft, although he is innocent of those

28. Regarding this generic category's use in the early black film wave, see Rhines, *Black Film/ White Money,* 89–90.

29. Lott, "A No-Theory Theory of Contemporary Black Cinema," 151.

crimes and guilty mainly, as he admits near the story's conclusion, of stupidity, gullibility, and an obstinate masculine unwillingness to openly express his emotions. Although a largely sympathetic character who is clearly trying to do what is morally right, Mathias misappropriates impounded drug money in a noble if errant attempt to help his lover, who then apparently dies in a blaze that engulfs her home, which Mathias's fire department colleagues confirm as arson. The money, of course, initially seems to have disappeared in the flames, just as hard-nosed DEA agents handling another drug case requisition it in order to help incriminate an even bigger dealer than the one Mathias arrested.

To make matters worse, Mathias was seen by a neighbor's visiting mother while searching for his lover at her house just prior to the fire. He thus becomes someone at whom all the evidence points and must try to solve the case and find the money before his estranged wife, Alex (Eva Mendes), an ambitious, rising homicide detective in nearby Miami, puts the clues together and discovers that the husband from whom she has recently separated is circumstantially the person most likely to have committed these crimes. In this sense, the film functions as a Hitchcockian thriller in that it follows an innocent man who desperately tries to clear his name while a web of suspicion closes in around him. Yet it is also *noir* in that Mathias himself is a generally sympathetic but morally ambiguous and flawed protagonist who is drawn into crime by his current lover Ann (Sanaa Lathan), who fits neatly into the mold of the *femme fatale,* with the twist that she possesses a certain humanizing desperation borne of poverty and, perhaps, domestic abuse. The film also trades on its story's deepening degrees of *noirish* deception, moral ambiguity, and determinism, even if it ultimately backs away from these elements in order to offer a neat and sunny resolution by the end, which, as noted earlier, is a possibility black *noir* has successfully revitalized.

In depicting these events, the narrative makes clear that race matters little to the residents of its fictional world and that in this regard they live lives of relative social harmony. Blacks, whites, and Latinos coexist peacefully and are relatively untroubled by ideas of racial prejudice or advantage. However, at one point the narrative nonetheless refers to some whites' inability to distinguish the features of black men, especially when considered as criminal suspects, a common feature of antiblack racism that black *noirs* have frequently addressed. Under this way of thinking, what matters is that the individual is black, which alone is thought to establish his guilt. So unimportant are the distinguishing features of different black men that whites frequently never learn how to do it, an incapacity that Lewis Gordon has argued is a form of epistemological "bad faith" that creates "an imaginary, 'magical' version of the world" in order to exclude blacks—particularly black men—as full-fledged members of humanity by presuming a generalized guilt for them all.[30]

In *Out of Time,* this inability to distinguish black suspects is played as a joke on the neighbor's visiting mother and displaced by having her daughter

---

30. Gordon, *Bad Faith and Antiblack Racism,* 103.

explicitly apologize for the fact that her mother "grew up in another time." Ironically, however, the older woman initially and accurately identifies Mathias as the man she saw lurking around Ann's house. But everyone laughs at the possibility that a respected chief of police could be considered the prime suspect in this case, even though she rightly indicates Mathias as the man she saw. But this character then ruins her credibility by going on to point to every other black man entering the police station as looking like the one she saw, once her initial identification is doubted. Nonetheless, this joking reference to white racial "bad faith" directs our attention, even if only momentarily, to the fact that problems of race are not completely resolved even in places of relative racial harmony such as that represented in the film, and that work remains to be done in order to fully eliminate such pernicious beliefs and presumptions.

Never Die Alone, on the other hand, tells the story of a young black criminal seeking to atone for his past misdeeds. The film unfolds using what its director Ernest Dickerson refers to as "that wonderful *noir* device of the story being told from beyond the grave, being told by a man who's already dead and we find out how he died."[31] Like *Sunset Boulevard, Never Die Alone* uses its voiceover to prompt a sense of bleak fatalism from the viewer and tinge its narrative with regret. These emotional overtones work in the story's favor because it focuses on a career criminal who realizes too late that his life was not one worth living, and will never be one worth living unless he "makes good" on his past mistakes. King David (DMX) seeks "redemption" for the many harmful acts he has committed over the years, but as the film illustrates, he greatly underestimates what "making amends" and "setting the record straight" will require. There are some actions that are so morally reprehensible, so horrendous, it is difficult to conceive how one could offer recompense for them, or receive forgiveness.

As the opening and closing sequences make clear, the story is about the moral weight of one's actions—"karma . . . payback," reaping what you sow. The filmmakers, of course, use these different cultural and religious terms to generalize the appeal of a claim that our actions carry with them a substantial moral significance. As King David tells us ruefully from beyond the grave, his tale is the story of one individual's evil deeds and how they return to haunt him, both metaphorically and literally. Based on the novel of the same name by ex-drug addict, pimp, convict, and writer Donald Goines, *Never Die Alone* draws its viewer into a *noir* underworld of life on the streets, where betrayals and scams are traded as freely as the drugs David deals, and where he lives up to his name as a king of deception.[32] After performing one too many scams, he must leave his home turf for the open city of Los Angeles, where he recreates the same circumstances and commits the same misdeeds that led him to

31. Ernest Dickerson, interview, *The Making of "Never Die Alone"* (no director listed, 2004), on *Never Die Alone,* DVD, directed by Ernest Dickerson (2004; Twentieth Century Fox, 2004).
32. Donald Goines, *Never Die Alone* (Los Angeles: Holloway House Publishing, 1974).

leave his home in the first place. Forced to flee once more, he drifts over the years from town to town committing the same rip-offs, deceptions, and street deals, only to find in examining his actions that the life he has lived is an empty one—and his fault, as he puts it, attributable to his own choices. Thus David returns home "to make good, make things right." But as other characters tell him, there are some things that can never be made good, especially when those toward whom one has acted immorally are unwilling to forgive or simply accept money as recompense.

One of David's fatal misjudgments is that even though he has decided to make up for his iniquitous past, he believes that mere sums of cash will do the trick, that "payback" may be strictly fiscal. Yet one of *Never Die Alone*'s themes is that some moral transgressions require much more, that certain immoral actions do not have simple cash equivalents. As King David assesses his life from beyond the grave, he conveys the rueful message that he would have done things differently if he had known during his life what he realizes now in death. Moreover, various film techniques communicate to viewers that the film's title is ironic because even though the main character's story tells us to "never die alone," that is precisely what he does. No one mourns David's passing. In fact, we hear characters agree that he "deserved to die." We also see his body robbed of its valuables by unscrupulous undertakers and callously stuffed into a cardboard box to be cremated, rather than buried in "hallowed ground," as was his dying wish as well as the paid-for funeral arrangement. We further hear in his final voiceover David wondering what will lie ahead for him on "the other side," as flames engulf the flimsy carton containing his body. The filmmakers then offer us a montage cataloging his iniquity, the sum total of King David's wasted, ruinous life, and the disastrous effects he has had on those around him. Given the flames, montage of images, and complete lack of those who grieve his passing, the viewer is left with little doubt regarding how David has died, as well as what lies ahead.

Like many of its black *noir* predecessors, the film seeks to turn the story of King David against itself by showing the other side of hustling life: one of nihilistic emptiness, meaninglessness, and devastation to others. It also seeks to reinforce this flipping of the story by employing the rap artist DMX in the lead role. As a performer who has made a great deal of money exploiting the "bling-bling" image of gangstas who live the high life of big money, expensive cars, and material gain from crime, DMX uses his charisma and charm to invest his part with some attractive features and draw viewers into the story. In spite of King David's horrendous treatment of others, especially the female characters whom he seduces and in two instances even murders, the character retains a certain attractiveness that minimally allies the audience with him. But the story uses the actor's charisma against the viewer in order to increase the emotional impact of depicting King David's ruinous life—the way in which it is rooted in gravely damaging others and gives its possessor nothing for which to live. Moreover, by killing off its protagonist, the film encourages viewers to reflectively examine the role of mistakes and misdeeds in one's life and the way in which they can drain it of significance. The film challenges the stereotypical gangsta life by turning it inside out, exposing it as a form of human existence that is fundamentally pernicious to oneself and others, and suggesting that many typical deeds that make up such a life have no worldly compensation.

On the other hand, one of the film's more interesting aspects is how race matters far less to its characters in their day-to-day lives than it did to characters depicted earlier in the cycle. As portrayed in the film, King David has on a routine basis much less trouble simply because he is black than Caine or Q did just a decade before. Still, even if the film eschews explicit depictions of everyday racism that figured crucially in earlier narratives, its story remains one steeped in problems facing the black underclass, which serve as the backdrop against which the film's events takes place.

Bamboozled by Blackface

Works like *Out of Time* and *Never Die Alone* reaffirm, even in their relative reluctance to depict the quotidian travails of antiblack racism, Spike Lee's more blunt and outraged assertion in *Bamboozled* (2000) that such phenomena remain serious difficulties, even if many might wish to downplay or ignore them. By framing his narrative in a way that, like Dickerson's film, explicitly references *Sunset Boulevard*,[33] Lee uses the rueful voice of a man already dead and reflecting on the events of his life to urge his viewers to consider how the legacy of blackface minstrelsy remains a destructive influence on both blacks and whites, even when they might want to believe that they have overcome such things. By employing the contemplative *noir* device of having a character tell his story from beyond the grave, *Bamboozled* encourages viewers to mull over difficulties faced during the past two centuries by African Americans, even while acknowledging that those difficulties have evolved into different forms. Here Lee emphasizes how the images and ideas that constitute the legacy of blackface minstrelsy must still be recognized for the damaging entities that they are, even though they may be submerged from our consciousness or evolved to the point that many people no longer recognize them or their influence. As the first homegrown form of American popular entertainment,[34] blackface minstrelsy remains a crucial part of the ongoing background to antiblack racism, Lee wants us to see, because minstrel images and their related

33. Lee acknowledges this influence in Gary Crowdus and Dan Georgakas, "Thinking About the Power of Images: An Interview with Spike Lee," *Cineaste* 26, no. 2 (January 2001): 9, and in Spike Lee, commentary, *Bamboozled*, DVD, directed by Spike Lee (2000; New Line Productions, 2001).

34. See Robert Toll, *Blacking Up: The Minstrel Show in Nineteenth Century America* (New York: Oxford University Press, 1974), and Alexander Saxton, *The Rise and Fall of the White Republic: Class Politics and Mass Culture in Nineteenth Century America*, (1990; repr., London: Verso, 2003), 165–81.

ideas, scenarios, songs, jokes, and presumptions comprise a pervasive aspect of American culture, even as their more contemporary forms are difficult to pick out and bring to the surface.

Lee calls these minstrel elements to our attention by having Pierre Delacroix (Daman Wayans) tell us the events that led up to his demise. Prior to his death Delacroix was a struggling, token black television writer who is unhappy with his job, so he thinks up the most racist idea for a TV show he can imagine, in the hope of being fired and receiving a comfortable severance package. Delacroix's idea is to present an unapologetic, unironic, and unrepentant blackface minstrel show, disingenuously titled *Mantan: The New Millennium Minstrel Show*, complete with "coon" routines, tap dancing, pickaninnies, Aunt Jemimas, Sambos, Rastuses, shucking-and-jiving, watermelon patches, and the whole litany of racist stereotypes, images, jokes, songs, and stock locations that owe their existence and vitality to this theatrical form.

To Delacroix's astonishment, his boss, the appropriately named Dunwitty (Michael Rapaport), a white producer who thinks he knows more about being black than Delacroix himself, loves the idea and fast-tracks it into production. In stunned horror Delacroix sees all the outrageous, hateful images he thought would get him fired paraded before his eyes, accepted and lovingly embraced by audiences, critics, and peers alike. *Mantan* and its blackface imagery become "the newest sensation across the nation," as he sullenly observes. As its creator Delacroix skyrockets to fame aboard a fad he cannot control, and, rather than dying the immediate death he believed it would bring upon itself, the program arises vampire-like to a voracious and frightening vitality. Like small-time Broadway producer Max Bialystock (Zero Mostel) in *The Producers* (Mel Brooks, 1968)—another admitted influence on Lee here[35]—Delacroix watches in shock and disgust an idea he thought would guarantee failure while assuring him a small profit achieve astounding success at the expense of personal catastrophe.

For a while, Delacroix believes that he can control the ugly, racial "Frankenstein" he has created. Seduced by the adulation that accompanies being the creator of a huge television hit, he looks forward to awards given to him "for all my hard work, my talent that had been previously overlooked," and becoming what he describes as "Hollywood's favorite Negro." But the show is so popular and so powerfully racist that it eludes his ability to guide it, and he conveys to us through his brooding and bitter voiceover that he realizes he has struck a racial "motherlode" buried deep in the American psyche, including his own. Audiences, both black and white, laugh at the coon routines and stereotypes in which the television show trades, not realizing that in doing so they reveal racialized aspects of their expectations and thinking about African-American capabilities that extend far deeper than almost any of them realize. By bursting into laughter when one of the show's characters evinces a slow-wittedness or infantile desire worthy of "Hollywood's favorite Negro" of the early 1930s,

35. Lee, commentary, *Bamboozled*, DVD.

Stepin Fetchit (whose real name was Lincoln Perry), these audiences reveal that they find such stereotypes enjoyable objects of pleasure and mirth.

I would further argue that in laughing at such sequences audiences reveal they find such characters comforting and nostalgic of a past that never existed, except in films like *Gone with the Wind* (Victor Fleming, 1939) or television shows like *Amos 'n' Andy* (1951–53), *Beulah* (1950–53), *Calvin and the Colonel* (1961–62), *Good Times* (1974–79), or their present-day equivalents,[36] "a simpler time when . . . nigras knew they place," as *Mantan's* Sleep-and-Eat (Tommy Davidson) tells the audience in minstrel dialect during the show's first taping, and current racial stereotypes such as those for urban welfare recipients and professional athletes may be forgotten, as he deftly points out. His partner, Mantan (Savion Glover), then picks up on this theme and advises the audience, "Cousins, I want you to go to your window, yell out, scream with all the life you can muster up inside your bruised and battered and assaulted bodies, 'I'm sick and tired of niggers and I'm not gonna take it anymore!!!'"

The implication of these remarks, of course, is that minstrelsy allows for the disregard of present-day stereotypes in favor of ones from the past that are more comforting and reassuring. Yet the comfort and reassurance that audiences find in these nostalgic racial images reveal their willingness to accept and think in terms of them, their eagerness to turn from existing racial realities—or racist delusions—and indulge in the consoling fantasies offered by blackface minstrelsy. The humorous, entertaining dimensions of blackface thus mask the fact that these fantasies necessarily presuppose the inferiority of an entire class of human beings, and that this presupposition causes nearly unimaginable damage to them by refusing to recognize, let alone acknowledge, their full humanity.

One noteworthy and daring feature of Lee's narrative is that he presses home the idea that such unquestioned presuppositions exist in the minds of not only whites, but blacks as well. He makes this point by showing members of both groups responding with uninhibited laughter to coon routines and generally enjoying the outrageously racist sequences of *Mantan*. Nearly everyone in the film finds them funny and pleasurable, in spite of the harm they cause.

Another way in which Lee explores the acceptance of blackface is through probing the psyche of his main character. As the narrative proceeds viewers see that in relation to his blackness Pierre Delacroix is a person attempting the

36. For more on the television programs mentioned here, see Thomas Cripps, "*Amos 'n' Andy* and the Debate over American Racial Integration," in *American History / American Television*, ed. John O'Connor (New York: Ungar, 1983), 33–54; Aniko Bodroghkozy, "*Beulah*," Museum of Broadcast Communications website, http://www.museum.tv/archives/etv/B/htmlB/beulah/beulah.htm (accessed February 7, 2005); Wil and Ron Kurer, "*Calvin and the Colonel*," Spud TV website, http://www.spudtv.com/features/primetimecartoons/calvinandthecolonel.html (accessed September 15, 2001); and Pamela S. Deane, "*Good Times*," Museum of Broadcast Communications website, http://www.museum.tv/archives/etv/G/htmlG/goodtimes/goodtimes.htm (accessed February 9, 2005).

impossible. He seeks to run away from that part of himself and thereby escape an aspect of who he is that has been imposed on him. We discover that in order to evade the racialized dimension of his identity Delacroix has changed his name, adopted a baroque, pretentious, and very "white" way of speaking, and generally eschewed dealing with anything stereotypically black. After witnessing a particularly garish audition for the show featuring a performer who hits all the base notes of the crudest form of gangsta rap, for example, Delacroix distastefully remarks, "I don't want anything to do with anything black for at least a week," as if he could escape his existence and live unracialized for a time. Although the narrative plays his comment as an amusing exaggeration from the foppish Delacroix, viewers come to realize that he also speaks from the heart in expressing this disdain for blackness, including his own.[37] His consistent use of the outmoded term "Negro," instead of "African American" or "black," further symbolizes his need to distance himself from racialization by displacing it into a past from which he sees himself as having escaped.

Once the show becomes a hit, Delacroix deludes himself into working to protect the monster he has created. He argues for its aesthetic, moral, and expedient exoneration on the shifting grounds of free speech, aesthetic freedom, and social necessity. Ever the opportunist, Delacroix employs any strategy he can in order to seek justification for his show and his actions in creating it. During a talk radio interview soon after his program has become a sensation, he asserts a thoroughgoing, simple-minded moral relativism: "Who is to judge? Who is to say that 'this is right' and 'this is not'?" Like many who have only thought superficially about morality, he espouses the stance that anything goes, even racist presentations of African Americans, because no one has the right or authority to determine what is moral, without seeming to realize that such a position also implicitly endorses the idea that the determination of morality would then be left to nodes of power that he himself will never possess.

He also argues that *Mantan: The New Millennium Minstrel Show* is "art, and that is what it should be called." Citing former New York City mayor Rudy Giuliani's 1999 rejection of African art in the Brooklyn Museum sight unseen, Delacroix asserts in contrast that, in the name of art, all must be permitted. Art may in no way be either censored *or* criticized on the grounds that it is immoral or promotes the injury and distress of others. Rather, it must be allowed to express freely and without criticism whatever it will, regardless of the consequences, apparently because Delacroix equates any sort of moral examination of art with its censorship, thereby failing to distinguish between two very different critical stances.

Mantan's creator also dismisses the issue of racialized slavery as a quaint historical problem that occurred "400 years ago. We need to stop thinking that way, stop crying over 'the white man this, the white man that,'" he lectures his talk show host. "This is the new millennium and we [meaning all blacks] must

---

37. See also Michael Sragow, "Black Like Spike" (interview with Spike Lee, 2000), in Fuchs, *Spike Lee: Interviews*, 193.

join it," presumably by "getting over" all past racial injustices, ignoring their legacies, and going on from where current circumstances have left African Americans—however unfair those may be. When his host points out Pierre's faulty arithmetic and the fact that he is seeking to excuse the black Holocaust that racialized slavery represents, Pierre dismisses it as "talking numbers . . . it doesn't matter. What matters . . . is slave mentality, and that is what must be broken." He goes on to tell a story about an aunt who refused to believe that anyone had ever walked on the moon and compares this aunt's unreasonable skepticism to those who believe that past racial injustice has had some meaningful effect on the present. "We must adapt to the times," he declares in his florid and overarticulated way. "Otherwise we will be left behind."

Delacroix's defenses of *Mantan* incorporate many of the standard arguments whites have employed to defend the idea that blacks are too sensitive about race in these postmodern times. His arguments in defending the television show presuppose that all major problems having to do with racial injustice have been solved, and that blacks need to "wake up," as he declares, and recognize the dawning of a new era, one in which race has been overcome. Sliding without conscience or scruple from one defense to the next as they are criticized and refuted, Delacroix argues that blacks should simply "get over" slavery, white supremacy, and long-enforced racial hierarchies because they happened a long time ago, they have no relevance to current circumstances, their memory imposes unfair obligations on the "freedoms" and advantages of others (i.e., whites), and, he implies, must be morbid preoccupation with the past or mental instability that causes blacks to remain so obstinately concerned with the oppressive dimensions of race and its consequences. As I have noted elsewhere in this book, these strategies are typical ploys mobilized to defend an epistemology of ignorance. They provide ways of recasting problems connected with race such that they may be rendered invisible to those who do not wish to think about them. Yet as Mills has explained, imposing nonracialized moral ideals on current racialized reality has the ironic effect of masking that reality and blocking the actual achievement of those very ideals.[38]

At a deeper level, however, what these defenses illustrate is Delacroix's own internalized racism, his inner self-hatred.[39] As someone who is forced to admit unwillingly that he constitutes a devalued and denigrated member of the society in which he lives, Delacroix shows clear discomfort over his blackness. Like Fanon's famous struggle to confront his racialization in "The Lived Experience of the Black," Delacroix finds himself at odds with what Mills refers to as "a depersonalizing conceptual apparatus . . . through which nonwhites must learn to see themselves" if conceptions of white supremacy are to be either explicitly or implicitly accepted by them.[40] But rather than struggle against this denigrating way of thinking, as Fanon did, Delacroix gives in to

38. Mills, *Racial Contract*, esp. 92.
39. Lee, interview, in Sragow, "Black Like Spike,"193.
40. Mills, *Racial Contract*, 87–88.

it. At a certain level, he embraces the social devaluation of blackness even as he must admit that he himself is black. This conflict creates "self-loathing," as it does for other blacks who similarly accept this white supremacist conception, such that they consent to think of themselves, at least on some level, as inferior and therefore undeserving of the regard and advantages equivalent to those granted whites.[41]

Understanding Delacroix's thinking in this manner clarifies how his justifications that the show is somehow satirical, an expression of aesthetic freedom, or that it offers insight into the new millennium for blacks are desperate self-deceptions rooted deeply in the conceptual acceptance of beliefs that undergird white supremacy and racial hierarchy, even as they violate the internal sense that most blacks—including Delacroix at some obscure and subterranean level— have of themselves as fully human. While acceptance of white supremacist beliefs typically causes soul-destroying conflict over one's own sense of self, the depersonalizing conceptual apparatus that makes possible acquiescence with white supremacy provides powerful tools for dealing with difficulties of self-inconsistency as well, such as scientific studies alleging inferiority for blacks on cultural, social, or genetic grounds, and their overall entrenchment and consistency with other historically embedded beliefs regarding African Americans.[42]

One way Lee's narrative depicts for viewers Delacroix's self-deception and self-hatred is through having its characters talk about, consider, and interact with the "Jolly Nigger Bank," a turn-of-the-twentieth-century toy that "reminds [us] of a time in our history in this country when [blacks] were considered inferior, subhuman, and we should never forget that," as Delacroix's assistant Sloan (Jada Pinkett Smith) notes when she gives him this collector's item as a symbol of his ambivalent success. The bank functions as what T. S. Eliot called an "objective correlative" for Delacroix's background assumptions, the beliefs he must accept if he is to advance, promote, and protect *Mantan*. Eliot defines his term as identifying something, such as an object, that may represent a particular emotion—or, by extension, belief.[43] Here the Jolly Nigger Bank represents the racist presumptions necessary to create Delacroix's hit TV show. Eventually objects like the Jolly Nigger Bank take over the television producer's office, literally colonizing his workspace, just as their intellectual counterparts come to dominate his thinking about blackness. He begins to imagine the Jolly Nigger Bank as having a life of his own, just as these presuppositions do, and just as his television show comes to have, once it becomes a sensation. This second correlation between *Mantan* and the bank further symbolizes the ways in which racist presumptions come to take over Delacroix's psyche and

41. Ibid., 89.

42. A fascinating precursor to this depiction of black self-deception, particularly in the face of "scientific racism," is J. Saunders Redding, *Stranger and Alone: A Novel* (New York: Harcourt, Brace, 1950). My thanks to Bill Lawson for bringing this example to my attention.

43. T. S. Eliot, "Hamlet and His Problems," in *The Sacred Wood: Essays on Poetry and Criticism* (London: Methune, 1921), 100.

put him wildly at odds with himself. It shows how some parts of his thinking are out of his control and he is losing his battle to coordinate all these disparate, racially inflected elements of his mental and emotional life.

In contrast, Sloan is the narrative figure who serves as the major conscience, the moral center, of the film. Lee has described her as "the most sympathetic and the most intelligent" character in the narrative,[44] for she realizes from the start that a television show such as *Mantan* could easily become unadulterated racist minstrelsy. Time and again she calls viewers' attention to its egregious stereotypical dimensions by indicating them to other characters in the narrative or through occasional voiceovers, such as when she describes the proper methods of burning and using cork to create blackface makeup. Other characters function narratively to morally orient viewers as well. For example, Tommy Davidson's character Womack, who plays Sleep-and-Eat in *Mantan*, eventually quits because acting the coon becomes too much for him. "It's the same bullshit! Just done over," he exclaims in frustration to the unbelieving Manray, who plays the eponymous Mantan and is the show's star. After going along with *Mantan,* its shucking and jiving, blackface, and cooning because it put a roof over his and Manray's heads, got them off the streets, and gave them something to eat, Womack realizes that there is nothing ironic, satirical, or positive about it. *Mantan* is just a straight-out racist minstrel show, doing the same damage to the concept of humanity as well as actual human beings that its predecessors have since the 1840s. Womack's sense of humiliation at putting on the coon act becomes so intense that he can no longer force himself to do it. He walks away from a show that offers him all the security, fame, and money he could ever have imagined wanting because he is overwhelmed by its racial degradation. After some earlier uncertainty he realizes that the shame and humiliation of portraying a subhuman stereotype throws not only his own humanity, but that of all blacks, into question.

Even the minor character of Delacroix's mother provides a crucial moment of moral centering for the audience. "You disappoint me," she sadly tells him when he tries to milk her for comforting maternal approval for his blatantly demeaning television program. The show's star Manray eventually sees the truth about *Mantan,* too: "No more buck dancing. No more blackface," he finally tells Delacroix after much soul-searching. Refusing to black up any more or don his minstrel costume, he appears in front of his television audience one last time, before he is fired and thrown off the set, in order to tell them, "Cousins, I want you all to go to your windows, go to your windows and yell out, scream with all the life that you can muster up inside of your bruised, assaulted, and battered bodies, 'I am sick and tired of being a nigger and I'm not gonna take it anymore!!!'" In doing so, he echoes verbally (only this time without using minstrel dialect) the earlier scene that he had played to introduce and justify the television show, as well as echoing in both instances Peter Finch's famously fed-up newscaster in *Network* (Sidney Lumet, 1976).

44. Crowdus and Georgakas, "Thinking About the Power of Images," 6.

By using some of the same camera shots, blocking, and gestures as the earlier scene, except in this instance with just enough variation to stress its seriousness, Lee and his collaborators further underscore Manray's change of heart, his realization that, as his old partner and friend Womack put it, *Mantan* is simply "the same bullshit," just done over.

Linked with these characters' realizations about the truth of *Mantan,* as in many of his other films Lee features a character who explicitly emphasizes education and learning. Earlier in the film Sloan tells Manray, "You should start reading," when he confesses a complete ignorance of past minstrel shows, their racist dimensions, and is disinclined to learn because reading "makes my head kind of hurt." The importance of knowing the past and reflecting on its effects in the present, as well as its likely influences on the future, are thereby underscored by means of Sloan's explicit emphasis on reading and learning, as well as her implied message that it is crucially important to think things through. Even though she facilitates the show's creation and production by doing research for Delacroix and goes along with *Mantan* because it promotes her career, she time and again emphasizes "telling the truth" about the program rather than sugarcoating it as alleged satire, or allowing the other characters' historical amnesia to pass unremarked. Through Sloan's repeated endorsement of education, learning, and the need to think, Lee provides his audience with a partial antidote to what he sees as the poisonous toxicity of blackface minstrelsy.

An additional feature of the narrative that shows how deeply racism has been internalized by more than just the primary characters is that, not only do the fictional television audiences demonstrate that they find the cooning routines funny, but the film prompts laughter from its own audience. One of the most audacious, courageous, and upsetting aspects of *Bamboozled* is that Lee allows some of these minstrel sequences to be humorous and entertaining for his own viewers. Even the character who provides the central moral orientation for the film, Sloan, laughs at least once during one of the classic coon routines, and the narrative has Delacroix point this out, so that its occurrence is not lost on viewers. We see as well one of the Maumaus, the self-righteous rap group led by Sloan's brother Big Black Africa (Mos Def), laugh at one of *Mantan*'s minstrel-derived sequences. These narrative details push the audience to reflect on why they would laugh at such racist humor themselves, in spite of the fact that it violates beliefs about equality and justice that most of them would otherwise explicitly uphold. Again, Lee urges his audience to seriously contemplate troubling dimensions of contemporary life in America by encouraging self-reflection about one's own presuppositions about race, specifically by reflecting on the conditions that make such laughter possible.

To further underscore these points, Lee makes a tonal shift in mid-narrative from biting comic satire to seriousness. Some critics have complained that this shift is where many viewers become lost or alienated,[45] but the change in

---

45. See, for example, Sragow, "Black Like Spike,"190, and Crowdus and Georgakas, "Thinking About the Power of Images," 8.

tone crucially highlights what Lee is up to in *Bamboozled*. The shift, which he refers to as "paying the piper" for the events that have preceded it,[46] functions to emphasize the negative aspects of the film's characters, which had been played for laughs earlier. It shows the other side of Delacroix's acquiescence to the presumptions of blackface minstrelsy, Manray's ignorance of his blackface predecessors, and the Maumaus' unknowing mimicking of that which they profess to reject. Like *Network* and *Sunset Boulevard,* the narrative of *Bamboozled* turns from the satirical fun of ridiculing its characters, their weaknesses, their gaps in knowledge or insight, and their self-deceptions, to showing the more serious consequences of such traits, which it does through violence (as did its antecedents) because Lee seeks to forcefully bring home their gravity. The director and his fellow filmmakers here transform those features that made us laugh earlier into the causes of several characters' downfalls.

Consonant with this goal and like many of Lee's earlier narratives, *Bamboozled* provides ways for its audience to see the actions of morally complicated characters as explicable but not justified. *Bamboozled* thus operates as a companion piece to works like *Do the Right Thing,* in that its amusing preceding events also aim to explain the subsequent violence. One strength of the later film is that, as in the earlier work, Lee does not allow viewers to avoid the ugly, hateful consequences of racism, here in the form of blackface minstrelsy and its damaging ongoing legacy. To drive home the impact of that phenomenon and the price of acquiescing with it, Lee felt the necessity of narratively depicting violent ends for Delacroix, Manray, and the Maumaus.

Viewers may readily comprehend why Delacroix and Manray should pay for having promoted and maintained minstrel imagery into the new millennium, why from the perspective of conventional morality their actions might require significant penalty. Both characters commit self-centered and seriously injurious actions toward others through either ignorance or willful self-deception, and this part of the film's moral structure implies, in agreement with the presumed conventional values of its viewers, that their transgressions should be punished. As Murray Smith has explained, classic Hollywood storytelling typically offers a system of values such that the moral structure of a narrative will be relatively clear. One option among others is a "Manichaean moral structure" through which the virtuous are rewarded and the evil punished, just as most of us would hope might be done in real life.[47] Lee invokes these conventional presuppositions here: narratively speaking, then, it makes sense to most viewers that Delacroix and Manray are punished for what they

46. Sragow, "Black Like Spike,"192; Crowdus and Georgakas, "Thinking About the Power of Images," 8.

47. Smith, *Engaging Characters,* 205–14. Smith argues against interpreting Hollywood melodrama *strictly* in terms of Peter Brooks's Manichaean moral structure (205ff.) and argues instead for a "graduated moral structure" for typical Hollywood films, especially melodramas. Obviously, I agree with Smith regarding this point. I merely point out here that in the cases of Delacroix and Manray, Lee invokes the Manichaean *option* of giving immoral or blameworthy characters their comeuppance.

have done to themselves and to blacks in general because audience members presumably hope and expect that evildoers will be punished for their transgressions. The violence of that punishment drives home Lee's point that their transgressions against the concept of humanity as well as actual human beings are severe. Here perhaps some may wish to argue that Lee's narrative morality borders on Old Testament harshness, but I think Lee would want to argue in response that an impression of harshness may well be due to a certain racial insensitivity to the dehumanizing and damaging effects of minstrel images.[48] The degree of harm and injury caused by such imagery is profound, a point Lee seeks to press home by means of the serious consequences visited on these characters.

Similarly, the Maumaus' anger at Manray as one of the chief vehicles for propagation of minstrel stereotypes is justified, even if their actions are not. Like Mookie's actions in *Do the Right Thing*, the Maumau's televised torture and execution of Manray may be seen from the moral perspective presumed by the narrative as actions that grow from preceding events, even as they remain unjustified and unfair. Even though Manray deserves to be punished for his feckless actions, what the Maumaus do to him is far worse than he deserves, particularly when one considers his belated realization that Womack was right. Some of the ways in which the Maumaus torture Manray are moreover racialized in just the ways they seek to criticize because, due to their lack of knowledge and insight about the past, they fail to recognize what they are doing is simply another version of blackface minstrelsy, a point the filmmakers emphasize by intercutting a cartoon version of their actions from the show that stresses the congruity of their actions with those typically portrayed on *Mantan* itself. In these ways *Bamboozled* makes Manray out to be something of a tragic figure, rather than endorsing the Maumaus' actions, even as it implies that Manray deserves serious retribution for his earlier complicity. Because Manray had seen the error of his ways and sought to make amends, the Maumau's literal and metaphorical blackface execution of him becomes that much more unjust, even if it remains explicable by means of the film's narrative details.

The Maumaus themselves, on the other hand, are then summarily massacred by the NYPD while resisting arrest. All but the one member who appears phenotypically white die in a hail of bullets as police raid their hangout just after they execute Manray. Their surviving member, One-Sixteenth Black (MC Serch), cries that he, too, should have been killed because he is himself black, and all it takes in America is "one drop of black blood." Viewers see narrative retribution visited on these characters for not only their treatment of Manray but also the misguided ways in which they ignorantly reenact aspects of minstrelsy themselves, such as their silly rejection of the letter "c" in the word "black" on the grounds that it is an instance of white oppression or the ways in which they enact the worst excesses of gangsta rap, the extremes of which Lee

48. See, for example, Spike Lee, interview, in *The Making of "Bamboozled"* (Sam Pollard, 2001), on *Bamboozled*, DVD.

FIG. 33   Sloan (Jada Pinkett Smith) forces Pierre Delacroix (Daman Wayans) at gunpoint to look at what he has contributed to by creating *Mantan*. Stepin Fetchit (Lincoln Perry) is on the monitor (*Bamboozled*, 2000).

has argued in interviews "has evolved to a modern day minstrel show, especially if you look at the videos."[49] While their intentions for rejecting *Mantan* and their anger at its demeaning imagery are justified, their actions of taking up a sort of gangsta-inspired vigilantism are not, for the narrative depicts their actions as unfair, excessive, and ignorant, rather than judicious, proportionate, and wise.

The narrative analogously explains without justifying Sloan's anger and act of killing Delacroix. Hysterical, she shows up at his office in her bedroom slippers after Manray's televised murder and carrying a gun because she knows that he has had a hand in both her brother's and Manray's deaths, as well as having contributed to the denigration of blacks generally through creating a profoundly racist television show. She feels as well that the only way she can get him to understand "what [he has] contributed to" is to force him, at gunpoint, to watch a compilation tape of demeaning minstrelsy images that show *Mantan*'s continuity with them. The *noirishly* unbalanced, off-kilter shots of this sequence underline her hysteria.

Once Sloan compels Delacroix to finally pay attention to the results of her research, he seems to realize his complicity. As he walks toward her while asking her to put the gun down, she warns him not to come any closer, and there is a sense in which the gun just goes off in her hand as he tries to

49.   Sragow, "Black Like Spike,"195; Crowdus and Georgakas, "Thinking About the Power of Images," 5. (Presumably this collapse of rap excess into modern-day minstrelsy is due to some artists not understanding the use of criminality as a pose for rejecting the status quo, or due to belief in their own hype.)

wrench it from her. As she screams at the gun's report it goes off once more, and her reaction to that second shot indicates she is surprised by it as well. When she apologizes for having shot him, he replies gently, "It's okay," as if he were comforting a child who was not responsible for what she did. Delacroix's forgiveness softens and to some extent exonerates Sloan's action within the fiction, as does the blocking of the shooting as accidental. These narrative elements still do not justify what Sloan has done, any more than the film does the Maumau's actions against Manray. Again, the narrative offers reasons why she shoots Delacroix without absolving her, for the film makes clear that, like the rap group which included her brother, she has acted excessively rather than in accordance with justice, even while it offers more comprehensive and mitigating reasons for why she acted excessively.

This question of what Delacroix appropriately deserves in consequence of his actions is further underscored by means of his dying soliloquy, in which he admits to his past mistakes and an overall negative judgment on his life: "As I bled to death, as my very life oozed out of me, all I could think of was something the great Negro James Baldwin had written. 'People pay for what they do and still more for what they have allowed themselves to become, and they pay for it very simply by the lives they lead.'"[50] Through these words and subsequent shots, the film openly prompts viewers to think about the kind of life Delacroix has led and what an appropriate judgment for it would be. These elements also more subtly prompt viewers to contemplate what kind of life they themselves lead in terms of the themes just presented, as well as what it would be appropriate for them to receive in having lived such a life. Is it one that somehow acquiesces with the sort of imagery promoted by *Mantan* or its real-world correspondents? Is it one intermixed with feelings of self-hatred and internalized racism, or one where unthinking acceptance of stereotypes has facilitated harm and injury to others? How free is one of background assumptions that make possible the unfair treatment of African Americans? Are there really adequate justifications for laughing at or finding pleasure in images of blackface minstrelsy, such as those with which the film ends? Just as Joe Gillis (William Holden) bitterly sums up his wasted, deluded life from the grave in *Sunset Boulevard,* so Pierre Delacroix assesses his own. By distancing himself from blackness and selfishly living his life in ways that damaged others, he has been bamboozled into making human existence worse for everyone, including himself, as he belatedly realizes.

The Baldwin quotation likewise underlines several other themes. One is a sort of *noir* fatefulness that *Bamboozled* directs at the consequences of going along with stereotypical images of blackface or its modern-day equivalents. Another is the need for education so that viewers may know the thoughts and insights of individuals such as Baldwin, and thereby have some hope of avoiding past mistakes. A third is that of taking seriously the need for contemplation

50. See also James Baldwin, "The Black Boy Looks at the White Boy," in *Collected Essays* (New York: Library of America, 1998), 386.

and analysis of the kinds of lives we lead, and what our actions say about our selves and our stance toward humanity in general. A fourth is that of remaining properly attuned to ongoing versions of racialized thinking and the effects such thinking may have on us. As a clip of Buckwheat (William Thomas) from the *Our Gang* serial mockingly tells the viewer, "Brother, this certainly gonna be a lesson to me!" Delacroix additionally tells us to "always leave them laughing" and follows with his own forced, bitter chuckling that merges into an obviously canned laugh track.

His acidic irony forces onto viewers an acrid aftertaste over having found amusement and pleasure in the images presented earlier in the narrative. Given the film's structure and the careful way in which it presents its tale of self-deception and casual dismissal of racism gone horribly wrong, the filmmakers intend for their audience to thoroughly experience that bitterness. In the end *Bamboozled* is a scathing, angry, *noir*-influenced satire that wishes to explicitly convey its fury over these matters, so that viewers might have some reason to think and act differently. Through carefully considering the film's narrative, they might grasp that Lee's aim here is a lesson that will turn them inward to contemplation of what made their earlier laughter possible, as well as to motivate them to actually do something about what they find within themselves.

A *Noir* Atlantic: *From Hell, Empire, City of God, Dirty Pretty Things, The Constant Gardener, Catch a Fire,* and *Children of Men*

Finally, in this chapter I wish to consider the internationalization of black *noir;* that is, the way in which filmmakers have applied aspects of African-American *noir* films, as well as other dimensions of *film noir,* to oppressions that reach beyond U.S. borders. Let me begin by briefly discussing the Hughes brothers' *From Hell* (2001). This film occasionally deploys black *noir* sensibilities to explore the contours of racism and classism in the context of a horror narrative set in late Victorian England. Based on a graphic novel that already betrays the influences of literary *noir,*[51] the Hughes brothers take these influences one step further by applying their cinematic counterparts to this tale about Jack the Ripper and how his detection was prevented by anti-Semitism and classist presumptions about who would be capable of such heinous acts as those performed by this late nineteenth-century serial killer, thus calling audience attention to forgotten dimensions of Victorianism's attitudes toward "the other" and implicating them in past injustices. As cultural historian Sander Gilman has shown, many contemporary depictions of Jack the Ripper were steeped in racist conceptions of sexually aberrant Jews, classist presumptions about working-class men, and these ideas' agglomeration in Lombrosian criminal

51. Alan Moore and Eddie Campbell, *From Hell* (1993; repr., Marietta, Ga.: Top Shelf Productions, 2004).

physiognomy, all biases which helped to prevent an impartial investigation of the famous Whitechapel murders.[52]

By telling most of the film's story from the perspective of the prostitutes being stalked, Albert and Allen Hughes depict another kind of dark underworld where a proper understanding of troubling murders becomes literally blocked by the walls of bigotry. Their depiction of late nineteenth-century London street culture and its accompanying violence, drug abuse, and sexual hypocrisy also bear striking parallels to their late twentieth and early twenty-first-century counterparts. By explicitly foregrounding prejudices against Jews, Asians, the Irish, the poor, and women, the random violence permitted by the police among these different underclass groups, and the abuse of various drugs that often accompanies living in such desperate circumstances, the Hughes brothers show that the streets of nineteenth-century Whitechapel were not so very different from the streets of twentieth-century South Central Los Angeles, near where these filmmakers grew up.[53]

The story revolves around an intricate attempt to erase one of the royal family's involvement with a Whitechapel prostitute. Edward (Mark Dexter), duke of Clarence and eventually king of England, falls in love with one of the many women he hires for sex or as models for his painting. He marries the Irish Catholic Ann (Joanna Page) and together they have a child, who would then have been heir to the throne. The royal family finds this prospect utterly repellant, so their minions go about eliminating everyone who could have known about the relationship, the marriage, or the child. Ann is lobotomized, and the women who witnessed her marriage to her rich gentleman—but who do not know he is the crown prince—are secretly murdered by an overzealous retainer because the idea of an Irish Catholic heir to the crown is abominable to those who fully embrace the litany of Victorian biases that underwrote *fin-de-siècle* London society. In addition, the moral corruption and hypocrisy of using other human beings as means, of considering them merely objects to be cleared from one's path to maintain one's social position, is something that goes all the way to the top, as the film depicts even Queen Victoria's involvement in this murderous secret plan that was misunderstood by the public as the work of a serial killer.

Visually much of the film is dark and *noirish* because it takes place at night, in rain, or in fog. It also cultivates suspenseful ambiguity and ambivalence by offering various different possibilities for whom the murderer might be and presenting few characters with whom viewers might straightforwardly ally themselves. Although the narrative does finally opt for one of its characters

52. Sander L. Gilman, "'I'm Down on Whores': Race and Gender in Victorian London," in *Anatomy of Racism*, ed. David Theo Goldberg (Minneapolis: University of Minnesota Press, 1990), 146–70.

53. For the record, the Hughes brothers grew up in Pomona (Gates, "Blood Brothers," 166, 169).

being Jack the Ripper, it also gives the impression that if it had not been him it would have been one of the other royal family's underlings.

Much of the story unfolds through the investigations of Scotland Yard Inspector Fred Abberline (Johnny Depp), an absinthe- and opium-addicted, working-class detective who deduces but cannot prove who committed these murders, because he cannot cross lines of Victorian propriety and status. Abberline arrives at his deduction because he is not only a detective, but also a clairvoyant: by means of his drug ingestion he dreams the murders before they happen. Yet he is unable to stop them, as his visions do not reveal enough about the murders for him to prevent them. Like many *noir* detectives who preceded him, he is ultimately powerless against the massive corruption against which he must operate. In general the film cultivates a *noirish* quality for its central mystery, its detective figure Abberline, its Irish Catholic prostitutes whose desperation force them into acts of sexual degradation just to survive, and the pervasive sense of moral corruption that circulates in this lightly fictionalized version of Victorian London.

From Hell thus borrows liberally from *noir* conventions in its black, classic, and neo-*noir* incarnations, even if it remains more a horror film than a *film noir*. The point I wish to stress here, however, is that the Hughes brothers use some black *noir* conventions to depict the social oppressions of the era. Viewers get a clear sense from the bottom up of how hierarchical beliefs about race, class, gender, religion, and other matters heavily influence many characters' perceptions and actions in the narrative, thereby exposing previously unknown parallels between social conditions in Victorian England, with its grab bag of social prejudices, and social conditions in America today. In this way it takes a modest step in the direction of pushing techniques developed through black *noir* beyond U.S. borders and toward creating a racially conscious, international sense of *noir*.

Similarly, writer/director Franc Reyes's *Empire* (2002) uses techniques developed in black *noir* to mount a critique of the raced and classed disadvantages faced by urban Latinos. Like *Double Indemnity* and many films that followed it, *Empire* exploits *noir*'s ability to make lawbreaking alluring and attractive. John Leguizamo plays Victor Rosa, a smart, ambitious South Bronx drug dealer who, having successfully mastered the heroin trade in his neighborhood, begins to see the limitations of what he does, longs to escape, and go legitimate by investing in Wall Street stocks. Although an accomplished master of street knowledge and the intricacies of illicit drug commerce, he is out of his depth when dealing with a corrupt white stockbroker, Jack Wimmer (Peter Sarsgaard), who swindles him out of four million dollars and disappears in the belief that Victor will be unable to either trace or prosecute him, since the money was obtained illegally in the first place and in Jack's judgment Victor is a "Spic . . . ghetto piece of shit" who lacks the intelligence or skills required to find him.

Told using the enthusiastic voiceover of someone who is proud of what he does and how good he is at it, *Empire* depicts the social disadvantages Victor must overcome as much more straightforwardly socioeconomic than racial.

As he declares from the outset, he believes that the American Dream is all about money. Immigrants do not come here because of the beautiful South Bronx views or quality of life, he tells us, but to make money. As the narrative proceeds, however, he relates how he has come to realize that even though that may indeed be the American Dream—or one version of it—the ideal is a hollow one and there is much more to life than financial gain. The narrative adds to the regret Victor expresses over not realizing this insight earlier by revealing at its conclusion that the entire film, in ways similar to *Sunset Boulevard, Menace II Society,* and *Bamboozled,* Victor has told in flashback as his life passes before him in the moment before he dies.

Like earlier black *noirs* I have discussed, *Empire's* narrative examines beliefs that some of its viewers might unquestioningly embrace, such as that what life is really all about is making money or that the glamorous gangster life Victor leads is somehow worthwhile, and tries to flip them into their opposites. A satisfying life cannot be based solely on the acquisition of money or the callous disregard for other human beings, but rather must be directed toward goals like having and cultivating friends, developing companionship, and "thinking about others," as Victor notes in his final reflections. These alternative ideals do not untrivially agree with assertions advanced by philosophers at least since Aristotle spent one-fifth of the *Nicomachean Ethics* arguing for the importance of these matters to a flourishing human life.[54] Unfortunately, Victor realizes this philosophical insight too late to do anything about it, but by telling his story in the way that they do the filmmakers hope to inspire their viewers into appreciating these alternative conceptions of a decent human life before it is too late for them.

Victor's difficulties are more a matter of having been born poor and in the wrong neighborhood than having been born Puerto Rican, although the latter factor is not discounted. As in *Never Die Alone,* race is less a story focus than its accompanying class-based complications of poverty, bad education, and lack of opportunity. However, the tentacles of race hold back Victor as well. He remains marked as a racialized member of New York City ghettos, as Jack points out, which the narrative uses to characterize his circumstances and their inherent unfairness in addition to the socioeconomic dimensions that it more centrally foregrounds. By using themes and techniques developed in black *noir* and applying them to a slightly different context, *Empire,* like *From Hell,* shows how this film form may be profitably employed elsewhere to portray the injustices facing other racially and class disadvantaged human beings and thus encouraging thoughtful reflection about differently nuanced social oppressions.

A film that even more fully realizes black *noir's* internationalization is Brazilian director Fernando Meirelles's *City of God* (2003). Its narrative uses themes and conventions developed in black *noir* in order to portray a rather different experience of race in Rio de Janeiro's poverty-strickened *favelas* (slums). Like many of its American predecessors the film depicts a story about

---

54. Aristotle, *Nicomachean Ethics,* 119–53.

astonishingly young gang members, their sense of entrapment and expend-ability to the society in which they live, and their desperate hopes for escape from the brutality and violence that permeate their lives. In this way the film-makers direct their viewers' attention to the unfair conditions established by means of another American hierarchy of race, namely that of Brazil.

As explained by political scientist Michael Hanchard, one's racial status in Brazil is established by means of conceptualizations of other human beings similar to but distinct from those found in the United States.[55] Like Charles Mills, Hanchard argues that modern conceptions of citizenship were deter-mined under presumptions of white supremacy. In Brazil this historical fact makes the achievement of full citizenship for Afro-Brazilians difficult because presumptions of whiteness remain in place socially, politically, economically, and epistemologically in contemporary Brazilian society.[56] In other words, this political correspondent to moral recognition of one's full and complete human-ity retains its power to determine the perceived status of Afro-Brazilians. Thus, even though Brazilian conceptions of race are not so narrowly pheno-typical as those found in the United States and tend to be more bound up with issues of class,[57] those of African descent nonetheless find themselves in the situation of being measured as Brazilian citizens by means of a stan-dard that, logically speaking, they cannot meet because, as blacks, they cannot be white. Even though a strange sort of alchemical economic exceptionalism makes it possible for a few very wealthy blacks to escape Brazilian presup-positions attached to blackness, in a broader sense the structural dimensions of race remain in place. Members of Brazilian society continue to perceive and understand blackness by means of the white supremacist presuppositions that historically established conceptions of who counts as a full citizen and who does not, which in turn are rooted in conceptions of who counts as a full-fledged human being and who does not. As Hanchard observes, "While the old Brazilian adage that 'money whitens' is true in certain cases, it is equally true that blackness taints."[58]

In order to portray dimensions of this differently racialized way of think-ing, *City of God* borrows from black *noirs*. Its narrative similarly focuses on the formation of gangs because of poverty and lack of opportunity, gang mem-bers' astonishing youth, their cartoonishly violent but all too real actions, and the overall futility of their attempts to escape the desperate circumstances of the *favelas* through criminality. The film contrasts these children's desper-ate hopes of freedom with their feelings of being trapped into an existence that offers little beyond the illicit paths they have already begun to tread. Like films such as *Juice*, *City of God* also focuses on these young gang members' need for human recognition, even if it is to be recognized as a criminal. For

55. Michael Hanchard, "Black Cinderella? Race and the Public Sphere in Brazil," in *The Idea of Race*, ed. Robert Bernasconi and Tommy L. Lott (Indianapolis: Hackett, 2000), 161–80.

56. Ibid., esp. 166–78.

57. Ibid., 174–75.

58. Ibid., 177.

example, what brings about gang leader Li'l Zé's (Leandro Firmino da Hora) downfall is that he wants his picture in the newspapers like his imprisoned opponent, Knockout Ned (Seu Jorge). He wants to be recognized as somebody, even if it is as a gangster, because that negative recognition would nonetheless acknowledge that he was seen as a being who possesses worth. Like Harry Fabian (Richard Widmark) in *Night and the City* (Jules Dassin, 1950) or Radio Raheem in *Do the Right Thing*, Li'l Zé longs for the ways in which others might see him as someone of value, even if that value is negative, rather than as a mere nobody, a two-bit hustler, or another member of the discouraged underclass, unworthy of others' attention.

These themes of recognition and acknowledgment, of course, have found expression in African-American literature from at least Ralph Ellison's *Invisible Man*, but black *noir* has given their articulation a peculiar form in the figure of the black gangsta. Many young black men condemned to urban underclass status find that among the easiest means to impress their existence on others is through mobilizing the most powerful emotions they already inspire, namely fear and hatred. Conveying this point was one of Spike Lee's aims in constructing the character of Radio Raheem for *Do the Right Thing*, and other African-American filmmakers have noticed this possibility and at times built it into their *noir* narratives, as I have outlined in previous chapters.

Lessons regarding how to exploit these emotions may also be traced back historically to "the folklore of black outlaws" from the late nineteenth and early twentieth centuries as described by Lawrence W. Levine. Stories and songs about bandits and lawbreakers symbolized a kind of "freedom from organized society . . . [and] statutory law." Such narratives also "express the profound anger festering and smoldering among the oppressed."[59] According to Levine, many outlaws portrayed in black folklore are violent, cruel, and without "socially redeeming characteristics" (420). Similarly, historian Eric Hobsbawm has argued that the lack of socially redeeming traits in folklore figures from Europe and elsewhere is because this kind of outlaw is "essentially a symbol of power and vengeance" for profoundly oppressed groups among whose very few resources are the capacities to be violent and cruel.[60] At the same time, black literature scholar John W. Roberts argues that despite a deep ambivalence on the part of black community members toward such characters, many tales provide evocations of sympathy and empathy for these bad men.[61] Overall, because the social order is in these oppressed groups' eyes so irredeemable, such figures represent what Hobsbawm calls "social justice [as] destruction,"[62] for currently existing society appears to these oppressed groups to lack both the possibility of being reconstructed justly and an elegiac past when justice allegedly prevailed and to which one might nostalgically return. Instead, one

59. Levine, *Black Culture and Black Consciousness*, 410, 417, 418.
60. Eric Hobsbawm, *Bandits* (New York: Delacorte Press, 1969), 55.
61. Roberts, *From Trickster to Badman*, 209–10.
62. Hobsbawm, *Bandits*, 56.

must destroy and begin again from scratch. If we look at the history of anti-black racism and its legacy as it proceeds into the twenty-first century, we may see similar feelings of despair and hopelessness, something that many of the films analyzed in this book reflect. In particular, we may begin to see how those trapped in inner city slums of the United States or the *favelas* of Rio de Janeiro might feel the way Hobsbawm describes, so their capacity to see this kind of outlaw as a hero begins to become clearer.[63]

As Diawara has argued, black *noir* takes up these themes of powerful violence, cruelty, and vengeance as expressive of black rage and desires for freedom from the confining circumstances in which many poor, urban African Americans find themselves. Specifically, these themes find their expression in the anger and brutality of young black gangsta figures.[64] In the same way that Chester Himes used the folklore strategies identified by Levine and Hobsbawm to express dreams of freedom and power in his novels, even when that violence and vengeance was directed at other African Americans, Diawara notes that black *noir* uses such strategies to evoke similar feelings in its viewers. The cruelty and violence expressed by black *noir* characters (and many hip-hop figures, for that matter) thus represent a powerful reactive stance toward race relations as they currently exist and anger at their seeming imperviousness to change.

These strategies are precisely what *City of God* appropriates in order to tell its story of the violent, brutal, and forgotten slums outside Rio de Janeiro. In telling the stories of Li'l Zé, Knockout Ned, and the conditions that create such individuals, the film appropriates conventions of *film noir* as filtered through the new black film wave, in particular its construction of the black gangsta. Such narrative ploys work to evoke the righteous anger that many viewers feel at the injustice of existing social relations. These narrative approaches also reaffirm why individuals trapped in such circumstances might crave any sort of acknowledgment and recognition as individuals of value, even if it is negative. Li'l Zé's desire to have his picture in the newspaper is a longing for those forms of human appreciation from others because they would mean that Li'l Zé was no longer an invisible member of the oppressed underclass, but a gangsta infamous enough to merit having his picture taken and prominently published, like his rival. It would mean others recognized and acknowledged Li'l Zé as a somebody, even if a notoriously bad and criminalistic somebody, rather than being unnoticed because he was a nobody.

City of God underscores Li'l Zé's longing for acknowledgment and recognition by presenting its realization amusingly as a problem for the young thug. No one in his gang knows how to use the camera they have, so they cannot take pictures of themselves to send to the newspaper. The only person they know who understands how to operate a camera is their old acquaintance

---

63. Roberts, *From Trickster to Badman*, 212–14, also notes how some in the black community took such characters as "models of emulative behavior."

64. Diawara, *"Noir* by Noirs," 268–69.

FIG. 34   Li'l Zé (Leandro Firmino da Hora), armed with rifle near right of center, and his gang pose for a photograph in *City of God* (2003). Five gang members hold their guns sideways in the manner of O-Dog (Larenz Tate) in *Menace II Society*.

Rocket (Alexandre Rodrigues), so he is summoned to photograph them. Li'l Zé and his gang then naïvely pose for Rocket with their illegal guns in all their gangsterish glory because Li'l Zé craves the sort of human recognition and acknowledgment he will get by having his picture published in the newspaper. When the gang runs into Rocket on the street a few days later, Li'l Zé is so pleased with the fact that Rocket's photo was printed on the front page that he again tells the young photographer to take their picture, and here several of them holds their guns sideways in the manner first established as a gangsta pose by the character O-Dog (Larenz Tate) in *Menace II Society* and now seemingly *de rigueur* for nearly all cinematic gangsters, from *The Usual Suspects* (Christopher McQuarrie, 1995) to *The Departed* (Martin Scorsese, 2006).

As viewers, of course, we understand that these young thugs' desperate desires for recognition and acknowledgment trump competing ones, as we are able to grasp from the outside that their desires, while understandable, are not in their best interests in terms of freedom or survivability, so it seems inevitable that Li'l Zé's wish to be seen and acknowledged becomes his downfall. With recognition comes recognizability, and because his war with Knockout Ned's gang has also attracted significant media attention by violently spilling out of the *favela* into the public's awareness, the corrupt and lazy police have to finally do something about all the mayhem the young thug has been causing. After still another violent confrontation with Ned's gang, Li'l Zé is caught, but his police captors release him when he pays them off with the last of his money. Because he is now broke and weaponless, and his gang has been decimated by recent encounters with Ned's gang and the police, younger, more ruthless child-thugs Li'l Zé himself had armed kill him, and thus the cycle of

FIG. 35   O-Dog (Larenz Tate) firing his gun sideways, thereby establishing a cinematic gangster image (*Menace II Society,* 1993)

poverty, racism, gangs, violence, and drugs goes on undisturbed by all these characters' misguided efforts to be seen as full-fledged human beings and escape the determinative traps of the *favelas*. The structural embeddedness of these institutional forms of social oppression remains undisturbed.

While some may object that these violent and cruel gangstas whose lives are driven by vengeance and desire for money do not deserve the same recognition as decent and law-abiding people, it is important to remember one of Mulhall's observations about the replicants in *Blade Runner*. Within the film these characters' humanity "is in the hands of their fellows; their accession to human status involves their being acknowledged as human by others, and if their humanity is denied, it withers."[65] So too, characters like Li'l Zé and his cohorts: without recognition and acknowledgment from others that they are fully human, their own humanity has withered from lack of attention, thereby making possible the brutality and violence that characterizes their actions. As beings who are seen by others as less than fully human, they see others as less than fully human as well. They are products of others' refusal to acknowledge them as fellow human beings, and their evil characters may thus be seen as a result of that failure.[66] If we ask ourselves why Li'l Zé and his fellow gangstas are able to act so brutally, we have an important part of the answer in realizing the consequences of such withholdings, for these actions reproduce what they enact. Again, this dimension of black *noir* revolves around empathy—the way in which we may see as viewers that it is withheld from these young characters,

65. Mulhall, *On Film,* 35.
66. Ibid., 34–35. As Mulhall notes (137 n. 5), Stanley Cavell provides an extended analysis of acknowledgment (including *inter alia* remarks on slavery and race) in *Claim of Reason,* 371ff.

even as the narrative itself cultivates a critical version of it in us for these needy, misguided, and damaged youth. We understand why they act as they do even as we recoil from their heinous deeds, and through this partial identification we feel, as they do, a certain anger at not only the individuals but also the institutions that withhold human acknowledgment and recognition from them.

Although in some respects it is a Brazilian gangster film about street children with guns à la *Pixote* (Hector Brabenco, 1981), the point I want to emphasize here is how *City of God* differs from its predecessor in that it appropriates many of the thematics and narrative structures of black *noir* in order to transpose its story of the Rio de Janeiro slums into a readily understandable narrative that may be recognized internationally. Like many black *noirs* that preceded it, *City of God* focuses on drugs, guns, gangs, and how criminality represents a seemingly attractive and glamorous way to put food on the table for its young, desperate characters. Criminality is presented as a profession that allows one to be recognized and acknowledged as a power, a person of value, in a society that would otherwise denigrate these individuals' moral status into that of expendable beings, more like a thing than a person, to use Kant's famous distinction.[67] The film also depicts a kind of pervasive moral corruption that is both made possible and encouraged by the society around it. The expendability of the *favela* residents serves a crucial function in Brazilian society. They are a cheap labor force, ready to do at any time tasks that no one else would want to do for such scandalously low wages. They also provide other services valued by bourgeois and upper-class members of Brazilian society, even when these activities are illegal and dangerous, such as distributing drugs or maintaining networks of prostitution. The racial oppression and human degradation portrayed in the film are the flip side of what W. E. B. Du Bois once called "the public and psychological wage" of whiteness.[68] They are, in other words, the results of the social and moral penalties of blackness in a world where human beings remain ranked according to attenuated conceptions of race and white superiority.

Even though the film is in one sense about the "success story" of Rocket's escape from this notorious slum because one of his photos of Li'l Zé and his gang fortuitously becomes valuable front-page news, the narrative makes clear how accidental that escape was—dependent on arbitrary whim and chance, not hard work, determination, and having the patience of Job. In no way does it recommend Rocket's story as a model for success or any sort of solution to the circumstances depicted in the slum. Rocket's escape from the *favela* remains a stroke of good fortune, a singular chance occurrence not likely to be repeated or emulated. Rather, the construction of *City of God*'s narrative calls for the viewer to reflect on the depths of moral depravity and callousness that

67. Immanuel Kant, *Grounding for the Metaphysics of Morals,* 3rd ed., trans. James W. Ellington (Indianapolis: Hackett, 1993), 35–36.

68. W. E. B. Du Bois, *Black Reconstruction: An Essay Toward a History of the Part in Which Black Folk Played in an Attempt to Reconstruct Democracy in America, 1860–1880* (New York: Harcourt, Brace, 1935), 700.

make such conditions possible. It places into question the presuppositions that undergird ways of thinking and acting such that places like Cidade de Deus may exist and thrive. In this way, *City of God* directs its viewers by means of black *noir* conventions to think reflectively and philosophically about how forms of racism different from those in the United States may contribute to the oppression of human beings on an even broader scale. It turns their attentions to worldwide racial oppression and to problems of the African diaspora in general, rather than parochial concerns limited to North America.

In this sense *City of God* represents a developing consciousness—a "*noir* Atlantic," a sensibility about the global connectedness of various oppressions, as well as an awareness of various shared values, ideals, and possible solutions that might remedy the social problems posed by such oppressions. As a combination of not only black critical perspectives on Western ideals but a thoughtful retention of some, such as justice, equality, and freedom, black *noir* represents what Gilroy has described as a hybridized way of thinking that could potentially exceed national borders and offer a politics and philosophy of transfiguration. Similarly, Tommy Lott has argued that black (American) film itself is a hybridized and polyvocal artform, making it generally amenable to black Atlantic–type concerns.[69] Consistent with the more explicitly philosophical work of Mills, Gordon, and others, black *noir* also embodies the sort of Du Boisian twoness or double consciousness that Gilroy argues is a dimension of some black music, which amounts to a popular "philosophical discourse that refuses the modern, occidental separation of ethics and aesthetics, culture and politics."[70] Although I would argue with Gilroy that Western moral philosophy is going through an agonizing transformation rather than its death throes, I agree with his analysis that some aesthetic cultural expressions, such as those found in black music, black literature, or black *noir*, offer crucial philosophical lessons that have escaped strangulation by means of myopic categorizations exemplified by much of the white philosophical tradition.[71] Thus I would argue that this internationalization of black *noir* represents the development of a "*noir* Atlantic," an American influence that is, for a change, liberating rather than oppressive.

Along with *City of God*, in regard to the development of a *noir* Atlantic we might also note white British director Stephen Frears's *Dirty Pretty Things* (2003), which many critics identified as a *film noir*.[72] This film examines the strained circumstances of illegal third-world aliens in first-world cities such as polyglot, multicultural London. In this manner its narrative prompts viewer realization about how desperate situations are for many such workers, whose labor makes luxury, comfort, and ease possible for those in the upper echelons of urban society. It also prompts reflection on how their desperation is

69. Lott, "Aesthetics and Politics," 288.

70. Gilroy, *Black Atlantic*, 38–39.

71. Ibid., 39.

72. See, for example, Elvis Mitchell, "Amid the Luxury, Immigrants in Peril," *New York Times*, July 18, 2003, E13, and Silver and Ursini, *Film Noir*, 9.

typically raced in newly evolved ways that would hardly have been imaginable a few years ago.

The film's main character, Okwe (Chiwetel Ejiofor), is a former doctor from Nigeria who was forced to flee his country and work illegally in the invisible economy of London. From the beginning the narrative presents Okwe as a good, decent human being who is surrounded by corruption and trying desperately to resist the easy immorality that confronts him at every turn. Like Easy Rawlins in *Devil in a Blue Dress* or Victor Dunham in *Clockers,* he is trying arduously to resist the evil temptations that could be his simply by not doing certain things, or that he could easily embrace because they would require the simple exercise of skills he already possesses. The film thus centers around the way in which Okwe maneuvers his way through this sea of moral sleaze, again making the point that chance plays a significant role in his circumvention of it, but offering more hope than *City of God* that human qualities such as resourcefulness and integrity may offer potential for making one's way through this twenty-first-century *noir* underworld.

While *Dirty Pretty Thing*'s narrative is racially inflected and recognizably *noirish,* it seems more of a first cousin to black *noir* than a member of the immediate family. Nevertheless, its story is arguably indirectly indebted to black *noir* in the sense that this film form has paved the way for popular understandings of cinematic narratives that incorporate critical dimensions of race by means of *noir* techniques. But the broader point I wish to make here is that I do not see the need to restrict the development of *noir* Atlantic films to black *noir* origins. Other sources may be enlisted as well, such as black *noir*'s inspiration, classic *film noir* itself, depending on the source's utility in depicting particular aspects of global oppression. *Noir* Atlantic films thus parallel many concerns examined by black *noirs* and at times borrow techniques from them, but that borrowing need by no means be exclusive. Depending of their usefulness, *noir* aesthetics techniques may be derived from elsewhere as well, even as black *noir* itself has prepared the cognitive soil for this international film form.

In this context, it is useful to consider Meirelles's more recent feature *The Constant Gardener* (2005), which parallels black *noir* concerns by employing more traditionally *noir* methods to convey startling depths of corporate corruption on an international scale, in particular its racial dimensions in using poor, desperate Africans as guinea pigs for experimental drugs. Although the film frames its narrative by focusing mainly on the tragic love story of white British characters Justin and Tessa Quayle (Ralph Fiennes and Rachel Weisz), it uses Justin's quest to discover the circumstances of his wife's murder to guide viewers through their own discovery of *noirish* iniquity on the part of unscrupulous pharmaceutical companies bent on profiting from their products, regardless of their safety or the human cost of testing them. Pressed into service as a detective to investigate Tessa's mysterious death, Justin traces her clandestine activities as a social activist who sought to make public one such company's transgressions. He therefore functions as a sort of "ordinary man" *noir* protagonist who is far out of his depth in dealing with the moral corruption he uncovers. Like Jake Gittes (Jack Nicholson) in *Chinatown,* he seeks to find the truth and do what is right, but is woefully unprepared to confront the profundity of human evil that hitherto he would have found unimaginable. Much of the film functions as a detective narrative, with the viewer's knowledge restricted to that of the protagonist's, so that when Justin discovers the gravity of evil in this pharmaceutical company's doings, as well as in his co-workers at the British consulate, who have colluded with this company, and the extent to which they will go in keeping their activities secret—including ordering the murder of Tessa—we are as surprised as he. In grief and shock, Justin nonetheless pursues discovering the truth, even after he has his passport confiscated, is beaten up, and is warned off the case repeatedly by those involved. He becomes more and more fatalistic about the realization that knowing the truth could result in his own murder, and once he fully grasps the danger he is in he seems to invite its inevitability. The narrative thus becomes increasingly deterministic as it wends its way to a conclusion, betraying still another debt to *noir* narrative.

On the other hand, the film is not discernibly indebted to black *noir,* except insofar as it similarly uses *noir* techniques to criticize problems focusing around race. Yet Meirelles's ability to make this film no doubt rested heavily on his success in using black *noir* conventions in *City of God.* In the guise of an international *noir* thriller based on John Le Carré's best seller of the same name, *The Constant Gardener* imparts a sense of outrage concerning the racial injustices caused by events taking place within its fictional world. Moreover, by virtue of its pointed analogies to real-life correspondents, it also conveys to viewers a similar sense of outrage regarding events taking place in the world around them. Corporate corruption and iniquity of this nature are not unknown to most viewers, so it would be easy for them to transfer their sentiments to actually existing counterparts.[73] Thus, like many black *noirs* this work aims to raise viewer awareness regarding hitherto unnoticed features in their lives to which advantage may have blinded them. In these respects, *The Constant Gardener* is a *noir* Atlantic film.

A further example is Australian director Phillip Noyce's *Catch a Fire* (2006), which depicts a sympathetic black male protagonist, Patrick Chamusso (Derek Luke), attempting to live an "ordinary" life under the extraordinary conditions of *apartheid* existing in South Africa during the early 1980s. When a bombing occurs at the coal gasification plant where he works, an antiterrorist police unit abducts and tortures him because he will not account for his whereabouts the night the bombing occurred, because he is attempting to hide the fact that

---

73. For some recent examples, see *Global Corruption Report 2006: Special Focus on Corruption and Health,* http://www.transparency.org/publications/gcr (accessed September 7, 2006). This concern for making people think about real-life correspondents seems to have been Le Carré's intention as well. See "Author's Note," *The Constant Gardener* (New York: Scribner, 2001), esp. 490–91.

he was visiting his young son, who was the result of an adulterous affair. Eventually the unit abducts and tortures his wife, Precious (Bonnie Mbuli), as well, at which point Patrick confesses to the crime so that they will let her go, even though he had nothing to do with the bombing. Because the head of the police unit, Nic Vos (Tim Robbins), now realizes that Patrick could not have taken part in the terrorist attack (the desperate husband confesses to the wrong way of admitting the terrorists), he lets the oil refinery worker and his wife go. Yet not only has damage of the physical kind already been done to Patrick, but psychological repercussions have been put into effect as well. Because he has been needlessly tortured and humiliated—and lost his job, this apolitical black man has finally appreciated the depth of evil embodied by the form of white supremacy under which he lives, so he leaves his family and trains as a terrorist in nearby Mozambique and Angola. Months later he secretly returns to the oil refinery to actually blow it up, thus enacting what he and Precious had been wrongly tortured for being complicit in earlier.

Catch a Fire may be considered a *noir* Atlantic film because it uses familiar *noir* techniques to depict its story regarding racist oppression and the main character's attempts to respond to it. Told in flashback and using a voiceover that gives the story a considered moral perspective, the narrative portrays a flawed character following a path of *noir* determinism that has been imposed on him by South African *apartheid*. The film depicts how even ordinary individuals could become terrorists, given the proper conditions, a possibility convincingly sketched by Adam Morton.[74] Based on the life of the real Patrick Chamusso, the film offers for our consideration the story of someone who joins the military arm of the African National Congress to overthrow the sitting South African government because he realizes that, from the perspective of the whites controlling the nation, it does not matter how he acts: they will treat him as a terrorist (guilty until proven innocent) anyway, so he might as well lend a hand in putting an end to such a socially oppressive institution. (So much for "constructive engagement.") In ways analogous to the manner in which black *noirs* like *Menace II Society* sought to make clear how oppressive social conditions could propel young black men into lives of crime, *Catch a Fire* shows how late-era *apartheid* readily produced the very individuals it hoped to eliminate—a lesson, perhaps, that other, more contemporary world leaders would do well to heed. By carefully building up details that curry not only our sympathy but our empathy for such a character, this narrative encourages us to side with a protagonist who is driven to terrorism by the blindness of whites in the grip of a particularly virulent form of racism.

Interestingly, the film also offers a white antagonist in the form of Robbins's character Vos, who is "the equivalent of a sympathetic Nazi," in the words of *Los Angeles Times* reviewer Kenneth Turan.[75] Convinced that what

74. Morton, *On Evil*, esp. 87–88.

75. Kenneth Turan, "*Catch a Fire:* Derek Luke does justice to tale of wronged man," *Los Angeles Times*, October 27, 2006, http://www.calendarlive.com/printedition/calendar/ cl-et-catch27oct27,0,7324199.story.

he does is righteous and will eventually lead to a better life for all, Vos care-fully manipulates his abductees in an effort to eliminate the leaders of the resistance, even to the point of taking Patrick to Sunday dinner so that he can soften him up for questioning later. As a man with children whom he teaches to shoot handguns efficiently in the possible event of their having to protect themselves from blacks, who outnumber whites by more than eight to one, Vos is portrayed as someone who has well-defined senses of compas-sion, justice, and the good life, but is horribly misguided by the racist ideol-ogy that structures not only his government but his thinking as well. In this way the moral distance between criminalistic, good-bad protagonist and police antagonist is considerably reduced (although not eliminated), which is again a common *noir* convention. At the same time, this move to similarly humanize both characters provides grounds for the possibility of reconciliation between the opposing sides these narrative figures represent, something that the film clearly seeks to advocate, as illustrated by its relatively uplifting black *noir* end-ing.[76] In this sense, the film seeks to both recognize a racist past and provide usable resources for a nonracist future.

Finally, let me suggest that *Children of Men* (Alfonso Cuarón, 2006) is a *noir* Atlantic film about white fears of the other. Set in a not-too-distant future Britain, the story explores how these fears could run rampant as a result of global catastrophe. Like *Summer of Sam* and *The Constant Gardener*, the film uses the vehicle of aligning viewers with a white male protagonist to explore these racial anxieties. Theo Faron (Clive Owen) is apathetically watching his world crumble around him when his long-departed ex-wife Julian (Julianne Moore) goads him into caring about its fate and helping her facilitate what amounts to a miracle—the birth of the first infant in this fictional world in nearly two decades. In the guise of an action thriller, we see paraded before us a catalog of white racial paranoia played out to its logical conclusion at the same time a motley group of barely organized rebels and malcontents try to assist a young pregnant black woman's escape from the British Isles to a possibly mythical safe haven, where she might raise her child without being exploited by ruthless groups with dubious political agendas.

Children of Men uses the presumed cinematic "universality" of Owen's white male protagonist to examine the reactionary explosiveness of anxiet-ies felt by many whites that they may be about to slip into their worst night-mare—minority status. While this is actually true globally as well as being a certainty nationally for the United States within the next half-century, white advantage has protected many whites from these facts. But *Children of Men* exploits the latent racial angst of white advantage and deploys it metaphorically against those in such positions of power while still providing hope that by working together humanity might yet free itself from a desti-tute, *noirish* end. Hailed by some critics as a *Blade Runner* for the twenty-first

76. Morton explores the possibility of reconciliation with evildoers as well; see *On Evil*, 104–35.

century,[77] this film also seems to have qualities that link it to black *noir* and its international descendant. With a cast and crew from around the Atlantic (Mexican, British, American) and themes of moral ambiguity, alienation, and dissatisfaction with the status quo interweaving with incendiary action sequences, Cuarón's film invokes thoughtful reflection about what could happen, given current racial conditions, if global catastrophe were to actually occur. Would, for example, unjust social institutions become even more so in conformity with existing preconceptions of race? Would extreme forms of white supremacy find currency and run rampant in ways that dominated countries where white advantage still retains an edge? The film uses our sympathetic and empathetic emotional responses to *noirish* underworld characters confined by circumstance to encourage us to consider a dystopic future where race has fundamentally determined the social order and promises to squelch all hope for humanity. A thematically and tonally dark film, *Children of Men* asks us to think about the possible consequences of our inaction about race and its effects on the environment, including the end of the human race itself, all for the sake of maintaining an idea that mainstream science itself has now proven conclusively to have no basis in objective reality.

Films such as these are capable of getting audience members who are not confined by nationalistic boundaries to scrutinize the dilemmas of African and other diasporic populations in general while at the same time embodying the sort of transnational and hybridized ways of thinking outlined by Gilroy as indispensable to overcoming problems of race. This development advances aesthetic capacities similar to those possessed by black *noir* in order to focus audience attention on matters of social disadvantage globally while indicating directions for resolution by means of ways of thinking that combine Enlightenment ideals with black critiques of their currently existing configurations. Again, like the work of recent philosophical theorists of race, *noir* Atlantic films provide not only anatomies of racism and other oppressions on the global stage, but in addition the hope that such social difficulties may be overcome. Crucial to the success of such liberatory projects is the identification, examination, and critique of various presuppositions about human beings embedded in the background of typical ways of thinking and acting, which not only black *noirs* but also *noir* Atlantic films seek to make evident. Utilizing readily accessible cinematic techniques derived from *film noir* to depict racial and other social oppressions, these films also push us to think philosophically. By goading us to use our mental powers to think deeply and reflectively about these matters and their importance to our senses of self and our lives, such films oblige us to achieve that level of profundity as they point us in the direction of greater realizations of humanity, both our own and that of others.

77. For example, Kenneth Turan, "*Children of Men*" (review), *Los Angeles Times*, December 22, 2006, http://www.calendarlive.com/printedition/calendar/cl-et-children22dec22,0,180035.story (accessed November 15, 2007).

CONCLUSION
race, *film noir*, and philosophical reflection

Let us use a little philosophy.
                                    —Frederick Douglass

In this book I have argued that *noir* cinema provides opportunities for thinking, believing, and knowing differently about race—for contributing to an
alternative naturalized epistemology such that apparently intractable problems of social disadvantage might be thoughtfully addressed and explored.
By possessing the capacity to encourage reflective examination of beliefs and
presuppositions that permit as well as maintain forms of disadvantage, this
popular art form has the potential to help viewers achieve greater insight into
what prevents our moral ideals, such as those for justice and equality, from
being fully implemented. While *film noir* may also be used in conservative or
reactionary ways to criticize "decadent" practices or register other grumblings
of the ideological right, many filmmakers find its techniques and themes
crucial for making visible new ways of seeing and understanding the role of
race in contemporary society. As such, the best of black *noir* and *noir* Atlantic
films can be seen as part of what Clyde Taylor calls an "imperfect narrative of
resistance," in which filmmakers use mainstream as well as unconventional
cinematic practices to subvert ideas that many people either would never think
of questioning or would accept at first glance as unobjectionable and nothing out of the ordinary.[1] These films thus defamiliarize us with what we take
to be "normal" (namely, typical presumptions regarding race, class, certain
kinds of individuals, and so on) in the fashion of philosophical thinkers such
as Thoreau, Cavell, Wittgenstein, Fanon, Mills, Gordon, and others.[2] By foregrounding considerations of race, many of these films help to break down the
dominance of the "white gaze" and permit greater acquisition of knowledge
concerning racialized experience "from the inside."

1. Taylor, *Mask of Art*, 254ff. See also Lott, "Aesthetics and Politics," 282–302.
2. Thoreau, *Walden*, esp. 1–64; Cavell, *In Quest of the Ordinary*, 9–25; Cora Diamond,
"The Difficulty of Reality and the Difficulty of Philosophy," in *Reading Cavell*, ed. Alice Crary
and Sanford Shieh (London: Routledge, 2006), 98–118; O'Connor, *Oppression and Responsibility*, esp. 1–20, 111–40; Ludwig Wittgenstein, *On Certainty*, ed. G.E.M. Anscombe and G. H. von
Wright, trans. Denis Paul and G.E.M. Anscombe (1969; repr., New York: Harper Torchbooks,
1972); Fanon, "Lived Experience of the Black," 184–201; Mills, *Racial Contract*; Gordon, *Fanon
and the Crisis of European Man*, 38–66.

In doing so, these new forms of *noir* cinema have not only exploited but expanded ways of eliciting empathy and sympathy for narrative characters by providing new and novel techniques to present them. By using the sort of "epistemological twist" described by George Wilson to make viewers see and understand characters in hitherto unconsidered ways, black *noir*, for example, has developed narrative methods for depicting sympathetic white characters and suggesting insights about the complicated ways their identities can be raced. By either distancing viewers from or drawing them closer to such characters, black *noir* narratives make available new perspectives on the diverse phenomena that comprise racialized moral thinking for different forms of whiteness.

It is worth noting that this technique can now be found in even more mainstream Hollywood film: the Academy Award–winning *Crash* (Paul Haggis, 2005), for example, offers at least two such sympathetic racist characters, LAPD officers Tommy Hansen (Ryan Phillippe) and John Ryan (Matt Dillon). It is instructive to contrast these uses of the character type with those in the films I have analyzed, as it shows a greater effectiveness of certain uses of this narrative technique over others. Let me first describe the relevant narrative details from *Crash*. Unable to control his boiling anger and resentment toward blacks, one night Officer Ryan pulls over the prosperous black couple Cameron (Terrence Howard) and Christina (Thandie Newton), knowing full well that their car is not the one just reported stolen. The film makes clear that Ryan's sole aim is to harass this couple, which he does to Christina in particular by molesting her under the guise of searching for weapons, as Cameron looks on, unable to protect his wife. The next day, after still more racial (and gendered) frisson resulting from a failed attempt to get help for his sick father from a female African-American HMO supervisor, Ryan comes across a traffic accident and finds himself in the middle of rescuing Christina. While he had begun his efforts to free her without knowing who she was, in this instance he carries on following his duty as a police officer and working to disentangle her from her jammed seatbelt, rather than act on his feelings as an antiblack racist. After a rather manipulative sequence Ryan manages to drag Christina from her flaming vehicle, even after she has screamed at him, tried to repel him, and asked for anyone else who might be able to help her.

Once he has carried her to safety, what he has done in spite of his personal biases seems to dawn on him. The camera lingers on his expression of surprised realization in a sort of abbreviated "scene of empathy," giving viewers a chance to contemplate and absorb his interior emotional experience.[3] Yet even though we are later given an additional glimpse of him thinking as he drives home that evening, the narrative never makes clear precisely what Ryan was feeling during those moments the camera lingered on his face. We are not provided with further elucidation of his realization, nor whether it will lead to any change on this character's part. Has he realized what a bigot he really is, such

3. Plantinga, "Scene of Empathy," 239–55.

that he feels he should now act differently? Has he seen the conflict between his personal prejudices and his duties as a police officer in a multiracial city like Los Angeles as a problem he must resolve? Has he at least realized that he has recognized Christina's humanity in spite of himself? Because we do not know enough about him as a character, the film does not make Ryan's inner experience transparent. As viewers we are left with a serious opacity regarding what he has ultimately learned by saving Christina. The narrative plainly signals that he has realized something, but specifically what never becomes clear, nor does what we as viewers are to make of this character twist.

His partner Hansen, on the other hand, the narrative takes in the opposite direction. Appalled by Ryan's overt racism, he has himself reassigned to his own squad car and the next day discovers himself facing a raging and despairing Cameron held at gunpoint by some fellow LAPD officers. Driven to the point of self-destruction by a seemingly endless stream of racist slights and affronts, Cameron has refused to cooperate with these officers surrounding his car after a wild chase through the LA streets caused by an attempted carjacking of this well-off black man's SUV. As he taunts the officers threatening him with their weapons, Hansen recognizes Cameron as the husband his ex-partner Ryan had humiliated the previous evening and intervenes in his favor, stepping into the line of fire so that his fellow officers would have to shoot him, too, in order to shoot this uncooperative suspect. The young police officer manages to defuse the situation, calm Cameron, and send him home with only a "harsh warning," rather than a "bloody stump for a head," as Hansen indelicately describes the likely outcome of this confrontation if Cameron does not stop insulting the angry policemen aiming their loaded weapons at him.

That night as Hansen drives home he picks up a black hitchhiker, Peter (Larenz Tate), with whom he has an escalating argument about whether blacks could like country music or hockey (Why does he object to these possibilities? What have we seen in his character that would lead us to believe he would do so?), and whose laughter at a religious statue in Hansen's car riles the young officer. A moment later, when Peter attempts to show him something, this off-duty cop, acting on his (and much of the audience's) presumption that a poor young black man is likely to be a criminal carrying a gun, shoots his passenger as Peter pulls an identical St. Christopher statue from his hip pocket. Hansen then dumps Peter's body in some roadside weeds and burns his car to hide his crime. The white character audiences had assumed to have had the greatest sympathetic understanding of blacks thus kills a young black man in the racist belief that he posed a greater physical threat to him than other human beings. Hansen, too, turns out to be a sympathetic racist character, although the opposite sort from his former partner Ryan. While the latter is like Rocco in *Clockers*—that is, a racist who at the same time is able to (occasionally) do good acts for blacks, Hansen turns out to be a sympathetic character, like Sal in *Do the Right Thing*, who also harbors racist beliefs.

In spite of the admitted salutary effects that "mainstreaming" such techniques will likely have, the awards given to this film, and high praise from critics like the *New Yorker's* David Denby,[4] I would argue that these characters do not function as insightfully as the sympathetic racist characters I describe in this book, mainly because *Crash* does not use its epistemological twists as effectively. The characters are not developed to an extent that the shock in realizing their opposing traits is more than surprising in an O. Henry-ish sort of way. Their actions remain to a significant degree incomprehensible, given what we know of these characters, because of less in-depth development and consequently more tenuous character engagement with them. The foregoing narrative motivates these twists too weakly. It is unclear what the filmmakers intend the viewers to learn from such narrative revelations, beyond the idea that characters may contain surprising racist or nonracist quirks. Why did Ryan choose to continue performing his duty as a police officer, rather than act on his raging hatred for blacks and simply give up? What does he learn from having done so? Will he act similarly or differently in the future? Do we, as audience members watching this character, learn more than we might from watching *Clockers* and reflecting on Rocco? What foreshadowing in Hansen's character do we have that he might harbor racist beliefs about young black men, beyond his rather surprising final argument with Peter and the ominous warning from Ryan that he really does not know himself? What do we learn about humanity or racism from Hansen that we could not already have learned—and learned better—from contemplating the characters of Sal, Hurricane, or even Todd Carter in *Devil in a Blue Dress?*

Contrary to Denby's assertion that *Crash* does better what Spike Lee has been doing for nearly two decades, I would argue the opposite—that Lee and other black filmmakers' deploy such characters *more* effectively because their uses involve much more developed, insightful, and comprehensible characters. We know Sal, Hurricane, Rocco, and even Carter well enough to grasp in detail whence their moral complications arise, unlike the cases of LAPD officers Ryan and Hansen. Thus we may achieve a more thorough understanding of the inner workings of white racism through the work of filmmakers like Lee and Franklin, who provide much more thoughtful acknowledgments that "the intolerant are also human," to use Denby's forgiving phrase (110). While wholly welcome as a continued cinematic exploration of xenophobia and its pernicious effects, the narrative of *Crash* seems at least in this respect less satisfying than those of *Do the Right Thing, One False Move, Clockers,* or *Devil in a Blue Dress* because these earlier films offer more perceptive, discerning, and intelligible uses of the sympathetic racist character type. In this sense, then, *Crash* could be seen as *Do the Right Thing* "lite," even if it deserves praise in other respects.[5]

Another crucial theme underscored by the films analyzed in this book is that *film noir* is often about empathy. As I have frequently noted, a considerable

---

4. David Denby, "Angry People" (review of *Crash*), *New Yorker,* May 2, 2005, 110.

5. Although I will not develop the argument here, I suspect that a more developed and insightful "mainstreamed" sympathetic racist character is Leonardo DiCaprio's Danny Archer in Edward Zwick's *Blood Diamond* (2006), which I also think qualifies as a *noir* Atlantic film.

number of *noir* narratives cultivate empathetic viewer responses for socially marginalized characters. This fact about *film noir* enables filmmakers to tell affecting stories about raced human beings: *noir* patterns for cultivating empathy thus allow for the presentation of pathways of understanding for audiences regarding how problems of race look from the underside, opening up the possibility for greater comprehension of the beliefs, situations, and decisions that blacks in America and elsewhere often face. For example, the films analyzed in Chapters 4 and 5 offer empathetic presentations and explorations of black nihilism, providing the possibility for viewers to imaginatively "slum it" and grasp the challenge of passive nihilism's allure for young black men. Of course, there exists the danger of generating desires to emulate this form of criminality in some viewers as well, but the best of these ghettocentric *noir* films clearly attempt to foreclose that possibility by suggesting that alternatives remain available.

Interesting to note in this regard is the recent biopic loosely based on the life of rapper Curtis "50 Cent" Jackson, *Get Rich or Die Tryin'* (Jim Sheridan, 2005). I agree with Roger Ebert that "A more accurate title might have been, *I Got Rich but Just About Everybody Else Died Tryin', and So Did I, Almost,*"[6] but what I want to stress here is how the film clearly alludes to the earlier *noir* cycle: it uses an extended flashback structure and protagonist voiceover to tell a dark and gritty crime-driven narrative in which drug dealing seems to be the only viable way out of the ghetto for young black men. In doing so, it underscores that nearly a decade and a half later many things still have not changed for them, such as the grinding poverty of growing up black, poor, and forgotten in urban neighborhoods. Some of its scenes rival those of *Clockers* in depicting the specious allure of drug dealing. "It's full of long, lonely nights—and hard days," the protagonist's early mentor Majestic (Adewate Akinnuoye-Agbaje) tells him. Later Marcus (played by Jackson himself) observes in his voiceover, "The thing about being a coke dealer on a corner, it was lousy pay. . . . If you added up all the hours and time spent waiting around, it was like minimum wage. And if you added in the time you were likely to spend in prison, it was less than minimum wage." Later, when crack revolutionizes drug-dealing and Marcus makes money hand over fist, he still reflects that "something was missing"—and eventually the narrative makes clear that it is a sense of connection to others, "love," in the term that the film itself offers. These observations hardly make drug-dealing as a way out attractive, even when compared to working at McDonald's. In addition, the film underscores this life option's brutal violence and likelihood of ending in death, as Ebert's alternative titling makes clear.

Yet the film adds an interesting plot development as well. Rather than have the protagonist die at the end of his extended flashback, as in *Menace II Society, Empire,* or *Bamboozled,* Marcus survives multiple gunshot wounds (as did

---

6. Roger Ebert, "*Get Rich or Die Tryin'*: Rapping His Way Outta the 'Hood," *Chicago Sun-Times,* November, 10, 2005, http://www.rogerebert.com (accessed September 21, 2006).

Jackson in real life) and gets a second chance to make things right. In the last twenty minutes of the film, we see that through caring about others, especially his long-time friend Charlene (Joy Bryant) and their infant son, he finds a way out of his passively nihilistic gangster life. In this fashion *Get Rich or Die Tryin'* seeks to go beyond *Menace II Society* in particular—to which it consciously alludes, as when Marcus has a prison conversation with his one-time boss and probable father, the drug kingpin Levar Cahill (Bill Duke)—by more fully actualizing the possibility for an active nihilism that begins to construct new possibilities for transvaluating values in ways that might be more humanly livable, an option that as I noted earlier Jacqueline Scott has outlined.[7] Many problems of nihilism's allure remain, to which the early parts of the narrative attest, but the filmmakers consciously try to reach past them and explicitly depict a positive alternative.

On the other hand, *Get Rich or Die Tryin'* provides limited insight regarding solutions that might be emulated in regard to the problems it so vividly presents, as Marcus's success depends fundamentally on chance. Like *City of God*, its protagonist's escape from grinding poverty and racism is not the kind that may be readily mimicked, but constitutes a singular solution dependent on its main character's unique abilities to rap and his extreme good fortune— for example, at not dying after having been shot nine times. Still, even given these shortcomings *Get Rich or Die Tryin'* shows that more recent black *noirs* remain worthy of our consideration. As a narrative that depicts a fuller sense of actively seeking ways out of the trap of passive nihilism than many of its predecessors, it offers more substantial hope that such potential exists, even if that option remains difficult to access—an insight that should surprise no one who has thought about these matters in any depth.

Black *noir* has, of course, also opened up possibilities for empathizing with still different kinds of human "others." *Noir* Atlantic films, as I argued in the previous chapter, provide ways to depict the global connectedness of various oppressions by means of accessible popular narratives that combine black and Western critical perspectives to reflectively assess and transfigure Enlightenment ideals such as freedom, equality, and justice, thereby bringing into focus possible shared values, ideals, and solutions. Given this characterization, I would argue that *Hotel Rwanda* (Terry George, 2004) may be read in part as a *noir* exploration of human corruption as generated by white supremacy. The fictionalized character of Paul Rusesabagina (Don Cheadle), who is of course based on his real-life counterpart, slowly realizes his faith in white European values leave him and everyone like him aside as humanly unimportant. As the leader of the token UN "peace-keeping" force, Colonel Oliver (Nick Nolte), bitterly summarizes for him, "We think you're dirt, Paul. . . . The West—all the superpowers; everything you believe in. . . . We think you're dung. You're worthless. . . . You're black. You're not even a nigger. You're an African." Unlike the first world's response to genocide in Bosnia just a few

---

7. See Scott, "'The Price of the Ticket.'"

years before, no troops will be sent to save the thousands and thousands of Tutsis being butchered in 1994 Rwanda. Rather, such a response is reserved for "whites only" because the full humanity of Africans is neither recognized nor acknowledged. As Rusesabagina is led to the depth of this realization and its roots in a banalized, "ordinary" evil of substantially devalued black life in comparison to white, so too is the audience. In this way *Hotel Rwanda* is an African *film noir* rather like *Coup de Torchon* (Bernard Tavernier, 1981).[8] While lacking many of the stylistic features of *noir*, thematically it shows viewers as much of everyday human evil's operation as works like *Chinatown*, with the proviso that its focus is racially motivated senses of human hierarchy and indifference insofar as they affect Africans.

At the same time, *Hotel Rwanda* is also at least related to *noir* Atlantic films by virtue of offering a global perspective on white supremacy and its pernicious effects, even to the point of depicting how such thinking affects Africans themselves regarding their sense of human worth, both in their own case and those of others. While still clearly valuing Enlightenment ideals like freedom, equality, and justice, it also presents a scathing critique of their differential application by means of aligning as well as allying its audience with an appealing "ordinary" black protagonist whose extreme courtesy and discretion draws viewers in, even as he learns the *noirish* consequences of differential human rights applications. While not a direct descendant of black American *noir* cinema, one could argue that its possibility depended on black *noir*'s preexistence and success, both economically and aesthetically, as it is unlikely that such a film could have been made without those films paving the way, both in general and in terms of Don Cheadle's achievement of stardom in part by means of them (e.g., as in *Devil in a Blue Dress*).

Cavellian Individualities and Film as Philosophy

Here it might be helpful to remind readers that these new forms of *noir* film facilitate the development of non-mainstream "individualities" in Cavell's sense by providing techniques for eliciting recognition and acknowledgment of full-fledged humanity in characters that many audience members might not ordinarily recognize or acknowledge, for example, gangstas, mentally ill black homeless persons, ex-cons, and other socially marginalized types. These films do so by means of providing analogical bridges to their characters' full humanity that viewers may utilize in grasping the deservedness of this status for all those represented by such narrative figures. This recognition and acknowledgment can thus easily transfer over to the actual actors who play

8. In a video interview for the Criterion Collection edition, Tavernier describes his film as "the first black African *film noir*," but one that "refuse[s] the conventions of the genre," which aptly describes *Hotel Rwanda* as well. See Bernard Tavernier, "Tavernier Interview" (Kim Hendrickson, 2000), on *Coup de Torchon*, DVD, directed by Bernard Tavernier (1981; The Criterion Collection, 2001).

these characters, such as Cheadle, Denzel Washington, Samuel L. Jackson, or Laurence Fishburne. These new forms of *noir* facilitate such a transference partly because they encourage reflection and expansion of various audience presuppositions regarding what it is to be human. They raise to viewer attention previously unnoticed presumptions about identity and race in ways that call for contemplation and revision, not only in cinematic viewing but real life. In reflecting on the humanity of *noir* characters, then, many audience members may come to grant more full-fledged recognition and acknowledgment to the actors who play these narrative figures.

Congruently, by foregrounding presuppositions regarding the "white gaze" as the dominant norm for cinematic viewership, black *noir* and *noir* Atlantic films may induce audience members, if properly disposed, to see the automatized belief schemata involved as typically even if also contingently raced, thereby giving them a *choice* regarding how they might wish to view cinematic narrative. Such a possibility represents an occasion for developing greater white double consciousness, something advocated by Alcoff, Sartwell, and others, as well as an occasion for dissolving the epistemology of ignorance. If white viewers take up the challenge to reflect here, they have the possibility of choosing whether to maintain their allegiances to whiteness and the prevailing norms of white identity. As Mills notes, this is not an easy choice,[9] but it is one that I would argue arises out of more nuanced understandings of race made available by many of these *noir* films.

These cinematic movements in America and elsewhere also highlight *film noir*'s overall capacity to elicit reflection and the possibility of raising it to the philosophical level, doing "Third Cinema" one better, so to speak. These new forms of *noir* have, in other words, pushed *film noir*'s potential for social criticism to the next level. As a set of techniques that can be effective in narratively depicting various forms of oppression, *film noir* has rarely been so sharply deployed. Of course, *film noir* has always had the potential to make people think. As critics have pointed out for decades, its focus on existential realities and dissatisfactions have been among the most distinctive *noir* characteristics. But black *noir* and *noir* Atlantic films show us rather startlingly how this film form may be not merely socially critical, but philosophical.

Here, I take the phrases "film as philosophy" and "films that philosophize" to mean mainly that films may evoke philosophizing in viewers, such as using our reasoning capacities to reflect on fundamental human questions like who one is or how one should live. However, films may also philosophize in the sense that they can provide us new ways to think, as Cavell and Mulhall have argued films often do, or by presenting "thought experiments," counterexamples, illustrations, or mimicking other dimensions of philosophical discourse.[10]

9. Mills, *Racial Contract*, 107.
10. Cavell, "Thought of Movies," 9; Mulhall, *On Film*, esp. 1–10; Mulhall, "Ways of Thinking"; Thomas E. Wartenberg, "Philosophy Screened: Experiencing *The Matrix*," *Midwest Studies in Philosophy* 27 (2003): 139–52; Baggini, "Alien Ways of Thinking"; the essays in the *Journal of*

With regard to the *noir* films I have discussed, the critical depiction of moral and aesthetic details urge viewers to reconsider and rethink their ordinary practices with regard to race such that full-fledged recognition and acknowledgment of other human beings may be more readily possible. *Noir's* techniques for defamiliarizing us with what lies before us here become focused on race, and as such encourage us to think hard and deep about the epistemological norms that typically govern our beliefs and actions (both conscious and unconscious) regarding the racialization of human beings through presumptions of white advantage, black inferiority, racialized criminality, and the like.

These new forms of *noir* thus bring to new prominence *noir's* general potential to induce serious and systematic reconsideration of matters concerning identity, social constitution, and Socrates' old question of how one should live. For example, by exploiting *noir's* possibilities for making its audience members think about specific social issues and their unacceptability as currently configured, black *noir* and *noir* Atlantic films have taken *film noir's* capacity for making people think critically about inconsistencies within existing social structures and refined it into a philosophical capacity to induce viewers into thinking about social injustices and the myriad ways in which they permeate our lives. As literary critic John Cawelti noted three decades ago regarding melodrama, these new forms of *noir* have become especially adept at bringing to its audiences' attention social contradictions that require thoughtful consideration and carefully outlined action to resolve.[11]

African-American *film noir* and its aesthetic descendants have thus promoted a better perception of social injustices as social contradictions by making these inconsistencies clearer and more glaring. This is a real advance in *film noir,* and we have many artists to thank for its development, among them Spike Lee, Carl Franklin, Kasi Lemmons, Ernest Dickerson, Bill Duke, Albert and Allen Hughes, Walter Mosley, Denzel Washington, Laurence Fishburne, and Fernando Meirelles. By taking *noir's* melodramatic roots seriously—that is, its origins in crime melodrama, female gothic, criminal adventure, and other subgenres of cinematic melodrama—black *noir* and *noir* Atlantic films have focused their capacities for aesthetic expression on that quintessential American experience, blackness, to reveal its complexity, ambiguity, and frequent outright contradiction with what are otherwise regarded as globally accepted human values such as justice and equality. Exploiting the development of graduated moral structures in melodrama that Murray Smith describes at length,[12] these new forms of *noir* have utilized the moral complexity and

---

Aesthetics and Art Criticism 64, no. 1 (Winter 2006); *Film as Philosophy: Essays on Cinema After Wittgenstein and Cavell,* ed. Rupert Read and Jerry Goodenough (Basingstoke: Palgrave Macmillan, 2005).

11. For melodrama's ability to bring social contradictions to our attention, see Cawelti, *Adventure, Mystery, and Romance,* 269–71.

12. Smith, *Engaging Characters,* esp. 196–97, 205–14; Neale, *Genre and Hollywood,* 196–202, esp. 197.

ambiguity of *film noir* in general to expose the complexities and paradoxes of race in America and the world, making possible the forceful presentation of racial injustice. Of course, these presentational capacities exist for viewers to discern or ignore, but the point I wish to emphasize here is that black *noir* and *noir* Atlantic films have both raised the stakes of ignorance and lowered the threshold for inducing reflection about these matters. Viewers ignore these possibilities at their own risk—specifically, the risk of leading a misguided, deluded life, which neither Socrates, Aristotle, Kant, Mill, Thoreau, Rawls, Joe Gillis, Socrates Fortlow, nor Pierre Delacroix would recommend.

Some of this philosophizing on the part of audiences will, of course, be affected by what the viewer brings to the narrative in the first place. It will also vary depending on how the film elicits parts of the viewer's automatized belief schemata as they watch the film or while they think about it afterward. Film as philosophy in general will thus be crucially influenced by what we bring to the screen, as well as what expectations and reflections it raises in us, as the relations between these dimensions of cinematic viewing are symbiotic. Invoking the appropriate parts of viewers' belief structures, particularly the racialized ones without alienating them, will be difficult. But at least some black *noirs* and *noir* Atlantic films seem to accomplish just that, as they frequently induce expanding rings of reflective analysis in many viewers.[13]

A Taxonomy of Empathy and Expanding Moral Imagination

The focus on marginalized individualities by these new forms of *noir* cinema also raises the issue of *how* viewers may generally empathize with fictional characters. Clearly, such responses will not be of the "Vulcan mind-meld" variety criticized by Carroll, but presume a separation of self from the character with whom one "identifies."[14] Empathy, then, requires only congruence or analogy with the other, not isomorphism between mental, emotional, or bodily states.[15] Empathy also seems to require "substantial characterization," as Peter Goldie has noted, as well as a grasp of the narrative in which the other is to be centrally imagined.[16] In addition, empathy seems to be a response that may be simple or complex; thus, it can be relatively straightforward and immediate or developed over time, as a result of extended thought.

The understanding of empathy I have in mind here is also broadly commonsensical in that it ranges over everyday uses such as those covering forms

---

13. A great deal more needs to be said about this symbiosis, but here I leave the matter open to further study and research.

14. Carroll, *Philosophy of Horror*, 89.

15. Coplan, "Empathetic Engagement," 143.

16. Peter Goldie, *The Emotions: A Philosophical Exploration* (Oxford: Clarendon Press, 2000), 195. I have loosened Goldie's third requirement because, like Bordwell and Wilson, I do not think that narration requires a narrator. Sometimes there are such entities, but sometimes there are not. See Bordwell, *Narration in the Fiction Film*, 61–62, and Wilson, "*Le Grand Imagier* Steps Out."

of emotional contagion, motor and affective mimicry, autonomic reactions, in-her-shoes imagining, emotional or mental simulation, and other responses that would fall within the category of taking on aspects of an other person's mental, physical, or emotional states. Of course, these different responses that fall under the umbrella of commonsense "empathy" may be distinguished and separately analyzed—in fact, I think they should be—but our common-sense conception seems to include parts of many if not all of these phenomena, and for this reason we should be receptive to the diverse complexity of what we mean by "empathy" and make every effort to incorporate it in our theoretical discussions. As Smith notes, "There is a consensus [even among scientists] that a certain range of phenomena are usefully gathered under" the term.[17] For example, film theorist Margrethe Bruun Vaage has argued for a kind of "embodied empathy" that accounts for many of our mirror reflex responses to film, based on recent research investigating "mirror neurons" and their role in our affective responses to others.[18] Similarly, there seem to be forms of "cognitive" or "narrative empathy" that operate much like what has been described as "mental simulation" which arise at least occasionally in film spectatorship.[19] In general our empathetic responses in the world represent complicated human phenomena, so in their employment while viewing film we should expect similar complexity.

The analyses provided in this book stress mainly three types of empathy: reflective, retrospective, and critical. For example, many of the black *noir* films I have examined urge us to empathize *reflectively*—that is, grant empathy to another after some considered thought regarding whether we should do so or not. Although this response may occur during the film, frequently such granting will be done *retrospectively* in consideration of our viewing experience once the film is over.[20] A narrative may challenge us to better figure out one of its characters, such as *Do the Right Thing* does regarding Sal. This form of reflective, retrospective empathy will ideally be philosophical, as it will not only induce us to transform presumed conceptions that are embedded dimensions of our automatized belief schemata, but will also transform our senses of who we are—our senses of self—and with that, our place in the world.

17. Smith, *Engaging Characters*, 96.

18. Margrethe Bruun Vaage, "The Empathetic Film Spectator in Analytic Philosophy and Naturalized Phenomenology," *Film and Philosophy* 10 (2006): 21–38.

19. See Goldie, *The Emotions*, esp. 194–203. For its application to film, see Smith, *Engaging Characters*, 95–102, and "Imagining from the Inside," in Allen and Smith, *Film Theory and Philosophy*, 412–30. Although I have reservations about the literalness of mental simulation, I do agree that narrative or cognitive empathy is often *like* mental simulation in that central imagining is crucial for both. For a thoughtful analysis of central imagining as simulation that nonetheless leaves conceptual space for the possibility that it could generate narrative knowledge even if literal mental simulation is false, see Jinhee Choi, "Leaving It Up to the Imagination: POV Shots and Imagining from the Inside," *Journal of Aesthetics and Art Criticism* 63 (2005): 17–25.

20. See also Murray Smith, "Empathy, Expansionism, and Expanded Mind" (paper presented at Empathy: An International Interdisciplinary Conference, California State University, Fullerton, Calif., June 23, 2006).

With reference to these new forms of *noir*, ideally racialized presumptions of privilege and advantage would no longer be embedded in viewers' thoughts and actions; and sensitivity to expectations of superiority or inferiority would become salient in their interactions with fictions as well as other people. As a result, viewers would see the world as a different place because they would understand themselves and their place in it differently.

In addition, many of these films call for our *critical* empathy; that is, our extension of congruence of thought or feeling while at the same time remaining critical of those thoughts or feelings. Given the proper sorts of narrative prompts, we may imaginatively build analogical bridges to another's situation, even as we remain conscious of the other's mistake in thinking or feeling as they do. Berys Gaut argues for this sort of empathy. He notes that even as we may be encouraged to respond empathetically to a character, we may still see that his or her actions are "in certain respects foolish and deluded."[21] Similarly, in many black *noir* and *noir* Atlantic films we are urged to grasp a character's cognitive or emotional state while still recognizing that what they do or think is wrong, such as when they give in to passive black nihilism, choose to become criminals, or act immorally. Critical empathy would also seem to be at least compatible, if not presupposed, by Kieran's and Smith's discussions of imagining immoralism and imaginative "slumming."[22] Moreover, such empathetic responses may be simple or complex by being evoked either during the movie itself or after we have invested some retrospective reflection in the matter. Of course, which is evoked will depend to some extent on us and what we bring cognitively, emotionally, and receptively to the film.

Finally, I would argue that the best of black *noir* as well as *noir* Atlantic films are about expanding our imaginations, broadening our horizon of human possibilities, an oft-noted feature of fiction here directed toward presumptions of race and white supremacy. Many of these films pluralize human rights and Enlightenment concepts like the person, autonomy, dignity, respect, equality, freedom, and justice. As works of art that encourage something similar to what Amy Gutmann has called the "identification view" regarding one's stance toward social justice, these films can help viewers to see "that their own interests are bound up with living in a more just society."[23] Of course, such interests may diverge as well, but Gutmann wishes to emphasize that frequently they do not, an insight that many black *noir* films in particular underwrite by linking one's view of others' humanity with one's own. In addition, their cultivation of empathy tends to support the commonsense conception of identification that Gutmann employs. Again, even though empathy may be used for just as well as unjust purposes, the best of these films seek to use it

---

21. Gaut, "Identification and Emotion in Narrative Film," 216. Of course, I reject Gaut's claim that "identification" may be rehabilitated theoretically to the status he claims for it, even if I agree with him that empathy can be critical.

22. Kieran, "Forbidden Knowledge"; Smith, "Gangsters, Cannibals, Aesthetes," esp. 223–25.

23. Amy Gutmann, *Identity in Democracy* (Princeton: Princeton University Press, 2003), 145.

in the interest of linking together justice with one's personal stake in human flourishing.

These films often imply further questions for their viewers' consideration. For instance, how could more satisfactory ways of human socializing be worked out? Are Enlightenment ideals the only ones worth considering in attempting to imagine new forms of socializing? Are they the best ones? *Noir Atlantic* films further add to this interrogation perplexities such as whether these ideals only work in the West, in Western-style democracies, or under Western capitalism. Imagination and the political are crucially linked, and ignorance often blocks their expansion. This connection frequently makes their extension an epistemological question, a point that has underwritten much of my project here.

Explicit presentations of such expansive possibilities include, I would argue, moments in Spike Lee's more recent *noirish* narratives in *The 25th Hour* (2002) and *Inside Man* (2006), which offer glimpses of a polyglot New York, where diverse human beings live side-by-side, even if not always harmoniously, in ways that illustrate possibilities for racial tolerance. By foregrounding allegiances with morally complex, good-bad or attractive-bad characters involved in plots of mystery and suspense revolving around crime, often taking place at night, in these films Lee goads us to imagine how we might work out more satisfactory ways of human socializing despite problems of race. While in no way dismissing racial matters, Lee also looks beyond them to a sense of how we might live together in the face of such social impediments. I take these possibilities to be the point of the montage of New Yorkers that Monty (Edward Norton) sees as he heads to prison at the conclusion of *The 25th Hour*, as well as his earlier profane tirade from the mirror against all the raced, classed, gendered, and miscellaneous "others" of New York—a tirade that he ultimately admits is false. Bringing these possibilities to viewer attention also seems to be the point of *Inside Man's* use of world music mixed with hip-hop on its soundtrack and its self-consciously matter-of-fact presentation of the city's "mongrelized," hybrid population: blacks, whites, Jews, Asians, Sikhs, Albanians, Russians, Italian-Americans, and on and on.[24] Like a rigorous Cavellian who has also been influenced by Gilroy, Lee integrates into these narrative moments the need to recognize *all* human "others" as *fully* human, to acknowledge our differences as well as our sameness by means of a more developed sense of tolerance as well as the human itself, and the need to take responsibility for our actions, even when doing so will cost us dearly. It is only through these ways of expanding our imaginations that we might finally get beyond race and see ourselves as well as "others" as full-fledged human beings, rather than as something more or less.

---

24. For more on the positive uses of the terms "mongrelized" and "hybrid," see Edward Said, "Europe and Its Others: An Arab Perspective," in *States of Mind: Dialogues with Contemporary Thinkers,* ed. Richard Kearney (New York: New York University Press, 1995), 46.

Black *noir* films and their cinematic descendants offer us ample opportunities to reflect philosophically on various forms of social oppression. Whether we accept those challenges is, of course, up to us, but doing so would make it much more likely that problems of race and other forms of disadvantage may, someday, be successfully resolved.

Alcoff, Linda Martín. "What Should White People Do?" *Hypatia* 13 (1998): 6–26.

Allen, James, et al., eds. *Without Sanctuary: Lynching Photography in America*, Santa Fe: Twin Palms Publishers, 2000.

Allen, Richard. "Hitchcock and Narrative Suspense: Theory and Practice." In *Camera Obscura, Camera Lucida: Essays in Honor of Annette Michelson*, ed. Richard Allen and Malcolm Turvey. Amsterdam: Amsterdam University Press, 2003.

Allen, Richard, and Murray Smith, eds. *Film Theory and Philosophy*. Oxford: Clarendon Press, 1997.

Altman, Rick. *Film/Genre*. London: BFI Publishing, 1999.

Alton, John. *Painting with Light*. 1949. Reprint, Berkeley and Los Angeles: University of California Press, 1995.

Ansen, David. "How Hot Is Too Hot; Searing, Nervy, and Honest." *Newsweek*, July 3, 1989, 65.

Appiah, Kwami Anthony. "Racisms." In *Anatomy of Racism*, ed. David Theo Goldberg. Minneapolis: University of Minnesota Press, 1990.

Arendt, Hannah. *Eichmann in Jerusalem: A Report on the Banality of Evil*. 1963. Reprint, New York: Penguin Books, 1994.

Aristotle. *Nicomachean Ethics*. Translated by Terence Irwin. Second edition. Indianapolis: Hackett, 1999.

———. *Poetics*. Translated by Stephen Halliwell. Excerpted in *The Philosophy of Art: Readings Ancient and Modern*, ed. Alex Neill and Aaron Ridley. Boston: McGraw-Hill, 1995.

———. *Rhetoric*. Translated by Lane Cooper. 1932. Reprint, New York: Appleton-Century-Crofts, 1960.

Arjouni, Jakob. *Happy Birthday, Turk!* Translated by Anselm Arno. Harpenden: No Exit Press, 1993.

Armour, Jody David. *Negrophobia and Reasonable Racism: The Hidden Costs of Being Black in America*. New York: New York University Press, 1997.

Bach, Craig N. "Nietzsche and *The Big Sleep*: Style, Women, and Truth." *Film and Philosophy* 5/6 (2002): 45–59.

Baggini, Julian. "Alien Ways of Thinking: Mulhall's *On Film*." *Film-Philosophy* 7, no. 24 (August 2003). http://www.film-philosophy.com/.

———. *What's It All About? Philosophy and the Meaning of Life*. 2004. Reprint, New York: Oxford University Press, 2005.

Baker, Houston A., Jr. "Spike Lee and the Commerce of Culture." In *Black American Cinema*, ed. Manthia Diawara. New York: Routledge, 1993.

Baldwin, James. "The Black Boy Looks at the White Boy." In *Collected Essays*. New York: Library of America, 1998.

———. *The Fire Next Time*. New York: Dell, 1964.

Bardaglio, Peter W. *Reconstructing the Household: Families, Sex, and the Law in the Nineteenth-Century South*. Chapel Hill: University of North Carolina Press, 1995.

Barefoot, Guy. *Gaslight Melodrama: From Victorian London to 1940s Hollywood*. New York: Continuum, 2001.

Barkan, Elazar. *The Retreat of Scientific Racism*. Cambridge: Cambridge University Press, 1992.

Barnes, Allison, and Paul Thagard, "Empathy and Analogy." *Dialogue* 36 (1997): 705–20.

Barnfield, Graham. "'The Urban Landscape of Marxist *Noir*': An Interview with Alan Wald." *Crime Time*, June 26, 2002. http://www.crimetime.co.uk/features/marxistnoir.html/ (accessed March 24, 2006).

Barstow, David, and David Kocieniewski. "Records Show New Jersey Police Withheld Data on Race Profiling." *New York Times*, October 12, 2000, 1+.

Bates, Karen Grigsby. "'They've Gotta Have Us': Hollywood's Black Directors." *New York Times Magazine*, July 14, 1991, 15–19+.

Beck, Robert. *Pimp: The Story of My Life*. Los Angeles: Holloway House, 1969.

———. *Trick Baby*. Los Angeles: Holloway House, 1970.

Bernardi, Daniel, ed. *The Birth of Whiteness: Race and the Emergence of U.S. Cinema*. New Brunswick: Rutgers University Press, 1996.

Bernasconi, Robert. "Kant as an Unfamiliar Source of Racism." In *Philosophers on Race: Critical Essays*, ed. Julie K. Ward and Tommy L. Lott. London: Blackwell, 2002.

———. "Who Invented the Concept of Race? Kant's Role in the Enlightenment Construction of Race." In *Race*, ed. Robert Bernasconi. Oxford: Blackwell, 2001.

———, ed. *Race*. London: Blackwell, 2001.

Bernasconi, Robert, and Tommy L. Lott, eds. *The Idea of Race*. Indianapolis: Hackett, 2000.

Berrettini, Mark L. "Private Knowledge, Public Space: Investigation and Navigation in *Devil in a Blue Dress*." *Cinema Journal* 39 (1999): 74–89.

Biesen, Sheri Chinen. *Blackout: World War II and the Origins of Film Noir*. Baltimore: Johns Hopkins University Press, 2005.

Bodroghkozy, Aniko. "*Beulah*." Museum of Broadcast Communications website. http://www.museum.tv/archives/etv/B/htmlB/beulah/beulah.htm/ (accessed February 7, 2005).

Bogle, Donald. *Toms, Coons, Mulattoes, Mammies, and Bucks: An Interpretive History of Blacks in American Films*. Fourth edition. New York: Continuum, 2001.

Borde, Raymond, and Etienne Chaumeton. *Panorama du film noir américain, 1941–1953*. Paris: Editions de Minuit, 1955. Translated by Paul Hammond as *A Panorama of American Film Noir, 1941–1953* (San Francisco: City Lights Books, 2002).

Bordwell, David. *Narration in the Fiction Film*. Madison: University of Wisconsin Press, 1985.

Bordwell, David, and Kristin Thompson. *Film Art: An Introduction*. Sixth edition. New York: McGraw-Hill, 2001.

Bordwell, David, and Noël Carroll, eds. *Post-Theory: Reconstructing Film Studies*. Madison: University of Wisconsin Press, 1996.

Borgers, Etienne. "*Série Noire*." In *The Big Book of Noir*, ed. Ed Gorman, Lee Server, and Martin H. Greenberg. New York: Carroll and Graf, 1998.

Boxill, Bernard. *Blacks and Social Justice*. Revised edition. Lanham, Md.: Rowman and Littlefield, 1992.

———. "The Morality of Reparations." *Social Theory and Practice* 2 (1972): 113–22.

———. "The Morality of Reparations II." In *A Companion to African-American Philosophy*, ed. Tommy L. Lott and John P. Pittman. London: Blackwell, 2003.

———, ed. *Race and Racism*. Oxford: Oxford University Press, 2001.

Boyd, Todd. *Am I Black Enough for You? Popular Culture From the 'Hood and Beyond*. Bloomington: Indiana University Press, 1997.

Brecht, Bertholt. *Brecht on Theatre: The Development of an Aesthetic*. Edited and translated by John Willett. New York: Hill and Wang, 1962.

Bruun Vaage, Margrethe. "The Empathetic Film Spectator in Analytic Philosophy and Naturalized Phenomenology." *Film and Philosophy* 10 (2006): 21–38.

Bryant, Jerry H. *"Born in a Mighty Bad Land": The Violent Man in African American Folklore and Fiction*. Bloomington: Indiana University Press, 2003.

Buss, Robin. *French Film Noir*. London: Marion Boyars, 1994.

Camus, Albert. *The Myth of Sisyphus and Other Essays*, trans. Justin O'Brien. 1955. Reprint, New York: Vintage, 1991.

Canby, Vincent. "Spike Lee Raises the Movies' Black Voice." *New York Times*, May 28, 1989, sec. 2, 14.

———. "Spike Lee Tackles Racism in *Do the Right Thing*." *New York Times*, June 30, 1989, C16.

Card, Claudia. *The Atrocity Paradigm*. New York: Oxford University Press, 2002.

Carroll, Noël. "Film, Emotion, and Genre." In *Passionate Views: Film, Cognition, and Emotion*, ed. Carl Plantinga and Greg M. Smith. Baltimore: Johns Hopkins University Press, 1999.

———. "Interpreting *Citizen Kane*." In *Interpreting the Moving Image*. New York: Cambridge University Press, 1998.

———. "The Paradox of Suspense." In *Beyond Aesthetics: Philosophical Essays*. Cambridge: Cambridge University Press, 2001.

———. *The Philosophy of Horror, or, Paradoxes of the Heart*. London: Routledge, 1990.

———. *A Philosophy of Mass Art*. Oxford: Clarendon Press, 1998.

———. "Prospects for Film Theory: A Personal Assessment." In *Post-Theory: Reconstructing Film Studies*, ed. David Bordwell and Noël Carroll. Madison: University of Wisconsin Press, 1996.

———. *Theorizing the Moving Image*. New York: Cambridge University Press, 1996.

Cavell, Stanley. *Contesting Tears: The Hollywood Melodrama of the Unknown Woman*. Chicago: University of Chicago Press, 1996.

———. *In Quest of the Ordinary*. 1988. Reprint, Chicago: University of Chicago Press, 1994.

———. *The Pursuits of Happiness: The Hollywood Comedy of Remarriage*. Cambridge: Harvard University Press, 1981.

———. "Something Out of the Ordinary." *Proceedings and Addresses of the American Philosophical Association* 71, no. 2 (November 1997): 23–37.

———. "The Thought of Movies." In *Themes Out of School: Effects and Causes*. Chicago: University of Chicago Press, 1984.

———. *The World Viewed: Reflection on the Ontology of Film*. Enlarged edition. Cambridge: Harvard University Press, 1979.

Cawelti, John G. *Adventure, Mystery, and Romance: Formula Stories as Art and Popular Culture*. Chicago: University of Chicago Press, 1976.

Chan, Kenneth. "The Construction of Black Male Identity in Black Action Films of the Nineties." *Cinema Journal* 37 (1998): 35–48.

Chandler, Raymond. "The Simple Art of Murder." In *The Simple Art of Murder*. New York: Ballantine Books, 1980.

Chartier, Jean-Pierre. "Americans Are Also Making *Noir* Films" (1946). Translated by Alain Silver. In *Film Noir Reader 2*, ed. Alain Silver and James Ursini. New York: Limelight Editions, 1999.

Choi, Jinhee. "Leaving It Up to the Imagination: POV Shots and Imagining from the Inside." *Journal of Aesthetics and Art Criticism* 63 (2005): 17–25.

Clarens, Carlos. *Crime Movies*. New York: W. W. Norton, 1980.

Cole, David. "The Color of Justice." *Nation*, October 11, 1999, 12–15.

Conard, Mark T. "Nietzsche and the Meaning and Definition of Noir." In *The Philosophy of Film Noir*, ed. Mark T. Conard. Lexington: University Press of Kentucky, 2006.

———, ed. *The Philosophy of Film Noir*. Lexington: University Press of Kentucky, 2006.

Cooper, John M. *Reason and Human Good in Aristotle*. 1975. Reprint, Indianapolis: Hackett, 1986.

Copjec, Joan, ed. *Shades of Noir*. London: Verso, 1993.

Coplan, Amy. "Empathetic Engagement with Narrative Fictions." *Journal of Aesthetics and Art Criticism* 62 (2004): 141–52.

Corliss, Richard. "Hot Time in Bed-Stuy Tonight." *Time*, July 3, 1989, 62.

Cottingham, John. *On the Meaning of Life*. London: Routledge, 2003.

Cowie, Elizabeth. "*Film Noir* and Women." In *Shades of Noir*, ed. Joan Copjec. London: Verso, 1993.

Cripps, Thomas. "*Amos 'n' Andy* and the Debate over American Racial Integration." In *American History/American Television*, ed. John O'Connor. New York: Ungar, 1983.

———. *Black Film as Genre*. Bloomington: Indiana University Press, 1978.

———. "Introduction to 1929–1940: Hollywood Beckons." In *Instructor's Guide to African Americans in Cinema: The First Half Century*, ed. Phyllis R. Klotman. Urbana: University of Illinois Press, 2003. CD-ROM.

———. *Making Movies Black: The Hollywood Message Movie from World War II to the Civil Rights Era*. New York: Oxford University Press, 1993.

———. "'Race Movies' as Voices of the Black Bourgeoisie: *The Scar of Shame* (1927)." In *American History/American Film: Interpreting the Hollywood Image*, ed. John E. O'Connor and Martin A. Jackson. New York: Ungar, 1979.

———. *Slow Fade to Black: The Negro in American Film, 1900–1942*. New York: Oxford University Press, 1977.

Crowdus, Gary, and Dan Georgakas. "Thinking about the Power of Images: An Interview with Spike Lee." *Cineaste* 26, no. 2 (January 2001): 4–9.

Crowther, Bruce. *Film Noir: Reflections in a Dark Mirror*. New York: Continuum, 1988.

Currie, Gregory. *Arts and Minds*. New York: Oxford University Press, 2004.

———. "The Film Theory That Never Was: A Nervous Manifesto." In *Film Theory and Philosophy*, ed. Richard Allen and Murray Smith. Oxford: Clarendon Press, 1997.

———. *Image and Mind: Film, Philosophy, and Cognitive Science*. New York: Cambridge University Press, 1995.

Dancy, Jonathan. *Moral Reasons*. London: Blackwell, 1993.

Davies, Martin, and Tony Stone, eds. *Mental Simulation*. London: Blackwell, 1995.

Davis, Angela. "Rape, Racism, and the Myth of the Black Rapist." In *Women, Race, and Class*. New York: Random House, 1981.

Davis, F. James. *Who Is Black?* University Park: Pennsylvania State University Press, 1991.

Davis, Mike. *City of Quartz: Excavating the Future in Los Angeles.* 1990. Reprint, New York: Vintage, 1992.

Davis, Zeinabu Irene. "Black Independent or Hollywood Iconoclast?" *Cineaste* 17, no. 4 (1990): 36–37.

De Certeau, Michel. *The Practice of Everyday Life.* Translated by Steven Rendall. Berkeley and Los Angeles: University of California Press, 1984.

Deane, Pamela S. *"Good Times."* Museum of Broadcast Communications website. http://www.museum.tv/archives/etv/G/htmlG/goodtimes/goodtimes.htm/ (accessed February 9, 2005).

Denby, David. "Angry People" (review of *Crash*). *New Yorker,* May 2, 2005, 110.

———. "He's Gotta Have It." *New York Magazine,* June 26, 1989, 53–54.

Dennis, Denise. *Black History for Beginners.* New York: Writers and Readers Publishing, 1995.

Desser, David. "Global Noir: Genre Film in the Age of Transnationalism." In *Film Genre Reader III,* ed. Barry Keith Grant. Austin: University of Texas Press, 2003.

Diamond, Cora. "The Difficulty of Reality and the Difficulty of Philosophy." In *Reading Cavell,* ed. Alice Crary and Sanford Shieh. London: Routledge, 2006.

Diawara, Manthia. "Black American Cinema: The New Realism." In *Black American Cinema,* ed. Manthia Diawara. London: Routledge, 1993.

———. *"Noir* by *Noirs:* Toward a New Realism in Black Cinema." In *Shades of Noir,* ed. Joan Copjec. London: Verso, 1993.

———, ed. *Black American Cinema.* London: Routledge, 1993.

Dickerson, Ernest. Interview by Linda Lynton, in Lynton, *"School Daze:* Black College Is Background." *American Cinematographer* 69, no. 2 (February 1988): 67–72.

Doane, Mary Ann. *Femmes Fatales: Feminism, Film Theory, and Psychoanalysis.* London: Routledge, 1991.

Doherty, Thomas. Review of *Do the Right Thing. Film Quarterly* 43, no. 2 (1989): 35–40.

Douglass, Frederick. *Narrative of the Life of Frederick Douglass, An American Slave, Written By Himself.* 1845. Reprint, New York: Anchor Books, 1989.

———. "Introduction." In Ida B. Wells, Frederick Douglass, Irvine Garland Penn, and Ferdinand L. Barnett. *The Reason Why the Colored American Is Not in the World's Columbian Exposition,* ed. Robert W. Rydell. 1893. Reprint, Urbana: University of Illinois Press, 1999.

Dray, Philip. *At the Hands of Persons Unknown: The Lynching of Black America.* New York: Modern Library, 2003.

D'Souza, Dinesh. *The End of Racism: Principles for a Multiracial Society.* New York: Free Press, 1995.

Du Bois, W. E. B. *Black Reconstruction: An Essay Toward a History of the Part in Which Black Folk Played in an Attempt to Reconstruct Democracy in America, 1860–1880.* New York: Harcourt, Brace, 1935.

———. *The Souls of Black Folk.* 1903. Reprint, New York: Signet, 1969.

Dyer, Richard. *White.* London: Routledge, 1997.

Ebert, Roger. *"Get Rich or Die Tryin':* Rapping His Way Outta the 'Hood." *Chicago Sun-Times,* November 10, 2005. http://www.rogerebert.com/ (accessed September 21, 2006).

Eliot, T. S. "Hamlet and His Problems." In *The Sacred Wood: Essays on Poetry and Criticism.* London: Methuen, 1921.

Ellison, Ralph. *Invisible Man.* New York: Random House, [1952].

———. "The Shadow and the Act." In *Shadow and Act.* New York: Vintage, 1972.

Elsaesser, Thomas. "The Dandy in Hitchcock." In *Alfred Hitchcock: Centenary Essays,*
ed. Richard Allen and S. Ishi Gonzales. London: BFI Publishing, 1999.

Estes, Steven S. *I Am a Man! Race, Manhood, and the Civil Rights Movement.* Chapel
Hill: University of North Carolina Press, 2005.

Eze, Emmanuel C. *Achieving Our Humanity: The Idea of a Postracial Future.* New York:
Routledge, 2001.

———, ed. *Race and the Enlightenment.* London: Blackwell, 1997.

Fanon, Frantz. *Black Skin, White Masks.* Translated by Charles Lam Markmann. New
York: Grove Press, 1967.

———. "The Lived Experience of the Black." 1951. Translated by Valentine Moulard.
In *Race,* ed. Robert Bernasconi. Oxford: Blackwell, 2001.

Farr, Arnold. "Whiteness Visible: Enlightenment Racism and the Structure of Racialized Consciousness." In *What White Looks Like: African-American Philosophers on
the Whiteness Question,* ed. George Yancy. New York: Routledge, 2004.

Farred, Grant. "No Way Out of the *Menaced* Society: Loyalty Within the Boundaries of
Race." *Camera Obscura,* no. 35 (May 1995): 7–23.

Feagin, Joe R., Hernan Vera, and Pinar Batur. *White Racism.* Second edition. New
York: Routledge, 2001.

The Film Encyclopedia. Edited by Ephraim Katz. New York: Perigee Books, 1979.

Fleming, Robert E. *Willard Motley.* Boston: Twayne Publishers, 1978.

Flory, Dan. "Black on White: *Film Noir* and the Epistemology of Race in Recent African American Cinema." *Journal of Social Philosophy* 31 (2000): 82–116.

———. "Race, Rationality, and Melodrama: Aesthetic Response and the Case of
Oscar Micheaux." *Journal of Aesthetics and Art Criticism* 63 (2005): 327–38.

Frank, Nino. "A New Kind of Police Drama: The Crime Adventure." In *Film Noir
Reader 2,* ed. Alain Silver and James Ursini. New York: Limelight Editions, 1999.

French, Peter. *Cowboy Metaphysics: Ethics and Death in Westerns.* Lanham, Md.: Rowman and Littlefield, 1997.

———. *The Virtues of Vengeance.* Lawrence: University Press of Kansas, 2001.

Fuchs, Cynthia, ed. *Spike Lee: Interviews.* Jackson: University of Mississippi Press,
2002.

Gaines, Jane. *Fire and Desire: Mixed-Race Movies in the Silent Era.* Chicago: University
of Chicago Press, 2001.

Garcia Espinosa, Julio. "For an Imperfect Cinema." In *Film and Theory: An Anthology,*
ed. Robert Stam and Toby Miller. Oxford: Blackwell, 2000.

Gates, Henry Louis. "Blood Brothers: Albert and Allen Hughes in the Belly of the
Hollywood Beast." *Transitions,* no. 63 (1994): 164–77.

———. "Statistical Stigmata." In *Deconstruction and the Possibility of Justice,* ed.
Drucilla Cornell, Michel Rosenfeld, and David Carlson. New York: Routledge,
1992.

Gaut, Berys. "'Art' as a Cluster Concept." In *Theories of Art Today,* ed. Noël Carroll.
Madison: University of Wisconsin Press, 2000.

———. "Film Authorship and Collaboration." In *Film Theory and Philosophy,* ed.
Richard Allen and Murray Smith. Oxford: Clarendon Press, 1997.

———. "Identification and Emotion in Narrative Film." In *Passionate Views: Film,
Cognition, and Emotion,* ed. Carl Plantinga and Greg M. Smith. Baltimore: Johns
Hopkins University Press, 1999.

———. Review of *Engaging Characters: Fiction, Emotion, and the Cinema,* by Murray Smith. *British Journal of Aesthetics* 37 (1997): 96–97.

George, Nelson. *Blackface: Reflections on African-Americans and the Movies.* New York: HarperCollins, 1994.

Gilman, Sander L. "'I'm Down on Whores': Race and Gender in Victorian London." In *Anatomy of Racism,* ed. David Theo Goldberg. Minneapolis: University of Minnesota Press, 1990.

Gilroy, Paul. *The Black Atlantic: Modernity and Double Consciousness.* Cambridge: Harvard University Press, 1993.

Glicksman, Marlaine. "Spike Lee's Bed-Stuy BBQ." In *Spike Lee: Interviews,* ed. Cynthia Fuchs. Jackson: University of Mississippi Press, 2002.

Global Corruption Report 2006: Special Focus on Corruption and Health. http://www.transparency.org/publications/gcr/ (accessed September 7, 2006).

Goines, Donald. *Black Girl Lost.* Los Angeles: Holloway House, 1973.

———. *Daddy Cool.* Los Angeles: Holloway House, 1974.

———. *Dopefiend.* Los Angeles: Holloway House, 1971.

———. *Never Die Alone.* Los Angeles: Holloway House Publishing, 1974.

———. *White Man's Justice, Black Man's Grief.* Los Angeles: Holloway House, 1973.

Goldberg, David Theo, ed. *Anatomy of Racism.* Minneapolis: University of Minnesota Press, 1990.

———. *The Racial State.* London: Blackwell, 2002.

———. *Racial Subjects: Writings on Race in America.* New York: Routledge, 1997.

———. *Racist Culture: Philosophy and the Politics of Meaning.* London: Blackwell, 1993.

Goldie, Peter. *The Emotions: A Philosophical Exploration.* Oxford: Clarendon Press, 2000.

Gombrich, E. H. *Art and Illusion: A Study in the Psychology of Pictorial Representation.* Second edition. Princeton: Princeton University Press, 1972.

Gooding-Williams, Robert. *Look, a Negro! Philosophical Essays on Race, Culture, and Politics.* New York: Routledge, 2006.

Gordon, Lewis. *Bad Faith and Antiblack Racism.* Atlantic Highlands, N.J.: Humanities Press, 1995.

———. "Critical Reflections on Three Popular Tropes in the Study of Whiteness." In *What White Looks Like: African-American Philosophers on the Whiteness Question,* ed. George Yancy. New York: Routledge, 2004.

———. *Fanon and the Crisis of European Man: An Essay on Philosophy and the Human Sciences.* New York: Routledge, 1995.

———. *Her Majesty's Other Children: Sketches of Racism from a Neocolonial Age.* Lanham, Md.: Rowman and Littlefield, 1997.

Gorman, Ed, and Lee Server and Martin H. Greenberg, eds. *The Big Book of Noir.* New York: Carroll and Graf, 1998.

Gossett, Thomas. *Race: The History of an Idea in America.* New edition. New York: Oxford University Press, 1997.

Gould, Stephen Jay. *The Mismeasure of Man.* Revised edition. New York: W. W. Norton, 1996.

Gracyk, Theodore. *Rhythm and Noise: An Aesthetics of Rock.* Durham: Duke University Press, 1996.

Grant, Barry Keith, ed. *Film Genre Reader III.* Austin: University of Texas Press, 2003.

Gray, Beverly. "Triple Threat: Interview with Carl Franklin." *Creative Screenwriting* 4, no. 1 (Spring 1997):15–21.

Green, George Dawes. *The Caveman's Valentine.* 1994. Reprint, New York: Warner
    Books, 1995.

Guerrero, Ed. "A Circus of Dreams and Lies: The Black Film Wave at Middle Age." In
    The New American Cinema, ed. Jon Lewis. Durham: Duke University Press, 1998.

———. *Do the Right Thing.* London: BFI Publishing, 2001.

———. *Framing Blackness: The African American Image in Film.* Philadelphia: Temple
    University Press, 1993.

———. Review of *Devil in a Blue Dress. Cineaste* 22, no. 1 (1996): 38, 40–41.

Guglielmo, Jennifer, and Salvatore Salerno, eds. *Are Italians White? How Race Is Made
    in America.* New York: Routledge, 2003.

Guralnick, Peter. *Last Train to Memphis: The Rise of Elvis Presley.* Boston: Little, Brown,
    1994.

Guthrie, W.K.C. *The Greeks and Their Gods.* Boston: Beacon Press, 1955.

Gutmann, Amy. *Identity in Democracy.* Princeton: Princeton University Press, 2003.

Hammett, Dashiell. "The Golden Horseshoe." 1924. In *The Continental Op,* ed. Ste-
    ven Marcus. New York: Vintage, 1975.

Hanchard, Michael. "Black Cinderella? Race and the Public Sphere in Brazil." In *The
    Idea of Race,* ed. Robert Bernasconi and Tommy L. Lott. Indianapolis: Hackett,
    2000.

Hardy, Paul-A. "Medieval Muslim Philosophers on Race." In *Philosophers on Race:
    Critical Essays,* ed. Julie K. Ward and Tommy L. Lott. London: Blackwell, 2002.

Haut, Woody. "Chester Himes." In *Pulp Culture: Hardboiled Fiction and the Cold War.*
    London: Serpent's Tail, 1995.

———. *Neon Noir: Contemporary American Crime Fiction.* London: Serpent's Tail,
    1999.

Hemingway, Ernest. *To Have and Have Not.* New York: Charles Scribner's Sons, 1937.

Higham, Charles, and Joel Greenberg. *Hollywood in the Forties.* New York:
    A. S. Barnes, 1968.

Hill, Thomas E., Jr., and Bernard Boxill. "Kant and Race." In *Race and Racism,* ed.
    Bernard Boxill. Oxford: Oxford University Press, 2001.

Himes, Chester. *My Life of Absurdity: The Later Years.* New York: Paragon House,
    1976.

Hirsch, Foster. *Detours and Lost Highways: A Map of Neo-Noir.* New York: Limelight
    Editions, 1999.

———. *Film Noir: The Dark Side of the Screen.* 1981. Reprint, New York: Da Capo
    Press, 1983.

Hobsbawm, Eric. *Bandits.* New York: Delacorte Press, 1969.

Hoffman, Martin L. *Empathy and Moral Development: Implications for Caring and Jus-
    tice.* 2000. Reprint, Cambridge: Cambridge University Press, 2003.

hooks, bell. *Yearning: Race, Gender, and Cultural Politics.* Boston: South End Press,
    1990.

Hume, David. *An Inquiry Concerning the Principles of Morals,* ed. Charles W. Hendel.
    Indianapolis: Bobbs-Merrill, 1957.

Hunt, Lester H. "Sentiment and Sympathy." *Journal of Aesthetics and Art Criticism* 62
    (2004), 339–54.

Itzkoff, Seymour W. *The Decline of Intelligence in America.* Westport, Conn.: Praeger,
    1994.

Jacobs, Harriet. *Incidents in the Life of a Slave Girl.* 1861. Reprint, Cambridge: Harvard
    University Press, 1987.

James, Joy. *Resisting State Violence*. Minneapolis: University of Minnesota Press, 1996.

———. *Transcending the Talented Tenth*. New York: Routledge, 1997.

James, William. *The Will to Believe*. 1897. Reprint, New York: Dover, 1956.

Jones, Janine. "The Impairment of Empathy in Goodwill Whites for African Americans." In *What White Looks Like: African-American Philosophers on the Whiteness Question*, ed. George Yancy. New York: Routledge, 2004.

Jones, Jacquie. "In Sal's Country." *Cineaste* 17, no. 4 (1990): 34–35.

———. "The New Ghetto Aesthetic." *Wide Angle* 13, no. 3–4 (1991): 32–43.

"Joseph Moncure March." *Contemporary Authors Online*, 2000. http://galenet.galegroup.com (accessed March 24, 2006).

Joyce, Cynthia. "Eve Gets Even." *Salon*, November 7, 1997. http://archive.salon.com/ent/movies/1997/11/07eve.html/.

Kael, Pauline. Film Note on *Double Indemnity*. *New Yorker*, November 29, 2004, 46.

Kant, Immanuel. *Grounding for the Metaphysics of Morals*. Translated by James W. Ellington. Third edition. Indianapolis: Hackett, 1993.

———. *Prolegomena to Any Future Metaphysics*. Translated by Lewis White Beck. New York: Liberal Arts Press, 1950.

Kauffmann, Stanley. "*Do the Right Thing*." *New Republic* 201 (July 3, 1989), 25.

Kearns, Cimberli. "Fascinating Knowledge." *Film and Philosophy* 3 (1996): 24–37.

Kellner, Douglas. "Aesthetics, Ethics, and Politics in the Films of Spike Lee." In *Spike Lee's "Do the Right Thing*," ed. Mark A. Reid. New York: Cambridge University Press, 1997.

Kempton, Murray. "The Pizza Is Burning!" *New York Review of Books*, September 28, 1989, 37.

Kennedy, Randall. *Nigger: The Strange Career of a Troublesome Word*. New York: Pantheon, 2002.

Khoury, George. "Big Words: An Interview with Spike Lee." In *Spike Lee: Interviews*, ed. Cynthia Fuchs. Jackson: University of Mississippi Press, 2002.

Kieran, Matthew. "Forbidden Knowledge: The Challenge of Immoralism." In *Art and Morality*, ed. Jose Bermudez and Sebastian Gardner. London: Routledge, 2003.

King, Martin Luther, Jr. "Letter from Birmingham City Jail." In *African-American Philosophy: Selected Readings*, ed. Tommy L. Lott. Upper Saddle River, N.J.: Prentice-Hall, 2002.

———. *Why We Can't Wait*. New York: Signet, 1964.

Klein, Joe. "Spiked? Dinkins and *Do the Right Thing*." *New York Magazine*, June, 26, 1989, 14–15.

Klemke, E. D., ed. *The Meaning of Life*. New York: Oxford University Press, 1981.

Knight, Deborah. "Aristotelians on *Speed:* Paradoxes of Genre in the Context of Cinema." In *Film Theory and Philosophy*, ed. Richard Allen and Murray Smith. Oxford: Clarendon Press, 1997.

Knight, Deborah, and George McKnight. "Whose Genre Is It Anyway? Thomas Wartenberg on the Unlikely Couple Film." *Journal of Social Philosophy* 33 (2002): 330–38.

Kripke, Saul A. *Naming and Necessity*. Cambridge: Harvard University Press, 1980.

Kroll, Jack. "How Hot Is Too Hot; The Fuse Has Been Lit." *Newsweek*, July 3, 1989, 64.

Krutnik, Frank. *In A Lonely Street: Film Noir, Genre, Masculinity*. London: Routledge, 1991.

Lawson, Bill E. "Microphone Commandos: Rap Music and Political Ideology." In *A Companion to African-American Philosophy*, ed. Tommy L. Lott and John P. Pittman. London: Blackwell, 2003.

————, ed. *The Underclass Question*. Philadelphia: Temple University Press, 1992.

Le Carré, John. *The Constant Gardener*. New York: Scribner, 2001.

Lee, Spike, with Lisa Jones. *Do the Right Thing: A Spike Lee Joint*. New York: Fireside, 1989.

Levin, Michael. "Responses to Race Differences in Crime." In *Race and Racism*, ed. Bernard Boxill. Oxford: Oxford University Press, 2001.

————. *Why Race Matters: Race Differences and What They Mean*. Westport, Conn.: Praeger, 1997.

Levine, Lawrence W. *Black Culture and Black Consciousness: Afro-American Folk Thought from Slavery to Freedom*. Oxford: Oxford University Press, 1977.

Lindo, Delroy. "Delroy Lindo on Spike Lee." In *Spike Lee: Interviews*, ed. Cynthia Fuchs. Jackson: University of Mississippi Press, 2002.

Lopez, Ian F. Haney. *White by Law: The Legal Construction of Race*. New York: New York University Press, 1996.

Lott, Eric. "The Whiteness of Film Noir." *American Literary History* 9 (1997): 542–66.

Lott, Tommy L. "Aesthetics and Politics in Contemporary Black Film Theory." In *Film Theory and Philosophy*, ed. Richard Allen and Murray Smith. Oxford: Clarendon Press, 1997.

————. "Hollywood and Independent Black Cinema." In *Contemporary Hollywood Cinema*, ed. Steve Neale and Murray Smith. London: Routledge, 1998.

————. *The Invention of Race: Black Culture and the Politics of Representation*. London: Blackwell, 1999.

Lott, Tommy L., and John P. Pittman, eds. *A Companion to African-American Philosophy*. London: Blackwell, 2003.

Lovibond, Sabina. *Realism and Imagination in Ethics*. Minneapolis: University of Minnesota Press, 1984.

Lowance, Mason, ed. *Against Slavery: An Abolitionist Reader*. New York: Penguin, 2000.

Lukes, Steven. *Individualism*. Oxford: Basil Blackwell, 1973.

Madison, James H. *A Lynching in the Heartland: Race and Memory in America*. 2001. Reprint, New York: Palgrave Macmillan, 2003.

March, Joseph Moncure. *The Wild Party / The Set-Up / A Certain Wildness*. Freeport, Maine: Bond and Wheelwright, 1968.

Markowitz, Jonathan. *Legacies of Lynching: Racial Violence and Memory*. Minneapolis: University of Minnesota Press, 2004.

Marling, William. *The American Roman Noir: Hammett, Cain, and Chandler*. Athens: University of Georgia Press, 1995.

Martin, Richard. *Mean Streets and Raging Bulls: The Legacy of Film Noir in Contemporary American Cinema*. Lanham, Md.: Scarecrow Press, 1999.

Mask, Mia L. "*Eve's Bayou*: Too Good to Be a 'Black' Film?" *Cineaste* 23, no. 4 (1998): 26–27.

Massood, Paula J. *Black City Cinema: African American Urban Experiences in Film*. Philadelphia: Temple University Press, 2003.

Mawakkil, Salim. "Spike Lee and the Image Police." *Cineaste* 17, no. 4 (1990): 35–36.

May, Lary. *The Big Tomorrow: Hollywood and the Politics of the American Way*. Chicago: University of Chicago Press, 2000.

McDowell, John. "Virtue and Reason." *Monist* 62 (1979): 331–50.

McGary, Howard. "The Black Underclass and the Question of Values." In *The Underclass Question*, ed. Bill E. Lawson. Philadelphia: Temple University Press, 1992.

———. "Justice and Reparations." In *Race and Social Justice*. London: Blackwell, 1999.

McNaughton, David. *Moral Vision*. Oxford: Blackwell, 1988.

"Mekhi Phifer." *People Weekly*, December 25, 1995, 124.

Mills, Charles W. "Dark Ontologies: Blacks, Jews, and White Supremacy." In *Blackness Visible: Essays on Philosophy and Race*. Ithaca: Cornell University Press, 1998.

———. *From Race to Class: Essays in White Marxism and Black Radicalism*. Lanham, Md.: Rowman and Littlefield, 2003.

———. "Kant's *Untermenschen*." In *Race and Racism in Modern Philosophy*, ed. Andrew Valls. Ithaca: Cornell University Press, 2005.

———. *The Racial Contract*. Ithaca: Cornell University Press, 1997.

Mitchell, Elvis. "Amid the Luxury, Immigrants in Peril." *New York Times*, July 18, 2003, E13.

Modleski, Tania. *Loving with a Vengeance: Mass Produced Fantasies for Women*. New York: Methuen, 1984.

Moody-Adams, Michele M. "Race, Class, and the Social Construction of Self-Respect." *Philosophical Forum* 24 (1992–93): 251–66.

Moore, Alan, and Eddie Campbell, *From Hell*. 1993. Reprint, Marietta, Ga.: Top Shelf Productions, 2004.

Morgan, Janice. "Scarlet Streets: Noir Realism from Berlin to Paris to Hollywood." *Iris* 21 (1996): 31–53.

Morrison, Toni. *The Bluest Eye*. 1970. Reprint, New York: Washington Square Press, 1972.

———. *Playing in the Dark: Whiteness and the Literary Imagination*. Cambridge: Harvard University Press, 1992.

Morton, Adam. *On Evil*. London: Routledge, 2004.

Mosley, Walter. *Always Outnumbered, Always Outgunned*. New York: Washington Square Books, 1998.

———. *Devil in a Blue Dress*. 1990. Reprint, New York: Pocket Books, 1991.

Motley, Willard. *Knock on Any Door*. New York: Appleton-Century-Crofts, 1947.

Mulhall, Stephen. *On Film*. London: Routledge, 2002.

———. "Picturing the Human (Body and Soul): A Reading of *Blade Runner*." *Film and Philosophy* 1 (1994): 87–104.

———. "Ways of Thinking: A Response to Anderson and Baggini." *Film-Philosophy* 7, no. 25 (August 2003). http://www.film-philosophy.com/.

Mulvey, Laura. "Visual Pleasure and Narrative Cinema." *Screen* 16, no. 3 (1975): 6–18.

Munby, Jonathan. *Public Enemies, Public Heroes: Screening the Gangster from Little Caesar to Touch of Evil*. Chicago: University of Chicago Press, 1999.

Murdoch, Iris. *The Sovereignty of Good*. 1970. Reprint, London: Ark Paperbacks, 1985.

Murray, Charles, and Richard J. Herrnstein. *The Bell Curve*. New York: Free Press, 1993.

Musser, Charles. "To Redream the Dream of White Playwrights: Reappropriation and Resistance in Oscar Micheaux's *Body and Soul*." In *Oscar Micheaux and His Circle*, ed. Pearl Bowser, Jane Gaines, and Charles Musser. Indianapolis: Indiana University Press, 2001.

Nagel, Thomas. "What Is It Like to Be a Bat?" *Philosophical Review* 83 (1974): 435–50.

Naremore, James. "American Film Noir: The History of an Idea." *Film Quarterly* 49, no. 2 (1995–96): 12–27.

———. *More Than Night: Film Noir in Its Contexts*. Berkeley and Los Angeles: University of California Press, 1998.

Neal, Mark Anthony. *Soul Babies: Black Popular Culture and the Post-Soul Aesthetic*. New York: Routledge, 2002.

Neale, Steve. *Genre and Hollywood*. London: Routledge, 2000.

———. "Melo Talk: On the Meaning and Use of the Term 'Melodrama' in the American Trade Press." *Velvet Light Trap* 32 (1993): 66–89.

Nehamas, Alexander. *The Art of Living: Socratic Reflections from Plato to Foucault*. Berkeley and Los Angeles: University of California Press, 1998.

Neill, Alex. "Empathy and (Film) Fiction." In *Post-Theory: Reconstructing Film Studies*, ed. David Bordwell and Noël Carroll. Madison: University of Wisconsin Press, 1996.

Neve, Brian. *Film and Politics in America: A Social Tradition*. New York: Routledge, 1992.

Nieland, Justus J. "Race-ing *Noir* and Re-placing History: The Mulatta and Memory in *One False Move* and *Devil in a Blue Dress*." *Velvet Light Trap* no. 43 (Spring 1999): 63–77.

Norman, Richard. *On Humanism*. London: Routledge, 2004.

Nussbaum, Martha. *Love's Knowledge: Essays on Philosophy and Literature*. New York: Oxford University Press, 1990.

O'Brien, Charles. "Film Noir in France: Before the Liberation." *Iris* 21 (1996): 7–20.

O'Connor, Peg. *Oppression and Responsibility: A Wittgensteinian Approach to Social Practices and Moral Theory*. University Park: Pennsylvania State University Press, 2002.

Ogunnaike, Lola. "Credentials for Pulp Fiction: Pimp and Drug Addict." *New York Times*, March 25, 2004. http://www.nytimes.com/.

Oliver, Bert. "The Logic of *Noir* and the Question of Radical Evil." *Film and Philosophy* 8 (2004): 122–37.

Oliver, Kelly, and Benigno Trigo. *Noir Anxiety*. Minneapolis: University of Minnesota Press, 2003.

Oppenheimer, David B. "The Movement from Sympathy to Empathy, Through Fear: The Beatings of Rodney King and Reginald Denny Provoke Differing Emotions but Similar Racial Concerns." *The Recorder*, June 9, 1992, 14.

Orr, David. "The Rural Noir of *One False Move*." *Creative Screenwriting* 7, no. 5 (September 2000): 55–59.

Oxford English Dictionary Online. http:// dictionary.oed.com.

Palmer, R. Barton. *Hollywood's Dark Cinema: The American Film Noir*. New York: Twayne, 1994.

Parks, Louis B. "Jackson Takes a Detour to the 'Bayou.'" *Houston Chronicle*, November 8, 1997, Houston Section, 1.

Perlmutter, Dawn. "Miss America: Whose Ideal?" In *Beauty Matters*, ed. Peg Zeglin Brand. Bloomington: Indiana University Press, 2000.

Pines, Jim, and Paul Willemen, eds. *Questions of Third Cinema*. London: BFI Publishing, 1989.

Piper, Adrian M. S. "Two Kinds of Discrimination." In *Race and Racism*, Bernard Boxill, ed. Oxford: Oxford University Press, 2001.

Pizzello, Stephen. "Between 'Rock' and a Hard Place." In *Spike Lee: Interviews*, ed. Cynthia Fuchs. Jackson: University of Mississippi Press, 2002.

Plantinga, Carl. "The Scene of Empathy and the Human Face on Film." In *Passionate Views: Film, Cognition, and Emotion*, ed. Carl Plantinga and Greg M. Smith. Baltimore: Johns Hopkins University Press, 1999.

Plantinga, Carl, and Greg M. Smith, eds. *Passionate Views: Film, Cognition, and Emotion.* Baltimore: Johns Hopkins University Press, 1999.

Plato. *Plato: The Collected Dialogues,* ed. Edith Hamilton and Huntington Cairns. Princeton: Princeton University Press, 1963.

Popkin, Richard H. "Eighteenth Century Racism." In *The Columbia History of Western Philosophy,* ed. Richard H. Popkin. New York: Columbia University Press, 1999.

Porfirio, Robert G. "No Way Out: Existential Motifs in the *Film Noir.*" In *Film Noir Reader,* ed. Alain Silver and James Ursini. New York: Limelight Editions, 1996.

Pratt, Ray. *Rhythm and Resistance: Explorations in the Political Uses of Popular Music.* New York: Praeger, 1990.

Price, Richard. *Clockers.* New York: Avon Books, 1993.

Pudovkin, V. I. *Film Technique and Film Acting,* Translated and edited by Ivor Montagu. 1958. Reprint, New York: Grove Press, 1970.

Quart, Leonard. Review of *Clockers. Cineaste* 21, no. 4 (1995): 64.

———. "Spike Lee's *Clockers:* A Lament for the Urban Ghetto." *Cineaste* 22, no. 1 (1996): 9–11.

Quart, Leonard, and Albert Auster. "A Novelist and Screenwriter Eyeballs the Inner City: An Interview with Richard Price." *Cineaste* 22, no. 1 (1996): 12–17.

Rabinowitz, Paula. *Black and White and Noir: America's Pulp Modernism.* New York: Columbia University Press, 2002.

Rawls, John. *A Theory of Justice.* Cambridge: Harvard University Press, 1971.

Read, Rupert, and Jerry Goodenough, eds. *Film as Philosophy: Essays on Cinema after Wittgenstein and Cavell,.* Basingstoke: Palgrave Macmillan, 2005.

Redding, J. Saunders. *Stranger and Alone: A Novel.* New York: Harcourt, Brace, 1950.

Rhines, Jesse Algernon. *Black Film/White Money.* New Brunswick: Rutgers University Press, 1996.

Roberts, John W. *From Trickster to Badman: The Black Folk Hero in Slavery and Freedom.* Philadelphia: University of Pennsylvania Press, 1989.

Roberts, Rodney C. "Justice and Rectification: A Taxonomy of Justice." In *Injustice and Reparations,* ed. Rodney C. Roberts. New York: Peter Lang, 2002.

———. "Why Have the Injustices Perpetrated Against Blacks in America Not Been Rectified?" *Journal of Social Philosophy* 32 (2001): 357–73.

Rose, Tricia. *Black Noise: Rap Music and Black Culture in Contemporary America.* Middletown: Wesleyan University Press, 1994.

Rothman, William. *The "I" of the Camera: Essays in Film Criticism, History, and Aesthetics.* Second edition. New York: Cambridge University Press, 2004.

Rushton, J. Philippe. *Race, Evolution, and Behavior.* New Brunswick: Transaction Books, 1995.

Russell, Bertrand. *The Problems of Philosophy.* 1912. Reprint, New York: Oxford University Press, 1959.

Ryle, Gilbert. *The Concept of Mind.* 1949. Reprint, New York: Barnes and Noble Books, n.d.

Said, Edward. "Europe and Its Others: An Arab Perspective." In *States of Mind: Dialogues with Contemporary Thinkers,* ed. Richard Kearney. New York: New York University Press, 1995.

Sallis, James. "Chester Himes: America's Black Heartland." In *The Big Book of Noir,* ed. Ed Gorman, Lee Server, and Martin H. Greenberg. New York: Carroll and Graf, 1998.

Sarris, Andrew. "A 10-Year-Old Murderer Propels a Nervy Debut Film" (review of
    Eve's Bayou). *New York Observer*, November 17, 1997, 37–38.
Sartwell, Crispin. "'Wigger,'" In *White on White/Black on Black*, ed. George Yancy.
    Lanham, Md.: Rowman and Littlefield, 2005.
Saxton, Alexander. *The Rise and Fall of the White Republic: Class Politics and Mass Cul-
    ture in Nineteenth Century America*. 1990. Reprint, London: Verso, 2003.
Schatz, Thomas. *Boom and Bust: The American Cinema in the 1940s*. New York:
    Charles Scribner's Sons, 1997.
Schrader, Paul. "Notes on *Film Noir*." In *Film Noir Reader*, ed. Alain Silver and James
    Ursini. New York: Limelight Editions, 1996.
Schwartz, Gary. "Toni Morrison at the Movies: Theorizing Race Through *Imitation
    of Life*." In *Existence in Black: An Anthology of Black Existential Philosophy*, ed.
    Lewis R. Gordon. New York: Routledge, 1997.
Scorsese, Martin. Interview. In *The Evolution of an American Filmmaker*. Directed by
    Lorna Anozie, 2003. On *The 25th Hour*, DVD.
Scott, Jacqueline. "Nietzsche and Decadence: The Revaluation of Morality." *Continen-
    tal Philosophy Review* 31 (1998): 59–78.
———. "'The Price of the Ticket': A Genealogy and Revaluation of Race." In *Criti-
    cal Affinities: Nietzsche and African American Thought*, ed. Jacqueline Scott and
    A. Todd Franklin. Albany: SUNY Press, 2006.
Scruton, Roger. *The Aesthetics of Music*. Oxford: Clarendon Press, 1997.
Shaw, Daniel C. "Lang *contra* Vengeance: *The Big Heat*." *Journal of Value Inquiry* 29
    (1995): 533–45.
Sheinkopf, Evy. "Who's the Babe? (actor Mekhi Phifer)." *Teen Magazine*, November
    1997, 46.
Silver, Alain, and James Ursini. "Appendix E1: Neo-Noir." In *Film Noir: An Encyclo-
    pedic Reference to the American Style*, ed. Alain Silver and Elizabeth Ward, 3rd
    edition. Woodstock, N.Y.: Overlook Press, 1992.
———. *Film Noir*, ed. Paul Duncan. Cologne: Taschen, 2004.
———, eds. *Film Noir Reader*. New York: Limelight Editions, 1996.
———, eds. *Film Noir Reader 2*. New York: Limelight Editions, 1999.
Silver, Alain, and Elizabeth Ward, eds. *Film Noir: An Encyclopedic Reference to the
    American Style*, 3rd edition. Woodstock, N.Y.: Overlook Press, 1992.
Simon, Scott. *Jackie Robinson and the Integration of Baseball*. Hoboken, N.J.: John
    Wiley & Sons, 2002.
Singer, Ben. *Melodrama and Modernity: Early Sensational Cinema and Its Contexts*.
    New York: Columbia University Press, 2001.
Sklar, Robert. *City Boys: Cagney, Bogart, Garfield*. Princeton: Princeton University
    Press, 1992.
Smith, Murray. "Empathy, Expansionism, and Expanded Mind." Paper presented at
    Empathy: An International Interdisciplinary Conference, California State Univer-
    sity, Fullerton, Calif., June 23, 2006.
———. *Engaging Characters: Fiction, Emotion, and the Cinema*. Oxford: Clarendon
    Press, 1995.
———. "*Film Noir*, the Female Gothic, and *Deception*." *Wide Angle* 10 (1988): 62–75.
———. "Gangsters, Cannibals, Aesthetes, or Apparently Perverse Allegiances."
    In *Passionate Views: Film, Cognition, and Emotion*, ed. Carl Plantinga and
    Greg M. Smith. Baltimore: Johns Hopkins University Press, 1999.

———. "Imagining from the Inside." In *Film Theory and Philosophy,* ed. Richard Allen and Murray Smith. Oxford: Clarendon Press, 1997.

Solanas, Fernando, and Octavio Gettino. "Towards a Third Cinema." In *Film and Theory: An Anthology,* ed. Robert Stam and Toby Miller. Oxford: Blackwell, 2000.

Spicer, Andrew. *Film Noir.* Harlow: Longman, 2002.

Sragow, Michael. "Black Like Spike." In *Spike Lee: Interviews,* ed. Cynthia Fuchs. Jackson: University of Mississippi Press, 2002.

Stack, George J. "*Vertigo* as Existential Film." *Philosophy Today* 30 (1986): 246–64.

Stoehr, Kevin. "Nihilism and *Noir.*" *Film and Philosophy* 8 (2004): 112–21.

Streible, Dan. "Race and the Reception of Jack Johnson Fight Films." In *The Birth of Whiteness: Race and the Emergence of U.S. Cinema,* ed. Daniel Bernardi. New Brunswick: Rutgers University Press, 1996.

Taylor, Clyde. *The Mask of Art: Breaking the Aesthetic Contract—Film and Literature.* Bloomington: Indiana University Press, 1998.

Taylor, Paul C. "Malcolm's Conk and Danto's Colors; or Four Logical Petitions Concerning Race, Beauty, and Aesthetics." *Journal of Aesthetics and Art Criticism* 57 (1999): 16–20.

Taylor, Quintard. *In Search of the Racial Frontier: African Americans in the American West, 1528–1990.* New York: W. W. Norton, 1998.

Thomas, Laurence. "Moral Deference." *Philosophical Forum* 24 (1992–93): 233–50.

———. "Moral Flourishing in an Unjust World." *Journal of Moral Education* 22 (1993): 83–96.

———. "Self-Respect, Fairness, and Living Morally." In *A Companion to African-American Philosophy,* ed. Tommy L. Lott and John P. Pittman. London: Blackwell, 2002.

———. "Split-Level Equality: Mixing Love and Equality." *Racism and Philosophy,* ed. Susan E. Babbitt and Sue Campbell. Ithaca: Cornell University Press, 1999.

Thoreau, Henry David. *Walden; or, Life in the Woods.* 1854. Reprint, New York: Dover, 1995.

Toll, Robert. *Blacking Up: The Minstrel Show in Nineteenth Century America.* New York: Oxford University Press, 1974.

Tunney, Tom. Review of *Always Outnumbered, Always Outgunned. Sight and Sound* 8, no. 11 (November 1998): 66–67.

Turan, Kenneth. "*Catch a Fire:* Derek Luke does justice to tale of wronged man." *Los Angeles Times,* October 27, 2006. http://www.calendarlive.com/printedition/calendar/cl-et-catch27oct27,0,7324199.story/.

———. Turan, Kenneth. "*Children of Men*" (review). *Los Angeles Times,* December 22, 2006. http://www.calendarlive.com/printedition/calendar/cl-et-children22dec22,0,1800835.story (accessed November 15, 2007).

Tuska, Jon. *Dark Cinema: American Film Noir in Cultural Perspective.* Westport, Conn.: Greenwood Press, 1984.

Ursini, James. "Angst at Sixty Fields per Second." In *Film Noir Reader,* ed. Alain Silver and James Ursini. New York: Limelight Editions, 1996.

Varouxakis, Georgios. "John Stuart Mill on Race." *Utilitas* 10 (1998): 17–32.

Vincendeau, Ginette. "Noir Is Also a French Word: The French Antecedents of Film Noir." In *The Book of Film Noir,* ed. Ian Cameron. New York: Continuum, 1992.

Wager, Jans B. *Dangerous Dames: Women and Representation in the Weimar Street Film and Film Noir.* Athens: Ohio University Press, 1999.

Walsh, Andrea S. *Women's Film and Female Experience, 1940–1950.* Westport, Conn.: Praeger, 1984.

Walton, Kendall. *Mimesis as Make-Believe: On the Foundations of the Representational Arts.* Cambridge: Harvard University Press, 1990.

Ward, Julie K. "*Ethnos* in the *Politics:* Aristotle and Race." In *Philosophers on Race: Critical Essays,* ed. Julie K. Ward and Tommy L. Lott. London: Blackwell, 2002.

Ward, Julie K., and Tommy L. Lott, eds. *Philosophers on Race: Critical Essays.* London: Blackwell, 2002.

Wartenberg, Thomas E. "Philosophy Screened: Experiencing *The Matrix.*" *Midwest Studies in Philosophy* 27 (2003): 139–52.

Watkins, S. Craig. *Representing: Hip-hop Culture and the Production of Black Cinema.* Chicago: University of Chicago Press, 1998.

Weitz, Morris. "The Role of Theory in Aesthetics." In *The Philosophy of Art: Readings Ancient and Modern,* ed. Alex Neill and Aaron Ridley. Boston: McGraw-Hill, 1995.

Wells, Ida B. "Lynch Law." In Ida B. Wells, Frederick Douglass, Irvine Garland Penn, and Ferdinand L. Barnett. *The Reason Why the Colored American Is Not in the World's Columbian Exposition,* ed. Robert W. Rydell. 1893. Reprint, Urbana: University of Illinois Press, 1999.

Wepman, Dennis, Ronald B. Neuman, and Murray B. Binderman. *The Life: The Lore and Folk Poetry of the Black Hustler.* Philadelphia: University of Pennsylvania Press, 1976.

West, Cornel. *Race Matters.* Boston: Beacon Press, 1993.

White, Alton Fitzgerald. "Ragtime, My Time." *Nation,* October 11, 1999, 11–12.

Williams, Bernard. *Problems of the Self.* Cambridge: Cambridge University Press, 1973.

Williams, Tony. "British *Film Noir.*" In *Film Noir Reader 2,* ed. Alain Silver and James Ursini. New York: Limelight Editions, 1999.

Wilson, Charles E., Jr. *Walter Mosley: A Critical Companion.* Westport, Conn.: Greenwood Press, 2003.

Wilson, George M. "Film and Epistemology." Paper presented at the sixty-second annual meeting of the American Society of Aesthetics, Houston, Tex., October 29, 2004.

———. "*Le Grand Imagier* Steps Out: The Primitive Basis of Film Narration." *Philosophical Topics* 25 (1997): 295–317.

———. "Transparency and Twist in Narrative Fiction Film." *Journal of Aesthetics and Art Criticism* 64 (2006): 81–95.

Wisdom, John. *Other Minds.* Berkeley and Los Angeles: University of California Press, 1968.

Wittgenstein, Ludwig. *On Certainty.* Edited by G. E. M. Anscombe and G. H. von Wright. Translated by Denis Paul and G. E. M. Anscombe. 1969. Reprint, New York: Harper Torchbooks, 1972.

———. *Philosophical Investigations.* Translated by G. E. M. Anscombe. Third edition. New York: Macmillan, 1968.

Wolfenstein, Martha, and Nathan Lietes. *The Movies: A Psychological Study.* Glencoe, Ill.: The Free Press, 1950.

Wollheim, Richard. *On Art and the Mind.* Cambridge: Harvard University Press, 1974.

———. *The Thread of Life.* Cambridge: Harvard University Press, 1984.

Yancy, George. "A Foucauldian (Genealogical) Reading of Whiteness: The Production of the Black Body/Self and the Racial Deformation of Pecola Breedlove in Toni Morrison's *The Bluest Eye.*" In *What White Looks Like: African-American Philosophers on the Whiteness Question,* ed. George Yancy. New York: Routledge, 2004.

———, ed. *What White Looks Like: African-American Philosophers on the Whiteness Question,* ed. George Yancy. New York: Routledge, 2004.

Selected Films

(The following DVDs contain materials that are referenced in the footnotes or the epigraphs.)

Bamboozled. DVD. Directed by Spike Lee. 2000; New Line Home Video, 2001.

The Caveman's Valentine. DVD. Directed by Kasi Lemmons. 2001; Universal Studios, 2001.

Coffy. DVD. Directed by Jack Hill. 1973; MGM Home Entertainment, 2001.

Coup de Torchon. DVD. Directed by Bernard Tavernier. 1981; The Criterion Collection, 2001.

Devil in a Blue Dress. DVD. Directed by Carl Franklin. 1995; Columbia Tristar Home Video, 1998.

Do the Right Thing. DVD. Directed by Spike Lee. 1989; The Criterion Collection, 2001.

Eve's Bayou. DVD. Directed by Kasi Lemmons. 1997; Trimark Home Video, 1998.

Menace II Society. DVD. Directed by Albert Hughes and Allen Hughes. 1993; New Line Home Video, 1997.

Never Die Alone. DVD. Directed by Ernest Dickerson. 2004; Twentieth Century Fox Home Entertainment, 2004.

New Jack City. DVD. Directed by Mario Van Peebles. 1991; Warner Home Video, 1998.

No Way Out. DVD. Directed by Joseph L. Mankiewicz. 1950; Twentieth Century Fox Home Entertainment, 2005.

Once in the Life. DVD. Directed by Laurence Fishburne. 2000; TriMark Home Video, 2001.

One False Move. DVD. Directed by Carl Franklin. 1992; Columbia TriStar Home Video, 1998.

Panic in the Streets. DVD. Directed by Elia Kazan. 1951; Twentieth Century Fox Home Entertainment, 2005.

Pickup on South Street. DVD. Directed by Samuel Fuller. 1953; The Criterion Collection, 2004.

Scarface. DVD. Directed by Brian De Palma. 1983; Universal Studios, 2003.

The Set-Up. DVD. Directed by Robert Wise. 1949; Warner Brothers Home Entertainment, 2004.

Training Day. DVD. Directed by Antoine Fuqua. 2001; Warner Brothers Home Video, 2001.

The 25th Hour. DVD. Directed by Spike Lee. 2002; Buena Vista Home Entertainment, 2003.